RUSI

and

BRASSEY'S

Defence
Yearbook
1991

Edited by

The Royal United Services Institute for Defence Studies
London

101st Year of Publication

BRASSEY'S (UK)

(Member of the Maxwell Macmillan Pergamon Publishing Corporation)

LONDON • OXFORD • WASHINGTON • NEW YORK • BEIJING
FRANKFURT • SÃO PAULO • SYDNEY • TOKYO • TORONTO

UK (Editorial)	Brassey's (UK) Ltd., 50 Fetter Lane, London EC4 1AA, England
(Orders, all except North America)	Brassey's (UK) Ltd., Headington Hill Hall, Oxford OX3 0BW, England
USA (Editorial)	Brassey's (US) Inc., 8000 Westpark Drive, Fourth Floor, McLean, Virginia 22102, USA
(Orders, North America)	Brassey's (US) Inc., Front and Brown Streets, Riverside, New Jersey 08075, USA Tel (toll free): 800 257 5755
PEOPLE'S REPUBLIC OF CHINA	Pergamon Press, Room 4037, Qianmen Hotel, Beijing, People's Republic of China
FEDERAL REPUBLIC OF GERMANY	Pergamon Press GmbH, Hammerweg 6, D-6242 Kronberg, Federal Republic of Germany
BRAZIL	Pergamon Editora Ltda, Rua Eça de Queiros, 346, CEP 04011, Paraiso, São Paulo, Brazil
AUSTRALIA	Brassey's Australia Pty Ltd., PO Box 544, Potts Point, NSW 2011, Australia
JAPAN	Pergamon Press, 5th Floor, Matsuoka Central Building, 1-7-1 Nishishinjuku, Shinjuku-ku, Tokyo 160, Japan
CANADA	Pergamon Press Canada Ltd., Suite No. 271, 253 College Street, Toronto, Ontario, Canada M5T 1R5

First edition 1991

Library of Congress Catalog Card no. 75–641843

British Library Cataloguing in Publication Data

RUSI and Brassey's defence yearbook 1991
1. Armed Forces—Periodicals
I. Royal United Services Institute for Defence Studies
855'.005   UI
ISBN 0–08–040710 2 (Hard cover)
ISBN 0–08–040729 3 (Flexicover)

Printed in Great Britain by B.P.C.C. Wheatons Ltd, Exeter

Contents

Defence Industries and the Market Place

The Place of the Military in Regional Stability

Signposts

Membership of the RUSI

As a working body engaged in the study of the wide range of issues affecting national and international security, the Royal United Services Institute has a large membership made up not only of those individuals and organizations with a professional interest in the field but also of those whose interest in the Institute's work is of a more general nature.

INDIVIDUAL

Anyone may apply for membership of the RUSI. All members, depending upon the terms they choose, receive a range of RUSI publications and have full access to the library and reading room in Whitehall. Members may attend the large programme of lectures, seminars and conferences organized on their behalf and have full voting rights at the Annual General Meeting. Application forms are freely available on request from the Membership Secretary.

ASSOCIATE CORPORATE

Embassies and High Commissions to London and other non-UK governmental organizations may apply for this category of membership. A number of representatives, designated as nominated members, receive the same privileges as members with the exception of voting rights and, in some cases, of attendance at certain functions. Please contact the Membership Secretary for detailed information.

CORPORATE

Any organization or company, if not subject to the Associate Corporate category above, may apply for corporate membership. Nominated representatives enjoy all the privileges accorded individual members with the exception of voting rights: each corporate member may cast only one vote. In addition, corporate members may take advantage of a unique range of facilities and services for research, meetings, briefings

and other events. The amount of subscription varies propor-
tionately with the likely call made upon the Institute by each
corporate member about which further information, in the first
instance, may be obtained from the Membership Secretary.

ROYAL UNITED SERVICES INSTITUTE
FOR DEFENCE STUDIES
Whitehall, London SW1A 2ET
England
Tel: 071-930 5854 Telefax: 071-321 0943

Introduction

Instability and International Security

DAVID BOLTON

Director, RUSI

Iraq's invasion of Kuwait provided both the catalyst and test for a new international order following the end of the Cold War. It also arrested what was in danger of becoming a headlong gallop in the West to cut back defence spending with the demise of the Warsaw Pact and East-West confrontation. Again weight was added to historical evidence that instability and prospective conflict can very quickly confound aspirations of peace and international order.

Potential instability abounds in Central and Eastern Europe. Even the cohesion of the Soviet Union itself has been called into question as it seeks to avoid economic catastrophe and the break away of its various Republics. Whatever the outcome of the Gulf crisis, the future stability of the Arab world too is at risk and, in turn, affects not only the Palestinian issue and Israel but, possibly, future American involvement in the Middle East, Europe, and elsewhere in the world.

In seeking to come to terms with a rapidly changing world, emphasis has again been given to the United Nations as well as, paradoxically, to a variety of regional groupings. In Europe, they proliferate. The Conference on Security and Cooperation in Europe (CSCE) will be strengthened; the European Community (EC) seeks to extend its interest into defence and foreign affairs; NATO wrestles with the problems both of defining its future and finding a military structure to support it; and all the while other associations are being developed amongst Nordic States, those in the Balkans, and in the Mediterranean area too.

As always, security is determined by the dynamic correlation of political, economic and defence interests. If the risk to peace and stability is no longer one of the Superpower confrontation, but rather of containing instability and localised unrest, then economic and political leverage will have important roles to play.

3

But, as the Gulf Crisis has shown, the threat to the free world's interests can be potent indeed. The spread of sophisticated weapons, sometimes coupled with large scale armies, means for the West a continuing reliance upon superior technology, rapidity of movement and, above all else, a security structure which guarantees the rapid assimilation and assessment of intelligence, political decision making, and the capability for nations to act together; that is if the interests of the free world are to be defended and sustained.

PROSPECTIVE INSTABILITY IN THE SOVIET UNION

With the demise of the Warsaw Pact as a cohesive military force—if it ever was that—then the risk of war as previously perceived has all but disappeared. Instead we are faced with the disintegration of the Soviet bloc and possibly, even probably, of the USSR itself; all at a pace when the previously unimaginable has already become commonplace. The prospects for self-determination and democracy are exciting and encouraging: in Eastern Europe it is the long delayed end of the Second World War, as the countries now seek to emulate the achievements of Western Europe over the last 45 years. But the problems to be faced are also tremendously daunting.

In seeking to rescue the Soviet economy, President Gorbachev has, over a period of five years, moved from policies of economic acceleration, through restructuring, the replacement of centralised control, and now to establishing a fully fledged market economy. Partial reforms such as limited decentralisation and privatisation have not worked: state orders still constitute the overwhelming majority of production demands. Yet inflation is increasing; the budget deficit is huge; and there is a vast rouble 'overhang', in excess of 300 billion roubles, with little to spend it upon. Shortages are chronic, generating both black and white markets, the latter covering the bartering of raw materials and other products. There are very real problems ahead, particularly through the winter, with prospects of food shortages, power breakdowns and inadequate transport. The crisis is acute; President Gorbachev himself, in obtaining powers to rule by decree, described the position as one of extreme danger.

The underlying problems are threefold. First has been the failure of the administration to commit itself wholeheartedly to a market economy and all that goes with it. In giving President

Gorbachev the power to rule by decree, the Congress of People's Deputies has at least realised the seriousness of the situation, even if they can't agree what to do about it; they have now tied the outcome to President Gorbachev himself. Besides this there has been the adverse attitudes of the people themselves to price rises and the other consequences of a free market. But even they now realise that something must be done and that matters can not be left to drift on down into economic chaos. Finally, there remains a general lack of entreprenuerial experience, even of a spirit of enterprise; though there are now signs that this might be emerging as the prospect of a reversal of policies become increasingly unlikely with the lack of other alternatives.

What is now needed is the removal of the central control of prices, wages, production and distribution. Concurrently, the basic elements of an economic structure have to be introduced; that is systems of taxation, banking, interest rates and the like, along with rouble convertability. The problem lies in its implementation. The option of a gradual approach has long passed and there seems little alternative to 'shock treatment'. Thus the attraction of a symbolic '500 day plan' or a similar time-scale, which provides positive indication of at least the prospect of a dramatic turnround, as well as implying that any suffering will only be for a further but limited period. The tragedy of the situation is not that the Soviet Union is a poor country; rather it is rich in resources, but it has been badly managed for so long.

The economic future of the USSR is now inexorably bound to the political cohesion of the Union itself. At essence is the relationship between the Soviet Republics and 'the centre': the tension between what Moscow sees as the devolution of certain powers from the centre, as opposed to the responsibilities which the Republics are prepared to allow the centre. Having stridently proclaimed their independence, if not the process by which it might be achieved, and the primacy of their legislation over that of Moscow's, the Republics have looked over the chasm and seen the chaos which the disintegration of the USSR could bring; this has brought about a tendency to seek a more managed reduction of central control. It should be noted, however, that the Russian Federation—not the Kremlin—is the real core of the Union. Russia now regards her surrounding republics less as a barrier against a hostile world or as a source of economic growth, but more as a drain on resources, jeopardising Russian interests.

Thus, Russia seeks a formal recognition of her predominance in her future relations, both with other Republics and the Kremlin itself.

There is wide-spread disillusion with the Communist Party, even though elements remain in positions of power and exercise influence in some of the Republics. In addition to ethnic tensions, there are also those in the Republics who resist change because it threatens their own positions of authority. President Gorbachev, however, continues to present himself as the supreme arbitrator between pressure groups, political movements, Republics and Parliaments, governing increasingly through the Supreme Soviet and the Congress of Peoples Deputies, the unelected President's Council, and by decree. It now remains to be seen whether he is able to produce a new democratic structure as the old Communist one collapses around him. His place in history is already assured, whether he and the Kremlin become increasingly irrelevant as events move out of their control is another matter.

The place of the Soviet military in this process of change is crucial. The strains within the Kremlin are also apparent in the military itself. There are those who see themselves as the ultimate defenders of the Motherland in its entirety, defending not only its borders but also its cohesion and discipline. Others within the military perceive the overwhelming need for a sound economy and support the means of achieving it. Moreover, for political and economic reasons, as well as facing up to reality, it is broadly recognised that the armed forces will need to move towards smaller, more professional services. The rising rate of refusals of conscription, particularly with the prospect of service outside their own Republic, points to this. With the possibility of unrest in the Republics this, in turn, has been matched by a dramatic growth in the troops of the Interior Ministry, rising from some 30,000 to over 300,000 in the last two years. Suffering from a sense of resentment at their loss of influence and prestige, the risk is that faced with a breakdown of law and order in a particular Republic, stemming from food riots or ethnic unrest, the military may be tempted to assume control or be ordered in to do so. A successful seizure of power in one Republic might be repeated in others. The deterrent to such action, however, lies in the sterility of any other economic solution other than the introduction of some form of market economy. Thus, without economic expertise, any seizure of power by the military is unlikely to be long-lasting.

Despite the economic and political constraints upon the military, the equipment production rates of the USSR, although reducing, are still impressive. In 1989, the last year for which figures are available, the following were produced in the Soviet Union: 10 submarines, 6 major warships, 50 bomber aircraft, 600 fighter aircraft, 1700 main battletanks, 450 ballistic missiles. Thus Soviet tank production albeit reduced to half of its previous level, is more than double that of the whole of NATO. Even recognising that, from a Soviet perspective, the 'buffer states' of Eastern Europe have gone and, at the same time, that it may be difficult to stop or convert major production lines with the attendant risk of further unemployment, the military production rates for the Soviet Union are formidable and represent a range of modern equipment sufficient to more than sustain the needs of the USSR, the Russian Federation, a Slavic state or group of states, or whatever might result from prospective realignments stemming from a breakup of the Soviet Union.

PROSPECTIVE INSTABILITY IN CENTRAL EUROPE

The economy was again the dynamic for political change in Eastern Europe and it remains central to the question of stability in that region. The Polish economy is still under considerable threat, despite substantial achievements. Romania lacks viable democratic traditions and, because of its mobilisation of mob rule to counter opposition to the Government, Western economic aid will be restricted. The foreign debt in Hungary remains extremely high and the Czechoslovak environment is very seriously damaged, as is that of East Germany; all of which will make considerable demands upon scarce economic resources.

Nevertheless, what has been achieved already is remarkable. In the first six months of 1990, hyper-inflation in Poland had ended and some 7600 state enterprises, 80 per cent of the economy, had been set on the road to privatisation. But this has been achieved at a considerable social cost: a 30 per cent cut in economic activity and unemployment in the region of 10 per cent of the work force. To set Poland's economic recovery in context, it should be noted that its GNP per capita needs to increase by some 700 per cent to match that of Belgium. Moreover, tensions have developed within 'Solidarity' and these will come to a head with the Presidential elections, where the main points of issue will be that the cost of economic reform is too high, and whether the old enemies of the Communist Party have disappeared, or even if it is right that they should do so.

Hungary is committed to a market economy, but is seeking ways to introduce it slowly. Harsh realities remain to be faced. Czechoslovakia, on the other hand has indicated that, like Poland, it will be going for shock treatment. However, it has yet to face up to the severe practicalities that this will entail. As elections in Bulgaria and Romania have shown, equality in misery is still an option, though perhaps not in the longer term. At the heart of the matter is that many in Eastern Europe equate democracy with prosperity. Instead, the future points to a time of unemployment, inflation, and harsh economic measures before there is the prospect of prosperity.

Overlaying potential economic instability in Eastern Europe is the prospect of ethnic unrest. Not one of the Eastern European states is ethnically homogeneous with the possible exception of Hungary, but she feels responsible for the fate of some three million Hungarians outside her frontiers. It is, moreover, only recently that Hungary has recognised her own very large gypsy population as an ethnic minority. Furthermore, no Eastern European state considers its present borders as either legitimate or permanent; Romania aspires to Soviet Moldavia; Bulgaria to Macedonia in Yugoslavia; Hungary to Romanian Transylvania; Czechoslovakia to the USSR's Carpathean Ukraine; and Poland dreams of its long lost Eastern territories. These ambitions are inseparable from the Eastern European national self-assertion which was started by the revolutions of 1989, and they are not yet over. A delayed revolution in Albania and the very serious prospect of an explosive disintegration of Yugoslavia, suggests that the Balkans will, again, become the focus of instability, unrest and violence.

Elsewhere in Eastern Europe it is possible that a protracted lack of prosperity could give rise to crises of expectation which, in turn, will put fledgling democracies at risk, with an attendant rise in the appeal of authoritarian regimes capitalising on ethnic strains. Under such circumstances, the call for a united Moldavia or a greater Hungary to protect their fellow countrymen could have a strong emotional attraction. Whilst any unrest or violence which might ensue could be limited geographically, it could certainly provoke fierce local conflicts, and stockpiles of redundant Warsaw Pact equipments could further fuel and spread that unrest.

PROSPECTIVE INSTABILITY IN THE MIDDLE EAST AND OTHER AREAS OF THE WORLD

There are many areas of prospective instability throughout the world. South East Asia, Southern Africa, Central and South America; conflict and violence could occur in any of these areas. Equally, it is likely to be contained, and its effects localised, without calling fully into play the world's major economic power blocs, or introducing large forces from outside the region. The same cannot be said for Iraq's seizure of Kuwait and the resultant Gulf crisis. This has prompted and hastened the development of an international order following the end of the Cold War. Certainly, the resolution of conflict and instability in the Middle East has far wider implications.

With his 'victory' over Iran and his rhetoric against Israel, Saddam Hussein had already established himself as a potential leader of the Arab world; a position reinforced by the large and well equipped military forces under his command. He had further enhanced his standing with his insistence that oil production quotas be adhered to, particularly bringing Kuwait and the United Arab Emirates into line. Why then invade Kuwait? Again, the motive was primarily economic. Faced with a stagnant economy and considerable debt, as well as difficulty in meeting his own oil production targets, Saddam saw that the takeover of Kuwait would largely resolve those economic difficulties, as well as putting himself in a position to be able to influence significantly, if not control, future oil prices. Moreover, as Kuwait's wealth and attitudes were largely resented by her neighbours, he perceived it would enhance his position as leader of the Arab world. With such a stroke, he would also meet his own strategic requirements of access to the Gulf, outside Iranian control, and resolve Iraq's long standing historical claim over Mesopotamia.

The United States was thus faced with the prospect of more than 20 per cent of the world's oil production in the hands of an unpredictable, unprincipled and war-like dictator, posing a threat to the oil supplies of Saudi Arabia and the Gulf states and thereby giving Saddam Hussein a stranglehold over half the world's oil supply, which could place the free world's economy in thrall. President Bush therefore launched an initiative to uphold international law and to protect those oil supplies by mobilising the United Nations and deploying military forces to the area. The aim was—and remains—the maintenance of international law by the restoration of Kuwait, and the neutralisation of Iraq's potential domination of the free world's oil.

The unprecedented response of the United Nations was evidence of a new era in international relations. With the Soviet Union putting its weight behind the organs of international law and diplomacy and the end of Superpower confrontation, the UN Security Council was no longer emasculated by an almost automatic veto from one or other of the Superpowers. As originally intended, the Security Council was able to give the lead to the United Nations General Assembly, rather than abrogating its responsibilities because of the veto, as it had done in the past. The prospect of a revitalised form of world order, under the aegis of the United Nations, as first intended by its founding fathers, is once again before us. Failure to give effect to the UN resolutions against Iraq, supported whole-heartedly by almost all of the United Nations membership, could only serve to denigrate that organisation once more into a 'talking shop' with little real power or influence.

The Gulf crisis has also served to expose the myth of Arab unity. Whilst the Palestinian cause might have provided a focus for Arab emotions and aspirations, it has masked the real security needs of the Arab states themselves. For Saudi Arabia and the Gulf states, the primary threat has been from the North in the shape of either Iraq or Iran. Facing up to that will determine future security policies in the area. With the combined population of Saudi Arabia and the Gulf States, which is less than half that of Iraq alone, as well as numerically inferior weapon systems and a limited capability to handle current and future high technology equipments, it is clear that the nations of the Gulf will require outside assistance for their future security. Whilst an Arab 'front' might come from Egypt and others, the necessary high technology weapon systems should come from the West, and that assistance will be needed for many years to come, no matter what the outcome to the current crisis.

SECURITY ARCHITECTURES

Should military intervention be required in any future dispute, most nations would be much more comfortable if this were achieved under the United Nations flag. If processes within the Security Council and the General Assembly of the United Nations become more practised and strengthened by success, prospective military deployments could be greatly facilitated by the re-establishment of the Military Staff Committee. Whilst it would take some time to establish procedures, a start could be made in that Committee on such matters as shared intelligence, command and control arrangements, logistic support and, possibly, even tentative rules of engagement, along with arrangements for joint training. A whole range of lessons will be forthcoming from the Gulf crisis: in the political-military as well as support areas, they could provide the basis for initial military staff work, in spite of the reluctance of nations to consider any formal allocation of forces to the United Nations itself.

Within Europe, and following on from the NATO Summit of July 1990 and its London Declaration, as well as the Conference on Security and Cooperation in Europe (CSCE) Summit in Paris in November 1990, it is evident that the CSCE itself will be strengthened to deal with such matters of security as concerns over border disputes and ethnic conflicts, as well as confidence building measures in relation to military affairs and arms control. Although the Council of Europe, and particularly the Court of Human Rights, could prove attractive institutions to Eastern European nations, fundamental freedoms and human rights are also already part of the CSCE process, as is cooperation in the field of economics, science and technology and the environment. But the CSCE is an organisation that operates on consensus; it has no structure or forces available to it to respond to crises. It offers an important forum for the airing of views and positions on potential or real conflicts and disagreements. Even a small secretariat will do no more than facilitate ministerial and other meetings. The fundamental question becomes one of whether nations will seek first to co-ordinate their positions before attending the CSCE, or whether they will be content to act as only one of its members.

The correlation between economic, political and defence issues will continue to play an important part in any future security arrangement; thus there could be merit in addressing these issues initially at a regional level. The Nordic Council has long established such a grouping as has, more recently, the Pentagonal group (Czechoslovakia, Hungary, Austria, Italy and Yugoslavia) in the Balkans, and the proposed wider Conference on Security and Cooperation in the Mediterranean. Furthermore, the linkage between political-economic and security matters suggests, albeit as part of a dynamic process, an overlapping of EC and NATO interests. The new groupings bring together East and West

Europe; the old divisions can not be seen to be maintained by the EC and NATO. It will therefore be necessary to develop a form of a loose but developing association, albeit without guarantees which could not be sustained.

The European Community is now facing fundamental questions over its future broadening and deepening. The previous economic dynamo provided by the former Federal Republic of Germany now faces the demands of sustaining social services and industrial development in the old German Democratic Republic, along with other investments throughout Eastern Europe, paying off the Soviets for the removal of forces from East Germany, and contributing to the underwriting of the costs of the Gulf crisis. This will give rise to an increased money supply, inflationary pressures and, possibly, higher interest rates in the new Germany. Thus, taking into account the wider economic climate and even with the Single European Act and 1992 in prospect, the pace of EC development could slow, despite rhetoric to the contrary, although this will be offset by those in Germany, and the other EC countries who wish to see Europe's leading power tied into Western institutions. These issues will be more clearly defined by the EC's intergovernmental conferences on future political and monetary union, as well as other discussions over constitutional reform, extending to an EC interest in foreign and security affairs.

In this last respect, the Western European Union (WEU) could be absorbed into the EC to provide a security and military structure. However, to give effect to such policies would take some years. Once more there is a danger that the WEU would become an organisation of last resort or, at least, of expediency. Coordinating mine sweepers in the Gulf during the Iran-Iraq war, seeking to establish command and control measures for maritime forces presently in the Gulf, and now seeking to develop a framework for a future European intervention force totalling up to 500,000 men—all fraught with considerable difficulties and arguments fuelled by national differences—do not bode well for the future. The prospects for some form of a European Defence or Security Community therefore looks remote; unless the Americans rush to pull out of Europe and hasten such a development within the EC.

So far as military alliances are concerned, the Warsaw Pact no longer exists. Its Eastern European members are concerned more with defending their own borders and reducing the size of their forces to adapt to the new political situation in Europe and their own national economic pressures. The prospect of a reconstructed Warsaw Treaty Organisation, giving emphasis to the political means of meeting the security needs of its members, is possible but unlikely. To many in Eastern Europe, the Warsaw Pact is synonymous with Soviet and Communist control and they want none of it. However, those same countries are anxious and wary of the possible breakup of the USSR and instability on their eastern borders. Thus, if a reconstituted Warsaw Pact saves the face of the Soviet military and seemingly, maintains their status by being involved in an international organisation, there may be some support for such an outcome. Certainly, Poland takes this view. Moreover, the Eastern European countries might also seek to co-ordinate their positions and attempt to resolve their ethnic disputes before raising them in the CSCE forum.

Before any formal demise of the Warsaw Treaty Organisation, its presence will be necessary to give effect to the reductions achieved in Vienna under the Conventional Forces in Europe (CFE) negotiations; though that must not become the rationale for the continued existence of the WTO or for retaining Soviet forces in Eastern Europe for any longer than absolutely necessary. The CFE process is important, if only because of the effort that has been invested in it. It is also important that an agreement which reflects the common concerns of both East and West, involving asymmetrical reductions in conventional forces, and which has resulted in extensive and intrusive verification measures, is given full effect. Thereafter, the process is in danger of becoming numerically irrelevant: national decisions will largely determine the numbers of tanks, aircraft and troops, post CFE. The necessary verification of these subsequent reductions could well be codified through the Confidence and Security Building Measures (CSBMs) of the CSCE process. In any event, and well into the 1990s, there will still be a great deal of sophisticated weaponry in Europe and the Soviet Union, and those totals cannot be lightly dismissed.

FUTURE DEFENCE REQUIREMENTS

Whatever may happen in the future, history tells us that reliance upon ad-hoc collective security arrangements is fraught with difficulties and dangers. In Western Europe we already have such an arrangement, tried and tested by different crises over many years, and possessing both the means of political consultation and direction, as well as a command and control system and military structure. Of most consequence is how NATO will respond and adapt to the changing situation now before it. The great danger is that its member nations will seek separately to assess their individual defence requirements; reducing the NATO consultative process to no more than an early warning to allies of what individual nations intend to announce. There are already signs of this 'renationalisation' of defence; for example, as the USA and the UK determine their own defence needs and structures, it remains to be seen how flexible they might be to fresh proposals stemming from NATO's defence review.

Nevertheless, it is possible to determine those principle considerations which are relevant to Alliance defence requirements. The threat or risk in Europe is one of potential instability, stemming from the economic and political strains facing newly democratic governments and exacerbated by possible ethnic disputes and unrealised expectations, all of which provide the breeding ground for unrest, violence and the risk of authoritarian regimes attempting to seize power. Not to be forgotten is the added danger of considerable numbers of conventional, as well as nuclear and biochemical military hardware, remaining in Europe. In the longer term, the possibility of a resurgent Russian military power must also be guarded against. Moreover, as events in the Gulf have shown, potential instability outside the NATO area cannot be ignored: high technology weapons are available to third world countries and large forces under arms exist. Thus with smaller forces, because of reductions, the demographic trough and possibly a disinclination to serve in the military or to continue with conscription, the Alliance will need to cover larger areas. The logistic requirements could also be immense, as the Gulf crisis again has shown.

The principles governing the structure of future armed forces are therefore clear. Emphasis will be upon the need for a sound surveillance and reconnaissance capability, perhaps linked with arms control verification and confidence building measures, possibly using commercial satellites. In responding to a threat of instability, both within the European theatre and outside it, the principles determining future force structures will be those of mobility, flexibility, along with 'reach' in their weapon systems and a high rate of accuracy and lethality in their smaller weapon stocks, and sound logistic support. The whole linked by responsive command, control, communications and intelligence systems and all backed by a minimal nuclear capability, which even the Soviets now recognise as necessary.

In meeting these principles, high technology will continue to play an important part; it will remain fundamental to future needs and thus the focus for research and development. Nevertheless, there will be much less emphasis upon platforms and much more on the weapon systems which can be 'strapped' to them. In more specific terms, with main battle tanks remaining in Europe and elsewhere, there will be a continuing need for others to counter them, at least for one further generation, but in far fewer numbers than might previously have been envisaged. Moreover, the requirements of mobility and flexibility suggest increased research into new, more powerful but lighter armour, coupled with greater tank speed. Similarly, artillery and possibly multiple launch rocket systems must also be mobile, with greater range and with very accurate submunitions. In the air, the armed helicopter continues to be particularly attractive. As far as air forces are concerned, there will be a continuing need for reconnaissance and air defence capabilities but requiring, perhaps, less offensive air support. Again, the need will be for reliable modern platforms upon which can be attached weapon systems to meet the demands of particular roles, thus giving emphasis to multi-role aircraft. With the prospect of 'out-of-area' operations, air transport will also be needed, possibly using civilian resources. Naval forces too, must meet European and wider requirements, but with a lower priority going to anti-submarine warfare in maintaining trans-Atlantic sea lines of communications. However, the prospect of sophisticated weapon systems in the hands of less developed countries much further afield will necessitate a reliance upon high technology in the maritime area.

Finally, looking at future force structures, priority, for both political and economic reasons, will be given to collective arrangements and, thus, the introduction and development of multinational forces. With ground forces, the basic building bloc will be of at least a brigade and, more often, a division. Whilst the NATO regions might continue in Europe, albeit with changed boundaries, national corps and corp areas will be phased out. In addition to other pressures, the military requirements will be different; there will be less reliance upon linear defence and more on constraining outbreaks of violence or, at worst, battles of manoeuvre. With greater warning time, it is now envisaged that reduced 'forces in being' would be expanded with reserve forces, should the need arise. For air forces, squadrons at least, if not wings, should retain their national identity, but air bases might be multinational in their administration, with wings being roled for specific functions. In all arms, a large measure of logistic support should be integral to national units, but inter-operability will be of the essence.

What is likely to be implemented is a multi-national force structure for Europe which would be fronted by a Reconnaissance Force, made up of national brigades, immediately backed by a Rapid Reaction Force of some eight to ten divisions grouped in NATO corps; all supported by Manoeuvre Forces in a skeletal organisation which would be filled out by reserves at a time of tension and need. Air forces would be brought together by the grouping of national wings or squadrons. With the London Declaration recommending such a broad structure, there will be a substantial reduction in current force levels along with, it is hoped, the publicly acceptable stationing of multi-national forces in Europe, and the capability to respond to situations in other NATO regions and, possibly, even beyond. The difficult question will be in determining the national contributions to the newly created multi-national forces. For example, it might be agreed that Germany should maintain a division in each of the NATO corps on its territory, with only one other country joining with it in each corp. However, whilst the Central Region is the main focus of interest, the flanks of NATO should not be overlooked. In the North, few difficulties might emerge, but in the Southern Region the introduction of multi-national forces, except perhaps on a bilateral basis between the host nation and the Americans, could cause considerable difficulties. On the matter of association with Eastern European countries, this could initially be met by an arrangement with ambassadors, which is already taking place, regular staff visits and attendance on courses and occasional joint training.

With sixteen sovereign nations in NATO, each must make its own initial assessments before entering into the Alliance defence review. National military contributions to meet wider responsibilities outside NATO, and in the nuclear field must also be taken into account. Yet, despite suspicions that some member states would rush head-long for the 'peace-dividend' door, and a disillusionment with past NATO staffing and decision-making processes, to finalise national force levels before a NATO review would put the Alliance itself at risk. Regeneration is on offer, but to 're-nationalise' defence and security whilst paying lip-service to NATO aims could sound the death-knell of the Alliance.

CONCLUSION

In summary and in addressing security issues, emphasis has very rightly moved to economic and political affairs as opposed to defence and military matters. Nevertheless, the place of the wider defence community is still of fundamental importance in safeguarding future security. Whilst maintaining a prudent caution at present, the future threat is likely to be one of containing instability and possible adventurism, extending beyond the NATO area, with the possibility of resurgent Russian military power in the longer term. Even after successful CFE negotiations, there will still be a great deal of sophisticated military hardware in Europe.

The outcome of the Gulf crisis could result in a strengthened United Nations, with its security element given greater cohesion by the regeneration of its military staff committee. Should Saddam Hussein even partially succeed in his seizure of Kuwait, then the United Nations might remain little more than a discussion forum. Such an outcome could also greatly affect the United States. The conflict between President Bush and Congress over the budget deficit, coupled to a breakdown of resolve over the Gulf crisis and a partial victory for Saddam Hussein, could result in President Bush becoming a one term President and a resurgence of American neo-isolationism. Within Europe, the future security architecture will be a developing CSCE, as this brings together the European nations, North America and the Soviet Union, but Western European interests will continue to be best served by an overlapping EC and NATO. However, neither of these organisations should be seen to be maintaining the division of Europe and therefore, an association of the Eastern European nations with both organisations will be necessary.

Finally, if political and public support for any necessary defence arrangements within an acceptable security structure is to continue, then an informed debate of the issues is a prerequisite. Thus, NATO must be seen to be responding positively and rapidly to the challenges it now faces: if it does not, its future is at best uncertain.

European Security

Eastern Europe: The Process of De-Colonisation

DR JONATHAN EYAL

Dr Eyal is Assistant Director (Studies) at the RUSI

When Mikhail Gorbachev assumed power in the Soviet Union in March 1985, he inherited not one, but three different domains. The first was Russia, heart of the Czars' possessions. The second was the territory surrounding Russia, acquired by expansion during the 18th and 19th centuries. Finally there was Eastern Europe, a vast expanse of lands bequeathed by Josef Stalin after the Second World War. All these principal domains and subsequent satellites (Cuba, Angola, Mozambique, Vietnam and others) were held together by a mixture of terror, cajolery, personal corruption and nepotism, justified in the name of a supposedly universal ideology which promised to 're-shape' history. These elements are hardly unusual, for most empires rely on a similar heady brew, and most also cloak this with an ideological veneer.

The difference here however, was that, while the French and British empires—to take but two fairly contemporary examples—never allowed ideology to interfere with cold strategic calculations (and therefore vacated territories when the benefits/liabilities balance sheet tilted against the colonial power), all Gorbachev's predecessors in the Kremlin assumed that the external uses of their ideology represented more than just a post-facto justification for what remained, essentially, geopolitical realities.

Unlike the French and the British, who toyed with ideas such as 'the white man's burden', 'free trade' and the benefits of 'culture and Christianity' which their rule was supposedly bringing to their subjects in the colonies, Marxist ideology (quite apart from the fact that it was never intended to apply to the Czar's domains) claimed to express a 'scientific' view of man's progress through history, a 'dialectical', inexorable march which may, under certain particular circumstances, be speeded up or hindered, but which cannot ultimately be halted or avoided. By adopting the Leninist variant of this doctrine as the bedrock of the Soviet state, the occupants of the Kremlin foreclosed any possibility of an orderly debate about geopolitical realities; by pushing themselves (for a whole host of reasons) into the position of leaders of a world movement with destiny on its side, they ruled out the flexibility required by any colonial power in managing its empire and adjusting its posture in accordance with new circumstances. This process of adjustment is never easy for any colonial power; in the Soviet Union, it seemed impossible.

Additionally, the adoption of a dictatorship by one party and—through a seemingly logical extension—ultimately by one man, (Lenin's greatest and most lethal contribution to the Soviet state) not only deprived the Soviet state of a framework for orderly political debate, but also stifled the means of communication and reliable analysis which are essential for the administration of possessions of such a magnitude. The leaders in the Kremlin never knew the size of their economy, the level of their defence expenditure, or the rate of their currency's inflation. They elevated the USSR's suffering in the Second World War to an act of martyrdom and a process of self-legitimation. Yet they never bothered to find out the exact number of those who perished in that conflagration and various other skirmishes in which the Red Army has been involved ever since. All these facts remained unknown because it was nobody's business to find out. In the name of 'progress' the empire marched backwards, sliding further and further away from reality. It was not only a matter of deliberate falsifications. True, Stalin was the 'Father of the People' when he murdered them by the millions and his country was promoting the 'blossoming of the nations' supposedly 'coming together' in creating the 'new Soviet man' at a time when entire nations were exterminated. Yet this mattered less than the gross strategic errors which the Kremlin committed because of its basic lack of information. According to all available evidence, military planners genuinely believed that the Soviet Union was poised to overtake the United States in industrial production and standard of living in 1960 (according to Khrushchev) or, again, in 1980 (*pace* Brezhnev). They honestly believed that possession of Eastern Europe was a strategic asset, that the Western powers were crumbling from within and therefore on the run throughout the world, and that the Soviet Union could maintain a Third World economy, but first-rate armed forces at the same time.

It was this nonsense which pushed the Soviet Union into world adventures and dictated one folly after another. African 'liber-ation movements' were supported partly because they appeared to justify Moscow-based interpretations of the spreading Marxist revolution; Afghanistan had to be occupied because Brezhnev was convinced that only this action would prevent the country's fall into American hands; the 1970s detente was sacrificed in order to maintain a vast military build-up and Eastern Europe had to be periodically invaded in order to maintain the integrity of the empire. Yet Eastern Europe had long ceased to represent a strategic asset for Moscow. The region's regimes persistently failed to acquire national legitimacy and their country's econom-ies, far from contributing to the colonial power's prosperity became a severe burden on Soviet coffers. Most importantly, in an age when missiles and aircraft take minutes to overfly Eastern Europe, the entire notion of creating a buffer zone between their country and the West—so dear to Soviet generals and party planners—became largely meaningless.

THE FRAMEWORK FOR GORBACHEV'S APPROACH

Gorbachev's greatest merit was that he was able to separate reality from the thick fog of official nonsense. Every Soviet or East European citizen who was not driven around in black limousines with drawn curtains and who did not benefit from purchasing rights in special shops, health care in 'closed' hospitals or have a datcha in the Crimea, knew the grim reality only too well. Remarkably, the relatively young party official from Stavropol did not forget this reality even after he stepped into the heavily gilded halls of the Kremlin. There are many reasons why reality became so compelling for Gorbachev. The technological gap with the West was growing all the time and, at least in military terms, quantity could no longer be translated into power without the help of quality. It was clear to Gorbachev that, in the absence of radical changes, the Soviet Union would, sooner or later, be relegated to a bitter reality regardless of what *Pravda* might print every day, and that reality would be one of a second rank power with little clout in the world. The starting point of Gorbachev's reforms was the preservation of all his country's domains. Upon his assumption of power, he did not give any indication that he intended to preside over the disintegration of his empire; what he passionately desired was this empire's modernisation from within, its preparation for survival well into the next century. In that respect, but in that alone, he conformed to the traditional pattern of most Russian reformers throughout the ages. Reality, however, turned out to be quite different and the loss of Eastern Europe provides the best illustration of how far Gorbachev was prepared to go in order to pursue his reforms.

WHAT KIND OF REFORM?

Essentially, the Soviet leader was tied to the classic problem of any dying empire. Realising that his country was overstretched, he wanted to cut his losses while maintaining the benefits of the colonies. Thus, while the Soviet leader was interested from the beginning of his rule in galvanising the creative energies of Soviet citizens, in Eastern Europe the Kremlin was primarily interested in stability. While at home Gorbachev had to start by imposing most of the reforms from above on a population used for hundreds of years to receiving orders, in Eastern Europe—where Stalin's system of government was only applied for the last 40 years—the pressure for greater economic and political freedoms came from below. There was also the difficulty of presentation. While Gorbachev could attack the policies of his predecessors, for which he was not responsible, the leaders in Eastern Europe could not, for they were Gorbachev's predecessors: they represented the policies which were under attack in Moscow after 1985. In short, like all imperial powers, Moscow discovered that circles could not be squared, and that colonial situations do not lend themselves to quick, fudged solutions.

Four different phases were discernible in Gorbachev's treat-ment of the region. The first phase—from 1985 to the end of 1986—consisted of giving all East European leaders assurances that their positions would not be threatened by the reforms undertaken in the USSR. It was the time when Gorbachev repeated promises about his intent to respect the 'sovereign rights' of his neighbours in an attempt to convey the message that *perestroika* was a Soviet affair. It was also the period when the Soviet leader visited all the Warsaw Pact capitals, electrifying local populations with his benign smile and attractive wife.

The second phase, lasting from early 1987 to mid-1988, entailed great efforts to reform Soviet-East European relations and place them on a more predictable and institutionalised level. These were the heady days of attempts to reform the Warsaw Pact and the Council for Mutual Economic Assistance (CMEA), the two institutionalised pillars of Soviet control in the region. A flurry of summits, photo opportunities and interminable speeches, as well as mountains of literature from a veritable army of Soviet international relations specialists and academics served to give the impression of a co-ordinated effort to understand and meet the needs of the East Europeans, to transform an empire into a 'commonwealth' and to replace force with mutual understanding and co-operation.

The third phase, which began in the second half of 1988 and lasted until the Spring of 1989, entailed the abandonment of some multilateral control efforts in favour of bilateral contacts. Massive projects for joint ventures were announced and much effort was expanded on discussing the state of bilateral trade with each East European country. Yet, the result was always a failure. With the benefit of hindsight, it is easy to see why: the regimes of Eastern Europe were simply unreformable. They relied on the implicit (and often explicit) threat of Soviet power. They did not solve, but merely compounded their countries' economic, political and ethnic problems. They were regarded by local populations as mere stooges of Moscow and knew no other instrument of social control but coercion and terror. Above all else, the entire political system which called itself 'socialist' or 'communist' was entirely discredited. Words such as 'comrade'; 'party'; 'party congress'; 'general secretary' and 'Soviet' are now used throughout Eastern Europe only in a pejorative sense. It hardly mattered that the Soviet Union militated for 'humane socialism', rather than 'barracks communism', as Gorbachev's assistants called the Brezhnevite version of Soviet control in the region. For the population of Eastern Europe, socialism with a human face was at best meaningless and at worse a contradiction in terms. After 40 years of deceit, terror and false starts in the race towards a 'new dawn', the populations of the region saw no need to believe promises uttered by their erstwhile masters: 'no more exper- iments' became the rallying cry of those East Germans fighting against their twice renamed communist party during the election campaign of 1990. The transformation of the East European possessions into truly independent states which would neverthe- less choose to remain tied to the Soviet 'commonwealth' was also a non-starter. Superficially, this offer was similar to that which the British Empire made after the Second World War. Yet the reality was completely different. For the former British colonies, the Commonwealth made some sense, at least for a period of time. For the East Europeans, association with the Soviet Union entailed no benefits at all. It promised the preservation of a tie with a weaker, rather than stronger economic power. It entailed the perpetuation of cultural and economic penury, the survival of a link which was abhorrent to most East Europeans.

Feelings and aspirations, however strong, were not enough to destroy the Empire. The outer ring of the Soviet possessions, the belt of East European states, was ultimately liberated by a combination of two developments: Moscow's decision that a cost-benefit analysis must apply to the region, and the East Europeans' own determination to seize upon this opportunity. Economic decay, the rising costs of occupation and the diminishing benefits from these possessions all played a part in the Soviet decision to relinquish control. However, the most important ingredient in the liberation of Eastern Europe was probably the West. By January 1989, the Soviet leadership was convinced of two things: that its economic reform at home stood no chance of success without the help of the West, and that this help would never be forthcoming without the abandonment of Soviet control in Eastern Europe. Soviet rule in the region not only served as a perpetual sore in East–West relations and as one of the primary causes for the break in the world communist movement during the 1960s and 1970s; it also prevented the establishment of a stable detente between the blocs. As long as the Soviet occupation continued, the West would wonder about Gorbachev's real long-term commitment to 'democratisation', not to mention democracy. And, as long as Moscow considered itself, and was seen as, responsible for the affairs of Eastern Europe, any crisis—be it in Hungary, Poland or Czechoslovakia—threatened to destroy in one stroke years of patient negotiations with the West.

The first real step in the avalanche of revolutions which marked 1989 was not—as the world media usually likes to suggest—the exodus of East German citizens and the collapse of the Berlin Wall. Although these episodes remain the most potent symbols in the liberation of the region, the process began imperceptibly with the elections in Poland in the Spring of that year. As part of a deal between the Polish communists and the Solidarity opposition, semi-free elections were held for the newly created two chambers of parliament. Although the communists still laid an *a priori* claim to a majority of the seats in the Sejm, those in the upper house of the Senate were open to free competition between all parties. The elections produced a stalemate: while the communists could rely on their pre-arranged, automatic majority in the lower house, they managed to lose no less than 99 out of the 100 seats in the Senate. Ostensibly, the Polish communists could have retained power; in practice, this power meant nothing but the perpetuation of their country's political divisions. Faced with this situation, Moscow had two choices. It could either insist that the Polish communists retain power, thereby assuming not only the risk of future violence in that country, but also undertaking the obligation to support Poland's bankrupt economy, or it could bow to the inevitable and allow the formation of a government in which the communists would be in a minority.

The Kremlin's decision to adopt the second option opened the East European floodgates. Throughout the region, local regimes relied on two different levels of repression in order to control their populations: actual force and deterrence. A bloated apparatus of secret police, informers and other organs of terror provided the obvious mechanism of social control. The danger of a Soviet invasion was the deterrence and, although less explicit, it was equally potent. Having witnessed the repression of the rebellion in Hungary in 1956 and the invasion of Czechoslovakia in 1968, most East Europeans concluded that there was little point in confronting their dictators with force. Even if a local regime could be overthrown, such a victory was bound to be short-lived, since it would merely invite another visit from the 'fraternal' Soviet tanks. Moscow's acquiescence in the removal of the Polish communist government indicated, for the first time since the late 1940s, that the USSR may be prepared to countenance the collapse of a communist regime. Once that was clear, the East Europeans gained confidence that their eventual victory against their own dictators could, at last, be meaningful and could be translated into real power. The disintegration of the Hungarian communists' control therefore accelerated and, after the fall of East Germany, Czechoslovakia's position became untenable. Bulgaria followed suit and even Romania made a dramatic dash towards democracy during the Christmas of 1989.

So, at least, it seemed at the time. The reality is, however, much more complex. Despite the fact that Gorbachev probably decided that, if challenged, the Soviet Union would give up its control of Eastern Europe, the Soviet leader, like any imperial overlord, was neither prepared to hasten the process of disintegration, nor was he indifferent about the future course of the region. Right until the end of 1989, the Soviet Union refused to reject explicitly the so-called 'Brezhnev Doctrine' which served as

a justification for Moscow's military intervention in Eastern
Europe. To do otherwise would have been tantamount to giving
up all influence in the region. Nor did the Kremlin indicate how
far the East Europeans could go without incurring Moscow's
wrath. Through this tactic, the USSR maintained a semblance
of stability in a year of revolutions. Opposition movements were
encouraged to be moderate in their expectations and the communist hard-liners throughout Eastern Europe could still believe
that, if the worst came to the worst, Moscow would still come to
their aid. That aid never arrived, but throughout Eastern
Europe, populations agreed that the military, the security services
and their countries' international obligations should not be
challenged too much. It was probably the best Moscow could
have hoped for under the circumstances and, as far as the
management of a process of imperial disengagement is concerned,
it was not too badly handled either.

Nor was the Soviet leadership disinterested in the political
succession in Eastern Europe. In at least three countries
(Czechoslovakia, Romania and Bulgaria), the KGB and other
Soviet agencies were actively involved in the promotion of certain
personalities to prominence. In all three states, the Kremlin's
original intention was to enforce the removal of former leaders,
in order to ensure the survival of communist regime and a smooth
transfer of power. In Czechoslovakia, the smooth transformation
succeeded, but communist power could not be preserved; in
Romania, a violent revolution took place, but masked communist
rule continues. Only Bulgaria appeared to have answered both
Soviet desires but even there, the rise of an organised opposition
threatens to shatter the continued control of the communists, now
impeccably entitled 'socialists'. The reasons for this different
performance are to be found in these countries' widely varied
political and historical experiences.

THE NEW AND OLD IN EASTERN EUROPE

Since 1945, the West has been accustomed to the concept of
Eastern Europe as a unitary region composed of states with fairly
similar outlook and problems. To a certain extent, this concept
was accurate. After all, the six East European states were
all controlled by one party, owed allegiance to the Soviet
Union, sealed off their frontiers and operated command econom-
ies. They therefore appeared to share similar problems and, as a

consequence, necessitated broadly similar solutions. True, Western states pursued a policy of 'differentiation' after the late 1960s, intended to enhance the individuality of each East European state by 'rewarding' those who progressed towards a pluralist society and democratic institutions. In practice, however, the policy ultimately served as an appendix to the West's wider security considerations vis a vis the Soviet Union and, as such, it still viewed Eastern Europe as merely a pawn in wider strategic manoeuvres. The most famous example of this remains, of course, Romania, a country which won great favours from the West until the mid-1980s, despite the fact that it operated one of the most grotesque dictatorships the continent has witnessed since 1945. President Ceausescu was not rewarded for his democratic credentials, but merely because he baited the Soviet Union and, as such, appeared useful to the West. Paradoxically, 1989 only served to reinforce the prevalent Western perception that Eastern Europe still represented an easily recognisable, fairly homogeneous entity. Throughout the year, and as levels of dissent rose in every state, Western governments (the British included) viewed this process of liberation with mixed feelings. They welcomed democratic institutions, but thought the East Europeans were proceeding 'too far and too quickly' on the road of freedom. The reason for this apprehension was, yet again, the basic view that Eastern Europe was part and parcel of a wider policy whose main aim was the Soviet Union and which remained predicated on Gorbachev's survival in power.

What most Western governments (and the British in particular) failed to understand, was that they were dealing with emotions and with the politics of the street. To paraphrase a current quip very popular in the Soviet Union, the West hoped that Eastern Europe would opt for a gradual and orderly divorce procedure from its colonial powers. The East Europeans, however, refused to consider divorce, for they never regarded their connection with the Soviet Union as anything more than rape, an act of force whose consequences should be erased as quickly as possible. Thus, Mrs Thatcher hoped as late as December 1989 that German unity would take '15 years'. In fact, it took less than 10 months. The pace of events escaped the control of both Western governments and the Soviet Union, and Eastern Europe essentially liberated itself. It hardly matters that many Western governments harboured reservations about the process and that many policy planners in chanceries arould the world bemoaned the passing of a predictable and 'stable' continent. Europe was not stable as long as the desires of many of its component nations were not articulated; it may not reach anything resembling stability even thereafter.

THE CONCEPT OF STABILITY AND THE FUTURE OF THE 'NEW EUROPE'

Once these facts were understood, Western leaders embraced the euphoria which joined all Europe. Although Mrs Thatcher could not bring herself to tour the Berlin Wall immediately, her Foreign Secretary did oblige by providing journalists with a 'photo opportunity' in front of the most potent symbol of the continent's division. And most foreign ministries did start to muse about a 'new' community of nations, a 'European space' and the 'integration' of a continent. Most of this talk is, of course, nonsense. Eastern Europe's economic reconstruction will take years and would have to be accomplished in a transition period during which the two halves of the continent would still move on quite different tracks and at various speeds. Whether their ultimate destination should be a united Europe is beyond the scope of this article but a few pointers about the future of the region could be given with some confidence. Quite apart from the process of economic reform, which would be painful and would entail a great deal of suffering, the most obvious division would be cultural and political. Put simply, Eastern Europe was never a coherent entity, and the West allowed itself to be blinded by the all too obvious but superficial similarities of communism. The area is divided historically, ethnically and religiously, and all these divisions are now becoming important.

Poland, Hungary and parts of Czechoslovakia are devoutly Catholic, a fact which denotes more than just allegiance to the Vatican. It also indicates a different level of political development and national aspirations. The Church in all these states was never as implicated in collaboration with the communist dictatorship as the Orthodox Churches in Romania and Bulgaria. Furthermore, the existence of a church structure which refuses to view its temporal authority on par with its spiritual and universal authority enhances Hungary's and Poland's chances of developing the civic society and institutions which would sustain democracy. The truth still is that a stable democracy is not only a matter of parliaments and responsible governments; it is also a question of the diffusion of power between various centres in the state, of a process whereby no institution has monopoly control and no one is able to impose individual rule.

None of the East European countries have reached this stage yet. In Poland, a government is responsible to the people more out of self-restraint, rather than because it encounters a strong opposition. In Czechoslovakia, the honeymoon with democracy continues, with the Civic Forum still concentrating more than one party under the same political umbrella. In both states, these amorphous bodies, born out of a single-minded opposition to one enemy—the communists—will disintegrate once it becomes clear that the old enemy is no longer dangerous. Politics will assume their own predictable course, with interest groups coalescing around people who can best represent their aspirations. The dangers in those countries—as, indeed, in Hungary— is from a proliferation of small parties and the consequent inability to form a coherent government, a situation described by a noted expert on the region as 'Italian politics without the Italian economy'. Nevertheless, it is possible to predict with some degree of certainty that Czechoslovakia, Hungary and Poland (in that order) are well on the road to a future democracy.

Romania and Bulgaria, on the other hand, have yet to reach the status of their previous comrades·in misfortune. This, again, is hardly coincidental. Both states have precious little experience of democracy. Both had almost no organised opposition to the communist regime. While Poland had Solidarity and its periodic food riots; while Hungary experienced a popular rebellion and years of slow reform throughout the last two decades; while Czechoslovakia had its intellectuals, uncowed by the 1968 invasion and years of repression; the Romanians and Bulgarians had precious few individuals who dared stand up to their dictators. The bravery of these people cannot be denied, but their actions were ineffective, disorganised and ultimately failed to create not only a viable opposition movement; they also failed to offer any alternative to the dictatorship. A 'return' to Europe is ardently desired in both Bulgaria and Romania, yet the concept remains a wish, not a programme for government. Both societies lack cohesion; the peasants have little in common with industrial workers, and town dwellers are different from those living in the countryside. The intellectual elite bickers not about the future, but about the past, and is constantly plagued by counter-accusation of collaboration with the previous dictatorships.

THE DANGERS THAT LIE AHEAD

The liberation of Eastern Europe is still fraught with dangers. Indeed, throughout the West, initial euphoria has been replaced by bewilderment and even despondency at the enormity of the task still facing the continent. The most obvious potential danger remains the restructuring of the economy, for although a large body of research exists about the transformation of a market economy to a socialist one, the world has no real experience of the reverse process. The example of the liberalisation of markets in France, Germany and Britain at the end of the Second World War is hardly relevant: these countries' economies were, indeed, under state control during the war, but their financial institutions, expertise, entrepreneurial spirit and property relations remained largely unaffected. The post-war liberalisation was precisely that: a removal of state shackles and a return to an economy in which the role of the state was containable and quantifiable. The situation in the East is hardly comparable. Currencies represent nothing but accounting units (and usually fail to perform even this humble task). The banking industry and financial services are in their infancy and although the entrepreneurial spirit does not appear to be non-existent, property relations have to be re-created from scratch.

All East European countries are convinced that only a vast privatisation of economic activities, coupled with integration into world markets, the establishment of a convertible currency and the introduction of the profit motive in all economic transactions would provide the higher standard of living their people desire. The problem is merely one of implementation. Poland, Czechoslovakia and Hungary have accepted that this massive transformation has to be implemented as quickly as possible and, preferably 'from below', through the privatisation of all enterprises, the elimination of state subsidies and the destruction of the old bureaucratic frameworks of control which provide much of the resistance to current policies. Predictably, Romania and Bulgaria are still toying with the idea launched by Gorbachev in 1985 and now thoroughly discredited, by which economic reforms of such a magnitude could be controlled and implemented 'gradually' from above. The chances are that these two Balkan countries would be disappointed and will discover that their bureaucratic machineries cannot be reformed from above, any more than the profit motive can be reinstated by decree.

The fear throughout Eastern Europe is, of course, of unemployment and inflation. The Polish 'shock therapy', implemented since January 1990, has given us some pointers. The Polish *zloty* appears to have stabilised and inflation seems to be under control. It is not entirely clear whether this is due more to the severe recession in the local economy, or whether a tight fiscal policy has succeeded. The bad news, however, is that unemployment is much higher than the Polish authorities envisaged. In the first six months of the year, unemployment climbed to 5 per cent of the workforce and is likely to continue its speedy rise. Similar unemployment figures are already discerned in the former territory of East Germany. The spectre of inflation and unemployment haunts all East European governments, and rightly so. Like any politician concerned with winning the forthcoming elections, the leaders of the region are painfully aware of one basic fact: for most of the East Europeans, 1989 represented not only delivery from dictatorship. It also held the promise of a prosperous life, foreign travel, Western fashions and unlimited opportunities. This, of course, is a dream which must remain unfulfilled for many years. However, its fulfilment remains the aim of every East European government and all the leaders of the region are painfully aware that, unless they show some immediate results, the entire experiment with democracy may come into question.

These fears are probably exaggerated. Certainly, the danger of populist and authoritarian leaders is there. Poland's Lech Walesa is already aiming to be elected as president on a political platform that amounts to nothing more than a cry of 'What About the Workers?'. A great deal of mischief could be created by the former communists in trade union organisations throughout Eastern Europe, as penury starts biting hard. However, it must also be remembered that in the case of Czechoslovakia and Hungary, democratic institutions appear fairly well-entrenched and would probably survive most of the immediate social and economic consequences of reform. The aim of all East European states must be the establishment of institutionalised channels of political debate, in order to prevent social tensions from spilling on to the streets. In the case of Bulgaria and Romania, no such channels exist. Indeed, in both these Balkan states, social tensions resurfaced even before economic reforms were implemented: the sight of miners beating up students in the streets of the Romanian capital are the best indication of this bitter reality.

The other major problem which will beset Eastern Europe is that of ethnic minorities. This is a complex issue, which strikes

right at the heart of the process of national redefinition undertaken throughout Eastern Europe in the last two years, involving
a mix of territorial conflicts, historical claims and economic issues.
Roughly two million Poles live in Western Ukraine, and in
Poland itself, an equal number of citizens claim to be of German
descent. Czechoslovakia is an amalgam of two nations; in Romania, more than 1 in 10 citizens is not a member of the ethnic
majority and the same applies to Bulgaria. Hungary remains a
special case. Although a fairly homogeneous state, more than 2
million of its kith and kin live in Romania, a further 700,000 in
the USSR; 600,000 in the Slovak lands of Czechoslovakia and a
similar number in neighbouring Yugoslavia. No democratically
elected government in Eastern Europe could ignore the issue of
ethnic minorities, for which a solution must be found. The
problem is, however, that no East European state would admit
to being a multi-national entity. Newly liberated and fiercely
proud of their regained independence, all the countries in the
region claim to be homogeneous.

   The free ballots which were held throughout Eastern Europe
during 1990 sought to ensure individual rights. They therefore
complied with the Western view of human rights, which tends to
regard the protection of the individual from the powers of his state
as paramount. This is not the experience of Eastern Europe.
Throughout the region, ethnic minorities require not only equal
rights for their members, but also group rights, mainly in order
to protect their separate identity, education, religious institutions
and economic base. The notion of the 'melting pot', of assimilation, is only likely to increase tension in the region. It has not
worked in the past, and is unlikely to do so again. However,
throughout 1990, the fundamental contradiction between individual and group rights has not been addressed. Some ethnic
minorities chose to support wider, national parties in their
countries of residence, while others have opted to create their
own, ethnically based political formations.

   The small German and Jewish minorities had few chances of
sustaining separate ethnic parties and therefore voted according
to their wider political convictions. Millions of Gypsies live
throughout Eastern Europe, particularly in Romania, Hungary
and Czechoslovakia. Yet even after the first free elections for
decades, they remain vastly unrepresented as a group in all the
region's parliaments. Technical difficulties are partly responsible.
In Hungary, the Gypsies were not recognised as a minority for
many years and in Romania, electoral rolls often omitted their

names. Nevertheless, the Gypsies that did vote tended to avoid their own parties and opted instead for supporting broader political movements. If they thought that by supporting these parties they would have a political voice, disappointment will follow. With no political awareness or cohesive organisation, the Gypsies will remain ignored and subjected to discrimination.

Much more important will be the Hungarian minorities of Eastern Europe, who opted for a diametrically opposed approach to that of the Gypsies, voting for their own parties. To a certain extent, their choice was dictated by sheer numbers: Romania has 2 million Hungarians. It was also influenced by the proximity of their nation state and a historical tendency to rely on group representation. Given the recently bitter relations between ethnic groups in Transylvania, the creation of a separate Hungarian party was never seriously questioned. In fact, the Hungarian Democratic Federation of Romania (HDFR) established its claim to voice the minority's demands well before the country's May elections. Unity brought its rewards: the HDFR obtained almost 1m votes and captured 29 out of 387 seats in the Deputies' Assembly and 12 out of 119 seats in the Romanian Senate. In Czechoslovakia, the Hungarians fared less well, but their party still polled a respectable 8.66 per cent of the Slovak vote, ensuring 3 per cent of the seats in the two chambers of the federal parliament in Prague.

The Muslims of Bulgaria were another important ethnic group to vote for their own party, if by rather tortuous means. Bulgarian electoral law upheld the notion that the country is ethnically homogeneous and therefore banned the registration of ethnic parties. Consequently, the Movement for Rights and Freedoms, led by Professor Ahmed Dogan, claimed to be aimed at all Bulgarian citizens. In fact, it gained the support of 400,000 local Muslims and is expected to use its 23 seats in the Bulgarian Grand National Assembly to advance ethnic rights. The Muslims and Hungarians, the two important minorities in south-eastern Europe, now have a coherent voice of their own. Whether this fact will lead to some internal stability remains to be seen. It could be argued that, by establishing their own political parties, these minorities may exacerbate future ethnic conflicts. Much will depend on the way the West chooses to handle such conflicts. Clearly borders cannot be re-drawn throughout the continent. Nor could such an option provide a solution even if it was implemented, for many of the minorities are intermingled with other ethnic groups. The solution must reside in rendering borders less important and in discouraging the Eastern Europeans from viewing the nation-state as the only political entity worth defending.

OPTIONS FOR THE WEST

Euphoria has produced many superfluous concepts. Throughout the continent, many schemes were devised, each one more incredible than the other. The bureaucrats of the European Community, with their usual care for elegant English, speak of the 'European Space'; politicians in the West mention a 'Europe of Nations' or a 'Community of Ideas', while their counterparts in the East seem enamoured by various plans concocted by Czechoslovakia's Vaclav Havel to unite the centre of the continent. All these schemes attempt to answer the following major difficulties:

☐ How to integrate a united Germany into the continent, without changing the balance of power in Europe and without allowing Germany a free hand in the East of Europe?

☐ How to convince the East Europeans that they are part of the same community of nations, without gravely impairing the progress towards economic and political integration achieved in the West of the continent?

☐ How to achieve both objectives without alarming the USSR about the Europeans' future intentions, and without excluding North America?

☐ How to make sure that Eastern Europe does not become an industrial wasteland, an area exploited for its cheap labour and low standard of living for the economies of the West?

   Indeed, all these problems may seem insurmountable, but they can be tackled with patience and clear vision. This vision should start from the conclusion that no option, however grandly entitled and however well-meaning, can tackle all the problems with one stroke. The East Europeans must be incorporated into a loose security arrangement which can guarantee their broadly-defined security arrangements. There is little need for details, nor is there any requirement for offering them clear-cut security guarantees, which most East Europeans instinctively know may not be respected anyway. In reality, the security requirements of the newly liberated nations of the continent are much more modest: they require a clear indication that, after 45 years of occupation, they have finally escaped Soviet control. This could be achieved through a myriad of contacts and institutions, all serving specific aims. The CSCE could offer a loose security framework; the European Community could offer trade agreements; and a wider group of industrialised countries, not only from within Europe, could render wider economic assistance. Much of this framework has already been adopted by the West in its dealings with Eastern Europe, yet much of the assistance is still hampered by a fundamental quandary: a definition of what the European continent stands for. Should the continent, for instance, include the Soviet Union, with its territory in Asia? The problems of this decaying empire certainly defy solutions through their sheer enormity, but the question of where Europe should end is largely irrelevant.

The frontiers of the continent should be dictated by one criteria alone: the establishment of durable democratic institutions. The act of helping Eastern Europe is not a matter of disinterested charity. Rather, it is born out of a realisation that unless peace reigns in the East, there can be no peace in the West either. It is becoming increasingly clear that the very notion of Eastern Europe should be discarded. After the latest round of general elections, Hungary and Czechoslovakia appear to have fairly stable parliamentary institutions, governments with handsome parliamentary majorities and, above all else, administrations that are perceived to be legitimate by their people. They will still face dangers, but these should be surmountable. In Romania, on the other hand, this has not happened. The falsification of electoral results, the heavy-handed tactics of the country's neo-communist rulers and the intimidation of the opposition ensured the government's victory. But this does not amount to a great deal of legitimacy, nor does it ensure internal stability. As the country's economy declines even further, unrest and violence are bound to increase. Bulgaria appears to be in a better position, partly because its neo-communist rulers enjoy a smaller majority and partly because the opposition is better organised. Nevertheless, the stability and democratic credentials of these two Balkan governments will need careful monitoring. The West should not become a prisoner of sentimentalism, of nebulous ideas about a united continent. In the coming years, Europe will be split not between East and West, but between north and south, between industrialised states with durable democracies and Balkan

countries still in the process of rebuilding their national cohesiveness. 'Europe' should therefore remain, on purpose and by design,
a flexible idea of relative prosperity and stable democracy. It
should expand or contract, not according to any geographic
definition, but as a function of what always lay at the heart of the
West's own cohesion: democracy and the maintenance of peace
and collective security.

The German Democratic Republic: a State Disappears

JOHN MONTGOMERY

John Montgomery is a researcher on the RUSI Soviet and East European Studies Programme.

The former leader of the German Democratic Republic, Erich Honecker, had few things to take comfort from during the spring of 1990. Early in life, Honecker had thrown in his lot with Stalin's Soviet Union and had paid for this with eight years internment in one of Hitler's concentration camps. Now, he was paying again as he watched, from his refuge in a Soviet Army Hospital in East Germany, the total ruin of his life's work as the 'first German workers' and farmers' state' slipped out of existence into the waiting embrace of the Federal Republic. Although small comfort, Honecker may, at least, have felt he had been proved right in resisting those who had urged democratic reform on him. Either the GDR meant the Berlin Wall and absolute rule by the Socialist Unity Party (Sozialistisches Einheitspartei Deutschlands, SED) or it meant nothing at all.

Honecker understood this only too well. Many of the new oppositionists in the GDR, who had hoped to retain a separate, albeit democratically socialist, second German state, did not and consequently felt embittered and surprised at the success of West German intervention, particularly in the first free elections held in the GDR on 18 March 1990. Traditional unease over the prospect of a unified Germany tempted observers in the West to overestimate the viability of the GDR as a separate state shorn of its more repressive aspects. Every call by a Western leader for an 'end to the Wall' was, in fact, an invitation for West Germany to subsume the GDR economically and politically. The fact that the Cold War was over and that the Soviet Union had lost it was only beginning to be fully recognised, with a corresponding failure to appreciate the USSR's much reduced power and will to do much to prevent German unity. It is not known at what stage the leadership in the USSR began to realise that they might lose East Germany, but it must have been clear to the more astute among them that the breaching of the Berlin Wall on 9 November 1989 (presumably sanctioned by the Soviets) would inevitably lead to German unification and, possibly, largely on West German terms.

NATION BUILDING: GDR STYLE

Under the leadership of the SED, the German Democratic Republic was founded on 7 October 1949 (with a nice sense of historical orderliness, SED power unravelled 40 years later, almost to the day). From the outset it was a creature of Soviet post-war policy towards Europe, being one of a band of satellite states buffering the Soviet Union from the West with their Soviet imposed and copied economic and political systems. The GDR differed, however, from the other satellites in that it did not represent a national entity as the others did. Poland remained Poland whichever political system it was under, as did Czechoslovakia, Hungary, Bulgaria, and Romania. In fact, playing up to nationalist sentiment became standard procedure in the manipulation of these populations by their ruling communist parties, a strategy utilised for example in a particularly calculating and effective way in Romania.

The GDR represented only the rump of what had once been the German Empire. History had left the new SED leaders with the task of building a state bereft of a sense of nationhood and, thus, cut the GDR off from one of the main currents in European development since the French Revolution. Although they made an attempt over 20 years later to tap German nationalism, this option was unavailable to them in their early years of power. First of all, German nationalism was something they would have had to have shared with the Federal Republic, founded a year prior to the GDR, with the consequent division of loyalty this meant for East Germans. Secondly, German nationalism was unacceptable to the SED leadership on ideological grounds, who regarded it as a source of German militarism and fertile ground for fascist recruitment. Even the possibility of fostering regional loyalties as a nation building exercise had to be ruled out. Although four of the traditional German Länder (Mecklenburg, Sachsen-Anhalt, Thuringia and Saxony) were entirely contained within the borders of the GDR, part of Brandenburg and most of Selicia and Pomerania had been settled on Poland as compensation for Polish territorial losses to the Soviet Union. East Prussia had been lost altogether.

Encouraging German nationalism or loyalty to the Länder held little advantage for the SED as it left it exposed to the nationalist claims of West Germany on the one hand, and brought it into conflict with the Soviet Union's post-war settlement on the other. (By contrast, West Germans were able to feel more at home with a muted form of nationalism in so far as nationalist excesses in the past could be blamed on Prussia, for whom the GDR, conveniently, could be held to have inherited moral responsibility). The East German communists, therefore, rejected German nationalism and, in 1952, dissolved the Länder by dividing the GDR into 15 administrative regions (Bezirke), which took their names from the principle town in the various regions. The SED was left with the dual burden of having not only the legitimacy of its rule questioned at home and abroad but also the very legitimacy of the country over which it presided. Hoping that time would win international recognition, the only course open to the party on the home front was to try to create a new sense of patriotism and identity which centred on the GDR.

If the Socialist Unity Party was ultimately unable to create a sense of national identity, it, nevertheless, had the power and the means to simulate the outward appearance of such an identity. Against the background of a seemingly permanent division of Europe and Germany by the Iron Curtain, this sleight of hand was in many ways quite convincing. In no aspect of East German life was this more evident than in the National Peoples' Army (Nationale Volksarmee/NVA). Founded in 1956, the NVA, comprising the Land Force, Air Force/Air Defence and Peoples' Navy, was viewed by the SED as the main vehicle for moulding successive generations of East Germans into the type of citizen and party cadre viewed as desirable. Political indoctrination, carried out by the NVA's Main Political Administration, was carefully monitored at each stage by SED members. Officers were, of course, party members but each new intake of conscripts was expected to exit, after their 18 months had been served, with a precise understanding and appreciation of the 'socialist achievements' of the GDR and the vital role which the NVA played in defending these achievements.

Service in the NVA was the time when the party could expect to have a citizen's undivided attention, but the SED sought to bring East Germans regularly into contact with military related training at various stages throughout their lives, either through the youth oriented, pre-military organisation, the Society for Sport and Technology, or through reserve commitments to the Nationale Volksarmee (NVA) or the paramilitary Kampfgruppen der Arbeiterklasse. This system produced the most efficient and disciplined armed forces in the Warsaw Pact and allowed the SED to draw upon Prussian historical tradition, in an indirect way at first, but later through direct reference to historical figures such as Frederick the Great.

Discipline and 'team spirit' were supposed to provide the social cohesion which nationality provided other countries. This permeated all aspects of GDR society. It lay, for example, behind the party's obsession with acquiring sports trophies and medals, which was relentlessly pursued through sports schools and associations of the GDR and resulted in GDR athletes returning home every four years with armloads of Olympic trinkets. The party ran the GDR, indeed, as a manager might run his team; with slogans, cajoles, threats, rewards, 'pep talks', and constant appeals to make that 'extra effort'.

All of this, however, failed to prove as effective in holding the GDR together as the closed border surrounding the country. As the SED, backed up by the Soviet Union, was the only thing which kept East Germans apart from West Germans, every attempt to create a national consciousness inevitably focused on the SED itself. The state was incapable of ever becoming anything more than the party. In the end, the GDR was not invaded, it was not conquered, it was not subverted or undermined—it simply evaporated once the party fell from power.

TRAVEL RESTRICTIONS

In order to halt the first exodus of Germans out of the Soviet Zone of Occupation, the Soviet Military Administration in Germany (SMAD) closed the border with the British, French and American occupation zones on 30 June 1946 and through directives, issued on 29 October 1946 and later on 23 April 1947, laid down conditions under which the other zones could be visited. An inter-zonal pass, valid for 30 days, might be obtained if the reason for the visit was considered to be sufficiently pressing. The pattern was thus set for a system which would attempt to box in East Germans, one way or another, and which would not be broken until the dramatic events of 9 November 1989, when East Germans regained freedom to travel when and for whatever reason they liked.

The exact number of Germans who fled West from the Soviet Zone between 1945 and 1949 is not known, but the figure is believed to be in excess of 438,700. The following table shows the number of registered refugees beginning with the founding year of the GDR until the final sealing off of the border with the building of the Berlin Wall in 1961:

September 1949	129,245
1950	197,788
1951	165,648
1952	182,393
1953	331,390
1954	184,198
1955	252,870
1956	279,189
1957	261,622
1958	204,092
1959	143,917
1960	199,188
1 January-15 August 1961	159,730
	2,691,270

The number leaving was highest in 1953 during the months leading up to the uprising in East Berlin on 17 June of that year (March was a record month, with 58,000 leaving). Of the 1,684,806 registered refugees between 1954 and 1961, over 40,000 professionals left for West Germany, including 17,082 engineers and other technicians as well as 3,371 doctors. This constituted a serious drain on the skilled work force of the GDR. The comparative openness of the border between the two halves of Berlin made this the favourite place for East Germans to cross from East to West.[1]

By the mid-1980s, the East German authorities had begun to give a more liberal interpretation to their regulations governing East German travel to West Germany. At the same time, an increased amount of emigration to the FRG was also allowed. In 1984, for example, 38,633 East Germans resettled in the Federal Republic. Four years later, the figure had risen slightly to 39,732. The majority, about 80 per cent, of these 'Übersiedler' (East Germans who came from over the border as opposed to the 'Aussiedler', emigrants of German origin from outside Germany) came after having applied for and been granted permission to

leave the GDR. The exact number of GDR citizens who had
applied to leave was always a closely kept secret, but, in 1989,
West German estimates suggested that there were, perhaps,
600,000 current applications on file in the GDR (some put the
number as high as 1.5 million).[2] Also kept secret were the exact
dealings between the Bonn government and East Berlin over the
question of Übersiedler. Bishop Forck of the Evangelical Church
in East Berlin claimed in April 1989, that Bonn had agreed a
quota with the GDR authorities on the number of East Germans
West Germany would accept but this was hotly denied by the
West German Ministry of Inner-German affairs.[3]

The number of East Germans coming to West Germany was
expected to increase in 1989 and, indeed, by the end of April,
15,300 had already been registered as refugees. By June, 44,200
had been registered and of these, 37,000 had been granted
permission by the GDR to do so. The remaining 7,000 had either
fled illegally or had simply not returned after having been
allowed to visit the Federal Republic. With 12,500, June registered the highest number of refugees in any one month since 1961.
Again, most of these, 10,000, had been able to resettle with
permission from the authorities in the East. If the East German
government was willing to increase emigration as a means of
deflecting domestic discontent or if, as some suggested, the motive
was to free badly needed housing, it was also increasingly selective
in who should be allowed to go. Those working in areas of the
economy where there was a considerable labour shortage continued to have their requests to emigrate refused on the basis of
possessing 'sensitive knowledge'.[4]

Furthermore, citizens of the GDR found that the new changes
in the travel regulations instituted in January and April 1989
restricted the categories of persons allowed to visit West Germany
rather than, as had been expected, continuing the trend towards
their liberal interpretation which had been evident since the early
1980s. The fact that over 3,000,000 East Germans were allowed
to visit the FRG between 1 January and 31 June 1989 only served
to increase the impatience and frustration of those who were not
allowed even to visit, let alone emigrate. Many of these were
among the East Germans holidaying in Czechoslovakia,
Hungary, or travelling through these two countries to Black Sea
resorts in Bulgaria in the spring and summer of 1989. Hungary's
decision to remove barriers along its 215 mile Western border on
1 May presented them with a temptation some could not resist.
The stage was set for the GDR to lose some of its citizens in a

dramatic and highly damaging way for an SED leadership strongly committed to resist any pressure for reform and unwilling to admit that any was necessary.

ESCAPE OVER THE HUNGARIAN BORDER

East Germans did not immediately rush to cross the Western border in Hungary and the GDR authorities, while uneasy, continued to issue transit and tourist exit visas to Hungary automatically. The Hungarians, for their part, continued to abide by the relevant protocol of the agreement for visa free travel, signed on 20 June 1969 with the GDR, which committed them to preventing East Germans leaving Hungary for the West without authorisation to do so from the GDR ('visa free' meant that East Germans still had to obtain exit visas from their own border guards).[5] Doing so, however, left them in an awkward position as they had recently signed the UN Convention on Refugees which would be binding for them as of 1 October 1989. Their open border policy was being compromised through the presence of GDR citizens. Rumours began to spread that the East German authorities would cease to issue exit visas to Hungary automatically after 30 September 1989.[6]

By mid-August, approximately 1,600 East Germans had, nevertheless, negotiated their way past Hungarian border guards and crossed over into Austria. GDR citizens, who had obtained West German passports at the West German Embassy in Bucharest, were apprehended at the border for failing to have an Hungarian exit visa as well. Hoping for an imminent solution to the problem, the Hungarian authorities tried to steer a course between East and West Germany. A 'blind eye' was sometimes employed at the border by Hungarian guards, while at other times shots would be fired above the heads of escaping East Germans. As a general rule of procedure, Hungarian guards were instructed to prevent East Germans from fleeing through force, but not lethal force. Those caught were, however, no longer returned automatically to the GDR and were let free to try again.

During the second half of August, it remained unclear how many of the 200,000 or so East German holidaymakers in Hungary would try to go West. Newspaper reports on 16 August estimated the number of East Germans in Budapest waiting to cross the border at about 4000. 800 East Germans in Budapest were reported to be living in tents when the Hungarian Prime

Minister, Miklos Nemeth, and the Hungarian Foreign Minister, Gyula Horn, made a surprise and secret visit to Bonn on 18 August to discuss the growing dilemma. By this time, the Hungarian and Austrian populations on both sides of the border had begun to lend support to the East Germans in their escape attempts. One of the most publicised examples of this complicity was the so-called 'Pan European Picnic', staged near Sopron, with the clear intent of allowing 600 East Germans to escape while Austrians and Hungarians formed a human chain straddling the border. On 30 August, the West German Government confirmed that an arrangement had been reached with Hungary that would allow 4,000-5,000 East Germans to leave. Following this initial release of refugees, Hungarian officials stalled for time during the following two weeks as it became apparent that thousands more East Germans still on holiday wanted to leave as well. Finally, at midnight on 10 September, Hungary opened its border to all East Germans who wanted to leave and by early October, nearly 31,000 of them had used Hungary as a stepping stone to the Federal Republic.

OCCUPATION OF WEST GERMAN EMBASSIES

Parallel to the developments along the Hungary/Austria border, East Germans also began occupying West German embassies, not only in Budapest, but also in Warsaw, Prague and East Berlin. The Prague occupation ultimately became the largest and most humiliating for the SED leadership in East Berlin. From 10 East Germans occupying the Prague Embassy by mid-August, the numbers began to swell after the Hungarian escape route was cut off as Hungarian border guards refused entry into Hungary without a valid GDR exit visa. By 26 September, the figure had risen to 900 and had reached 1,300 two days later. The Czechs took the position that this was a political issue to be settled between the two Germanys and did little to prevent East Germans from entering the embassy grounds.

Four thousand East Germans were camping inside the perimeter fence of the embassy before it was announced that the Honecker leadership had agreed to let them pass to the FRG on specially arranged trains of the GDR's Deutsche Reichsbahn. On 1 October, the first group of 800 were taken out and over the next few days, hundreds more East Germans attempted to join the trains either in Czechoslovakia or as they passed through the

GDR. The East Berlin government suspended visa free travel to Czechoslovakia on 5 October and in so doing, reduced to nought the states to which East Germans could travel freely. Several thousand East Germans already inside Czechoslovakia, however, continued to pour into the West German embassy or to wait around outside it, hoping to get on one of the trains going to the FRG (by 11 October, 13,000 had escaped via the West German embassy in Prague).

Honecker's rule had always depended upon West and East Germans accepting Soviet backing for the regime as a fact of life. This arrangement was now becoming unbalanced. The spectacle of the Prague embassy occupations was extremely damaging to the SED's reputation at a time when the party leadership was preparing festivities in East Berlin designed to celebrate the 40th anniversary of the founding of the GDR on 7 October. The Soviet Union had now clearly demonstrated that it was not prepared to come to the aid of Honecker by not using its still considerable influence on either Hungary or Czechoslovakia. To many East Germans, this was a signal that the Soviet Union might countenance anti-Honecker agitation inside East Germany. An event potentially more threatening to SED rule than either the Hungarian or Czech dramas, took place on the night of 5 October: 10,000 East Germans marched through the streets of Leipzig demanding change.

THE 'PEACEFUL REVOLUTION' IN THE GDR

Although small in scale compared with the monster marches that would soon become a regular weekly feature in Leipzig, this demonstration held the distinction of being the first large public display of anti-government sentiment in the GDR since the workers' rebellion of 1953. Embarrassing and economically harmful though the haemorrhaging of population to West Germany was, it presented the SED with a problem which had, at least, a temporary solution in a sealed border and which, with luck, could be put off to another day, rather as a bad housekeeper might sweep dirt under a carpet. In so far as malcontents were skimmed off GDR society, the process was even of benefit to the SED (and, indeed, was deliberately employed by the SED towards this very end from time to time). A direct challenge, however, to SED authority within the GDR by East Germans, who gave the impression of not wanting to emigrate, was a different matter altogether.

Leipzig exploded the myth that the majority of East Germans, i.e. those not contemplating emigration, were a complacent people, happy to allow the party its monopoly of political power in exchange for a modest level of prosperity and social security. GDR dissidents commonly held this view, as did many foreign observers. It was also shared by the SED leadership. A Politburo member, Horst Sindermann, said:

> We (the party leadership) overestimated our successes, we exaggerated the successes, which there doubtlessly were, and kept quiet about the problems. In the end we were faced with a popular opinion which, in reverse, only recognised the problems and no longer the successes.[7]

Following the pattern set the previous spring in China, opposition groups, most notably the recently founded New Forum, saw the visit of Mikhail Gorbachev in East Berlin to take part in the '40th Anniversary of the GDR' celebrations as an opportunity to mobilise demonstrations in support of reform. Shouting 'Gorbi, Gorbi!', 'New Forum, New Forum!', 'Freedom, Freedom!', thousands of East Germans took to the streets not only in Leipzig on 5 October, but in other East German cities over the next two days. The Honecker government responded with police repression and attempted to keep foreign journalists out of the country. In spite of the demonstrations, the official celebrations took place as planned, including a torch lit parade by 200,000 members of the Free German Youth (the communist youth organisation), watched by Honecker with Gorbachev at his side. Although official East German reports of the talks between Honecker and Gorbachev stressed the Soviet intention to abide by its 1975 mutual aid treaty with the GDR and the two countries' highly valued strategic alliance, Soviet Foreign Ministry spokesman, Gennady Gerasimov, hinted that in private discussions Gorbachev had expressed his unease over the anti-reform stance of Honecker. In a speech at East Berlin's Palace of the Republic on 7 October, Gorbachev reaffirmed his position that the GDR leader could expect no Soviet support in dealing with the possible consequences of this stance, '. . . questions to do with the GDR will be decided, not in Moscow, but in Berlin'.[8]

Two days after Gorbachev's departure there was an anti-government demonstration of some 70,000 in Leipzig, a city which was beginning to establish itself as the trend-setting city during the turbulent autumn of 1989. This was followed by a continuing series of demonstrations throughout the GDR, culminating in a march of 120,000, once more in Leipzig, on 16 October. Erich Honecker, who, so long as he had been able to present himself as leader of a united party and a complacent population, had successfully stood up to Soviet pressure to introduce East German versions of 'glasnost' and 'perestroika', was left exposed and vulnerable by the show of popular discontent which the mass marches represented. Basically Honecker had two options open to him: a vicious repression (along the lines of the so-called 'Chinese solution') or caving in to the reformists.

Shooting at the crowds would have been the only possible way to clear the streets of demonstrators at this stage, but such a policy would have shattered at a stroke the extensive network of economic aid agreements with West Germany upon which the GDR economy depended and, additionally, would have embroiled the Soviet Union in a German crisis which it had every reason to want to avoid. Realising that such a policy assured disaster, the majority of Central Committee members opted for an attempt at reform, which, although dangerous, would buy them some time and give them some scope for manoeuvre. Excusing himself on grounds of ill health, Honecker was pressured into tendering his resignation as General Secretary of the SED and as head of state (Chairman of the State Council) at a meeting of the party's Central Committee on 18 October 1989.[9]

THE NEW OPPOSITION GROUPS

This was the period in which the new opposition groups came to the fore. New Forum had been founded in September 1989, originally to act as an umbrella group for the various strands of dissident groupings in the GDR. As such, its founder members did not regard it as a political party with a specific programme of reform to be advanced. Its leaders were largely artists and intellectuals, who, had they lived in the West, might have found their natural political home in movements such as West Germany's Green Party. Having had their first application to become a registered political grouping declined by the authorities on the rather quaint grounds that there was no 'social necessity' for such a grouping, they proceeded with a very successful campaign to collect signatures of their supporters and by November had the names of some 200,000 GDR citizens willing to be identified as New Forum 'members'.

Democratic Awakening (Demokratische Aufbruch) had its origins in a church-based citizens initiative group that had been founded in June 1989. Unlike New Forum, Democratic Awakening reconstituted itself as a political party at a delegated meeting on 30 October 1989 and developed a corresponding political platform which included separation of party and state, multi-party elections, an increase in co-operatively and privately owned property, and a reduction in the role of centralised economic planning. During its first month as a party, DA was able to attract in the neighbourhood of 20,000 members. Rainer Eppelmann, an East Berlin clergyman who was later to become the defence minister in East Germany's first democratically elected government (ironically having been imprisoned as a conscientious objector in the 1960s) sat on the executive committee of the newly founded party.[10]

The Social Democratic Party in the GDR was founded on 7 October 1989 by members of a similar milieu to that which founded DA. Indeed, most of the newly forming groups had their origins in either the church centred, unofficial peace movements or in human rights groups such as the Initiative for Peace and Human Rights. Originally using the initials 'SDP', the Social Democrats quickly changed it to 'SPD' in order to stress what they felt to be their historical link with German Social Democracy (the SPD in the GDR was forced to amalgamate with the communists after the war in order to form the communist led Socialist Unity Party). The Social Democrats, who within a month of their founding could claim 10,000 members, advocated an 'ecologically conscious, social market economy'.

A further group, the Citizens Movement 'Democracy Now', founded 12 September 1989, again largely from members of the Initiative for Peace and Human Rights, was one of the first groups to raise specific political demands such as the creation of a round table consisting of representatives of the SED, its alliance parties in the East German parliament (Volkskammer), the church and members of the new opposition groups. The circumspect approach many of these groups took towards the SED initially is illustrated by Democracy Now's early suggestion that a national referendum might be held on the question of Article 1 of the GDR's constitution which gave the SED a monopoly on political power.

Many other smaller groups also formed during this period, including the United Left, the Initiative for Founding a Green Party and numerous local 'citizens initiatives'. In general, all the new opposition groups articulated the demands that were most prominent amongst the crowds on the streets: freedom to travel, more democracy, and an end to the abuse of public office, including abuse of power by the Ministry for State Security (the much disliked 'Stasi'). Furthermore, they all still took some form of socialism for granted and spoke only of renewing it in some way. None of the groups, as yet, spoke of German unity. Some, indeed, such as the Social Democrats, actively disassociated themselves from the idea and any of its potential adherents.[11]

THE LAST DAYS OF THE WAY THINGS WERE

Honecker's successor as General Secretary and Chairman of the State Council, Egon Krenz, initiated what he must have hoped would be an exercise in damage limitation. Overnight, the party leadership refuted the previously held contention that party policy had been correct and that East Germany had been constantly building upon one success after another. A critical view of GDR society became the order of the day for party members and Krenz announced the SED's intention to enter into a dialogue with those marching through the streets beneath banners proclaiming 'We are the People'. If the hope had been to re-establish the credibility of the SED by attempting to place it at the forefront of the reform movement, the effort backfired as the party found itself unable to keep up with the social dynamic that had been set in motion. The subsequent history of the GDR was characterised by the ever increasing speed at which it inevitably slid towards unity with the Federal Republic. The disintegrating Soviet control over Eastern Europe left the GDR shorn of its special role as a strategic linchpin within the Warsaw Pact and with it, the only real justification for its existence. Without the threat of Soviet intervention, each new freedom introduced by the authorities in East Berlin brought the East German people another step closer to the realisation they didn't really need the GDR at all.

Egon Krenz retained Honecker's offices for only seven weeks before he was forced to resign, first as General Secretary of the SED, along with the entire Central Committee of the party on 3 December 1989, and then as Chairman of the State Council and of the Council for National Defence three days later. The resignation of the Central Committee and the calling of an extraordinary party congress of the SED for the 16-17 December (in fact its first sessions were brought forward out of necessity to 8 December) signalled the final recognition by the party that the fundamental changes which had taken place in the GDR over the past two months required a fundamental change in the party itself.

The old leadership tried to hold on to power by sacrificing some of its own number. Honecker, Joachim Herrmann (propaganda) and Günter Mittag (economy) were the first to go but more followed. Krenz, in his speech to the Central Committee on the day of Honecker's resignation has declared that 'the door was wide open, in line with our policy of continuity and renewal, for serious inner-political dialogue'.[12] Unfortunately for the party leadership the resulting dialogue contained much criticism that was far from friendly and which, once begun, was impossible to control. Hoping to deflect public anger towards their selected scapegoats, they set in motion a process which began to lift the lid on the whole corrupt nature of SED rule. East Berlin's *Berliner Zeitung* had taken advantage of the new press freedom and began investigating a case of alleged fraud involving former trade union boss, Harry Tisch. Soon other papers, including the Free German Youth's *Junge Welt* and the radio and television were competing with one another to uncover unsavoury facts about the GDR's former and present rulers.[13] Whether the charges raised were true or not became less important than the general picture which began to emerge of a leadership which, cosseted by comparative luxury and easy access to the best Western goods, was rapidly losing any moral right to govern in the eyes of a citizenry, that by ever increasing thousands continued to march through the streets of East Germany demanding change, or that continued to pour out of the country by thousands into West Germany.

In what may have been the single largest pro-reform demonstration that autumn, an estimated half a million people marched through the Alexanderplatz in East Berlin on 4 November. Nevertheless, within two days of this demonstration, the Politburo showed that it still believed that the game was being played by the old rules. The draft of the long awaited freedom of travel law was published on 6 November. Although far more liberal than the existing law, the right to travel when and where one wished continued to be conditional on state approval. Also, according to Article 6, paragraph 1 in the draft, an exit visa could continue to be denied on the, in the past, much abused grounds of protecting 'national security, public order, health or morality or rights and freedoms of others'.[14] Interviewed on television,

GDR Interior Minister, Army General Friedrich Dickel helpfully explained that applications for foreign travel would be processed within 30 days and for repetitive foreign travel within three to six months.[15] This proposal did nothing to stem the growing impatience of the population and demonstrations broke out again that evening, including one in Leipzig approaching the 4 November East Berlin march in size.

Events moved quickly after the popular rejection of the draft travel law. Willi Stoph, the Prime Minister, resigned along with his entire Council of Ministers on 7 November. On the same day, a crowd of several thousand protested outside the SED Central Committee building in East Berlin, denouncing the 7 May 1989 local elections as having been fraudulent (a direct stab at Krenz, who had been responsible for pronouncing the elections fair) and demanded free elections in the GDR. Finally, on 8 November, the entire Politburo resigned and the Central Committee elected a new one. Instead of 21 full members, the new Politburo consisted of only 11 and, in addition to the re-election of Krenz and six others, contained three new names, including the Dresden party leader, Hans Modrow, long held to have Gorbachev style sympathies for reform.[16] Realising that the time had come for a bolder stroke, Politburo member and Central Committee press spokesman, Günter Schabowski, announced on the evening of 9 November that the Council of Ministers intended to introduce a new travel law allowing exit visas to be issued, without conditions, at border crossings. This declaration of intent was sufficient to send thousands of East Berliners rushing to the Wall, forcing the SED to re-open traffic arteries that had been closed for the past 28 years.

Ironically on the same day, members of the opposition group New Forum had earlier received confirmation of their application to become a registered group from Army General Dickel's Interior Ministry. Would they, the Ministry requested, please submit their founding documents within the next three months, at which time they could receive official recognition.

THE MODROW GOVERNMENT AND THE WANING OF COMMUNIST POWER

Once the Wall had been pierced, the clearer heads in the SED knew that the real division of Germany had come to an end. The crowds in the street had wrung from the SED old guard a de facto freedom of speech, freedom of assembly and freedom to travel. Henceforth, SED members would have to work hard to maintain their positions of power as political life flowed back into the GDR for the first time in decades. Egon Krenz remained party leader for the next three and a half weeks and head of state for a few more days. During this time, the focus of political power in the GDR began to shift away from the SED and its internal wranglings towards the country's previously only rubberstamp of a parliament, the Volkskammer, which, at its 11th sitting on 13 November had elected Dr Günther Maleuda as its President and Hans Modrow as Prime Minister (Chairman of the Council of Ministers), charged with forming a new government.

Under the old regime, in addition to the SED and representatives of the mass organisations (most of whom were SED members), the Volkskammer was composed of representatives from the four parties allied to the SED; the Christian Democratic Union (CDU), the Liberal Democratic Party of Germany (LDPD), the National Democratic Party of Germany (NDPD) and the Democratic Farmers' Party (DBD). These parties, each allowed a set number of seats, lent substance to Honecker's claim that the GDR had been a multi-party state. Completely subservient to the SED in the past, they had begun to act more independently since the start of the crisis.

By no means a democratically elected body, the Volkskammer nonetheless was to provide an institutional framework through which the country could be governed until free elections could be held. The task facing Modrow and the reformers in the SED was to learn quickly how to make use of the parliament in a way advantageous to the party. This had to be achieved without increasing the popular suspicion of the Volkskammer due to the overwhelming predominance of SED members in it. On 1 December, the Volkskammer removed the SED's guaranteed sole right to run the country by striking out Article 1 of the GDR constitution.

Offensive though this may have been to old-fashioned party hardliners, it was, in fact, a clever move. By separating the administration of the state from the party's internal matters, it allowed Modrow and the SED members in the Volkskammer to dominate affairs of state for the duration of the parliament, at a time when the party needed to begin transforming itself into the sort of political machine capable of functioning effectively in, what now appeared to be, the inevitable future free elections. The necessary changes and experimentation within the party could take place without unduly affecting the efforts of parliamentary party members to explore ways of using leftover privileges from the old days.

The SED began to sort out its own house by making a visible break with the past. The exact form and timing of the break was presented to the party by the street crowds. Amid rumours that the Ministry of State Security was destroying documents necessary for the prosecution of corrupt officials (including stories of a document laden airplane destined for Romania having been impounded by ground staff at East Berlin's Schönefeld Airport)[17], large demonstrations formed outside Ministry of Security buildings in a number of cities and the Central Committee of the SED became the target of popular anger and suspicion.

On 3 December, the entire Central Committee resigned and 12 leading party members were expelled. Günter Mittag and Harry Tisch were arrested. The next few days saw further expulsions and arrests, including that of the former leader of the party and the country, Erich Honecker. A temporary steering committee was chosen to lead the party until a hastily called 'Extraordinary Party Congress' could be convened. The purpose of all this was to make the GDR's failures the result of mismanagement and corruption by the 'the Stalinists', i.e. the disgraced former leaders. On 6 December, Krenz, no longer General Secretary since the resignation of the Central Committee, also resigned from his state offices of Chairman of the Council of Ministers and Chairman of the National Defence Council. Manfred Gerlach, leader of the LDPD and one of the first members of parliament to call for reform two months earlier, was chosen to succeed Krenz as head of state. Krenz had become a liability to the Modrow government while Gerlach, as titular head of state, strengthened its prestige and increased the stake of the other parties in the survival of the parliament. The Volkskammer was further buttressed when its members agreed to the suggestion, put forward by the new opposition groups, that a 'round table' be set up composed of their delegates and representatives of the parliament. The Modrow leadership quickly saw this as a way to avoid or postpone any direct challenge to the legitimacy of the Volkskammer and the SED's pre-eminent position in it.[18]

At the time Modrow had three advantages. First, the old coalition parties of the SED felt compromised by their past subservience and were wary of change taking place too quickly lest they too should fall victim to it. Second, international opinion was not yet ready to accept the possible consequences of a political vacuum appearing in East Germany. Towards the end of November, a new slogan had begun to appear in the mass marches, 'Deutschland, Einig Vaterland!'. At first introduced by right wing elements, it appeared increasingly to be striking a popular chord, especially in cities nearer the West German border in the south, such as Dresden and Leipzig. Third, in groups such as New Forum, Modrow faced a new and inexperienced opposition more easily convinced of what it could not do than what it could. Still overawed by communist power on the one hand, and alarmed by any prospect of German unification which would threaten their hopes for an environmentally friendly, alternative form of socialism 'with a human face', on the other, many among the new opposition were convinced that immediate, direct elections could only end in a communist victory and a possible collapse of the GDR. As a result the Modrow Government was lent sufficient legitimacy to govern (in consultation with the Round Table) in spite of its undemocratic origins.

Although there had been considerable grass roots support among SED members to disband the party, the 'Extraordinary Party Congress' held in mid-December proved to be a measured success. Dissolution was avoided and the party was restructured and relaunched with a new chairman, Gregor Gysi, an East Berlin lawyer who had had a record of defending dissidents under Honecker. With a new name, Socialist Unity Party/Party of Democratic Socialism (later just Party of Democratic Socialism/PDS) the party groped its way towards a programme which it hoped to present to the GDR electorate as a 'third way' between Stalinism and capitalism. By the end of December, it appeared as if the communists in the 'new' PDS had weathered the storms of the autumn. This respite was, however, short-lived.[19]

In January, the Modrow Government was rocked by popular accusations that it was trying to revive the hated Ministry of State Security ('the Stasi') under a new form. Under the octagenarian Politburo member, Erich Mielke, the Stasi had built up secret police files on over half the GDR's population in its attempt to monitor and repress 'anti-socialist' activity in East Germany. With a regular staff of 80,000, 30,000 of whom were employed in the huge Normanenstrasse headquarters in East Berlin, and a further network of an estimated 150,000 informers, the Stasi had also been responsible for the GDR's espionage operations in West Germany and abroad.[20] Although the government had announced its intention to dissolve the Stasi in December, its true intentions were left unclear by later statements of Modrow's on the desirability of an internal security service to be in operation prior to the scheduled free elections in the Spring. The opposition members of the Round Table feared that this meant retaining the existing apparatus in some form and, indeed, Peter Koch, in theory charged by the government to supervise the dismantling of the Stasi admitted that 'it would be absolutely foolish, if one were to totally dissolve something, only to found it anew'.[21]

Modrow could hardly have picked a more sensitive issue with which to overstep the limits placed by public tolerance on his transitional government. Warning strikes by workers directed against the Stasi and continued communist influence in state agencies began to take place. On 15 January, a large demonstration formed outside the Stasi headquarters in East Berlin and succeeded in occupying the building. This pattern was repeated throughout the GDR as citizens' initiative groups assumed responsibility for guarding Stasi files and documents. In the end, Modrow was forced to back down on the question of an internal security service, but the very precarious position of his government had been exposed and highlighted the need for free elections to take place quickly. The date for the elections was moved up from 6 May to 18 March.

THE GROWTH IN SUPPORT FOR GERMAN UNITY

Between the first call for free elections in October and the final setting of a date on which to hold them, their significance underwent a change. By February, it was clear that the main task of a freely elected government in the GDR would be to represent East German interests in negotiations which would, in some manner, result in unification with the Federal Republic. As such, any new government would have a transitional character similar to the caretaker government of Hans Modrow. The idea of the GDR having a viable future as a separate, sovereign state was being shed by most of the political groupings in the GDR as a clearer picture of the real state of the economy after 40 years of 'real existing socialism' emerged and as, on average, two thousand East Germans per day continued to pour into the Federal Republic. Furthermore, the government of Helmut Kohl in Bonn was coming under considerable pressure to engineer a means of stopping East Germans from voting with their feet by persuading them that, not only was political change in the GDR guaranteed, but that their standard of living would improve quickly. German unity increasingly came to be viewed as the only realistic way of giving East Germans hope. Kohl had anticipated this development earlier when, on 28 November 1989, he surprised the world with his 'Ten Point Programme for Overcoming the Division of Germany and Europe' in which he declared his government would strive for a confederative status with the GDR that would ultimately, should Germans want it, result in unity.[22]

The actual development towards German unity (both East and West German politicians came to speak exclusively of 'unity' rather than 're-unification' in deference to Polish sensitivity over the question of its formerly German territories) proceeded at a rate which quickly outpaced the rather leisurely schedule envisaged by Chancellor Kohl's 10 points. But their pronouncement at such an early date, little over a month after Honecker's downfall, had the effect of bringing the question of German unity into the open as a realisable political goal. Except for a few isolated groups on the extreme right, the new East German political activists tended to view the issue of unity as a 'taboo' subject which only the politically irresponsible called for. There were, for example, embarrassing scenes during the mass marches in Leipzig, when outnumbered activists tried in vain to prevent chants demanding unity from being taken up by the crowds in the street. Kohl's 10 points allowed many of them, especially those in political sympathy with mainstream conservative politics in West Germany, to break through this psychological barrier by legitimising the question in their eyes. Furthermore, Kohl's action, undertaken without any prior consultation with the 'Four Powers' of Britain, France, the United States and the Soviet Union, was a clear statement that the right to self-determination of the German people took precedence over any residual rights to determine the future of Germany still held by these countries as post Second World War occupying powers.

THE FIRST FREE ELECTIONS IN THE GDR

Against this background the development of party politics in East Germany quickly began to take on the general contour of the political scene in West Germany. Additionally, it became obvious to parties in the GDR that 'partner' parties in West Germany constituted a desirable election asset, not only because they were a source of additional manpower, equipment, money and campaigning experience, but because backing by a West German party was increasingly becoming the most important factor in establishing credibility with the East German electorate. The West German parties, with future pan-German elections in mind, also realised that political co-thinkers in the East would be advantageous.

On the 11 February, Modrow and Kohl had agreed to establish a committee to implement the introduction of the West German Deutsche Mark into the GDR as a replacement for the weak East German Mark. Additionally, the government in East Berlin (expanded to form a 'grand coalition' since the inclusion of representatives from the Round Table on 5 February) was by now committed to introducing a market economy into the GDR. The success of both these ventures clearly depended upon smooth political relations between Bonn and East Berlin but, at the same time, there was growing uneasiness among East Germans over the social costs that the impending economic shakeout in the GDR would entail, in terms of unemployment resulting from East German factories shedding work force or closing altogether.[23]

At the start of the campaign, the East German Social Democratic party was riding high in the opinion polls, some of which were predicting a majority of over 50 per cent for the SPD (East).[24] The SPD's advocacy of extensive social security safeguards, linked to the gradual introduction of economic union with West Germany, was in contrast to the programme of the Alliance for Germany, a coalition between the Christian Democratic Union (East), which had been reformed under the leadership of Lothar de Maiziere, and the newer parties, Democratic Awakening and the German Social Union. The German Social Union, formed just prior to the election, was supported and largely created by the Bavarian Christian Social Union. The Alliance, backed by the West German CDU, campaigned for quick economic union, followed by quick political union achieved through East Germany joining the Federal Republic by means of Article 23 in the West German constitution. In line with their gradualist approach, the SPD favoured Article 146 which foresaw the drawing up of a new constitution for a united Germany, a much lengthier process than simply extending the existing Federal constitution to the East.

Twenty-two parties, in addition to the front-running Alliance and SPD, contested the elections. The remaining Bonn parliamentary parties, the Free Democrats and the Greens, had by this time also found GDR election coalitions to support. The original human rights activists, who had played such an important role in the earlier stages of the 'peaceful revolution' had banded together, without a backer in Bonn, to form Bundnis 90, which linked New Forum, Democracy Now and the Initiative for Peace and Human Rights. Similarly the PDS stood alone.

After intense personal campaigning throughout the GDR, the election results gave Chancellor Kohl what he wanted; confirmation that his approach to German unity was the most popular and a political grouping in power in East Berlin with which he could expect to work. The CDU (East) received the largest percentage of votes cast with 40.91 per cent. Together with the votes cast for its two coalition partners, the Alliance for Germany received a total of 48.15 per cent. The Social Democrats fell far short of their expected results with only 21.84 per cent. The former communists, the PDS, came third with 16.33 per cent of the vote. The coalition led by New Forum, who once had been able to gather the names of tens of thousands of East Germans declaring themselves to be members, received a tiny 2.90 per cent.[25] What the elections showed was that by German unity, most East Germans understood this to mean becoming, in effect, West Germans. Significantly, in areas where factory workers constituted more than 45 per cent of the electorate, the vote for the conservative Alliance was highest.[26] The old SED had given preference to the industrial sector of the economy at the expense of other sectors, with the result that industrial workers far outnumbered those employed elsewhere (contrary, for example, to the pattern in West Germany). Ironically, it was these people who felt most strongly that the future social market economy in the GDR should be in the hands of people who understood such things. In the Federal Republic they had a model of a successful market oriented society which was now being offered to them by the Christian Democrats. After 40 years of one unsuccessful social experiment, most East Germans saw little reason to delay their 'Anschluss' any longer than necessary.

NOTES

[1] Table in *Der Bau der Mauer durch Berlin*; *Die Flucht aus der Sowjetzone und die Sperrmassnahmen des kommunistischen Regimes vom* 13. *August* 1961 *in Berlin*, Bonn, Federal Ministry for Inner-German Relations; 1986, pp. 15-26; *Die innerdeutsche Grenze*, Bonn, Federal Ministry for Inner-German Relations; 1987, pp. 5-22;

Gert Ritter and Joseph Hajdu, *Die Innerdeutsche Grenze*: *Analyse ihrer raumlichen Auswirkungen und der raumwirksamen Staatstätigkeitin den Grenzgebieten*, 2nd., enlarged edition Geostudien no. 7, Cologne, (Dr Karl-Gunther Schneider and Dr Bernd Wiese), Dürenerstr. 249, D-5000 Köln 41, 1982, pp. 20-35.

[2] *Welt am Sonntag*, 26 March 1989, p. 2 (based on information alleged to have come from the Federal Intelligence Service-Bundes Nachrichtendienst (BND); *Die Welt*, 20-21 May 1989, p. 1.

[3] Foreign Broadcasting Information Service/FBIS, EEU-89-083, 2 May 1989, p. 12; FBIS, WEU-89-085, 4 May 1989, p. 2.

[4] *Die Welt*, 20-21 May, 1989, p. 1; Barbara Donovan, 'New East German Travel Regulations', Radio Free Europe Research, RAD Background Report/61, 6 April 1989.

[5] United Nations Treaty Series, 1975, vol. 986 I, Treaty No. 14407. The protocol to this agreement, meant to be secret, was published by the Hungarians in 1975.

[6] *Der Spiegel*, 3 July 1989, p. 16.

[7] The interview in *Der Spiegel*, 7 May 1990, pp. 53-66, was given six days before Sindermann's death.

[8] *Neues Deutschland*, 9 October 1989, p. 4.

[9] *Ibid.*, 19 October 1989, p. 1.

[10] Eppelmann was the main author of the 'Berlin Appeal' of 1981, an influential document in the history of the GDR's unofficial peace movement. For a discussion of its impact in East Germany at the time see, Vladimir Tismaneanu, 'Nascent civil society in the German Democratic Republic', *Problems of Communism*, March-June 1989, pp. 96-98.

[11] Hubertus Knabe, editor, *Aufbruch in eine andere DDR*; *Reformer und Oppositionelle zur Zukunft ihres Landes*, Reibek bei Hamburg, Rowohlt, December 1989, p. 158.

[12] *Neues Deutschland*, 19 October 1989, p. 2.

[13] Harry Tisch had already resigned (2 November 1989) as leader of the Free German Trade Union Federation (FDGB) by the time of the newspaper investigations into his activities. At a meeting of the National Executive Committee of the Free German Trade Union Federation on 9 December 1989, Tisch's successor reported that he had had at his free disposal a fund of 500,000 East Marks per year. For a report on the NEC meeting see FBIS, EEU-89-236, 11 December 1989, p. 61.

[14] *Neues Deutschland*, 6 November 1989, p. 1.

[15] *Ibid.*, p. 3.

[16] For a critical view of Modrow's 'pro-reform' role, particularly during the demonstrations in early October 1989, see *Der Spiegel*, 12 February 1990, pp. 98-100.

[17] For text of West German press agency report citing 'artists' circles' as the source and the East German press agency carrying the SED denial see FBIS, EEU-89-232, 5 December 1989, p. 34.

[18] The Round Table was set up on 7 December 1989 in the Dietrich-Bonhöffer-House at the invitation of the Evangelical Church. In addition to the Church and representatives of the government, participants included representatives

from the SED and its former bloc parties—New Forum, Democracy Now, Democratic Awakening, the Green Party, the Initiative for Peace and Human Rights, the SPD, and the United Left.

[19] The Extraordinary Party Congress took place on the weekends of 8-10 December and 16-18 December 1989. For various reports on the individual sessions see FBIS, EEU-89-236, 11 December 1989, pp. 48-57 and FBIS, EEU-89-241, 18 December 1989, pp. 35-53.

[20] For a detailed account of Stasi operations and organisation see the three part series in *Der Spiegel*, 5 February 1990, 12 February 1990 and 19 February 1990.

[21] *Süddeutsche Zeitung*, 8 January 1990, p. 1.

[22] For text of Kohl's speech to the Bundestag outling 'Ten Points', see Presse- und Informationsamt der Bundesregierung, 'Bulletin', no. 134/S. 1141, 29 November 1989.

[23] According to a report by East German Secretary of State for the Economy, Günther Krause, only 32 per cent of GDR firms were financially viable, 14 per cent were beyond all help and the rest might be saved with financial assistance from the state and access to credit. See *Der Spiegel*, 14 May 1990, pp. 122-123.

[24] The Central Institute for Youth Research (Zentralinstitutes für Jugend- forschung) in Leipzig, for example, carried out a poll which showed 54 per cent of GDR citizens planning to vote SPD. See *Neues Deutschland*, 7 February 1990, p. 2. The same poll showed 12 per cent for the PDS, 11 per cent for the CDU and 4 per cent for New Forum.

[25] *Süddeutsche Zeitung*, 20 March 1990, p. 6 (full results from the 15 constituen- cies).

[26] *Ibid.*, 21 March 1990, p. 6.

Human Rights As *Realpolitik*
The United States in the CSCE

CAROL O'HALLARON

Darwin College, Cambridge University

After the Soviet acquisition of atomic weapons, fear of nuclear war clouded the recognition by the West of the link between respect for human rights by governments and international security interests. As missiles stockpiled in the 1960s, the democracies decreased their criticism of repressive regimes in the East and instead pressed their leaders to ease tension and control the arms race through a *modus vivendi* with the Soviet Union. In response, western ministers eschewed a combative posture toward the East and endorsed a qualified policy of co-operation with the communist bloc which, they claimed, would lead to a more productive relationship. But, by the mid-1970s, the reaction of the West to the USSR grew more complex with acknowledgement that the fall-out of détente was further repression of civil and political rights in the East bloc. Ultimately, revulsion by the Western public against the Soviet Government's policy toward its citizens, coupled with anger over Soviet surrogate intrusion into the Third World proved stronger than anxiety over nuclear war. Thus, the Western delegations of the Conference on Security and Co-operation in Europe (CSCE), which convened in 1972 upon a Soviet initiative for recognition of the post-war *status quo*, infused the negotiations with demands for recognition of Western political values. In 1975 the 35 participating states from East and West Europe and North America signed the Helsinki Final Act which combined Soviet security concerns with Western principles on human rights.

The Helsinki Final Act and the CSCE implementation reviews contributed to a re-evaluation of human rights as an instrument of foreign policy by the United States. Over the last 15 years, the US and the Soviet Union have manifested an extreme confrontational posture inside the CSCE meetings. Suppressed during the era of détente, the subliminal ideological differences surfaced

63

inside the closed-door sessions of the reviews. But Western polemics on the dependence of international security on recognition of civil and political rights by governments would not remain compartmentalised in the CSCE process for long. The American public's support for pressure on the Soviet Union turned the human rights issue into a dimension of US *realpolitik*. The Soviet Union was compelled to take heed and US diplomatic efforts on the human rights issue in the late 1980s would accelerate Soviet domestic reform. But the road to acknowledgement by the Superpowers of the identity of peace and human rights was a jagged one and detours still lurk ahead.

The concept of a European Security Conference harks back to the 1954 Foreign Ministers Meeting of the Big Four when Soviet Foreign Minister Molotov proposed a non-aggression pact 'instead of plans for the creation of a European Defence Community'. The collective security Pact would replace the two alliances 'until the conclusion of a peace treaty with Germany and the reunification of Germany into a single state'.[1] Although NATO was consolidated in May 1955 with the inclusion of West Germany, the Soviets reiterated their proposal at the Geneva Summit in July and the follow-up Foreign Ministers Meeting in October. There the West counter-proposed a Treaty of Assurance, which would maintain the two alliances and become effective upon agreement regarding the reunification of Germany under supervised elections.[2]

The Treaty was similar to Molotov's Pact with regard to its provisions for the renunciation of force, no assistance to aggression, a zone within which special measures are taken, agreed limits of force, reciprocal inspection on verification and withdrawal of foreign forces not part of collective security. And while the Soviet Pact envisioned expansion of economic trade and cultural relations, the West proffered 17 items to encompass the east bloc specifically relating to human rights, including freedom from fear of arrest, exchange of ideas, freedom of movement, and reduction of radio jamming. Molotov responded that:

> We have never in the past and never will in the future picture to ourselves such a 'freedom of exchange of ideas' which could consist of free war propaganda or the misanthropic propaganda of atomic attack.[3]

Only minor cultural agreements were signed by the Big Four and all of these meetings in the mid-1950s ended in deadlock, primarily over the terms of German unification.

Although historians have dismissed the three meetings as unsuccessful, the conferences marked the first time the principles of the United Nations Declaration of Human Rights were discussed at the highest official levels since the Cold War began. Additionally, the meetings contained the seed sown by the Soviets for a security conference which would evolve into the CSCE. Unfortunately, discussion of the core differences between East and West—how governments should treat their citizens— would not crop up again in serious negotiations for another 15 years. In effect, the CSCE simply picked up the agenda the Big Four dropped in 1955. In the meantime, arms control issues eclipsed political debate in diplomatic discourse.

The decision by the Western Powers after the Korean War to cut expensive conventional forces and to rely on the cheaper deployment of nuclear weapons contributed to public worry about armaments, which would express itself in a demand for détente. Secretary of State, John Foster Dulles, foresaw the political problem that reliance on nuclear weaponry could create: '[S]triking power was apt to be immobilized by moral repugnance. If this happened the whole structure could collapse'.[4] The constituencies pressured their leaders to find ways to ease East- West tension as scientists publicised the grisly details of the effects of strontium-90. The launching of Sputnik in 1957 and Khrushchev's threats to the status of Berlin in 1958 exacerbated fears over nuclear engagement and offset the West's outrage against the Soviet government's repression of Hungarian revolutionaries in 1956. By 1959 the emotional climate shaped Western preparations for the Paris Summit. Although Dulles warned against 'spreading the impression that only power rivalries, and not basic principles create present tensions,' the United States removed the fundamental issue of the two German states from the agenda and human rights concerns were not considered.[5] Instead, Eisenhower planned to propose an 'atoms for peace' programme had the Summit not abruptly ended over the U2 incident.

'Basic principles' melted under the glare of the nuclear weapons problem, and over the next decade the new realists of foreign policy would relegate Dulles' remarks to the amusing rhetoric of Cold War ideology. But once diplomats diminished the primacy of Western ideology, then human rights as a dimension of that ideology would be devalued as well. Describing President John Kennedy, Arthur Schlesinger wrote that:

> The John Foster Dulles contrast between the God-anointed apostles of free enterprise and the regimented hordes of atheistic communism bored

him . . . With his historian's perspective, he was disposed to view the conflict in national rather than ideological terms.[6]

POLICY OF PEACEFUL COEXISTENCE

Although Kennedy had campaigned on a pledge to fill the 'missile gap', it was the Soviets who suffered a five to one inferiority in inter-continental ballistic missiles (ICBMs) and sea-launched ballistic missiles (SLBMs) in the early 1960s.[7] These security problems, along with an impending split with China, drove Premier Nikita Khrushchev to pursue the policy of 'peaceful coexistence' with the United States. Amenable to détente, Kennedy told Khrushchev in Vienna in 1961 that his interest was the maintenance of the *status quo*, a standstill in the spheres of interest and a nuclear test ban treaty. Concerned about communist insurgencies in the Third World, particularly in Laos, Kennedy advised his counterpart that the two powers shared the obligation to conduct the competition of ideas without involving vital interests.[8] Kennedy's approach to the Soviet Union hardened after the Berlin crisis in 1961, and anti-communist sentiment permeated his State of the Union addresses. However, after the scare of the Cuban missile crisis in October 1962, 'peaceful coexistence' was back on track and a partial test ban treaty was signed by the US and USSR in 1963. Probably more psychologically important for the public, hot line telephones were installed in the White House and Kremlin.

'Communication' appeared to provide the answer to the East-West conflict and this notion would further degrade the concept of human rights as a viable aspect of foreign policy. 'Those exchanges of ideological rhetoric accomplished nothing except to stir up angry emotions on both sides', wrote President Lyndon Johnson.[9] Eschewing the rhetoric also meant refraining from freedom and democracy themes in dealing with the Soviets. As a remedy to the East-West divide, the President proposed in 1964 to 'build bridges of trade, travel and humanitarian assistance . . . across the gulf that divided us from Eastern Europe'.[10] Johnson was forgetting Prime Minister Harold Macmillan's complaint to Molotov at the 1955 Foreign Ministers Meeting that exchanges should be the 'very reverse of officially sponsored or arranged visits' and his warning that multiplying group visits without reducing obstacles to free communication is to 'aim at the superficial and ignore the essential'.[11] Instead, Johnson signed more agreements on official exchanges with the Soviets, easily controlled by the state, than all previous Presidents combined.

Johnson had announced to the United Nations that his priorities were arms control and nuclear non-proliferation. In his meeting at Glassboro with Prime Minister Alexei Kosygin, Johnson did not discuss human rights but instead focused on the Middle East, Vietnam and strategic arms limitation talks.

In a speech in October 1966 to American newspaper editors, Johnson expanded on his humanitarian theme and said that the East-West environment must be improved in order that the unification of Germany could take place 'in the context of a larger, peaceful and prosperous Europe'.[12] In the same address he said that 'One of the bedrocks of our foreign policy was opposition to the use of force to change existing frontiers'.

Johnson's remarks dovetailed with the renewed Soviet campaign, expressed at Warsaw Treaty Organisation (WTO) meetings, for a European security conference, similar to the 1954 proposal. They called for the abolition of the alliances, to be replaced by a pan-European collective security arrangement and recognition of existing European frontiers. The new items on the Soviet agenda consisted of recognition of the German Democratic Republic (GDR) and prohibition of the acquisition of nuclear weapons by either German state. The Soviets still did not include full US participation in the proposed conference at their WTO meeting in Bucharest in July 1966 or Karlovy Vary in April 1967.[13] The Soviet objection to an American role would change, however, after the invasion by the USSR of Czechoslovakia, precipitating the President's suspension of strategic arms limitation talks (SALT). At the Budapest meeting in 1969, the WTO scrapped its insistence on the dissolution of the alliances, and invited the US as a full participant at the proposed security conference.

During this period the Allies undertook several measures in support of the continuation of détente. In July 1968 NATO called for mutually balanced force reduction (MBFR) talks. Wary of the near parity of ICBMs between the Soviet Union and the US (1050 to 1054, respectively), NATO issued the Harmel Report in 1969, calling for 'progress towards a more stable relationship'. In May 1970, the Western Alliance signalled support of the European Security Conference if the agenda for talks contained items on freedom of movement, ideas and information.

The Soviet Union, assisted by the West German *Ostpolitik* policy of Chancellor Willy Brandt, had actually achieved the same goals it had outlined for a European Security Conference through negotiations between the USSR and the Federal Republic of Germany (FRG) leading to the Moscow Treaty of 1970. Along with the Warsaw Treaty of the same year, signed by the FRG and Poland, the signatories recognised the inviolability of the East-West frontiers including recognition of the Oder-Neisse line and the GDR. Significantly, they contained human rights provisions with regard to visitation and travel arrangements among ethnic Germans. But bilateral agreements were insufficient for the Soviets and they sought multilateral recognition of their hegemony over East Germany, particularly from the other three countries sharing rights with the Soviet Union over the German states.[14]

In 1969 National Security Advisor and later Secretary of State Henry Kissinger wanted to begin formal SALT, the vehicle for the new Nixon Administration's pursuit of détente, but he was sceptical about the assembly of a European Security Conference. But the US was isolated among the Allies on the issue, so Kissinger decided to accept the conference, if linked to concessions by the Soviets. Besides a settlement of the Berlin question, 'our strategy', wrote Kissinger, 'was to tie the European Security Conference to talks on troop reduction and both of them to an end of the Vietnam war'.[15] By presenting the US public with the possibility of bilateral troop withdrawals through negotiations, Kissinger could effectively douse cold water on Congressional calls for unilateral withdrawal of troops from Europe.

Marking the importance of the conference for the Soviets, the USSR agreed to Kissinger's demands and guaranteed unhindered access by the West to Berlin through the Quadripartite Act signed in September 1971. They also agreed to MBFR talks to begin six months after the European Security Conference, to be called the Conference on Security and Co-operation in Europe (CSCE), scheduled to begin negotiations in September 1972.

The West European delegations insisted on detailed negotiations to be conducted on human rights topics when they sat down at the CSCE to negotiate the Helsinki Final Act. Kissinger was unenthusiastic and played down the importance of the conference. James Maresca, US negotiator at the CSCE wrote:

> The low profile was a reflection of Kissinger's desire to have a positive working relationship with the Soviet leadership, and to be able to negotiate with them on a broad range of issues... Kissinger regarded the CSCE basically as a concession to Soviets.[16]

Kissinger's approach to the conference would change, however, under the failure of Soviet reciprocity in the context of détente and under domestic pressure. The 'broad range of issues' was not resolving, as US Congress members and their constituents watched the US position in the Vietnam War deteriorate toward a complete withdrawal. The American public began to believe that détente benefited the Soviets and Moscow's official journal *International Affairs* would concur:

> The objective conditions for international détente are inherent in the material might and growing prestige and influence of the socialist community and in the growing strength of the whole anti-imperialist front.[17]

Nuclear holocaust was still a threat and Kissinger had issued an alert during the 1973 Middle East War, but the Western reaction became more differentiated. The public responded less to fear and more to the realities of Soviet expansionism and repression of its own citizens.

The USSR's invasion of Czechoslovakia renewed the ranks of Soviet dissidents, which had been depleted after the crackdown on publishers of unofficial magazines and demonstrators in support of the Soviet constitution in the mid-1960s. In 1969 dissidents organised the Action Group for Defence of Human Rights and they petitioned the UN Commission on Human Rights to investigate abuses in the USSR. The UN did not respond but Soviet security police did and heavy harassment by the authorities culminated in new arrests. In June 1971, the Human Rights Committee founded by Andrei Sakharov, established links with the New York-based International League for the Rights of Man and disseminated documentation on trials and incarcerations of activists through the dissident journal *The Chronicle of Human Events*. The outreach to the West, precipitated interest by the major newspapers and proved crucial in undermining the premises of détente. 'Relaxation of tensions' between East and West meant increased vigilance against 'infiltration' of Western ideas by Soviet authorities.[18]

The drumbeat of the dissidents reverberated in the West and first manifested itself politically when US Senator Henry Jackson and Representative Charles Vanick tied granting most favoured nation status to increased emigration of national minorities from the Soviet Union. Kissinger viewed the public raising of human rights violations of the Soviet Union as provocative and liable to jolt the international order, thus risking nuclear war. He pointed out that his quiet diplomacy with the Soviet hierarchy had resulted in unprecedented numbers of Jews being allowed to emigrate (35,000 in 1973 with promise of more).[19] 'If baiting Moscow led to increased Soviet adventurism, which of the crusaders for human rights would support our determination to resist it?' Kissinger asked.[20] Still, Congressional conservatives and liberals coalesced to pass the Jackson-Vanick Amendment to the 1973 Trade Bill, with the support of their constituents, plus the *New York Times* and the *Washington Post*.

By 1973 a new awareness of the significance of the human rights question to the American constituency influenced Kissinger and the new administration of President Gerald Ford, inaugurated in August 1974 after the Watergate scandal. 'This attitude was increasingly visible in the CSCE toward the end of the negotiations', wrote Maresca. 'The overall slippage in American relations with the USSR coincided with a growing domestic political need'.[21] By the spring of 1975 the US had retreated from Saigon and Cuban surrogates of the Soviet Union had penetrated Angola. The 'domestic political need' compelled Ford, to drop the word 'détente' entirely from his public pronouncements.

By the summer of 1975, the 35 CSCE delegations had negotiated a document reflecting a state of East-West détente with strong reservations. The Final Act is a morally obligating but legally non-binding document containing three 'Baskets' expressing Soviet security needs and Western human rights concerns.[22]

Basket I includes the Soviet desire for statements regarding the inviolability of existing frontiers; obligations to refrain from the threat or use of force; recognition of territorial integrity of states; the need for peaceful settlement of disputes; non-intervention in internal affairs; and the Western concerns for freedom of thought, conscience, religion or belief, equal rights and self-determination of peoples. Importantly, while negotiating Basket I, the FRG steadfastly rejected the Soviet concept of 'immutability' of borders and instead insisted on the right to 'peaceful change' of frontiers.[23] Under this principle, the CSCE should be able to 'bless' the reunification of Germany. To counter the Soviet emphasis on the security measures of Basket I, the West also insisted that this Basket contain the statement that all the principles therein were of equal significance. As a practical security measure, Basket I provides for the notification to all CSCE states 21 days in advance of major manoeuvres exceeding 25,000 troops. Participating states are also encouraged to 'invite'

voluntarily, on a bilateral basis, observers (outside their grouping) to the manoeuvres.

Basket II contains provisions regarding co-operation on
trade, technology, environment, education and culture.

Basket III delineates obligations to improve human contacts, including the reunification of families separated by the Cold
War, freedom of movement and information.

Most importantly, the signing of the Helsinki Final Act in 1975
reinvigorated dissidents in the Eastern bloc who formed groups
to monitor implementation of the accords. Reports on the plight
of these individuals stimulated Congress to establish a 'Helsinki
commission' composed of legislative and executive branch members to monitor the implementation of the Final Act. V. Chkhukvadze wrote in *International Affairs*:

> Never in the history of the rivalry of the two social systems has there been
> a political force to compare with the sanctimonious 'concern' over 'human
> rights' presently in full swing in the capitalist countries. Influential political
> groups in the West, the United States in particular, are sparing neither funds
> nor efforts to poison the international climate, undermine détente and
> resurrect the Cold War.[24]

During the Carter Administration, human rights did not
eclipse arms control, but the two issues became closely entwined
in the conduct of American foreign policy over the course of
Carter's term. He had campaigned for office eschewing the
expedient balance of power politics of the Nixon-Kissinger era,
and pledging public diplomacy on human rights in the international sphere. In the few weeks after the inauguration, the
President wrote to General Secretary Leonid Brezhnev calling for
respect for the Helsinki Final Act, and replied to Andrei
Sakharov's letter of congratulations. Then, days before the SALT
II talks were scheduled to resume in Moscow, the President
invited to the White House the first dissident released since the
signing of the Final Act, Vladimir Bukovsky. These incidents
drew Soviet fire and Brezhnev warned Carter in a letter of 25
February not to correspond with 'renegades', and, moreover, he
'would not allow interference in our internal affairs, whatever
pseudo-humanitarian slogans are used to present it'.[25]

The Soviets' harsh response, along with a letter from Prime
Minister Callaghan reporting both Helmut Schmidt's and Brezhnev's concern with Carter's new emphasis on human rights,
calmed the President's rhetoric.[26] Carter's main goal, not unlike

his predecessor, was to obtain a SALT treaty and he attempted
to mitigate the effect of his earlier statements on Soviet human
rights violations by insisting his human rights policy was global.[27]
Thus, when the Soviet Government aroused the American public
by further arrests of dissidents, National Security Advisor, Zbigniew Brzezinski admitted, 'we deliberately muted our reactions to
avoid further friction'.[28]

In March, when the Soviets rebuffed Secretary of State Cyrus
Vance's alterations of Ford's Vladivostock agreement on SALT
II to include ceilings on nuclear launchers, Foreign Minister
Andrei Gromyko said 'all that talk' about rights poisoned the
atmosphere of the SALT discussions. 'How could that help in the
resolution of other problems, including those touching on strategic weapons?' he asked.[29]

The first CSCE review meeting, assembling in October 1977
at Belgrade, manifested the changed attitude toward détente. The
fundamental issues which divided East and West erupted in
acrimonious debate, having been repressed for 20 years in the
dialogue of détente. The agenda of the meeting, like all the
following CSCE reviews, broke into three parts: review of implementation; submission of new proposals to strengthen the
Helsinki accords; and the drawing up of a document.

In the nine weeks of review of implementation, the US
delegation led a strong attack on the Soviet record of non-compliance and emphasised that respect for human rights was an
essential factor of détente. The Soviet delegation retorted that
raising human rights issues constituted a violation of the principle
on 'non-intervention in internal affairs'. Interpreting non-intervention as 'use of force', US Ambassador Goldberg complained
that raising a subject about fulfilment by another state of
commitments which both have undertaken cannot be considered
coercion, but rather normal diplomatic discourse.[30] He and other
Western delegations cited the cases of persecution of Helsinki
monitors and those incarcerated for their political or religious
beliefs.

But the Soviets conceded the issue when they broke their own
rule of refraining from raising human rights matters of another
state. By denouncing the US on problems of unemployment and
racial discrimination, the Soviet delegation could no longer claim
at the CSCE that human rights fell under the rubric of domestic
jurisdiction of states.

Both NATO and the Warsaw Pact had complied with the
provisions on notification of manoeuvres of Basket I and during

the Belgrade meeting, the Soviet Union invited the US as observers to Warsaw Pact military manoeuvres for the first time.[31] The Soviet delegation used their implementation of this provision as a basis for attempting to divert the human rights debate to security issues. They primarily promoted the concept of the irreversibility of détente, non-first use of nuclear weapons, prohibition of the expansion of political and military alliances (Spain was applying to become a member of NATO), and the dangers of the neutron bomb, a device which Carter had advocated for NATO.

The CSCE, operating under a consensus rule, could not agree on any proposals except for the assembly of three 'experts meetings' on (1) peaceful settlement of disputes; (2) economic, scientific and cultural co-operation; and (3) a scientific forum. The results of these meetings were to be reported to the next CSCE review scheduled to meet in Madrid in November 1980. The 35 issued a three-page document which asserted the Western bias that détente was dependent on the implementation of the Final Act.

In fact, the Belgrade review revealed that hard words on human rights by the US would not sabotage SALT II, and Carter stepped up his ideological attacks on the Soviet Union, backing them up with demands for concessions on human rights issues. Within weeks of the close of the Belgrade meeting the Soviet Union meted out harsh prison sentences to Anatoly Sharansky and Yuri Orlov, Soviet monitors of the Helsinki accords, and Carter retaliated by ordering a ban on export to the USSR of oil production technology and computer material. '[T]he President,' admitted Brzezinski, 'had to take into account the impact of any decision on our difficult SALT negotiations.'[32] On 2 June 1978, Carter called the Soviet system totalitarian and repressive and gave the Soviets a choice of 'co-operation or confrontation'.[33]

More significantly, in October of 1978, Carter attached pre-conditions of his signing of the SALT II at the Vienna Summit, scheduled for the spring of 1979. Unless dissidents were released from prison and the death sentence commuted on a Soviet spy convicted of espionage for the United States, Carter would not sign SALT II. By May, the Soviet Government released five incarcerated dissidents to the West and lifted the death sentence on the Soviet spy.[34] Also, in the course of 1979, Soviet emigration authorities permitted 50,000 Jews to leave the country.

But even with the signing of SALT II, in May of 1979, the policy of détente was becoming threadbare, as Vietnam installed a government in Cambodia and the Soviet Union supported Cuban troops in Angola and Ethiopia.

In Europe, NATO grew alarmed at the fast-paced Soviet deployment of intermediate range missiles in East Europe, a class of nuclear firepower they could not counter in Europe. In December 1979, the Allies decided that if the Soviet weapons could not be negotiated away by the autumn of 1983, NATO would deploy 108 Pershing II missiles to replace the shorter range Pershing I launchers and to add 464 ground launched cruise missiles in Western Europe.

Détente snapped between the Superpowers when the Soviet Union invaded Afghanistan on 25 December 1979. Among other sanctions, Carter imposed a grain embargo against the USSR and ordered a boycott of the Moscow Olympics. He also informed the Soviet Union that the bilateral General Agreement on Contracts, Exchanges and Co-operation would not be renewed. Finally, Congress would decline to ratify SALT II.

Soviet relations with the US deteriorated further in August 1980 over findings of a Soviet brigade in Cuba. In August 1981, the Soviets breached the security provisions of Basket I when they failed to provide 'required' information concerning a large-scale exercise in the Byelorussian and Baltic military districts and on the Baltic sea.[35] Furthermore, the activities of the independent trade union Solidarity in Poland provoked the Soviet government to deploy divisions on the Polish border in December 1980. In this acid atmosphere, the second CSCE review opened at the end of the Carter years, November 1980, two months before the inauguration of President Ronald Reagan.

Reagan filled the ranks of his Administration with staff opposed to détente. When Secretary of State Alexander Haig described Chinese concerns about US foreign policy, he was certainly just as accurately describing the disposition of the White House: 'Certain Chinese leaders, among others, believed that US diplomacy in the later Vietnam period had moved America toward strategic partnership with the Soviet Union through such measures as the Helsinki accords, SALT, détente, and increased credits and trade'.[36] In December 1982, National Security Directive-75 listed three objectives of the Administration: 1) to contain Soviet expansion and to moderate Soviet international behavior; 2) to encourage, by the limited means at the disposal of the United States, change in the Soviet system towards greater liberalism over time; and 3) to negotiate agreements that were in the interest of the United States.[37]

Unlike his predecessors, Reagan dismissed SALT talks as unimportant. This unnerved the Soviets, who wanted to renew discussions. Haig claims that Reagan planned to build up US defence again in order to enhance its bargaining position at new strategic arms talks with the Soviets.[38] Accordingly, the US would reveal a tough stance in opposition to the Nicaraguan government, an El Salvadoran guerilla movement, and a communist régime in Grenada.

Despite the intent not to negotiate too early, the US was compelled to sit down with the Soviets by the NATO decision in 1979, which called for a dual track of deployment and negotiation. In addition, the US needed to counter Soviet propaganda fuelling a growing peace movement in the West which opposed NATO's deployment of the intermediate-range missiles. Furthermore, gestures of peaceful purposes were needed to ameliorate careless remarks by the Reagan Administration on contingency plans for a nuclear war limited to Europe. Thus, in November 1981, the US began negotiations with the Soviets on intermediate nuclear forces (INF) and began talks on strategic weapons (START) in June 1982. The US also endorsed the French proposal, raised at the Madrid CSCE, for a Conference on Disarmament in Europe (CDE).[39]

Citation at Madrid of human rights violations by the Soviet Union would also serve to buttress the decision to deploy INF. The NATO countries did not have to look far for examples—the Warsaw Pact imprisoned over 500 human rights activists and religious believers during the course of the meeting, the Polish Government imposed martial law to suppress Solidarity in December 1981, and Vaclav Havel managed to smuggle a letter to the CSCE from his prison cell in Czechoslovakia.[40] In addition, Soviet dissidents in exile assembled in Madrid, lobbied Western delegations and called for abrogation of the Helsinki Final Act for Soviet non-compliance.

In particular, the Western delegations raised the cases of 43 incarcerated Soviet Helsinki monitors. When the Polish Government cracked down on the 9 million strong Solidarity group, US Ambassador to the CSCE Max Kampelman decided that negotiating a document on human rights in such an atmosphere was cynical and the accords would lose public support if the meeting continued. The West German delegation, on the other hand, wanted the conference to continue because of the crisis and saw Madrid as a handy forum for criticizing Warsaw. In the end, the Western delegations decided that they would no longer negotiate in the thrice-weekly sessions of the document drafting committee in protest against martial law in Poland.[41]

'In a typical session', wrote a Radio Liberty reporter, 'the Soviet Union and some of its allies—particularly Bulgaria and Czechoslovakia—begin with a demand for negotiations. The West sits in silence. Possibly one of the neutral and non-aligned, usually Malta, makes a one minute statement about how something should be done. Then there is silence again and the meeting breaks up.'[42] Because the CSCE operates on a consensus rule, no country could terminate a meeting without agreement from the other 34. The Warsaw Pact did not want the meeting suspended in March over martial law in Poland, but as the silent sessions continued, they yielded when the 35 agreed to reconvene in November 1982.

When the 35 reassembled, the West continued to cite human rights violations in the East, but negotiations stepped up on France's CDE proposal. The proposed conference would convene in two stages. First, the participating states would strengthen confidence and security building measures (CSBM) from the Atlantic to the Urals, thus increasing the coverage deeper into Soviet territory as well as the adjoining sea and air space of the Atlantic.[43] The next CSCE review, scheduled for Vienna in 1986, would assess the progress of the first stage of the CDE and consider means to continue efforts toward security and disarmament in Europe. The Soviets countered the French agenda with proposals on a nuclear free zone, and declaration on non-first use of nuclear weapons. The West rebuffed these plans, and the Soviets agreed to accept the French proposal.

But the US held off agreement to the CDE until the East agreed to strengthened human rights language in the document covering free trade unions, plus an agreement to balance the CDE forum with the convening of three meetings on human rights, human contacts and a cultural forum, before the next CSCE review scheduled for November 1986 in Vienna.[44] The Soviets accepted the new language and meetings.

The CDE forum grew in importance when the Soviets walked out of the INF, START and MBFR negotiations in the fall of 1983 over NATO's decision to go ahead with plans for INF deployment. On 17 January 1984, in the first stage of CDE in Stockholm, the 35 began discussion of confidence and security building measures primarily based on a Western agenda of security concerns: to create greater openness and more predictability in military activities which would reduce the risk of surprise attack; to diminish the threat of armed conflict from miscalculation; and to inhibit the use of force for the purpose of political intimidation.[45]

The CSBM negotiations proved quite an achievement, adding significant new military measures to Basket I by requiring states to invite all CSCE states to all notifiable activities above a certain threshold, by requiring an exchange of calendars yearly with a list of planned military activities, and by granting each participating state the right to conduct inspection on the territory of another when compliance is in doubt.[46] The success of the CDE contrasted with the lack of progress at the experts meetings on human rights and human contacts, and the cultural forum. Although General Secretary Gorbachev had made only a few token releases of political prisoners, such as Anatoly Sharansky and Yuri Orlov in 1986, the Stockholm Agreement was signed anyway in September, in time for the opening of the third CSCE review in Vienna. The strengthening of the security provisions of the Final Act, without corresponding gains in the human rights field, threatened the balance of the three baskets.

The emphasis on arms control without political progress appeared to be returning to the East-West relationship, as Reagan met twice in 1986 with Gorbachev in Geneva and Reykjavik to discuss nuclear force reductions. But in the course of the Vienna CSCE review, which opened on 4 November, the imbalance was rectified by Western insistence on performance by the Soviet Union in implementation of human rights principles in the Soviet Union. The Western delegations were assisted by the desperate state of the Soviet economy, which would need Western credits, trade and technology to survive. Without a change of the Soviet image on human rights, the USSR could not expect help from the West. Moreover, the Soviets wanted to cut armaments, since their budget could not continue to withstand its vast military expenditures, much less compete with Reagan's SDI programme announced in March of 1983.[47]

Thus, Foreign Minister Eduard Schevardnadze opened the Vienna CSCE with a call for a human rights meeting to be held in Moscow and for arms reductions.[48] These proposals provided the levers for the West to demand from the Soviets performance on their human rights obligations in addition to a substantial document in Vienna on human rights. The US and the West pushed for the release of 750 Soviet citizens, incarcerated for political and religious reasons, an end to Articles 70 (anti-Soviet agitation), 190.1 (anti-Soviet slander), and to psychiatric confinement of dissidents, the resolution of separated family cases, and an end to the jamming of Western broadcasts.[49]

The pressure on the Soviets began to work and on 17 January 1987 the Soviet Ambassador to the Vienna meeting confirmed that political cases were under review 'because they had been causes of some discomfort in the past, and caused tensions in our relations with other countries'.[50] In early February, the Supreme Soviet issued special decrees releasing 140 prisoners convicted under Articles 70 and 190.1. In March, the Soviets resolved 137 bilateral family cases, raised by the US 'Helsinki commission'.

When Gorbachev decided to drop his insistence on the abandonment of the SDI programme and agreed to negotiate the removal of INF over a five year period, Secretary of State George Shultz brought the Assistant Secretary of State and head of the Human Rights and Humanitarian Affairs section of the State Department, Richard Schifter, to the major INF talks at Moscow in April 1987. Both Shultz and Schifter raised human rights issues and lists of political prisoners were handed to Soviet officials. The inclusion of human rights in sensitive INF negotiations did not backfire and Tass characterized the meetings as 'very positively assessed.'[51]

After the signing of the INF treaty in 1987, the Soviet Union pushed harder for the Moscow human rights conference, a conventional arms mandate and the end of the meeting. In July of 1988, the US nearly yielded to pressure from other NATO countries, including West Germany and France, who pressed hard to end the Vienna meeting before the other human rights demands of the Soviet Union were fulfilled. The 'Helsinki commission' pressed the State Department to stay in Vienna and the United Kingdom and Canada also strongly urged the US not to sign off on a conventional arms mandate or a Moscow human rights meeting until the Soviets complied more thoroughly to the human rights provisions.[52]

In early November 1988, when it became clear that the US, the United Kingdom and Canada would stand fast on more performance by the Soviet Union, Shevardnadze inquired from Shultz what specific concessions were needed.[53] Shultz reportedly replied by letter that all political prisoners would have to be released, *refuseniks* and other nationalities allowed to emigrate, bilateral cases resolved, an end to radio jamming, and a firm commitment by Gorbachev to human rights.[54]

On 28 November all radio jamming by the Soviet Union of Western broadcasts ended. The following month the Supreme Soviet decreed the release of all those left under Articles 70 and 190.1 and other political articles. By January of 1989 the Soviet

Union had released 600 prisoners since the opening of the CSCE, allowed 18,965 Jews to emigrate in 1988, and even more Armenians and Germans. Finally, after announcing at the United Nations in December a unilateral cut of 50,000 troops and removal of 5000 tanks from Eastern Europe, Gorbachev made extensive commitments on human rights including no future incarcerations of political or religious prisoners.[55] After Gorbachev's UN speech, the Soviet delegation in Vienna were willing to sign off on a substantial concluding document which virtually exhausts the area of human rights.

In turn, the Soviets received their human rights meeting in Moscow scheduled for 1991 and a conventional force mandate, which ordered that conventional ground forces from the Atlantic to the Urals, not including chemical, nuclear or naval weapons, would be the subject of negotiations to begin formally in May 1989. The aim of the mandate was to reduce the threat of surprise attack and large-scale military assault.

The 35 attempted to balance the conventional arms negotiations with a series of three meetings on the 'human dimension' in Paris 1989, Copenhagen 1990, and the final Moscow meeting in 1991. Importantly, since the revolutionary changes in Eastern Europe, these meetings have upgraded the vocabulary of human rights and focus on broader aspects of democracy such as rule of law, free elections, and minority rights.

But with the euphoria over the collapse of communist régimes in the Eastern bloc, a complacency has set in the West with regard to the lack of political progress in the Soviet Union and, to a certain extent, Romania and Bulgaria. Thus again, arms control outpaces the resolution of the political problems of the USSR. The conventional forces in Europe treaty promises the most dramatic cuts in armed forces in Europe since the Cold War began. In June 1990 President George Bush and Gorbachev drew up plans for deeper cuts in nuclear arsenals and signed a chemical weapons treaty, along with protocols under negotiation for verification of nuclear tests.

In addition, the old problem of the terms of unification of Germany pushes the CSCE deeper into the military realm. When the Soviet Union was yet unwilling to see a unified Germany as part of NATO, Gorbachev proposed at the June Summit in Washington the enhancement of CSCE into a 'Greater European Council' which would safeguard borders and assist in the resolution of conflicts. The Council, according to the Soviets, should schedule regular meetings and enact a broad mandate.

Historically, the United States has taken a stand against any proposal which would supplant NATO, increase the Soviet role in Western Europe, and dilute the US status there. With the US outside the EEC, and NATO's significance diminished, Secretary of State James Baker has emphasized the importance of the CSCE, which keeps an American foothold in Europe. But, in general, the US favours the flexible character of the CSCE and has been reluctant to introduce bureaucratic elements into the process, which may precipitate inertia. Even so, Bush agreed, as a concession to the Soviets at the June Summit, to render a permanent secretariat to the CSCE and improve its responsibilities and effectiveness.[56]

West German Foreign Minister Deitrich Genscher has strongly advocated the institutionalisation of the CSCE, which appears to be a major policy thrust of the FRG. Besides calling for a pan-European institution in the CSCE for the protection of human rights. Genscher also calls on the CSCE to establish 'a European centre for the early detection and political settlement of conflicts.'[57]

But before any of the above pan-European security arrangements are developed, consistency in democratic principles of all participating governments must be established. While the CSCE discusses self-determination of peoples at Copenhagen following the June Summit, it should be remembered that the Soviet Union has had five of its 15 republics under martial law at one time or another since the close of the Vienna review. Moreover, the Soviet Ambassador to the Vienna review and the Paris human dimension meeting noted in the March 1990 issue of International Affairs that 'Legislation on human rights is a neglected—if not the most neglected—component of our legal reform ... While the [Vienna] document was adopted more than a year ago, no new legislation has yet been passed on the majority of issues ... Some bills, such as those on freedom of conscience or social associations have not been discussed in parliament so far.'[58]

The success of the CSCE in the future will depend on the vigilance of the 35 with regard to the adherence by all participating states to their commitments on human rights. As the late Nobel Prize Winner Andrei Sakharov stated, 'If the Helsinki accords were complied with, arms control agreements would be unnecessary, and we would, in fact, have the reality of peace'.

NOTES

[1] Command Paper 9080. *Documents Relating to the Meeting of Foreign Ministers of France, the United Kingdom, the Soviet Union and the United States of America. Berlin, 25 Jan.–18 Feb.* 1954 (London: H.M. Stationery Office 1954), 10 Feb. 1954, pp. 109-111.

[2] Command Paper 9633. *Documents Relating to the Meeting of Foreign Ministers of France, the United Kingdom, the Soviet Union and the United States of America. Geneva, 27 Oct.–16 Nov.* 1955 (London: H.M. Stationery Office 1955), 28 Oct. 1955, p. 2.

[3] Ibid., 14 Nov. 1955, p. 151.

[4] Stephen. E. Ambrose. *Eisenhower the President. Vol. II* (London: George Allen and Unwin 1984), p. 284.

[5] W.M.B. Bader. *Austria Between East and West* 1945–1955. (Palo Alto: Stanford University Press 1966), p. 203.

[6] Arthur M. Schlesinger, Jr. *A Thousand Days, John F. Kennedy in the White House.* (London: Andre Deutsch 1965), p. 271.

[7] C. Brown & P.J. Mooney. *Cold War to Détente.* (London: Heinemann Books 1987), p. 81.

[8] Schlesinger, p. 326.

[9] Lyndon Baines Johnson. *The Vantage Point: Perspectives of the Presidency* 1963-1969. (Weidenfeld and Nicolson 1971), p. 463.

[10] Ibid., p. 471.

[11] Command Paper 9633, Oct. 1955, p. 137.

[12] Johnson, p. 474.

[13] WTO Political Consultative Committee Official Communique, 'Budapest Appeal'. *Survival.* Vol XI, No. 5, May 1969.

[14] Harold S. Russell. 'The Helsinki Declaration: Brobdninag or Lilliput?' *American Journal of International Law.* April 1976, p. 245.

[15] Henry Kissinger. *The White House Years.* (London: Weidenfeld and Nicolson and Michael Joseph 1979), pp. 1249–50.

[16] John J. Maresca. *To Helsinki: CSCE 1973–1975.* (Durham: Duke University Press 1985), p. 45.

[17] M. Kudrin. 'Objective Factors of Détente.' *International Affairs.* (Moscow: All Union Zaniye Society March 1975), p. 54

[18] Frederick C. Barghoorn. *Détente and the Democratic Movement in the USSR.* (New York: The Free Press 1976), pp. 31–33.

[19] Henry Kissinger. *Years of Upheaval* (London: Weidenfeld and Nicolson and Michael Joseph 1982), p. 986.

[20] Ibid., p. 252.

[21] Maresca, p. 46.

[22] Russell, p. 242.

[23] Stephen J. Flanagan. 'The CSCE and the Development of Détente,' *European Security: Prospects for the 1980s,* ed. by Derek Leebaert, (Heath and Company 1979), p. 196.

[24] V. Chkhukvadze. 'Human Rights and Non-Interference in the Internal

Affairs of States.' *International Affairs* (Moscow: All-Union Zaniye Society Dec. 1978), p. 22.

[25] Brzezinski, Zbigniew. *Power and Principle: Memoirs of the National Security Advisor 1977–1981.* (New York: Farrar, Straus, and Giroux 1983), p. 155.

[26] Ibid., p. 165.

[27] Adam Ulam. *Dangerous Relations, the Soviet Union in World Politics 1972-1982.* (New York: Oxford University Press 1983), p. 168.

[28] Brzezinski., p. 174.

[29] Adam Ulam, p. 172. (Quote from Pravda 1 April 1977).

[30] U.S. Commission on Security and Co-operation in Europe. *The Belgrade CSCE Follow Up Meeting: A Report and Appraisal (Unpublished Draft)*, p. 49.

[31] Ibid., p. 56. Also, see Dept of State Special Report. No. 45. June 1978. (Wash, D.C.: U.S. G.P.O. 1978), p. 2.

[32] Brzezinski, p. 323.

[33] Ibid., p. 320.

[34] Ibid., p. 339.

[35] John Borawski. *From the Atlantic to the Urals, Negotiating Arms Control at the Stockholm Conference.* (Washington, Brassey's (US), 1988), p. 29.

[36] Alexander M. Haig. *Caveat.* (London: Weidenfeld and Nicolson 1984), p. 106.

[37] Garthoff, Raymond. *Détente and Confrontation, American-Soviet Relations from Nixon to Reagan.* (The Brookings Institution, Wash., D.C., 1985.) p. 1012.

[38] Haig, p. 228.

[39] Borawski, p. 26.

[40] Gordon Skilling. 'CSCE in Madrid.' *Problems of Communism.* Vol 30. No. 4. July-August 1981, p. 8.

[41] Michael B. Wall. 'Western Disagreements.' *Helsinki, Human Rights, and European Security*, ed. by Vojtech Mastny (Durham: Duke University Press 1986), p. 245.

[42] Borawski, p. 30.

[43] Borawski, p. 30.

[44] U.S. Commission on Security and Co-operation in Europe. *The Madrid CSCE Review Meeting.* (Wash., D.C. Nov. 1983), p. 9.

[45] Borawski, p. 38.

[46] Ibid., pp. 105–106.

[47] Carol O'Hallaron 'Risky Business: Linking Human Rights and Defence Issues at the Vienna CSCE.' *Cambridge Review of International Affairs.* Vol. 4, No. 1, Spring 1990, p. 27–40.

[48] Pravda, 6 Nov. 1986.

[49] United States Commission on Security and Co-operation in Europe. *The Vienna Review Meeting of the CSCE. Compilation of Speeches. Nov.* 4 1986 *to Dec.* 28 1986. (Washington, D.C., 1987.)

[50] Bill Keller. 'Dissidents Sentences are Said to be Under Review.' *New York Times.* 17 January 1987, p. 3.

[51] Tass, 16 April 1987.

[52] Interview, Canadian Ambassador to the Vienna CSCE, William Bauer, 12 May 1989.

[53] Roland Eggleston, '*NATO Allies Drawing Up Conditions for Moscow Conference*,' Radio Liberty 517/88, 10 November 1988.

[54] Don Oberdorfer and Lou Cannon, 'Moscow Conference Endorsed,' *Washington Post*, 4 Jan. 1989, p. A1.

[55] Soviet News, No. 6455, 14 December 1988, p. 459.

[56] Edward Cody. 'Kohl Says Summit Shows Unification Problems Can be Solved in Time.' *International Herald Tribune*. 4 June 1990, p. 1. Also see David Hoffmann and Don Oberdorfer. 'U.S. Offers Soviets a 9 Point Plan on Germany.' *International Herald Tribune*, 4 June. p. 5.

[57] Deitrich Genscher, Minister of Foreign Affairs of the FRG. Speech delivered on 6 April 1990 at the Annual Meeting of American Society of Newspaper Editors. Unpublished.

[58] Yuri Kashlev and Andrei Zagorsky. 'The Human Dimension of Politics.' *International Affairs* (Moscow: All-Union Zaniye Society March 1990), pp. 67-68.

Future Defence and Security Needs: Military Roles and Requirements

GENERAL HANS-HENNING VON SANDRART

The author is Commander-in-Chief, Allied Forces Central Europe

It is difficult for me as a simple soldier and as an operational commander at my subordinate level to comment on future political, strategic and conceptual operational planning, before the political and military leadership of the Alliance has given clear guidance where to go and within which parameters we must work to change the central region posture and security concepts. As a soldier, I am a believer in the hierarchy of responsibilities and levels. This is the hour of the responsible and imaginative politician, and not of the General.

Before we can plan regional operational concepts in detail, there must be a clear definition of the overall political and security framework of Europe, and Central Europe in particular. There must also be agreement on the future role and structure of the North Atlantic Treaty Organisation (NATO), and on the basic principles of a revised NATO strategy. It is almost stating the obvious that the final agreement on the future security status of a unified Germany, as a result of the Two plus Four talks, will be the corner stone around which Central Region planning will have to be arranged. These thoughts are offered merely as a contribution to the dialogue about some of these issues.

The Central Region comprises almost all of West Germany and Benelux and its eastern borders currently run from the north of Germany to the Alps. To the north is Allied Forces Northern Europe (AFNorth) in Oslo, responsible for Schleswig Holstein, Denmark and Norway. South of the Alps, beyond neutral Switzerland and Austria, is Allied Forces Southern Europe (AFSouth), with its headquarters in Naples, which is responsible for the Mediterranean area. Historically, the greatest threat of major conflict has been considered to be against the Central Region, consequently both sides have concentrated their forces, in Central and Eastern Europe. The subordinate headquarters to Allied Forces Central Europe (AFCENT) include the northern and central army groups, responsible for their respective sectors, and Commander, Allied, Air Forces Central Europe (COMAAFCE), who in turn commands the headquarters of 2 and 4 Allied Tactical Air Forces. Each army group has four National Corps, and my reserves include a further US Corps and might include, following an appropriate political decision, First French Army, supported by Forces Aeriennes Tactiques (FATAC).

Defence plans developed over the years have the wartime deployment of the corps in the well known 'layer cake' layout, as close to our eastern borders as possible. This concept met the requirements of both Flexible Response and Forward Defence in the Cold War period, as the borders had a front line character and we were facing a massive offensive Warsaw Pact posture with an offensive doctrine. Our defensive capabilities, embodied in a multinational integrated structure and as part of a defensive, war-preventing strategy, have contributed significantly to maintaining peace and freedom over the last 40 odd years and indeed to the dramatic changes which we are seeing now. Even today there remain some 530,000 soviet troops in Eastern Europe and 380,000 in East Germany. So far my mission stands unchanged.

Having been a soldier throughout the Cold War, I am delighted to see what is happening. At the same time however, I am aware that we have entered what might be a long transition period, which may go through phases of instability and even regional strife. Therefore, while we must adapt our security arrangements to the new situation, in the spirit of the 'message from turnberry', we must also continue to provide a stable basis for the secured transition towards a new European order.

Foremost among the processes which have created all this welcomed change towards what is hoped will be a free, democratic and undivided Europe, is the change of attitude of the Soviet Union. In my view, the Soviet Union had no option but to adopt a different approach to its political, economic and military strategy, if it was to maintain its power status. It is fortunate that the charisma and judgment of President Gorbachev has led to the direction of the necessary change, appearing to be positive and constructive. The need to alter Soviet policy has enabled the very welcome process of Democratisation in Eastern Europe and has led to some Unilateral force reductions and to the Conventional Forces in Europe (CFE); and other arms control negotiations. However, Gorbachev's policies have brought to the surface the very considerable internal difficulties within the Soviet Union, with which we are all familiar, and together with unknown developments in South Eastern Europe, could confront us with instability and even regional conflicts in the future. In order to master these challenges in a climate of secured dynamic stability, the free Western Democracies have to maintain their cohesion building on the proven structures of NATO and the European community as pillars of stability and confidence, and these should be the foundations of a wider and progressively institutionalised European Peace and Security order, based on the Conference on Security and Cooperation in Europe (CSCE) process. Whatever happens, the Soviet Union will remain the strongest military power in Europe, both in conventional and nuclear terms.

The difficulty in withdrawing Soviet troops from the forward areas back into the homeland is of particular military significance. The withdrawal has slowed, or stopped from East Germany. This may mean that substantial numbers of Soviet forces will remain in the forward areas for a considerable period. We must bear this in mind and find a way to counterbalance it in our own force and operational planning.

The changes in the Eastern European countries have had the effect of drastically altering the balance of forces available for offensive operations. Most of the former Warsaw Pact states indicate that their forces would participate solely in the defence of their own territory. As the East German Army can no longer be considered a threat the short term risk of a major reinforced attack on Western Europe is negligible. This must have a fundamental effect on our own security planning.

The unification of Germany and the advent of free elections in Czechoslovakia means that the Central Region's eastern boundaries lose their front line character. Our present 'layer cake' deployment would no longer be forward in Germany. Or, in the South, aligned against a state which, depending on the policies of the democratically elected non-communist government in the USSR, will seek friendly ties with the west. A retention of the 'layer cake' in these conditions would not only be of questionable military utility, but would also offer the wrong political signals and would reduce NATO's credibility.

Another factor of crucial importance is the arms control process. Should agreements be reached on conventional, chemical and nuclear weapons, we shall have to implement them carefully retaining an acceptable balance and mix of forces with respect to the remaining Soviet military capabilities. The reductions should be in concert with the NATO Nations within the NATO force planning process, especially in the Central Region. This will not be easy, because of National budgetary pressures and the need for forces which have sovereign utility. We must ensure that the forces left after the reduction process and national restructuring represent a balanced posture for the range of missions considered necessary within the frameworks of a revised NATO strategy and a coherent, multinational western security structure, which fits into an overall European security system based on the CSCE process. In that context, we could adapt the existing structure of forces in the Central Region to accommodate the implementation of the present CFE negotiations, and this course of action would be sensible during the transition period to which I have referred. Following a CFE agreement, it is likely that there would be further conventional force reductions and a drastically altered political environment. With these deeper force cuts, I believe we will be made to abandon our present force structure, a move which will probably become a political imperative in due course anyway.

The importance of public perceptions and opinions should not be under-rated. In the present environment, it is far too tempting to divert defence resources towards economic, social and environmental programmes, and especially into economic cooperation and stabilisation programmes for a changing Eastern Europe. The capacity of each nation to fund such projects relies on the ability to run its own economy in guaranteed security, with a free hand in the international community, and access to raw materials and free trade. This is only possible with peace and stability—in other words by the provision of national and international security. Therefore, defence spending must continue to be complementary to other funding priorities. Disarmament and conventional parity have never guaranteed peace alone. The difficult task of balancing national budgets is not an 'either/or' issue, but one of obtaining the right compromise based on future-orientated political decisions.

Another aspect of public perception involves the need for us all in the greater military community to conduct ourselves very carefully throughout our range of activities, from the occupation of barracks to field training, respecting public sensitivities and the environment. We must avoid presenting a warmongering image by avoiding the use of warrior terminology and by adopting a considered approach to our public image and, to our advertising in industry. However, we must not be timid in stating hard facts in an unbiased and reasoned way, for it is only by doing so that we shall be able to inform those outside our community of the security situation in the reality of a world which is still not safe and far from being ideal.

The role of armed force has changed. It is no longer the principal tool of power and policy projection, which is now better achieved by economic, technological and political instruments. Instead, armed forces offer the means of providing stability and security by denying any potential aggressors the prospect of profit by military adventurism. Thus the need for a sufficient level of armed forces of all types is a vital component in the provision of security. In this context, the retention of a balanced nuclear capability, maintained at minimum but credible levels, and controlled by a mutually agreed arms control system, is the 'ultima ratio' of war prevention and stability. For the last four decades the NATO nations have developed a highly refined political and military structure, unprecedented in history. We have achieved this not only by a clear identification of the need to cooperate in the light of the former Warsaw Pact's military might, but also by free discussion, acceptance of compromise, and dedication to our cause, even at times when national priorities threatened our delicate coalition posture. In my view, the success of NATO is the principal reason for the peace and relative prosperity we have enjoyed for the last 40 years and for the changes which we are witnessing now. A major factor has been the inclusion of North America, whose involvement, assured by the presence of stationed forces, has enabled us to match the strategic depth of the Soviet Union, and I anticipate no change in the need for this component of our alliance in the future. There are those who hold that NATO has not, or shortly will not have, any relevance in the new Europe, and that it should be totally replaced, perhaps, by the results of the CSCE process, in order to overcome the 'two military blocs'. However, this reasoning, putting NATO and the Warsaw Pact on the same qualitative level, neglects the fundamental difference between the two systems, which has caused the success of NATO and the failure of the Warsaw Treaty Organisation.

The 'message from turnberry', expressed the desirability of complementary roles for Western political, economic and security organisations, like NATO and a European Community, and an institutionalised CSCE process, for the whole of Europe. This progressive undertaking, to develop an institutionalised CSCE structure for cooperative European security management, will be essential to satisfy Soviet security interests and to involve them, together with our Trans-Atlantic partners, in a future European structure.

Having described some of the relevant factors which must play a part in our considerations for the future, what could be the way ahead for the Central Region? The last round of ministerial meetings have led to the request for a review of NATO's strategy, concepts and force composition, in particular greater multi-national integration. In order to contribute to this undertaking, I set in hand studies within my own headquarters to examine options for the future, for it is only by early study that we can offer our advice to our political leaders and national defence planners at the right time. I am very well aware that whatever emerges will be the result of the ongoing political negotiations, and must be based on the consensus of the sovereign NATO nations, for NATO itself is the expression of it's nations acting in solidarity. Even under changed conditions, I suspect that the Central Region will remain a single entity at the operational level, and my thoughts on how we might alter our stance are based on that premise.

Our present deployment plans involve a 'layer cake' of national corps and divisions deployed alongside each other and forward along our eastern borders. Therefore, our first area of study is concerned with adapting the present 'layer cake' format to accommodate lower force levels. This approach is evolutionary, making best use of existing arrangements, and will have applicability in the early stages of transition. However, from what I have said, you will gather that I believe the 'layer cake' will become obsolete, for both political and military reasons. We must prepare for a different future and a smooth transition to it; to paraphrase A Supreme Allied Commander Europe (SACEUR), we should have a vision of where we are going, of what final lasting security arrangement we wish to achieve. What I seek to avoid is a series of consecutive changes, which will only serve to confuse service-men and citizens alike. In this context we have to realise that we speak in time horizons which are already more limited than those of normal mid-term defence planning.

Although we are hoping to see a marked reduction in the capability component of the military risk in the Central Region, there are no indications so far that there will be a commensurate decrease in Soviet military capabilities on NATO's flanks. Indeed, some commentators suggest that while the likelihood of political crisis with a military conflict potential in Central Europe is drastically reduced, the risk of regional conflicts is increasing. At the operational level, this factor must be borne in mind, it might be that we have to plan for an improved reinforcement capability outside the central region, instead of concentrating everything into it.

The new political and military situation seems to provide increasing warning time which will be linked more and more to political and economic indicators. However, warning time will only become relevant in the context of an emerging political crisis, which carries the potential for an armed conflict. With the objective of reducing tension and preventing such conflict, politically controlled crisis management might call for graduated military options in the fields of readiness and mobilisation, and also for available, ready forces of high flexibility, and of a multinational character, to signal solidarity. This military element of crisis management has to become an important part of operational art, and should receive greater prominence within our revised NATO strategy.

So where does this lead us? Our considerations are still far from being fully developed, and are based on political and strategic principles as laid down in recent NATO documents and declarations.

I see the need to provide capabilities for various levels of political/strategic action:

- [ ] a visible multinational posture of demonstrated vigilance in peacetime;
- [ ] graduated military options as part of interactive crisis management;
- [ ] a reconstruction of defence capabilities in times of crisis and threat;
- [ ] a flexible deployment concept of counter-concentration options against any kind of threat and in any actual conflict, in what we used to call 'direct defence', against any kind of aggressive action;
- [ ] a controlled and measured capability for escalation, both conventional and nuclear;
- [ ] and of course provision for de-escalation and conflict termination.

All this must serve the overall objective of secured mutual security and stability in and around Europe in fluid and uncertain times.

This leads us to a second area of study, begun to develop an operational concept beyond the 'layer cake'. The underlying requirements for such a concept are:

☐ to retain the fully integrated, collective, multinational approach to the NATO force structure to include all the central region's nations' armed forces, even at reduced force levels;
☐ to offer a graduated system of military options for political use in crisis management;
☐ to provide the required minimum level of forces and the necessary mobilisation and reinforcement capability to meet any military risk at the correct time and in the most cost effective way;
☐ to have sufficient operational mobility and flexibility to meet possible commitments both within and outside our region;
☐ and to ensure that our military arrangements are politically and publicly acceptable and in accord with arms control treaties and environmental requirements.

One possible way of organising our Central Region forces in trying to meet these requirements might be by the establishment of the following structures and formations:

☐ a ready covering or guard force, which should comprise elements of all the Central Region nations, and which would be deployed on and over NATO territory. Its role would be to signal vigilance and readiness and to provide an initial collective NATO response against any aggressive effort. Such a force would have to have very considerable surveillance, reconnaissance, target acquisition and communications support linked to long range firepower and barrier capability. Its peacetime locations should be primarily dictated by its role;
☐ A rapid reaction force capability controlled by a high command level, which would be able to deploy for a number of purposes, but principally to provide rapid support to the areas of most danger, as identified by the covering or guard force. Its availability and peacetime locations would have to be matched to its role. The structure of such a capability is still an open question, but the requirements for in-place, ready, flexible forces and high mobility are already clear. They could very well have a multinational character;

☐ manoeuvre forces, concentrated in assembly areas in depth, for deployment forward to where they are required. These should be major national or multinational force groupings, relying substantially on reservists and mobilisation or re-inforcement forces, but with in-place headquarters, reception staffs and field units around which the forces would form. Bearing in mind that these major force groupings would need to start from concentration areas in depth, opportunities arise for their peacetime stationing in several NATO states.

Some of my staff officers are beginning to refer to this concept as the 'currant bun' option as opposed to the 'layer cake'. At this stage it is too early to discuss detailed structures and we are only considering options which will require thorough analysis and eventual political approval, but there is a strong case for more multinational integration of forces, as communicated by the ministerial Defence Planning Committee (DPC) on 23 May. There would also be implications for command structures and headquarters in addition to field units.

The UK is fully involved with our study into the formation of a multinational airmobile division, on light scales and with limited logistic support, for principal employment in the NORTHAG sector. We shall learn from this study much which will be useful in the political and military evaluation of bigger, mechanised multinational formations. Indeed, the standing planning group in my headquarters has the remit to examine the feasibility of developing the airmobile division into an airmechanised division, with more punch and better support.

I would like to outline two political aspects of multinational force structures. Firstly, greater integration of our forces will reinforce the unity and the mutual dependence of the alliance, and will clearly signal these aspects to both our own citizens and political opponents. This is entirely in accordance with the present trend towards greater political, social and economic cooperation in Western Europe and is compatible with, and complementary to, the CSCE process for the provision of an overall European security system. Secondly, it will increase the political acceptability of stationed forces in a time when citizens question the need for foreign troops to be based abroad. The importance of public opinion in this area must not be underesti-mated and we should do all we can to ensure that we respect these sensitivities. We should encourage a widespread understanding of the concept of European forces on European territory, or even better, Atlantic forces on Atlantic territory. In this context the wide distribution of national flags is of crucial importance.

Even though it is early in our studies, I can make some general comments about the likely implications of such a change in stance:

☐ with reduced force levels and a more dispersed deployment, relying very much on mobilisation and reinforcement, it is essential to maintain a structure of well trained multi-nationally integrated staffs, who know each other and can work together, to demonstrate the political and military solidarity of the NATO nations;

☐ the air and land commanders in this new environment will have to be trained in much more complex tasks and decision making, which will require greater imagination, and mental agility. In addition we should increase 'jointness' between land and air operations generally and at lower levels;

☐ whatever forces are available, should be modern and well equipped. Forces with ageing or obsolete equipment are not really worth their cost;

☐ mobility, also in trans-region terms, will be critical. Forces will be useless if they can't get to the right place in time, and the problem increases as force levels fall and the distances between formations increase;

☐ electronic and electro-optical systems will increase in import-ance, particularly for verification, surveillance, target acqui-sition, fire control, command, control and information systems. The information aspect is complex, requiring col-lection, fusion, collation and dissemination throughout national and international headquarters, but it is essential if tomorrow's commanders are to make best use of lower force levels. The communication problem will also increase with the wider dispersion of fewer forces;

☐ flexible long range firepower, both land and air delivered, and readily controlled will be essential;

☐ there will be a continued requirement to train our forces at all levels and especially our integrated staff structure. This will require a lot of imagination on our part, in order to reduce the environmental burdens and costs, but it will also require an understanding on the part of our citizens and political leaders, that training is part of their security guarantee. Here we have to exploit to the maximum the opportunities offered by modern computer and communications technology, in the field of operational level exercises and simulation. Inter-operability in this area is crucial too; While some useful progress has been made in inter-operability and standardisation among our air forces, the situation in the land forces is still disappointing throughout almost all areas. Unless we make major steps forward in this field, the concept of greater multinational integration, which is both militarily and politically desirable, will remain only a fashionable catchword.

I emphasise this aspect most strongly. We must rely on the will and determination of our nations to do better in this crucial field, especially in the general areas of C31, logistics, training and major weapon systems, or at least in their major components. Without success here, multinational forces will lead to inefficient use of manpower and additional costs and effort.

One area of particular importance is the ability for our intelligence systems to work together. I have already stated the increased role of information gathering, fusion, collation and dissemination in a post-CFE environment. In order to make best use of our assets they must be able to communicate with each other; intelligence systems have long been somewhat jealously guarded, often for very good reasons, by individual nations. However, we must attempt to overcome these difficulties. I am pleased to note the recent memorandum of understanding between Royal Ordnance, Giat and Rheinmetall to work together on the next generation of tank main armament and ammunition. This is a positive and welcome step and must hold promise for the future.

The ability of forces to work together is a complex subject. Equipment and logistic support systems must meet each others needs, while doctrine, tactics, language and training all need to have a common base. This cannot be achieved by groupings of companies alone. A successful working partnership between defence staffs, research and development establishments and industry must exist between the nations of the alliance—we have all had bitter experience of collaborative failures, resulting from a range of factors. However, we cannot allow these failures in the future, if we are to achieve the minimum, sufficient level of security in the most cost-effective manner. We must seek to compromise on individual national priorities in the light of seeking to achieve overall efficiency in our Alliance defence procurement.

In my review of possible implications of post-CFE and beyond, I have touched lightly on the more important areas. There will be a host of other factors to consider and accommodate, and their relative priority will change with time. We must remember that while we have seen very welcome changes to Eastern Europe, we do not yet have a CFE agreement. Beside the positive developments in Central and Eastern Europe, which are key to the future security landscape, the success of our alliance arrangements will be fundamentally influenced by our will to maintain our cohesion. This includes the cohesion of our security efforts, expressed by our multinational integrated structures. If we maintain that cohesion, then I am confident that we can look forward to continued peace and, I would hope, prosperity.

I conclude with a quotation from General Galvin's recent article referring to the battle of Waterloo; 'peace remains a delicate flower. So many times it has been allowed to wither and die because we lacked the foresight and wisdom to preserve it. Each time the price of our neglect has been tragic.'

Security Policies
and
Military Concepts

Defence in a Changing World

REAR ADMIRAL E. S. J. LARKEN and AIR COMMODORE A. G. HICKS

Rear Admiral Larken's last appointment was as Assistant Chief of the Defence Staff (Overseas). Air Commodore Hicks served as Director, Rest of the World. Both have recently retired from military service. The views expressed in this article are entirely their own.

For the past 25 years or so the basis of British defence policy has been commitment to the West and our essential contribution to the bi-polar balance between NATO and the Warsaw Pact. Certainly in providing forces for the Alliance we have at the same time maintained a balanced range of capabilities that could be used, and indeed have been, in a wide range of emergencies out of area (OOA). In practice, UK security policy has *never* been wholly confined to NATO: we have always had significant national concerns OOA—albeit not such as to pose a fundamental threat to the fabric of the nation. Now, however, we have been thrust into a period of headlong change.

The first momentous development is that we are nearly in a position where we can think, indeed must think, what has been until recently the unthinkable. We owe the colloquial use of this phrase to Herman Kahn. It became current in 1962, the year of the Cuban missile crisis, in association with Kahn's seminal work on the effects and consequences of thermonuclear war. But there are numerous indications that the unthinkable is back through the looking glass. From the terrifying possibilities which Kahn tried to tame intellectually, we are returning to a curiously familiar environment in which old wisdoms have suddenly regained their youthful vigour. We are able at last to turn our minds a little from a hybrid world in which thermonuclear war on the scale feared by Kahn, and once confronted by President Kennedy, has been our one mainstream strategic consideration. In its place we would appear to be entering, to use a phrase of Eric Grove's, 'an age in which nuclear weapons have not gone away but in which they are regarded as having little or no operational utility and in which their overall deterrent effect is, therefore, more subtle and elusive'. In consequence our circumstances require a great deal of rethinking, and as a matter of some urgency.

REVIVAL OF THE BALANCE OF POWER

It is now well recognised that we are moving rapidly from a relatively simple two-bloc strategic system, where all has been subject to a dominant symmetrical bi-polar confrontation, towards a more polycentric global arrangement. The Soviet Union faces an extremely uncertain future, including a degree of instability exceedingly disturbing in a nation still possessed of huge armed forces and a Superpower nuclear arsenal; beyond question, however, it is attempting to come to terms with its impaired economic situation. Eastern Europe is in disarray, with all the worries attendant upon such uncertainty. The USA has emerged in a military class of its own. Those concerned that unbalanced martial power is inclined by its nature to be unhealthy will be relieved that fiscal imperatives are already bearing upon the US military establishment. This process is induced particularly by the economic power of Japan—now judged on several criteria to be the world's foremost economy. Europe too is making somewhat elephantine progress, not just economically but towards a degree of identity which could become national, subject to the evolution of the new German dimension. Some other nations are gaining increased prominence, notably China and India, if not yet Brazil. Prospective groupings also need to be considered. Perhaps some formal Muslim understanding could develop, possibly against elements of the old West and a reformed Russia, or even around the Indian Ocean to counter expansionary aspirations by India itself. A loose coalition of prosperous Pacific-rim states could serve to balance the different pressures of China and of Japan. At the other end of the scale, sub-Saharan Africa is showing marked signs of becoming an underclass of backward nations, rich in resources but quite possibly in the process of extensive depopulation due to AIDS. From all this, a fresh coherence is beginning to emerge. The form is not totally unfamiliar, even if the geography itself is novel. It is the revival of the classic balance of power as the basic substance of world politics, albeit perhaps conditioned by a very different and possibly more co-operative international dimension; and confined in this new incarnation by the limits of the global envelope itself.

In trying to place some intellectual bounds on all this, it is a revealing discipline to tackle the problem from the outside and move inward—starting with global perspectives, and working towards CFE and our immediate preoccupations, before drawing some tentative conclusions. Essentially our external security policy is based, as it must be, firmly on self-interest. But in the famous words of John Donne 'No man is an island, entire of itself', and we are becoming increasingly aware that myopia and parochialism will no longer do in a number of respects. The confines of the global envelope are, increasingly clearly, not only relevant but somewhat fragile, and no major nation, even of the second or third magnitude, can any longer afford to disregard them.

GLOBAL PERSPECTIVES: ENVIRONMENT AND RESOURCES

Such an approach must start from those major trends in the geo-political circumstances which are likely to affect the condition of *homo-sapiens* on the planet. This means the environment itself, and the question of resources. Two major problems are attracting much international (and indeed media) attention—the apparent depletion of the ozone layer and global warming. Both the origins and solution to the ozone problem may be fairly straightforward; those associated with global warming most assuredly are not. Some predicted effects, in particular the melting of the ice caps, are dire. If you are an optimist, who moves above the mere details of human management and misfortune, you could perhaps balance constructively the advantages of opening up huge areas of Canada and Siberia for agriculture and comfortable habitation against the flooding of coastal areas and parts of major cities. But in practice quite small excursions from established temperature profiles can create serious problems: weather and rainfall patterns are disturbed, ocean currents can deviate a little. Routines of agriculture and fisheries still underpin much of our economic well-being and, crucially, the coherent development of the poorer and less technically capable countries. Yet global warming is by no means the well-established phenomenon that dogmatic doomsayers would have us believe: most certainly it is not fully understood. Our ability to make temperature measurements of the necessary accuracy, in particular from the sea, is comparatively recent, and thus the long-term data base upon which judgements need to be made has, to put it mildly, an uncertain provenance. But the dilemma is acute. International action may be needed urgently if serious effects by the middle of the next century are to be avoided, even if they are not already inevitable. On the other hand, unnecessary action, which would certainly involve a hugely costly revolution in fuel usage (imposing an especially heavy relative handicap on the developing countries), will impose a serious gratuitous constraint on economic progress.

A number of other environmental and resource problems, some related to global warming directly, are important. In particular: day-to-day pollution, which includes not just industrial and domestic waste but the indiscriminate use of fertilisers, pesticides and herbicides; forestation, which has of course major climatic and agricultural associations; fresh water supplies; food itself; energy (global warming again); and non-fuel minerals. In suggesting that the problems concerning all these global commodities are quite containable by good national and international management, it is important to avoid complacency: in many areas management is failing manifestly and outcomes may well be disastrous. Population is also of course a major worry. There are however quite strong indications that world population will reach a steady state at between 10 and 15bn, some two to three times the present 5bn. There is considerable evidence that this would be supportable, again given good management of both environment and resources. There is also a great deal of evidence that an approach to world population stability will bring a degree of convergence of disposable wealth—towards, gratifyingly, a higher material standard than we here enjoy today. Moreover, the same process should foster stable international relations. Herman Kahn was again very much to the point in saying that:

> It is a great virtue of the post-industrial economy that there are very few conditions under which war pays—or even seems to pay—as opposed to the situation that has applied during much of the pre-industrial and industrial eras.

Full attainment of this Eldorado can, however, only be a number of centuries away—shall we say at least two. Moreover it assumes a triumph of international good sense over discord, and even then it begs the question of consensus, and of whether coercion of some nations or groups of nations by others might well be seen to be necessary. There is equally the possibility that all could go terribly wrong. The point that must be emphasised at this stage is that the world really is a finite envelope. We shall continue to debate vigorously the question of global warming, together with all the other major environmental and resource effects. These may in aggregate prove to be more or less serious than we expect; but the clear fact is that mankind's routine activities—as we move towards some equilibrium of population and prosperity—will increasingly influence vital natural global phenomena, and we shall disturb their equipoise at our peril.

ECONOMIC INEQUITY AND ITS CONSEQUENCES

Turning to the question of economic inequity, it is not the function of the military, certainly not in relatively advanced and stable democracies, to tackle such problems directly. But much of the practical work of the military practitioner is liable to be the containment of their secondary effects. The sort of global factors we shall need to accommodate may often mean that things will get worse before they get better. Serious inequities in economic and social conditions give rise to misery, envy, political conflict (or suppression) and strife: and we are in for plenty of all of them. Widespread poverty will remain for the foreseeable future a source of instability in large areas of Asia, Africa and South America—as for example in sub-Saharan Africa which has endured a decade of falling per capita income, accelerating ecological change and now AIDS. The situation in many countries is very serious.

One evident consequence of severe social and economic deprivation is migration. On any scale, and in the absence of national kinship, this rapidly overcomes the hospitality and tolerance of host nations—as we are seeing with the Vietnamese Boat People, despite the modesty of scale in absolute terms. There are other current examples of course; for instance the steady drift of population from the countries of the Maghreb to Southern Europe, and (increasingly significant) the new mobility of population in Europe from East to West. Given the heightening racial conflicts all over the world often associated with changing political and economic orders, not least within and around the USSR, we can expect to see further problems of this nature and perhaps on a greatly increased scale. We would do well to remember the human cost of the partition of India in 1947.

Another rather different by-product of economic and social inequity is the illegal drug trade and its expansion. Often seen in purely regional terms, it is in practice all-pervasive and global in its connotations. Moreover, while the cost in terms of human misery and degradation is already unacceptably high and increasing, the large scale institutionalised criminal activity which international drugs traffic provokes—accompanied by wide-spread intimidation and corruption—undermines societies in a quite fundamental way. The sums of money involved are huge, forming significant proportions of the Gross National Products (GNPs) of, for instance, Bolivia, Peru and Colombia (not to speak of the United States). Effective policing and the administration of justice are likely to be but two casualties; the scale of resources involved is such that no-one, at any level, is immune from the risk of coercion. Within states therefore, the situation equates to a particularly insidious form of civil war in which people do not declare their allegiance. Extrapolating these levels of disorder internationally, the fight against drugs can be seen as a coalition of more or less resolute and effective governments ranged against multinational cartels, which may themselves operate coalitions of one sort or another. It is, therefore, not surprising that this conflict has become an important item on the agenda of inter-national security, with all that this implies for resource allocation. It is only necessary to point to the markedly increased US military involvement in anti-drugs operations (culminating most recently and dramatically in Panama), and to UK assistance in Colombia, to emphasise that the future development of the drugs threat must be addressed resolutely, both nationally and internationally.

It is salutary to conclude this catalogue by pointing to the continuing plague of what can best be called 'ideological unrea-son', which forms a seemingly irrational threat to the sensible co-ordinated approach to global problems which we clearly need. It remains endemic in many parts of the world, and shows little sign of diminishing. Indeed—and perhaps as a means of venting frustrations engendered by some of the inequities just outlined—it seems sadly to inflame all too readily tensions latent in religious or sectarian issues. In the Middle East, the main focus of Islamic fundamentalism has been Tehran, but fundamentalism continues to be exported (and with it a rabid hostility to the West, which Russia too is starting to feel). Equally in India, Hindu communal-ism looks set to place increasing pressures on the structure of a broadly secular and democratic society; and nearer to home the deep and violent divide in Northern Ireland seems likely to remain unresolved. The rump of the fragmenting communist world too will itself be a focus for further disruption. We are beginning to see already the consequences of the Balkans un-leashed, as Professor Freedman has pointed out recently; and indeed current events in the Baltic states, albeit under fragile control at the time of writing (May 1990), do not augur well for the future stability of the Soviet world. Equally, major disturbances may have been quelled in China for the time being, but the sheer weight of 'people-power', should the villages be mobilised in revolution, would make for a very different situation, as we have seen in Romania. The military practitioner can thus draw little of immediate comfort in the coming post-totalitarian world.

Where then do our vital interests lie? Major factors point strongly to the importance of maintaining an expansionary world trading regime of an essentially free-market nature, and tuned to steady economic growth. Such a process will lead to increasing economic interdependence, which will require, and to some extent impose, enhanced political stability. All this seems to focus quite logically on the need to support consistently, and indeed robustly, a world order edging towards a post-totalitarian (as well as post-industrial) 'Enlightenment', based broadly on modern and measured capitalist economic principles. This practice is not new: indeed an established foreign policy aim of the UK government is to promote stability in areas important to our interests, and to the wider interests of the West as a whole. But the practical application of this objective may well develop new dimensions.

BROADER ASPECTS OF NATIONAL DEFENCE

Turning to specific questions of national defence, the requirement to maintain our territorial integrity and to defend our population and homeland is fundamental and uncontroversial. However, our broader interests today give rise to many current parochial issues. These do not need to be rehearsed here in detail. Suffice to say that our *present* defence policy rests four-square on the NATO Alliance. Whatever uncertainties lie ahead, it is inconceivable (albeit after a year of the almost-inconceivable) that our *future* defence policy could fall outside a similar ultimate identity. Meanwhile, the sometimes alarming efforts of the media in recent months to postulate a basic defence review, based upon snapshots of rapidly moving events, need to be put into a longer-term perspective. The discussion so far outlines the more substantial backdrop we have described. Four major practical concerns emerge. These are:

☐ the maintenance of stability for economic activity, and the means to trade and convey goods at will;

☐ a constructive accommodation to major political changes, which have their most intense epicentre currently in the Soviet Union;

☐ the management of arms control; and

☐ the need to cope with the diffusion of advanced military capabilities to medium and small powers;

and all seen in a perspective comprehending the global envelope.

First, our national logistics and sustainment. It has sometimes been argued of course that the pattern of UK trade is increasingly centred on Western Europe, and that we are therefore becoming steadily more insulated from the unpleasant realities of economic life in the wider world. This is a delusion. Certainly it is true that some 75 per cent of our visible trade will probably remain with the countries of the European Community. But Europe is itself in many respects an island in economic terms. Our continent depends fundamentally therefore on the use of the air and the sea for its security. It is heavily dependent on imported fuel (as will be the UK itself from around the year 2000) and, although largely self-sufficient for food, it requires substantial imports of phosphates for fertilisers. Equally, Europe remains import-dependent for a range of non-fuel minerals; and although stockpiling can moderate strategic vulnerability, the significance remains. So we must secure our air and sea routes. Commercially this means basically air for people (except on short haul) and sea for things; some 99.5 per cent by weight of all trans-ocean cargo is carried in ships.

So here in another sense we need to remind ourselves that the economic security of the UK is very much bound-up not just with Europe but also with global dimensions and patterns. A key interest will remain access to stable markets worldwide, and this will include both their promotion and safeguarding. It follows that we may need to do our best to help stable and prosperous trading partners to avoid upsets and degeneration, and in this there are bound to be some unpleasant surprises.

What then are the key centres of uncertainty and disruption? First, the maelstrom of change in the Soviet Union defeats any detailed prognosis. As the recent pseudonymous article in *Daedalus*, the journal of the American Academy of the Arts and Sciences, puts it: 'The Soviet's transition to normality will be a long time coming'. It may well prove to be a period of opportunity for Western interests; but it could equally be a period of great danger. One already-visible result of the Soviet government's

enforced preoccupation with internal affairs is its almost precipitate retreat from the Third World. This does not mean that the
Soviet Union will necessarily not develop a more cohesive
capability for sustained military operations beyond the Eurasian
land mass. There is some substantial evidence from open sources
that the massive arms reductions taking place disguise a continuing process of modernisation and restructuring, which James
Sherr believes could come to fruition in some 10 years time. In
the meantime, quite possibly Western conflicts of interest with the
Soviet Union will concern competition for political and economic
influence rather than direct military confrontation—with collat-
eral opportunities for building a genuine partnership in both
senses. Amongst satellites and surrogates, Soviet withdrawal will
certainly cause some continuing instability. Looking beyond
Eastern Europe and the prospects of some Balkan shambles,
Afghanistan, Angola, Vietnam, Ethiopia and Nicaragua are
amongst the most distressed countries on the planet, and Cuba
looks increasingly uneasy. The West may well have to concern
itself with a nasty harvest of violence, terrorism and general
aggravation. Its aim will be to encourage and promote the
growth of ordered democracy and civilised prosperity above
tyranny and chaos—and obviously we must travel optimistically,
yet be wise in retaining our safeguards.

The area of arms control, however, presents the shift in current
strategic alignments that may have the most immediate effect on
future military concepts for necessary intervention capabilities
beyond the current NATO area, as well as nearer home. Most
analysts agree that there could be overall advantage to the West
in the CFE proposals as currently envisaged—always provided
that we continue to underwrite the credibility of our strategy of
forward defence and flexible response. We can expect a significant
reduction in Western holdings of all Treaty Limited Equipment
(TLE) categories. As a result, in order to concentrate forces
rapidly and fight effectively on a prospectively much thinned-out
battlefield, we shall increasingly have to emphasise mobility,
flexibility and enhanced Surveillance Target Acquisition (STA).

The third main area of concern stems from the problems caused
by the wider diffusion of the latest military technology. It is
perhaps ironic that Third World nations are increasingly gaining
access to advanced weapons capabilities just as we seem to be
moving towards a genuine reduction in forces at the major
Alliance level. Of most concern of course is the proliferation of
nuclear technology, which will inevitably become more difficult

to limit as the civil use of nuclear power spreads. Equally, ballistic missiles, with warhead options including chemical or biological munitions, are becoming a beguiling possibility for smaller nations. Many nations have the capacity to move into the field of chemical weapons, as demonstrated in the Iran-Iraq war in an appalling way; and every use tends to lower the threshold for future conflict. The attempted acquisition by Iraq of high technology nuclear triggers and the so-called 'super-gun' serve only to enhance these concerns. The consequences for the West in considering our strategy are significant. We have seen that our interests lie in promoting political and economic stability in areas of concern to the UK, implying the need to cope thereby with some varied and unpredictable circumstances. When disputes do arise, a main objective must be to avert conflict wherever possible; or, where this cannot be achieved, at least to contain it at the lowest possible level of intensity. In short, here again the principles of deterrence will remain alive and well: and these will extend from low-intensity operational capabilities up to nuclear deterrence. Because, whatever accommodation is hammered out by the Superpowers, we (begging the question, for the moment, of who 'we' may turn out to be) must never be open to blackmail by a rogue nuclear power. All this may well imply continuing readiness both for involvement in regional defence arrangements, such as the South-East Asian Five Power Defence Arrangement (FPDA), and to deploy forces to odd parts of the world to demonstrate commitment, which is itself simply a form of deterrence. We cannot escape a possibility that, at some point in the future, we shall be faced with the prospect of operations Out of Area. It remains of course a matter of judgment as to what level of operations we need to be prepared for, and as to the resources in terms of capability and sustainability we must therefore provide. In this connection too, we may need to take a long as well as a short term view in deciding the future of those of our overseas bases over which our tenure is still indeterminate.

FUTURE DEFENCE STRATEGY

From all these threads, the implications for our future defence strategy are beginning to become clearer. First it is very much to the West's advantage that the equipments necessary to achieve the conceptual evolution which Arms Control will necessitate are certainly within our technological grasp—although the costs involved are likely to be very high. It is thus already emerging that the developments necessary to maintain credible deterrence and flexibility in-area beyond the hopes for arms control agreements (many pioneered from the advanced concepts of attacking Soviet follow-on echelons in a potential Central Region battle under the old dispensation) should also provide a significantly enhanced capability for more distant operations. With in-place forces in Europe being reduced, it follows that trans-Atlantic reinforcement will become correspondingly even more important to stability. At the same time, in broader strategic terms, both airborne and amphibious elements of our forces are likely to remain crucial, especially to give us the flexibility and reach to meet future contingencies both within Europe (not least on the flanks) and further afield. And it is worth emphasising that these airborne and amphibious capabilities are complementary, and not alternatives. The potential convergence between 'in' and 'out of' area capabilities will also make it easier for us to develop and afford the appropriate levels of command and control, and commensurate logistics and sustainability. This will demand sufficient airlift and sealift, both specialist and with backup from trade. We shall need flexible multi-role ship and aircraft systems with appropriate access to intelligence, and surveillance and targeting data. In terms of land-force structures, we shall need improvements in firepower and manoeuvre capability for operations around the forward edge of battle area (FEBA) or equally in depth, either into enemy territory or beyond the seizure of an entry point.

It is finally necessary to hazard an answer to the question who are 'we', and what is a useful world role for 'us' in the matter of security? The problem, in a nutshell, is to insure against present dangers and to contribute to the maintenance of world stability to a degree essential if Kahn's Eldorado—perhaps in some two centuries time—is to be attained. This implies, in a word, 'policing'. Now there exist, in some quarters, profound misgivings over any suggestion of a world policing role for the UK, and some abhorrence—felt passionately by sectors of the political spectrum—of any form of quasi-imperialist revisionism. In any case, in purely practical terms, it is self-evident nonsense that the UK should adopt a self-appointed and self-financed world policing role. The fact remains, however, that the ring must be held in this finite world, for there will be increasing incidence of unacceptable anti-social national behaviour, both by the so-called rogues and by others who should know better. A latter day parable would perhaps not be out of place here. It starts in a flourishing game reserve in Kenya—a country where a great many species face extinction. A local shoot-to-kill policy has been authorised, and in this case it is properly provisioned and commands respect. Consequently no-one seems to be getting shot, and no poaching occurs. The wild animals, who are not stupid, are congregating. True, they go on as wild animals always will: herds abound and have ways of protecting themselves, predators eat this and that (much as institutions rise and fall in a free-market environment), and the elephants spectate and demolish the vegetation. By and large everyone is happy. Further south on the Zambesi, an ineffective shoot-to-kill policy is in operation. It is not respected. Lots of people get shot. Game is poached. Everyone is unhappy. It is not a bad analogue.

Fortunately there are some clear pointers as to the direction in which we should be moving. Not the least of these is the great success of the UK's modest programme of military assistance overseas. The demeanour of our military assistance teams abroad ensures that we are in brisk demand, not least by post-colonial countries who have tried the poisoned chalice of other helpers; we are welcomed back now as colleagues in a joint venture. The regional impact of recent deployment exercises is also very readily apparent. Thus the regular programme of Royal Navy task force exercises world-wide, together with recent long range deployments of RAF combat aircraft supported by tankers, have been clear demonstrations of the potential reach and capability of UK forces—as indeed was 1988's air-mounted reinforcement exercise in the Falkland Islands. Army exercises too—ranging from the Caribbean, through Africa to the Far East—all serve to contribute to regional stability and deterrence. Finally the immense success of our low-key Armilla operations in the Gulf is very widely recognised. This has been a classic deterrent campaign to protect our vital trading interests which, intriguingly, were almost as much European as British. Moreover, this crisis may prove to have been, writes Eric Grove, the catalyst for the beginning of a 'European Navy', not some grandiose bureaucratic structure, but a flexible framework of co-operation between separate national forces. Indeed, if a general lesson is to be drawn in this context, it is surely that a fundamental divide exists between the mounting of a polyglot force to underpin some ceasefire or disengagement process under reasonably benign conditions, which a miscellaneous group of nations under UN auspices can reasonably undertake; and actual intervention or other forceful peacekeeping military operations. The latter can only be achieved upon the basis of current doctrines, frequent practice amongst the forces concerned and firm command and control arrangements. The NATO nations (or, alternatively, the Western European Union (WEU)) and their close friends are within reach of this sort of capability; perhaps some time in the future it could gather some measure of UN authority. Arguably the British, and in their slightly different way the French, at our best excel at both the diplomacy and the practice. If the substance in the case presented here in predicting a fairly brisk return to something closely akin to balance-of-power politics, now within more-or-less the totality of the global envelope, there cannot actually be much doubt as to where our national identity will ultimately fit: we are Europeans, and it cannot be sensible to evade this conclusion. There are, however, some natural contributory roles in which—if specialisation is to mean any-thing really relevant—we can help Europe to apply itself most constructively.

'No man is an Island, entire of itself; everyman is a piece of the Continent, a part of the Main; if a clod be washed away by the sea, Europe is the less'. Everyone knows the rest of the quotation: we should cleave to our neighbours, and contribute our best talents whilst accepting theirs. Moreover, in the famous words of Benjamin Franklin at the signing of the Declaration of American Independence, 'We must indeed all hang together, or, most assuredly, we shall hang separately'. We must ourselves also cultivate the best of terms with all nations, especially the West and the developed world, for reasons Herman Kahn articulated so well. Benjamin Franklin's advice still bears upon us at more than just the one level. Charity may still begin at home; but we must all now learn where to fit into the world as a whole.

The Nature of Attack
And Defence

JONATHAN R MOORE

Jonathan R Moore is a civil servant

> The man who would be able to balance defence against attack, would be
> more of a god than a human being.
>
> Francesco di Giorgio Martini

In an era of rapid change, when the long-held security policies
of NATO and the Warsaw Pact are undergoing profound and
critical examination, particularly in the light of political movements in Eastern Europe and a real breakthrough in arms control
in the form of the Conventional Forces in Europe (CFE) negotiations, it is perhaps wise to examine some of the basic assumptions which underlie present military thought in both East and
West. The much vaunted change in Soviet military strategy, from
one based on decisive offensive action to one of 'defensive
sufficiency' begs the question—what is the nature of the 'defence'
and the 'attack'? This question, regardless of its fundamental
importance, is surrounded by mis-conceptions and a lack of either
rigour or clarity in modern military writing.

We can describe attack and defence as two of the six fundamental elements of war[1]. These elements exist independently of the
nature of the military organisation. As a consequence, they
possess characteristics which ultimately define the nature and
course of all military activity. However, the interrelationship of
attack and defence, and their interaction with conditions and
circumstances[2], is dependent on the military culture and the
forms and concepts of war adopted by the organism[3]. The attack
and the defence do not exist in a vacuum, or as abstract ideas
conjured by the military theorist, but are the very essence of
warfighting.

The key element in understanding the nature of attack and
defence lies in their respective relationship to the ability to engage

in combat and the particular purpose combat seeks to achieve. This ability we can describe as 'fighting power'. Essentially it consists of the capability to induce stress (through a variety of physical and moral means—fire, shock, mass and so on) against an opposing structure, until the cohesion of that organism breaks down. The cohesion of an organism is the product of its training, leadership, morale and motivation; it is the means to withstand the stress of battle. The cohesion of a unit enables the effective, and hopefully decisive, use of weapons on the battlefield. At its simplest, the difference between attack and defence is based on the priority given at any particular point in time, and at any level of war, to the inducement of stress (the attack) or the maintenance of cohesion (the defence).

We illustrate this in the diagram opposite, which shows the relationship of purpose, function and structure and the variable conditions of time and space. It should be noted, that the purpose of an organisation is simply what its seeks to achieve, in this case the end of military activity. The purpose of an army can be, for example, the defeat of a neighbouring state, to deter war or to suppress an insurgency.

The functions are the means by which the purpose is realised and are derived from the forms of war adopted by that army, and reflected in the concepts and techniques employed. Examples of the forms include linear and manoeuvre war. Concepts are the means by which forms are carried out in practice, for example, elastic defence or encirclement. Techniques are the basic tools which, in turn, enable concepts to be realised; the construction of strongpoints, the use of infiltration, the particular use of the machine gun, are all examples of techniques. Techniques and concepts, by their practical nature, tend to be more easily recognised and understood.

Structures we describe as the physical organisation through which functions are carried out. They are reflected in the tables of organisation and equipment and orders of battle. In the case of attack and defence, purpose, function and structure are defined opposite.

It will be noted that the functions and the response of the organisation to the variables is defined by the particular military culture of the organism, and the consequent forms and concepts of war it adopts. The manner in which the problems of time and space are approached and overcome is determined by the character of the organism and the various approaches to warfighting which it possesses through its training, methods of problem

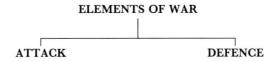

ELEMENTS OF WAR

ATTACK   **DEFENCE**

PURPOSE

1. Seeks to impose maximum   1. Seeks to maintain the cohesion
stress on the enemy   of own organism

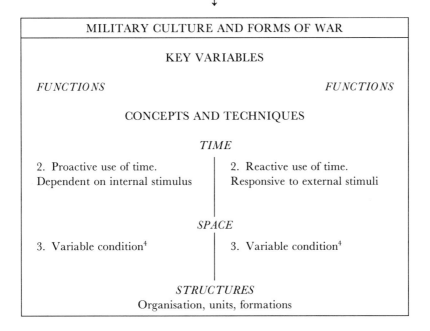

MILITARY CULTURE AND FORMS OF WAR

KEY VARIABLES

FUNCTIONS   *FUNCTIONS*

CONCEPTS AND TECHNIQUES

TIME

2. Proactive use of time.   2. Reactive use of time.
Dependent on internal stimulus   Responsive to external stimuli

SPACE

3. Variable condition[4]   3. Variable condition[4]

STRUCTURES
Organisation, units, formations

solving, techniques and technology. Quite simply, each unit has a battlefield function or functions as a means of realising its overall purpose. For example, artillery has the function of providing fire support in combat; the manner in which this is achieved is in turn a product of culture, forms and concepts. It can, for instance, be used by an attritional military culture as the main weapon for the wearing down the enemy's physical strength. In contrast, the mobile culture will use artillery, for example, to lend immediate, concentrated fire shock as part of an all-arms combat team carrying out the *Blitzkrieg* concept of war. It is the interplay of functions with conditions and circumstances that is the key to the actions of the military organism on the battlefield.

THE ATTACK

The attack, or the offensive[5] as it is commonly understood, suggests dynamic action with the aim of, to paraphrase Sun Tzu, seizing or destroying that which the enemy holds dear, through movement or 'shock' effect. In this case, should the purpose of the attack be movement against the enemy? If we define purpose as the inducing of stress within the enemy cohesion, then is movement in whatever manner, the defining function of the attack? Clearly this is not the case. Stress can be induced by a variety of means—by fire for example. This does not necessarily require movement against the enemy, the Somme offensive of 1916 being a case in point. The key function of attack in this example is best described by the phrase 'Artillery conquers, infantry occupies'.

Certainly, at the level of function, movement is valuable, but purely as a means of increasing the possibility of inducing stress upon the enemy, whether by manoeuvring fire or shock power or, as we would describe it, fighting power. The definition of attack in this fashion moves away from understanding the offensive, not by the variable MEANS of battlefield function, but by the ultimate END of the action, that is, purpose. Whether attempting to seize ground in a linear 'push', or using manoeuvre to attack the enemy's weaknesses on his flanks and rear, both are attempting to achieve the same purpose, that is, to break the enemy's internal cohesion. It is ultimately the only way in which a decision is reached, regardless of ground taken or units destroyed, although these may be steps toward that objective. Unless the enemy's cohesion is broken, he retains the ability to resist. In brief, we are faced with a complex phenomenon, which is a product of the organisms response to conditions and circumstances via its culture, forms and concepts of war, using technical and material possibilities.

THE DEFENCE

In the case of the defence, common perception suggests an element of passivity, normally viewed as the retention of ground. Even that most authoritative of commentators, Clausewitz himself, suggests this, describing defence as the 'parrying of a blow' and the 'awaiting of a blow'[6]. By our definition, Clausewitz is describing not the purpose, but identifying a particular battlefield function, in this case physically waiting for and attempting to absorb the stress imposed, with one's own cohesion, as is found in the positional and linear forms and concepts of war. In reality, the purpose of defence can be realised by a variety of functions, for example, the linear defence based on physical security provided by such means as fieldworks, the mobile defence carried out by manoeuvring formations eschewing the holding of ground, or a 'sword and shield' combining elements of both. In all these cases, the purpose is the maintenance of the cohesion of the WHOLE organism, the cohesion of the tactical unit adding to the total cohesiveness of the army. The defender will in turn be placing stress on the opponent by the use of fire, manoeuvre or shock, but this is in RESPONSE to the attacker's action, it is a means of preserving one's own cohesion by reducing the capability of the attacker to impose stress. Consequently, the use of defensive fire or shock is determined simply by the need to protect the cohesion of those forces.

The question of the level of decision, that is, the strategic, operational and tactical levels of war, adds a further element of complexity to our definition. Different functions can clearly be carried out at different levels of decision and at different times, yet within the same organism. For example, a strategic offensive may involve, at the operational level, passing at key phases to the defence, that defence may be attained by the use of 'mobile' or 'active' defence.

What then of such concepts as the mobile or active defence? Clearly, at the tactical and operational level they will involve the functions of the attack. However, the defining purpose will be realised, not by tactical conditions, but the operational and strategic context. As a result, these actions will take place to preserve and maintain the cohesion of the operational or strategic level of organisation. For example, a mobile defence will use manoeuvre concepts and techniques as a means of counteracting the enemy's fighting power, and hence his ability to impose stress on one's forces. In the sense that it should increase fighting power relative to the enemy, it is magnifying the ability of the army to withstand stress imposed by the enemy. Yet it achieves this by reducing the enemy's ability to impose stress by diminishing in turn his cohesion.

Similarly, the 'attacker' may be seeking to protect key national resources and territory, or form a protective 'buffer', by a preemptive 'offensive' on a neighbouring state. The purpose is defensive, as it seeks to maintain the cohesion of the military organism by reducing the enemy capability to produce strategic level stress by the seizure of vital sustaining forces. At the tactical and operational level, the functions are offensive, but they are defined by the overall defensive strategic purpose.

To briefly summarise our argument. The purpose of attack is realised through battlefield functions carried out externally to the organism, that is, against an opposing organisation. In contrast, defence is directed internally, within the organism, to preserve the coherency of the unit, formation or army.

COUNTER-ACTIONS

Perhaps a word should be added at this point to describe the nature of 'counter' moves in this analysis of attack and defence. Regardless of the specific conditions in which they take place and their ostensibly offensive nature, they are *DEFENSIVE* actions. They are, however, characterised by the adoption of offensive functions by forces in a defensive mode but with the purpose of preserving cohesion. What differentiates the counter-action from the pure attack, with which it has clear similarities, are the following:-

☐ *TIMING*—The point in time at which a counter-action is initiated is reactive, in that it is a response to the prior actions of the attacker.

☐ *OBJECTIVE*—This is of limited scope—it seeks to restore the loss of cohesion (either physical or moral) inflicted by the enemy. Only once a suitable correlation of forces (that is, comparative fighting power) has been achieved, is it then possible to transit to the offensive. It should be noted that the counter-action operates against an opponent who has 'risked' his cohesion in the attack for example, through the disordering effect of movement, exposure to fire, logistic 'stretch' etc. and consequently reduces his capacity to face stress placed on his own organism.

As for the counter 'attack', 'stroke' and 'offensive', these are techniques of war which are culturally determined through the form and concept of war used by a particular army. For example, in British army parlance, they are respectively directed at 'ground', 'forces' and aim to 'seize the initiative'. To the Soviet army, in contrast, they are representative of a scale of action from the tactical, through operational to strategic levels; the tactical level pertaining to the actions of the division and below, the operational to armies and fronts, and the strategic to theatres of Military Operations.[7] In this case, they do reflect the paradigm we have described, in that they seek to restore or maintain cohesion at a given level of organisation.

In contrast, the British definition suggests that the level of decision at which an action takes place is linked to a specific battlefield function. Our model indicates otherwise: for example, counter attacks can be directed against enemy forces or to gain the initiative, or the offensive may be directed to regain lost ground. The British approach tends to straightjacket the functions available to an army. The art of success in battle, the acme of good generalship, is to maximise available functions at all levels, not restrict them to particular fixed objectives.

THE CULMINATION POINT

Of particular importance is that, by analysis of purpose, we have a means to identify the key point when the counter-action of the defence transits to the attack. It becomes possible, in the case of complex and often continuous operations, when there is no clear break in activity, to identify the vital 'culmination point' of that activity. The culmination point we define as:

☐ The point in time when the stress induced by the attacker exceeds the ability of the defenders' cohesion to resist, resulting in a collapse in organism.

☐ When the cohesion of the defender exceeds the ability of the attacker to induce stress.

Simply, the culmination point is the moment when victory, defeat or even stalemate is decided upon the battlefield. Success is a favourable outcome in either attack or defence in the interaction (the transition) between stress opposed to cohesion of the combatants.

An early identification of such a transition is of key importance in assessing the correlation of forces and in planning new action and counter-moves to carry out a successful defence or attack. It enables the vital moment to be identified when a transition should be made from the attack to defence or vice versa. Too many battles, campaigns and wars are lost by the inability to recognise the point when a change in purpose is needed, even if only as a temporary measure to restore a favourable situation or force ratio. It should be noted that the time required to reach the culmination point varies according to the forms and concepts of war used and particular battlefield conditions.

BATTLEFIELD VARIABLES

The demands of imposing stress or maintaining cohesion naturally influence the nature of command and control. In the case of the attack, emphasis is placed upon the initiation of actions which allow the use of fighting power. In defence, *control* is emphasised, that is, the influencing of actions, in particular the interaction of one's own forces with those of the enemy. By being responsive to enemy action it is naturally reactive in the use of time. This may not be such a disadvantage if the defending forces have a command and control system which is more efficient and responsive than that of the attacker. Particularly as the latter will normally be signalling his future intentions by the accumulation of forces, logistic preparations and so on, thus allowing a defender to carry out such measures as to strengthen his cohesion. The Soviet army's emphasis on surprise as the key means to success in battle, reflects the need to avoid giving the defender the opportunity to improve his cohesion, by signalling intentions, and maximising the stress which can be induced on the defence through the unexpected, so achieving a more favourable correlation of forces.

The ability of an organism to carry out a successful defence or attack is further limited by the interaction of its fighting power and command and control system, with the 'space' available. In this case the form or concept of war adopted will be constrained by the type of terrain with which the organism is confronted. What strengthens the defence will often provide an obstacle to the attack. Likewise, an extensive theatre of war will reduce force-to-space ratios, providing opportunities for the use of a mobile concept of war, thus exacerbating the difficulties faced by an attritional based military organism seeking to impose its own combat functions and unfavourable conditions on its opponent.

TECHNOLOGY AND THE ATTACK AND DEFENCE

As we have touched upon conditions and circumstances, the influence of technology on attack and defence must be discussed. New forms of technology do NOT influence attack and defence as fundamental elements of war. There is no such thing as a defensive or offensive weapon, contrary to popular belief. New weapons influence the CONCEPTS of war used by an organism and, as a result, strengthen or weaken that concept relative to opposing concepts of war. The attack and defence continue to exist as the interaction of stress and cohesion; what changes is the most cost effective and decisive means of realising the attack and defence in battle. For example, the machine gun reduced the capability for decisive tactical and operational movement, forcing armies to adopt attritional concepts of war and provoking a strategic stalemate. The development of armoured vehicles made possible the creation of new concepts of war such as *Blitzkrieg*, adding a new dynamic to war. Likewise, new technology may undermine the *Blitzkrieg* concept demanding that the attack be realised by a return to attritional means, as the Iran-Iraq war illustrated.

What is clear is that the nature of attack and defence as we have described remains unchanged. What technology provides is the potential for new concepts of war to develop or existing forms to increase or decrease in power, and they can conceivably be rendered obsolete. For example, a successful defence by an army lacking tanks is as impossible to envisage today as is an offensive without the same technology. Armour is central to the validity of existing concepts of war, whether they belong to the mobile or attritional cultures.

CONCLUSION

The above model of attack and defence, seeks to define their essential nature and remove them from a superficial analysis based upon task, movement or position, to one of purpose and its proper relation with function and military culture. It provides a simple paradigm which can be applied at all levels of decision and with all concepts of war.

It is clear that by this definition NO military formation can be described as purely defensive or offensive, as some commentators wish to believe. Any unit possessing fighting power has the ability to attack or defend, induce or withstand stress. Its capability to do both is determined by the desired battlefield function, that is, to produce stress or maintain cohesion. It should be mentioned that any individual unit will have a varying capability for attack and defence, a product of its training, leadership and concepts of war. For example some units, such as a German Panzer division of 1940, will have a greater capability for attack than, say, a French fortress division of the same year. This merely reinforces the fact that attack and defence are products of unit battlefield function, that is, the method by which fighting power is used. A unit, formation, army or military alliance will be defensive because it seeks to preserve its cohesion. It may eschew attack for political reasons or because it lacks sufficient fighting power to generate enough stress to have a decisive effect on its opponent, in other words, achieve victory. Any army or alliance which tried to dispense with the capability to attack or defend would merely lose the capacity to fight, and with it, the ability to wage or endure war.

NOTES

[1] These elements we can identify as the creating and sustaining of forces, that which enables a state or people to organise forces and maintain them in the field in peace and war. Attack and defence, which we describe in the above article and command and control, which are respectively the ability to initiate an action and to influence that action once it is embarked upon. They are means by which the forces raised by the creating and sustaining elements are used on the battlefield. These elements do not change with the evolution of the methods of war. The elements must be used in order to make war. They reflect the basic nature of warfare in all ages.

[2] Conditions are the immediate external and internal factors acting upon military organisation, and, more specifically its units and formations. For example, terrain, time, resources, the air situation, logistics etc. They tend to change quickly and demand continuous re-evaluation. Circumstances are the wider factors influencing the whole military organism, for example geography, the national economy, presence of allies etc. These factors tend to change more slowly, and are beyond the immediate influence of the army.

[3] See Maj RAD Applegate and JR Moore, 'Warfare: an option of difficulties', *RUSI Journal*, Vol. 135, no 3 Autumn 1990 pp 13, for a detailed exposition of these concepts. Briefly, the culture of an organism represents its ideas, beliefs, prejudices, perceptions and determines the relationship between its constituent parts. We can identify two distinct military cultures—the attritional and mobile, and from culture emerges the form of war an army uses. The forms of war represent a particular theoretical approach to battle, from this we can derive concepts, the application of theory into practice.

[4] Space includes not just distance but terrain, climate, the primary mobility (that is, the capability to move at a rate at least equal to the enemy in the primary ground conditions of the area of activity) of the organism in specific conditions. It includes the room to manoeuvre, and the disordering effect on cohesion of movement. Likewise, limitations in space influence key force-to-space and force-to-force ratios. Terrain also provides physical protection and consequently increases mental security and with it cohesion, providing one of the strengths and attractions of the positional defence. Space is both a powerful determinate asset and a threat. At the simple level of decision making, it involves the weighing of opportunities and dangers. The response is a product of the

organisation of military culture and forms of war. For a more detailed analysis of this see Maj RAD Applegate and JR Moore, Op. Cit.

[5] The attack and the offence or offensive, are used throughout as interchangeable terms.

[6] C. von Clausewitz, *On War*, Princeton, 1976 p. 357.

[7] See HF Scott and WF Scott, *The Armed Forces of the USSR*, Arms & Armour, London, 1984 pp. 74–75.

I would like to thank Mr Michael Elliott-Bateman of the Department of Military Studies, Manchester University for his insights into the characteristics of Purpose, Function and structure and the influence of Military Culture. Also Major R A D Applegate RA for his valuable comments and encouragement.

Defence Industries
and the Market Place

Future Defence and Security: Military and Industrial Needs in the 1990s.

SIR PETER LEVENE, KBE

The author is Chief of Defence Procurement at the Ministry of Defence. This contribution stems from a lecture at the RUSI Summer Conference 1990.

I believe that the Procurement Executive is in a better position than ever to react to external changes and I intend to show how, through development of our procurement policies, the Procurement Executive has arrived at its present position. I would also look at some of the specific initiatives we have in mind which will change the way we buy defence equipment and defence research. Finally, I will look at international procurement as I believe the 1990s should be marked by an increase in cross-border purchasing.

Much has been written on the political changes in Europe and how they may affect the Alliance; clearly, they will also have an impact on how we procure defence equipment in the UK. Precisely how these developments will affect the UK and individual allies is as yet unknown. NATO has already made some changes—it has now agreed that the collective 3 per cent annual increase in defence budgets can be dropped—but there is clearly potential for an enormous change in the nature and size of forces in Europe. Among the European nations there will be varying degrees of enthusiasm to reduce defence spending and thus equipment programmes; perhaps some countries will be looking for relatively rapid reductions. Germany has the additional problem of finding money to finance the reconstruction of the Eastern part of the country following unification, and it is clear that this will increase pressure on their defence budget.

In the UK, the MoD is currently examining options for change in the defence programme. This has been prompted by the welcome changes in Eastern Europe and the prospects of a Conventional Forces in Europe (CFE) agreement. We recognise that there are implications for the deployment and structure of

127

our forces which are likely to affect the balance of expenditure in the equipment programme. So the likelihood is for smaller equipment expenditure by European countries, joined by the US, at a time when there is already over-capacity among Western defence manufacturers.

The outcome must be rationalisation by industry. Cross border mergers like the GEC/Siemens takeover of Plessey are likely to become more common. Some will pursue the strategy of building up their strength in defence, both by acquisition and the formation of joint venture companies with suitable partners—we have seen Thomson CSF of France follow this path. But of course companies may also choose to leave the defence market and I think we shall see other firms following Philips' lead in selling their defence interests and concentrating solely on the civil market.

As the result of rationalisation, there may also be factory closures and redundancies. These are always painful and should they occur there is bound to be pressure brought to bear on the MoD to preserve jobs through preferential contract awards. We can expect special pleading to be made which emphasise the particular strategic necessity for UK suppliers in any and every area. We must, however, resist any pressure to award contracts to those who do not provide value for money. It would be foolish to waste the limited defence budget on maintaining uneconomic, uncompetitive suppliers. Our approach will be to hasten changes and to encourage firms to restructure; not to try to hold back the tide.

CHALLENGE OF THE NEW ENVIRONMENT

For the Procurement Executive, the challenge of the 1990s may well be to operate with a reduced budget and programme and a rationalised defence industry. This will provide a greater incentive than ever to obtain the best value for money. Whereas the changes of the last five years were, in part, internally generated to improve efficiency, during the next five years we shall have to adapt to a greater degree of external pressure.

So what are the policies which have placed us in a good position to succeed in coping with the new environment? What have we achieved? The primary objective of the Procurement Executive remains a simple one; to acquire for the UK Armed Forces the equipment they need, when they need it, with the best value for money. We must obtain the best value for money not only so that the taxpayer knows his money is being spent responsibly, but also to enable us to meet the rising cost of defence equipment with a finite defence budget. Increased examination of the way the defence budget is applied will make it even more imperative that we achieve this value for money. To obtain the best possible value for money the PE has a commercial approach to its work. The key to this policy is competition. I am convinced that competition is the most effective way of searching out value for money. Market forces can be relied upon to encourage bidders to offer the best value they can. Of course, this does not mean buying the cheapest equipment on offer. We must assess the value offered by a bid in terms of running costs, the contractor's ability to deliver the goods, the technical risk involved and a whole host of other factors. These may show that the cheapest purchase price on offer would not provide us with good value for money. This commercial approach benefits not only the MoD. By encouraging more efficient use of resources by our UK suppliers we have increased their international competitiveness to the point where the UK is one of the most successful exporters of defence equipment in the world.

True and effective competition can only work if there is a wide supplier base and we have paid great attention to this over the last few years. We have been successful in a number of initiatives to increase the number of suppliers tendering for MoD business. In 1987 the Small Firms Advice Division was set up. This was so successful that at the end of 1988 its role was expanded and it was renamed the New Suppliers Service. Its work continues to include giving advice to small firms but now also involves the wider issue of encouraging firms of all sizes to compete for defence contracts. Suppliers are made aware of MoD contracts through the *MoD Contracts Bulletin* which includes notice of almost all contracts valued at more than £500,000—there are currently over 2500 subscribers. The *Contracts Bulletin* has been very effective at advertising contracts not only to prime contractors, but also to possible sub-contractors. We ask contractors to seek competition at sub-contract level whenever possible and we place particular emphasis on this when it has not been possible to place the prime contract competitively. Indeed, on contracts of over £1m, we review with the prime contractor his plans for placing sub-contract work. The success of the New Suppliers Service can be gauged, to an extent, from the growth of the Defence Contractors List which now exceeds 10,500:

the number of contractors added to the List each year is about 700.

In looking at our supplier base we must not forget the international scene; procurement is firmly international and we are also encouraging overseas companies to bid for requirements when appropriate. I will return to this in more detail when I consider international developments in procurement.

Our commitment to seeking value for money through competition is evident in the impressive growth in the value of contracts placed by competition or otherwise by reference to market prices. Eight years ago 36 per cent of contracts by value were let in this way and by 1989/90 it hit a record of 67 per cent by value and 86 per cent by *number* of contracts placed. However, it is not enough just to *search* out value for money: we must also *secure* it through the application of taut contracts where the risks are clearly identified, understood by both sides and firmly placed on the contractor. Our commercial approach has led us to develop taut contracts which seek to minimise the procurement risk to the MoD and to focus responsibility for whole systems on a prime contractor. We have moved away from cost-plus contracting to the use, wherever possible, of firm and fixed price contracts. If fixed or firm price contracts are not appropriate, we prefer to use contracts where the MoD and the contractor share, not necessarily equally, any cost overruns or underruns. The choice of contractual regime simply reflects an agreement between both parties on the perception of risk in the project; timescale risks, technical risks and the associated costs.

CHANGE IN STYLE

Our style of operation has changed considerably with the use of firm and fixed price contracts. The careful focusing of responsibility onto the supplier has led to a 'hands off' approach to project management. However, defence procurement is not a matter of giving a cheque to the contractor, even for a firm price, and then have him turn up when he is finished. The supplier has to demonstrate against contractual payment milestones that he is making satisfactory progress towards achieving the specification on time. Clearly our contracts require not only 'hands off' but also 'eyes on' project management. We are monitoring the progress of major programmes that have been contracted for in the last five years. These are proceeding within the original costs and virtually all to time. In the very small number of cases where some delay is apparent, there is no increase in the acquisition cost to MoD, all additional costs being borne by the supplier.

How will our policies develop in the 1990s? As I have said, we will continue to develop a commercial approach and we shall make significant efforts to achieve better value for money. Specific cases will help my argument here. Reliability and Maintainability of defence equipment is currently receiving particular attention within the MoD. The Services acknowledge that much of their current equipment lacks the required levels of R&M (as I shall call it for convenience). This of course has a direct impact on our operational capability. With force reductions in Europe, it will be even more important for each of a smaller number of weapons and equipment to work when needed. But a second and very significant factor upon which R&M has a direct bearing is cost of ownership. The cost of operating and supporting our equipment is a critical issue. The MoD estimates that unreliability currently costs the taxpayer £1bn per year. Although this is a very broad estimate, it does show the size of the problem, and there is no doubt that we have to reduce this figure substantially; indeed, our aim is to halve it, although this may take some years to achieve.

RELIABILITY

We now consider reliability as a key parameter when assessing competitive bids. As I have said, better value for money does not mean simply seeking the lowest acquisition cost: operating costs rank high among the factors taken into account and reliability is now considered on a par with performance. We are taking steps to increase the MoD's R&M capability and we have appointed a Director of Reliability and a number of specialist staff to lead our drive for improved reliability. In line with our commercial approach we are developing a strategy for contracting for reliability which will make reliability a specific term of contract, deliverable in the same way as performance, rather than a 'design aim' as it has tended to be in the past. We are also placing greater emphasis on the estimation of equipment Life Cycle Costs as an essential part of the value for money judgement. Thus specifications are now drafted in terms which explicitly enable life cycle cost implications to be weighed, either in the evaluation of bids or in the structuring of contract terms, underpinned as far as possible by arrangements which place continuing responsibility on the contractor after the equipment has entered into Service. So the 1990s will see contracts coming to fruition which incorporate our new approach to reliability but of course the benefits will extend well into the next century.

Our search for value for money has significantly changed the relationship between the MoD and its suppliers of equipment, but it hasn't stopped there. The commercial approach to procurement is also being developed within the MoD for the procurement of defence research. 1991 in particular will see the formation of a Defence Research Agency (DRA) out of four of the Research Establishments. The aim in establishing the DRA is to improve value for money on defence research and project support. We think it essential to make a clear distinction between responsibility for the efficient internal management of the Agency, and the responsibility for tasking it. Therefore, a key feature of the changes we are making is to focus on the roles of the MoD as customer and the DRA as supplier. This will be achieved firstly by forming the DRA as an organisation clearly distinct from the rest of the MoD. In charge of the DRA will be a Chief Executive reporting direct to the Secretary of State for Defence and clearly accountable to him for the day to day internal management of the Agency. Secondly, the DRA will have a proper taut, commercial relationship with its customers whether in the MoD or elsewhere. Dealings between the DRA and MoD will be on the basis of arrangements directly comparable to the commercial contracts which apply in other areas of Defence Procurement, in which the scope, price and terms of all work carried out by the DRA will be specified. Money will actually change hands from the customer to the DRA in exchange for services performed. From the outset there will be scope for significant competition in direct support to procurement projects, and although the scope for primary competition for advice and research on specialist defence topics is likely to be modest initially, it is expected to grow. Wherever feasible, MoD work will be open to private and public suppliers alike and, where a choice exists, it is intended that competitive tendering procedures should be the normal mechanism for placing work. Where primary competition is not feasible, secondary competition will be adopted with the maximum competition at sub-contract level. The DRA will also be encouraged to widen its customer base to make better use of its intellectual and physical resources for the benefit of the economy as a whole and to spread overheads, normally subject to the outside customers funding any additional investment needed.

Much work remains to be done, and there are many issues still to be decided, but the formation of the DRA provides a real opportunity to improve efficiency and effectiveness for all concerned in the MoD, DRA and the defence industry.

RELOCATION OF THE PROCUREMENT EXECUTIVE

If I were to select one other initiative which will make a great impact in the 1990s it would be the relocation of the Procurement Executive itself. The location of large numbers of staff in London and the London area have weighed heavily on our running costs and the 1990s will see an even greater increase due to the double factors of major rent reviews on most of our London buildings and a reduction in the availability of staff, due to the effects of the demographic downturn. It was for this reason that I set in hand studies which examined our options for the future, with particular emphasis on our ability to recruit good quality staff for the future. The resultant reports recommended *collocating* the Headquarters of the PE in the Bath/Bristol travel to work area. Sea Systems will be concentrated in this area, moving a further 1200 posts from Portsdown and Portland in 1992, whilst Land Systems and Air Systems, accompanied by the central contracts organisation and the Ordnance Board, will move in 1993. The main reasons for the choice of location were the existence of a major portion of the PE in the locality, the excellent road and rail links, and the ability to recruit as necessary for the future.

INTERNATIONAL PROCUREMENT

My final topic, as promised, is international procurement. Like it or not, defence procurement is becoming increasingly international, and the future of many sectors of British industry hangs on their reaction to this development. We have long recognised the military, economic and industrial advantages of international co-operation in defence procurement. Indeed, perhaps the first example, at least in modern times, was in 1918 with a collaborative tank, appropriately known as the 'International'. Since the 1960s, we have played an important role in a number of collaborative projects which have produced excellent results, and we have worked with partners from both sides of the Atlantic. A number of Anglo-French projects—Jaguar, Lynx, Puma and Gazelle—set the pace. They proved that collaboration can produce excellent equipment which, in most cases, others would want to buy. We therefore remain firmly committed to collaboration, wherever appropriate, as it can be a highly effective way of procuring defence equipment. Collaboration can also serve to increase standardisation, and to strengthen the bonds between allies. It helps to eliminate unnecessary duplication in research and development and to reduce unit costs through increased production runs.

But we must apply stringent criteria to our involvement in individual projects to ensure that we achieve value for money. We do not believe that just because a project is international, we should ignore the lessons learned in domestic procurement. And the complexity and particular problems of collaboration makes it all the more important that we observe the same good management practices: competition where possible, at prime and subcontract level, and incentive pricing. For competition also has its role to play in the new generation of collaborative projects, providing keener prices, and enabling us to achieve better value for the money available to meet our defence requirements. While collaboration is an important element in our international procurement strategy, it is not an end in itself, and it is only one of the procurement options that we consider when deciding how to achieve the best value for money on a particular project.

When we talk of co-operation, we must have in mind not just collaboration on joint projects, but a willingness to buy each other's equipment 'off-the-shelf'. For this, co-operation is not an alternative to competition; rather, we must regard the Alliance as a whole as our industrial base and work for a truly open and competitive defence equipment market across all of the Alliance. Our traditional national markets are individually too small to sustain efficient production runs, and no single country's industry can offer best value for money in all areas of defence procurement.

INCREASED COMPETITION

In the 1990s there will be more scope for increased competition in European defence procurement. The future is being shaped by initiatives such as the Anglo-French Reciprocal Purchasing arrangements and the Independent European Programme Group (IEPG)'s open European defence equipment market. The Anglo-French Reciprocal Purchasing initiative, launched in late 1987, is a specific example of this approach. We now do about £60m or FF600m of trade with the French through this agreement, and my staff are in no doubt that, as far as I am concerned, French industry is now considered, together with the UK's domestic procurement base, for products falling within the arrangement. In some ways these arrangements agreed between Britain and France provide a smaller scale prototype for certain features of the action plan for the progressive opening of the defence equipment markets of the IEPG nations. We have made real progress in the last year towards promoting the same equivalence of treatment and visibility of opportunity across all the IEPG nations. Five years ago it would have been unthinkable that we would run a genuine international competition for the British Army's new main battle tank; yet we are, and the jury is still out on the final choice. If, at the end of the day, Challenger 2 were to emerge as the winner, there is absolutely no doubt in my mind that the Army will get a far better product as a result of Vickers' having been exposed to the full blast of competition.

Of course nobody should underplay the difficulties of opening up defence equipment markets to international competition, but neither should the problems be used as an excuse for preserving the status quo. It is inevitable that nations will be keenly interested in the performance of their own industry. But we must remain equally aware of the consequences for procurement budgets of the traditional concern for exact reciprocity and workshare. These principles have resulted in inefficient practices that have cost us dear.

My emphasis on openness in defence procurement is very much in tune with the developments in civil industry as it gets ready for the Single Market after 1992. For though these initiatives to establish a more open European defence equipment market must be clearly distinguished from the EC's '1992' programme, they share the same belief that open market, competitive principles are the best means of achieving an efficient and healthy industrial base, and that this approach will benefit us all. There are political pressures for international co-operation in defence procurement: Europe must continue to demonstrate, both to its American allies and to the Warsaw Pact, that it is ready for collective and effective response. Equipment co-operation and more efficient use of industrial resources are two ways of doing this. Our efforts here can make a particularly important contribution to the debate on transatlantic burden-sharing.

To summarise, there are great challenges ahead, both for defence industry and for the PE. Clearly, our commitment to achieving value for money continues and the 1990s will see renewed efforts to reduce running costs within the PE and added commitment to open competition: competition not only within the UK but also on an international scale.

Innovation, Investment and Survival of the UK Economy

I. R. YATES, CBE, FENG

Ivan Yates is Deputy Chief Executive (Engineering), British Aerospace, Deputy President of the Society of British Aerospace Companies and Chairman, Eurofighter G.m.b.h.

One of the major tasks which I believe faces British industry, is to bridge the gaps in understanding between what we might call 'political speak' and the words and terminology of the industrialists, economists and engineers. It is difficult enough to bridge some of the different concepts between economists and engineers, as I know from a number of meetings over the last year or two, but I do believe that achieving an understanding between those two disciplines is an essential step towards making real progress for the future. Because we are trying to understand an exceedingly complex problem, I feel I can best help this process by applying what I might call an engineer's analysis of the situation. In particular, to apply the thought processes that control systems engineers apply to control nuclear power stations, complex chemical plants, or designing and flying aircraft. So expect to hear terms like 'feedback', 'time-constant', 'oscillation', and 'response time'. And perhaps I should apologise in advance to the economists present as I stray into waters which are uncharted except by their own efforts.

As a backdrop, let us examine a plot of the growth of Gross Domestic Product per head for a number of countries over the last 30 years. (Figure 1) You can see that the UK has been steadily overhauled since the 1950s successively by Germany, France and Japan. By the end of this decade we may have been passed by Singapore. These facts are not new, clearly there has been evidence of this for many years, but the perpetual puzzle is why is the UK economy relatively so unresponsive? One of the reasons why this poor performance is not a matter of continued public concern is that the slope is positive upwards which means that we are always better off than we were a few years ago. The decline is *relative* to other countries, and therefore only evident by direct, personal contact at more than a superficial level.

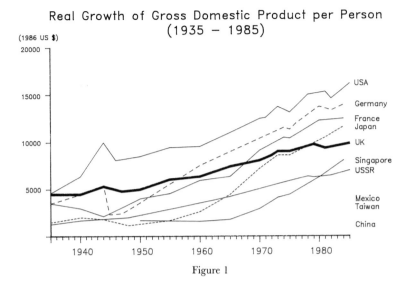

Figure 1

And there have been other distractions; within the lifetime of people still living there have been two major World Wars which have caused major upheavals and which can be seen in the economic indicators. We have made the transition from being a major world power with a huge empire which substantially protected much of our trading and our industrial exports, into being just another European power. More recently, we have had the great good fortune to enjoy the benefits of oil from the North Sea, but as we shall see later, this particular anaesthetic is beginning to wear off.

Analysis of the various problems associated with the economy is not new; There are many articles, lectures and books, all of which have made contributions to understanding and highlighting some of the critical aspects. As long ago as 1886, the commission of enquiry into the economic depression noted that 'more active rivals with better equipment are springing up and leaving us behind'. In 1925, Churchill commented that he 'would rather see finance less proud, and industry more content'. We had Industry Year only three years ago, so there should be no lack of awareness of the problems.

Ten years ago Sir Nicholas Henderson's valedictory dispatch included a classical analysis of the structural problems of British society and its attitude to the modern world.[1] Martin Wiener[2] and Correlli Barnett[3] continued that process. I might paraphrase one aspect of the latter by saying that after the last war, the British decided to give themselves an excellent health service and a new education system, without at the same time addressing the economic imperatives which faced them. We did not set out to provide the basic long-term wealth creating processes so that we could afford to pay for these other objectives.

Speaking in 1980 at the Graham Clarke lecture, Sir Frederick Page[4] referred to many of the problems, including effective management of innovation, lack of adequate capital investment, and management locked in battle with the unions fighting out the battles of the years before. He went on to say that what was needed was a very radical change in our attitude, one so radical that it amounted to a 'new industrial revolution'. Without this we were 'on the brink of the precipice and could only be saved by our own efforts'.

Since then, much has been done and the present government can take rightful credit for this. To speak of being on the brink of our precipice may have seemed alarmist then and equally so today. But many of those same fundamental problems remain; they are very deep seated and are at the root of today's discussion.

COMPLEXITY AND RESPONSE TIME

We are dealing with something, i.e. the economy, which is *enormously complex* and really not properly understood at all. And yet we have to reduce these complex matters to something which can be discussed. But we must be careful. Nobody would suggest regularly driving their car having ripped out all but one of the instruments, for instance the water temperature indicator. To exhibit the same behaviour when trying to fly a modern airliner, which is at least a thousand times more complex, would be even worse. But a modern aircraft is many times simpler than the economy. And yet we do hear people talking about trying to steer this horrendously complex non-linear interactive system by relying on only one or two parameters.

Another important aspect is that in the real world of industry it takes far longer to do things than the man in the street, or the politician realises. Even with an existing factory it takes a lot of time, several years—and a great deal of hard work—to build up a position in the market. To talk of 'switching' from the home market to exports, as if it is something which can be done almost between successive sets of trade figures, is totally unrealistic.

So we must be very careful about the *timescale* for the operation of the various phenomena we are talking about. They are nearly all longer than the annual budget cycle, and frequently longer than the life-time of a parliament.

THE STRUCTURE OF INDUSTRY

In any session like this we inevitably have to take a number of aspects for granted, but even the simplest 'engineering approach' requires more work, and I hope we can find time for this over the next few months. For instance, we should be clearer about the separation into the 'services' and the 'manufacturing' sectors of the economy: the canteen in a factory is really a service, but is a software or systems company all manufacturing although it clearly has many of the characteristics of that activity. Again, within manufacturing there are distinct differences between the 'process industry' which tends to be close to the science of chemistry, and engineering, which tends to work with separate 'technologies' and techniques which are more closely related to physics. And this latter industry appears to have a more complex structure, with more 'layers' of sub-contractors and suppliers and so forth.

We must be careful to avoid falling into the trap of thinking any one of these sectors is 'better' or more worthy than any other. The point I wish to make is simple—we need to do a lot more work to understand some of the relationships in these areas. It is time for engineers and economists to get together so we have a better understanding on which to base future policy decisions. I hope the studies I have already put in hand will, over the next few months, set the basis for this work.

For now I shall concentrate more on the engineering sector of manufacturing, which is where, for whatever reason, most of our UK difficulties lie.

BRITISH INDUSTRY PLC

At the centre of the manufacturing industry is engineering, which has been defined as using nature to provide wealth. At the heart of this process is what I call the 'development investment cycle'. This is the sequence, illustrated in Figure 2, of research, development of technology, development of the first product or

Typical Development Investment Cycle

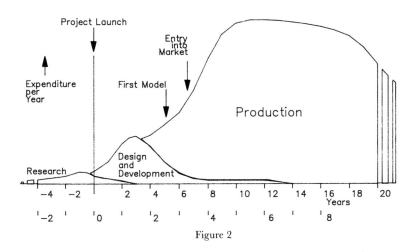

Figure 2

prototype which a company intends to market, and then the preparation for production and the launch into the market. After a year or two, or three, there is a need to embellish or update that product to keep its attraction in the market place; then that market penetration has to be continued in order to obtain from profitable sales the return on the original investment.

In the case of the aerospace industry, this development investment cycle can take some five years from the start until the first product is in the air, and another five years, even if you take quite a lot of risk in the programme, before it is really appearing in any number in the market place. Production might well go on for another 10 or 20 years. So a time horizon of 10–20 years is quite normal in the aerospace industry.

The same sort of cycle applies to power generation, nuclear power stations, electronic computer systems, and much of manufacturing industry, each exhibiting its own time-constant. If you are setting up something new, even if it is only relatively medium technology, such as a knitwear factory, you have to train people, get in the infrastructure, and get a product which is competitive in order to get it into the market place. It is not easy and it always takes time.

The next point I want to make is the relationship between the initial investment and the return which comes from profitable sales later, on—the so-called Virtuous Circle illustrated here (Figure 3). The Virtuous Circle refers to the profits which are fed

Virtuous Circle of Investment

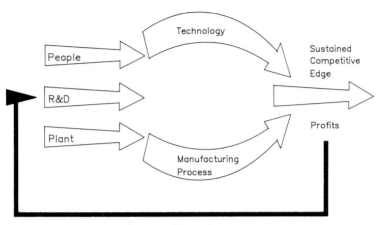

Figure 3

back into the next cycle of investment leading to further profits, steady growth in the company or the industry to which we are referring, and steady rewards for the shareholder. Inside this is a more complex process, deeply tied up with the internal investment and strategy of the company. At the top there is the investment in the technology of the product under consideration. Keeping the product, because that is what people buy, competitive in the market is one of the most fundamental objectives of industry. But in the lower circle, industry must also be seen to be continuously updating and improving its manufacturing processes, so that by improved quality and reduced cost it further improves its competitive edge in the market.

These two things go hand in hand and when successfully completed, give the company its sustained competitive edge, and from that, its position in the market with profits to feed back into investments. These investments are in research and development for both technology and the manufacturing process, in people and their training and education, and in the plant and infra-structure of the whole company.

Let us now turn to the performance of UK in the world market industry over the years. Some sectors have been very successful in maintaining their share of this market; aerospace, pharmaceuticals, chemicals, for instance. Others have been less successful, in particular, the automotive industry has lost market share dramatically, and this is also true of much of the mechanical engineering and the general manufacturing sector. This declining share of the world market is associated with a general contraction of parts of the industrial base, and today the manufacturing sector is down to around 23 per cent of our Gross Domestic Product, whereas in the middle 1960s it was something like 32 per cent. It also means that our good are less attractive in many cases, and industry is not able to supply even the home market; eventually loss of home market share usually goes hand in hand with loss of world market share.

DOES INDUSTRY MATTER?

Now these comments immediately beg the question, does it really matter if our industrial manufacturing base *is* declining? Many of us believe that it *does* matter a great deal, so there then arises the next question—what shall we do about it? To answer that question we need to look a bit further to try and understand some of the reasons for the decline. It is a truism to say—thanks to the jet airliner and electronics—that the world has shrunk, and with this has disappeared the spare 'headroom' of the 19th century provided by unexplored or subjugated territories. To help clear the mind, I find it a useful working hypothesis to assume that in the second half of the 20th century the pressures of rivalry between vigorous nations are translated into vigorous economic aggression, with the military spearhead of 50 years ago replaced by the competitive cutting edge of high-technology, excellent quality and careful differentiation in the market, supported by continual improvement in productivity and reduction in manufacturing costs. I do not mean trade wars, although they may break out from time to time, but I mean a ruthless, continuous, competitive economic advantage. Now some of our own industries clearly got the message in time, have reacted accordingly, and are healthy, with a good share of the world market. Others either did not get the message early enough, would not or could not respond in time, and have either been massively reduced, or as in the case of the motorcycle industry and some of the major players in the mechanical and electronic sectors, have been virtually wiped out.

Given this new set of rules, let us now look at some of the parameters which may well have influenced the strategic decisions and hence the fate of these industries over the last two or three decades. If we look at the previous plot of Gross Domestic Product (Figure 1) and enlarge the scale we can see more clearly

UK — GDP Growth and Growth Rate

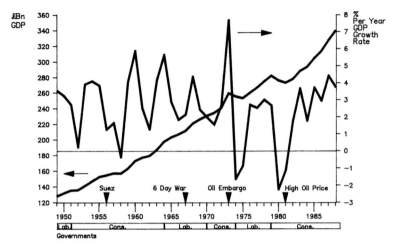

Figure 4

the large fluctuations in the 1960s reflecting the quite vicious stop-go cycles; (Figure 4) then in later years the huge overswings caused by the first and second oil crisis and the sharp rise in oil prices. More recently there are smaller fluctuations, and slightly increasing mean rate of growth during the last five or six years. Faced with these large and rapid variations in the economic health from economic stop-go cycles, it is hardly surprising that companies were wary of entering into long-term investments. The oscillations themselves are not the whole problem, because they are compounded by the fact that the general level of growth is low, only about 2 per cent on average. In these circumstances there is a high risk to long term investment based on domestic demand. On the other hand, the oscillations in the Japanese economy are also quite large, but here against a background of a much larger organic growth of 4-6 per cent, and in these circumstances you can be much more confident of seeing a good return on the investment much more quickly.

The same sort of oscillations occur in currency, and it is hardly surprising in the late 1970s, when the exchange rate of the pound against the dollar varied between $2.4 and $1.05 to the pound, that the boards of directors of nearly every UK company would be extremely wary of investing in projects which can only be sold into the American or dollar-denominated markets. (Further, if ever there was a justification for launch aid for long-term civil aircraft projects, this is it.) So UK industrial investment was squeezed by low growth at home, and extreme currency uncertainty for overseas prospects. Hardly surprising then when you examine the relative rates of investment, in capital, education and training, and particularly in new products, that UK industry has generally invested between one-third and one-half of the level of its competitors in other countries.

Now I do not want to pretend that there is a simple explanation—the truth of course is far more complex than I have just outlined. Factors such as good design, the lack of awareness of the world market, lack of marketing skills and the general social perception that engineering and industry were careers to be avoided, have all played their part. Market awareness, quality, better design and the underlying manufacturing productivity, have all improved over the last few years. Government economic policies, and the persistent campaigns, such as Industry Year in 1986, have been welcome. So we ought to find that things are better, but are they?

INNOVATION

Let us look at a comparison of investment in research and development. (Figure 5) This shows a comparison of the invest-

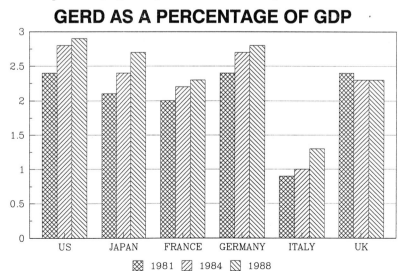

GERD AS A PERCENTAGE OF GDP

▨ 1981 ▨ 1984 ▨ 1988

Source: Annual Review of Government Funded R & D, HMSO 1988 & 1990

Figure 5

ment in 1981, 1984 and 1988, being the latest date for which consistent data is available, between UK, France, Germany, Japan and the US. It is clear that four of the countries have clearly got the message about sustained competitive edge and the need to keep their technology at the very leading edge in order to sustain their position in the market. It is a very clear sign, unfortunately, that the UK has simply not got the message. On the face of it the percentage of GDP at about 2.3 per cent is not terribly out-of-step with the others, but the trends are adverse. Furthermore, there is a fallacy in the figures which is particularly great in the case of the UK. That is because the civil R&D is in each case added up with the military, which of course is largely government funded. If we adjust for the military factor, the picture is substantially worse.[5]

Turning to industry, those parts which have received a degree of government support, like the aerospace industries and also those which are closely associated with the defence sector, such as certain sections of mechanical engineering but particularly the electronics industry, have levels of R&D investment which are at least consistent with the best in the world. Not surprisingly, therefore, these industries are those which have tended to maintain their share of the world market. By contrast, I believe it is a fact that the relative lack of civil R&D investment in certain sectors of industry, primarily 'medium' and 'low' technology which is associated with relative lack of innovation, leads to lack of competitive edge, loss of market share and subsequent decline—the so-called vicious circle.

PROFITABILITY

A vital element in our Virtuous Circle, is the return on investment. (Figure 6) This illustrates the return on fixed capital over the period 1972-1986. It compares UK manufacturing industry with that of Germany and the US. Manufacturing rates of return, net of depreciation at replacement cost in 1985 are 9 per cent in Britain, 18 per cent in West Germany, and 16 per cent in the US. With no figures for 1986 for West Germany, US remains about constant and the UK has improved to some 11 per cent. A rough estimate for 1988 on the basis of the general profits increase shown in company accounts would put the UK at about 13 per cent. So generally speaking it looks as if we are converging on about the same figure as Germany and the US. On almost any

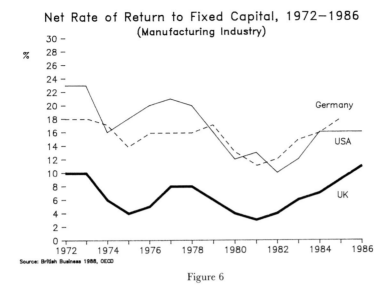

Figure 6

data, and even accepting that international comparisons are notoriously difficult and might be misleading, nevertheless Japan still appears to be way out in front.

Our profit performance of course is a measure of a number of factors, only one of which is prior investment. Nevertheless, the poor performance throughout the 1970s until the mid 1980s, (we are only now getting back to the sort of profit levels industry was enjoying in the 1960s) is consistent with low investment over the earlier period. But it is very disturbing to note that the steadily improving profit performance during the period 1982-1986 does not appear to be associated with an improving investment in research and development. Remember R&D investment in the UK has fallen in the 1980s. There must therefore be very serious concern about the future competitive capability of our manufacturing industry in the 1990s. It is very difficult to separate out cause and effect. One explanation could well be that the improving profitability has been partly achieved at the expense of investment in R&D. Whatever the explanation, this clearly is cause for concern.

Turning to investment in plant and machinery in the economy as a whole, (Figure 7) and comparing it with expenditure on acquisitions and mergers, it is interesting to note from the lower curve on this graph that there has been a great upsurge during the last few years in activities associated with acquisitions and

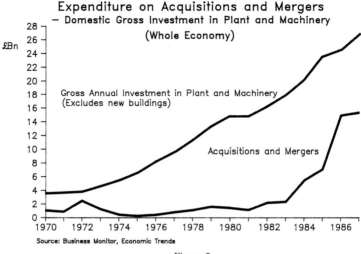

Source: Business Monitor, Economic Trends

Figure 7

mergers. The size of both investment and mergers is in money terms, not corrected for inflation. What is important is the relative size of each, year by year, and this clearly focuses interest on the rapid rise in acquisitions and mergers in the last few years. Looking at this data it is not unreasonable to say that in the economy as a whole, we appear to be spending almost as much on acquiring each other as on buying new plant and machinery.

CAPITAL PLANT

Also of concern is the lack of capital investment in manufacturing plants and machinery. (Figure 8) This figure shows that investment in manufacturing was effectively negative over the period 1980-1984. These statistics are of course only for the UK. You do not find similar trends in Japan, Germany, France or Italy. In the two years, 1986–87, companies were spending almost as much on acquisitions as they were on new plants and equipment. Yet it is only the latter that produces organic growth which can increase output and make a major contribution to wealth and the production of tradeable goods.

One of the effects of takeover activity is a tendency to focus too much management effort and time on short-term profitability to avoid the possibility of a takeover. Naturally under these pressures, one of the casualties is investment in research and

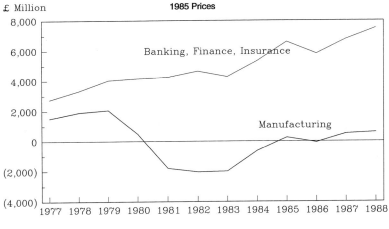

Figure 8

development, as well as in capital plant and equipment. But does the threat of a bid also help to keep management on its toes? Clearly yes, but we are surely entitled to ask also 'at what cost?' and, 'could we do the job better?'. John Kay, Professor at the London Business School, is quoted as saying that Britain spends about 10 times as much on takeover activity, as it spends on management education. Can we confidently say that bids produce 10 times the long-term benefit to British industry that the otherwise improved management skills would have brought? Personally, I doubt it. It is something we should examine further.

UK LTD

There is the irony that companies who manage their cash well, end up sitting on a cash mountain, producing short term profits which compare well with those companies investing their money in R&D and capital facilities. At the same time, it helps companies which are acquisitive, and which achieve their over-all objective of satisfying their shareholders by takeover rather than by organic growth. I know all this is fairly simplistic, and leaves a number of questions unanswered. It also leaves a number of questions unasked. I believe there is clear evidence that if we wish to increase both the efficiency and the size of our industrial base, then it means a massive increase in capital investment. This will only be possible from the market if it is supported by the appropriate level of profits. So we have to find a solution to a *three-pronged problem*—massively increasing our investment in industry—finding the best long-term way of both satisfying our shareholders, *and* being prepared to ride short term difficulties whilst gaining a greater share of the world market. I believe this represents one of the most important aspects which we need to address.

Another important factor is Government Tax Policy. This is because it affects retaining earnings, which in turn directly affects a company's propensity to invest long-term out of its profits. This is directly related to research and development which has to be written off year by year. Figure 9 shows taxes on corporate income as a percentage of GDP over the period 1980-1986. The first thing to note is the apparent difference between Japan and the rest of the European countries and the US. But bear in mind, first, that Japanese industry is a larger proportion of their GDP and also appears to be more profitable and, second, there are many other differences in the financing mechanisms open to Japanese companies, which makes direct comparison difficult, not least the quite unique saving system which has enormously supported Japanese industry over the last

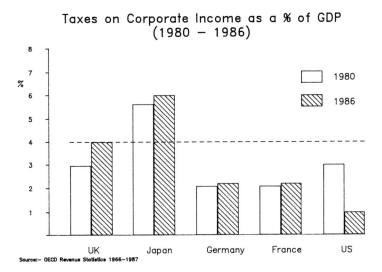

Figure 9

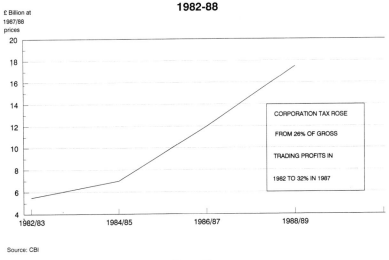

UK Corporation Tax Payments

1982-88

£ Billion at
1987/88
prices

CORPORATION TAX ROSE

FROM 26% OF GROSS

TRADING PROFITS IN

1982 TO 32% IN 1987

Source: CBI

Figure 10

decade. The various ways the Japanese system operates, to effectively encourage ralther than discourage R&D investment, by tax incentives for R&D amongst other arrangements, makes a direct simple comparison virtually impossible.

A more useful comparison is between the UK and Germany, France and the US. In the case of the latter, there has been a sharp reduction over this period in corporate tax. Contrast that with the UK, where there has been a 33 per cent increase over the period 1980–1986. In Germany and France there has been a negligible increase in the tax burden. It is interesting to compare the actual UK tax-take over the period 1982–1988 (Figure 10) and you can see it has risen over two and a half times, and this is at 1987/88 prices. Corporation Tax has risen from about a quarter of gross trading profits in 1982 to about a third in 1987, and is still rising. Compare it with the industry funded R&D figure of £5.5bn in 1985.

Clearly there is a case for further examination with some of these statistics, and a better understanding of the effects of the tax system. I doubt if the Treasury wish to re-examine this aspect, but it must surely be one of the most important areas for further study. This must then be linked to study the effects of all types of investment and the other associated factors such as dividend policy, and general performance of the stock market.

NATIONAL 'FINANCIAL ENGINEERING'

A lot of things have changed during the last few years, and there is very significant evidence of a very strong growth in manufacturing over the last five years. But this growth is from a much lower base following the 1980-84 so called 'shake-out'. This growth is accompanied by improved profitability in the manufacturing sector. But this raises key questions: *first*—is higher profitability really reflecting improved efficiency trends, or just the one-off benefits of the shake-out? (and how much from company 'financial engineering' arising from takeovers and mergers, already discussed); and *secondly*—why has there been no commensurate rise in product or technological investment in R&D?

One encouraging thing, in addition to a much better overall economic environment in the UK, should be the fact that the sums of money required to turn around the levels of investment, in R&D for instance, are not very large in relation to some of the other sums. For example, an extra £1.5bn a year would totally transform the R&D scene, bringing the UK well up to the international standards. The sums of money in the total defence budget, or the National Health Service, or Department of Education and Science, are all of the order of about £20bn a year. Similarly, the current corporation tax, is of the order of £15bn a year. Total tax take by the government this year will be £157bn or thereabouts.

On the face of it, with such large rivers of money flowing, it should not be too difficult to build up the banks of the river here or deflect a little of it into a trench dug over there, to make the right amount of money available for these purposes. I accept it is not quite as easy as that. But we must seriously examine each sector of industry to see whether and where in the long-term the UK is being seriously disadvantaged, relative to the opposition, possibly accidently, simply by the nature of our own tax structure. And there are other burdens on industry which have grown up over the last four years—the CBI calculate that the true growth is about £1000 per year for every person employed—which equates to something like half the net profit of many companies.

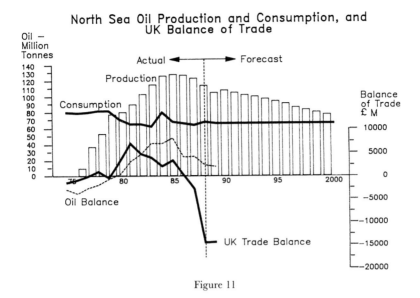

Figure 11

THE OVERALL ECONOMIC SCENE AND THE BALANCE OF PAYMENTS

Turning to the global scene of UK Ltd, one of the key adverse symptoms of the present economic scene in the UK is the trend in the balance of trade. (Figure 11) The underlying negative balance is strongly affected by the increasing negative balance in manufactures, which directly results from the lack of competitiveness and the massive reduction in the manufacturing base in the UK during the early 1980's. These things are very difficult to measure, but what we do know is that the UK manufacturing base is simply not large enough, nor does it produce the right goods, to prevent massive imports of foreign goods to satisfy domestic demand. Nor does it have sufficient positive trade balance in the areas where it does produce the right goods, to counterbalance the effects of all the imported manufactures. Unless the rest of the world will endlessly finance us to live beyond our means, we have to reverse this trend. British manufacturing industry and its associated tradeable services have to be better, and larger. To put things in context, if manufacturing is to fill the gap in tradeable exports it has to return towards, say, a 30 per cent share of GDP. Obviously this requires very rapid growth between now and the end of the century. If manufacturing were to achieve a share of 30 per cent by AD 2000, in a context where

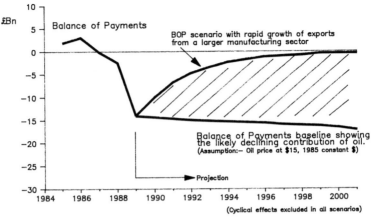

Figure 12

GDP is increasing at 2.5 per cent per annum, then the manufacturing sector must itself grow at about 5 per cent per annum. If it expanded its exports at this rate, it could achieve the scenario depicted here comfortably (Figure 12), all other things being equal. Against this background we must recognise that our national income from oil is declining, and depending on the oil price and the exchange rate assumptions at any time, the situation could deteriorate more or less rapidly.

This also begs the question what can be done to expand the services sector. The facts are that, broadly speaking, it is not large enough, and perhaps more important, only a small fraction of it is tradeable. So there is no conceivable way in which it can grow in order to fill the gap. What is more, the trade balance of the services sector has actually worsened over the last four years and the potential for productivity improvement, by applying modern technology and methods, is much less clear than in manufacturing. The gap I have shown is of course only indicative—the economic cycle, changes in terms of trade and so on, will ensure that the path back to equilibrium is an uneven one. The only conclusion one can arrive at is that the manufacturing sector itself, currently employing some 5m people, somehow has to grow to fill that gap. To do this, a growth rate as high, or higher, than that reached over the last few years is needed, supported by several times the rate of investment achieved during the last two or three years. Returning to my 'Virtuous Circle' again, we need higher sustained profits from organic growth if this increased investment is to be attractive to the capital markets.

The other major factor is the number of people involved. It is quite clear that we cannot employ another two to four million people in the economy in manufacturing, which is what simple growth from 23 to 30 per cent would require. So it is clear that we also need to sustain and perhaps accelerate the improvement in productivity which has been achieved in recent years. This itself will require additional levels of investment, which further factor up the estimates of investment required to achieve growth in the size of the manufacturing sector.

But suppose for the moment, we solve the problem of financing this investment, which should not be too difficult given that we are in a favourable position for inward investment, we are operating in a world economy with massive financial resources available, and with all the city's expertise for financial management. The real problem will be the physical resources, and more particularly, the intellectual resources, in short, people. We are now back to the vexed problem of the time constants to which I referred earlier. The fact is that it takes years to match people and a new plant, and get the product to the market even under the most favorable circumstances.

INWARD INVESTMENT

On the other hand, instead of starting with entirely new products at the research and development end, we can put into production articles which are already developed. For instance, the inward investment, by the US, Europe and the Japanese, in the electronics and the automotive industry in the UK, is having precisely this favourable effect. (Figure 13) The estimate for all foreign inward investment in 1988 was £8bn. This assistance in building up an efficient manufacturing base is obvious and should be encouraged. But it does beg two further questions.

First does it matter who owns this investment? I think most people will answer by saying that it is not critical, given that the UK owns such significant assets overseas. The *second* question is more difficult. Does it matter who does the R&D, and where? The answer to this is, I believe, that it does not matter too much about the R, but the D is important. In the medium to long-term it is important for the overall health of the UK economy that we

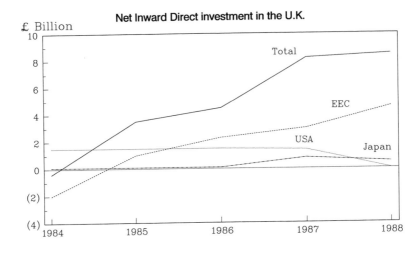

Figure 13

have a balance between our research centre, our development capability and the manufacturing capacity. So I believe that these new manufacturing facilities must develop their relationships with the universities and other research centres in this country; and sooner rather than later build up their own R&D facilities in the UK. Failure to achieve this will in effect be cutting off the blood supply to part of the brain and we know that, except for a very short time, this is quite unacceptable. Put another way, this could develop into industrial colonisation of the UK, bringing it into the status of a country being exploited only for its relatively cheap labour, unless the rules are defined.

It is true that one of our major advantages is the fact that at the moment, certainly in the automotive sector, wage levels are the second lowest in Europe (the exception is Spain). We have other major advantages such as the English language, good communications, a relatively well-trained and experienced workforce, good access to an excellent higher education system, and a generally very open economy which welcomes such inward investment. Subject then to the proper balance between R&D and manufacturing in the medium and long-term, such inward investment is unquestionably welcome. We must maintain a balance between such transplanted industry and new, organic growth with its roots in the UK.

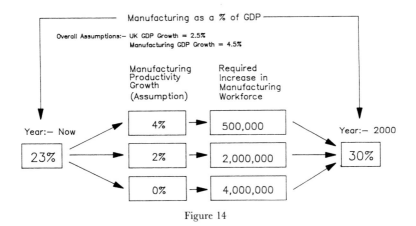

Figure 14

PEOPLE

We now need to turn our attention to the third aspect, and perhaps the most complex, with its own set of time constants. That is people, and the matter of education and training. Just to deal first with total numbers, (Figure 14) it is clear that with zero productivity growth we would require a further 4m people by the year 2000, to move from where we are now to a manufacturing sector. 30 per cent of GDP, 2 per cent growth, which is modest, would make this figure 2m. But with a manufacturing productivity growth of 4.0 per cent, year on year, there would still be a required increase in the manufacturing workforce of 0.5m by the year 2000. Such productivity growth is very demanding indeed and has never been sustained for long. However, it is *not* impossible, given all the means now open to us in manufacturing systems and technology and a more widespread awareness of what has to be done to manage it.

One of the difficulties, of course, is the availability of trained people and their availability distribution in the population. We are all aware of the demographic effect, whereby there is a 28 per cent reduction in the number of 16-19 year olds by the middle of the 1990s. This graph (Figure 15) is relative to an index of 100, for each line, in 1980. The total labour force will be increasing, partly accounted for by general ageing of the population (20–59) and the increasing number of women who, it is believed, will wish to come back into productive employment, shown as separate

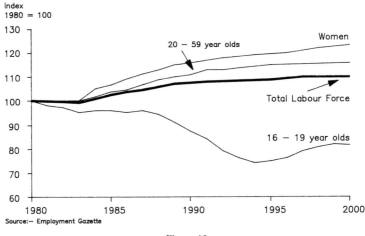

The Changing Labour Market

Figure 15

lines. So whilst there will be a major redistribution in terms of the age levels and in the types of employment in various sectors, *overall* the situation, providing we can maintain the 4.0 per cent improvement in productivity, does appear to be manageable.

But the major difficulty lies in the skills and in the training of the workforce. Employment patterns have been responding to major structural developments in the UK economy and there will be no let up in the impact of technological advances, linked with market pressure for product innovation and sophistication. External pressures will continue and there will be increasing competition at home from the effects of completing the internal market in Europe in 1992. In the future, individuals are less likely to be recruited to undertake a specific task, but are more likely to be hired to help achieve overall company objectives requiring the commitment of abilities, ideas and skills. There will be many changes, and much more flexibility in people's contributions will be central to the drive for productivity, efficiency, quality and service.

An indication of the changing structure of the engineering workforce is given in Figure 16. In particular the impact of the supervisors, skilled and the semi-skilled, is such that the numbers will reduce relatively, whilst the importance of the technically qualified, the technicians and the engineers, will become increasingly important as we have more automation and higher technology in the manufacturing process itself. The leverage from our

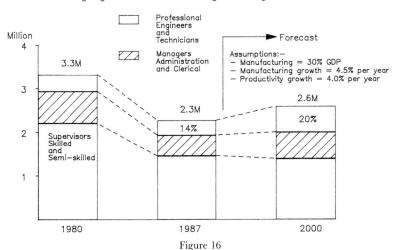

Figure 16

qualified engineers is going to be significantly increased. In other words, the flexibility and education of people have become the key to competitiveness. Companies must organise their employment policies and their strategies to utilise individuals effectively and nowhere are these messages more clearly written than in relation to training and the development of people.

INTERNATIONAL COMPARISON

Unfortunately, a number of studies have indicated that the UK workforce in terms of education, training and qualifications does not compare well with our industrial competitors. There is no space to go into this here, but we do have the results of an education system which has tended to aim at meeting the needs of the more academic, leaving the majority as a relatively poorly-educated national resource. As a nation we have tended to discount skills and professionalism, and to pay too small a premium for them.

Despite spending about £12bn per annum, vocational training has tended to produce a lower level of qualifications in traditional occupations rather than sufficient high levels of skill in the newer industries. This can be seen by a comparison (Figure 17) for 1985 between UK and the US, France, Germany and Japan. The figures are for qualifications in degrees, technicians and

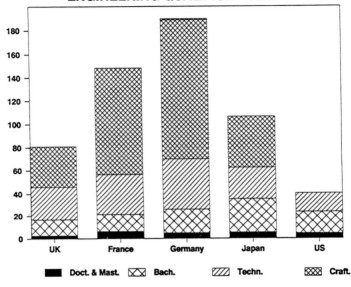

Figure 17

craftsmen. Again we need to treat the Japanese figures with some reservation, because of the immense amount of in-company training, whilst the US figures reflect the fact that they have never had a national craft apprenticeship scheme.

One thing industry must do urgently is to obtain a measure of true costs of training and education: we must make sure that there are no hidden burdens in British Industry PLC which place it at a disadvantage relative to the international competition. And we must not be surprised to find quite significant differences between sectors of British Industry.

CONCLUSIONS

There seems to be room for a fresh approach, which is why I have tried what can be called an 'engineering' approach. *First*, because looking at a lot of sometimes conflicting data and trying to make some sense of it is what engineers are professionally qualified to do. *Second*, because some 'control systems' thinking, ideas such as feedback, time constants etc. can be useful concepts. *Third*, because it might help to move the debate to new ground and avoid the polarisation of politics, or the sometimes conflicting—and frequently strongly held views—of the various schools of economics! There is also a *fourth* reason—that it is time for engineers to come out from behind the drawing boards, or electronic work stations, and take a hand in a vital debate.

There is little that is new in my message, but perhaps it is the first time the scale of the problem has been linked back—however crudely—through industry to the overall macro economic scene. We cannot afford to wait for market forces to reach levels which become irresistible before we act. The British always tend to be 'too little, too late' in their reactions to any situation. We are good in a crisis, none better, but this time if we wait until we have a crisis before we act, it will be one crisis too many. We need to heed the 'feedback' from the signals displayed today. When driving our motorcars, none of us wait to hit the kerb or be rammed by another car before we take avoiding action—we look beyond the end of the bonnet and use the feedback from our eyes, our ears, and all our senses. So if there is a *single-line message* it is let us think hard about the feedback signals *now*, and take some action.

NOTES

[1] Henderson, Sir Nicholas. 'Britain's Decline; its causes and consequences.' The Economist, 2nd June, 1979.

[2] Wiener, M. J. 'English Culture and the Decline of the Industrial Spirit 1850-1980.' Penguin, 1985.

[3] Barnett, C. 'The Audit of War.' Macmillan, 1986.

[4] Page, Sir Frederick W. 'Towards a New Industrial Revolution.' 24th Graham Clark Lecture.

[5] Yates, I. R. 'Defence, Development and Economics.' A lecture given to the EIRMA Annual Conference, Brussels, 31st May, 1989.

Conventional Arms Verification— The Status and Potential of Space Synthetic Aperture Radar Technologies

SIR PETER ANSON, Bt CB

The author is Chairman of Marconi Space Systems.

The aim of this paper is to outline the current status and potential of West European spaceborne Synthetic Aperture Radar (SAR) technologies in the role of CFE (Conventional Forces Europe) verification.

ASSUMED OPERATIONAL OBJECTIVES

Primary surveillance area:	Eastern Europe to the Urals and Caspian Sea (see Figure 1)
Surveillance targets:	Tanks Armoured Vehicles Artillery Combat helicopters Combat aircraft

These are the pinpoint verification targets. It is assumed that the surveillance of force concentrations, major fixed installations, infrastructure nodes and choke points etc. would be a primary element of the verification process.

Operational date:	As early as possible after 1991, the proposed CFE treaty ratification date.
Frequency of observation:	To meet operational specifications with a day/night baseline, increasing in frequency of revisits for sensitive targets ('hotspots') in times of tension.

It is also assumed that the space and ground segments would not require hardening against physical or electromagnetic attack.

163

CFE
VERIFICATION FROM SPACE

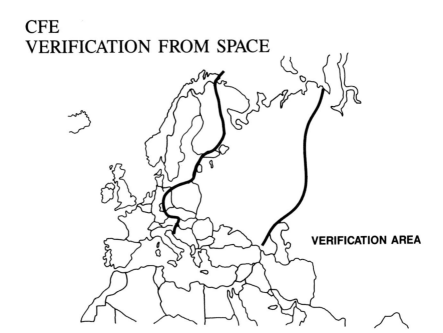

VERIFICATION AREA

THE ELEMENTS OF A SPACE BASED
VERIFICATION SYSTEM

The essential elements of a space based verification system are described below and illustrated in Figure 2.

- ☐ Low earth orbiting satellites carrying either optical (visible or IR) or SAR instruments, or both combined, together with their data transmission payloads communicating either directly to the ground or via a Data Relay Satellite (DRS).

- ☐ Data Collection Ground Stations (DCGS) to collect the raw radar data either directly from the surveillance spacecraft or via a DRS.

- ☐ Real-time image processing facilities.

- ☐ Satellite telemetry, tracking and telecommand (TT&C) ground stations.

- ☐ Satellite operational monitoring and control stations.

- ☐ Mission operations control.

- ☐ Target/data dissemination facilities.

FIGURE 2: ELEMENTS OF A SPACE BASED VERIFICATION SYSTEM

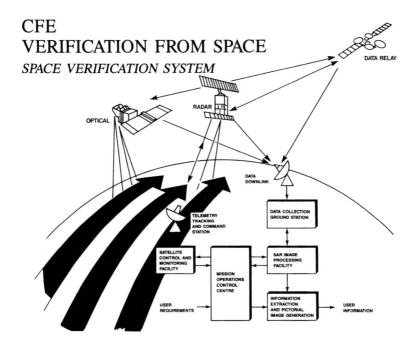

THE CHARACTERISTICS OF SPACE SURVEILLANCE

Space based surveillance systems are characterised by these primary features:

☐ *Non-intrusive.*
These are the only surveillance instruments which will allow verification without the cooperation or acquiescence of other parties.

☐ *Global potential.*
This characteristic embraces global flexibility —the inherent capability to survey threats from other sources and areas. A European space surveillance system could be equally effective in verifying any proliferation of arms in other parts of the globe.

☐ *Large area cover and fine resolution.*
The facility to cover vast areas in a short time, coupled with the resolution to detect small targets. By way of an example, a reconnaissance aircraft such as the recently retired US SR71 is capable of filming 250,000 sq.km in one hour; the French Spot satellite can cover 1,500,000 sq.km in the same period with a resolution down to 10m^2; and the European ERS1 spacecraft 500,000 sq.km in 10 mins with resolution down to 30m^2.

CFE
VERIFICATION FROM SPACE

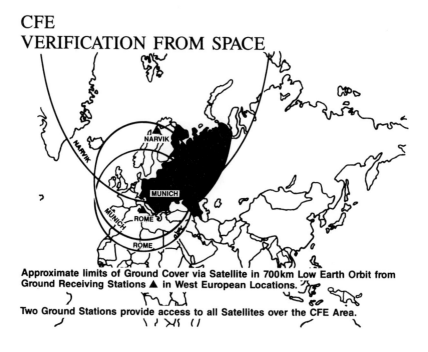

Approximate limits of Ground Cover via Satellite in 700km Low Earth Orbit from Ground Receiving Stations ▲ in West European Locations.

Two Ground Stations provide access to all Satellites over the CFE Area.

☐ *Real time response capability.*
  The potential to process and disseminate real-time observations.

☐ *Durability.*
  The space platform is virtually immune to the disruptions that could be instantly imposed on on-site inspections and overflying rights.

☐ *Global communications cover.*
  As Figure 3 shows, two DCGS's would be sufficient to maintain direct communication with a verification satellite in Low Earth Orbit (LEO) throughout its observation of the entire CFE area. For communications contact extending over the full global orbit, DRS satellites could provide a virtually unlimited space relay service.

SYSTEM CHARACTERISTICS

Ground Coverage

   Civil earth observation satellites typically operate in polar orbits between 700-850 km. The extent of ground coverage is

FIGURE 4: SWATH COVERAGE OF A SYNTHETIC APERTURE RADAR

CFE
VERIFICATION FROM SPACE
SWATH COVERAGE OF A SYNTHETIC APERTURE RADAR

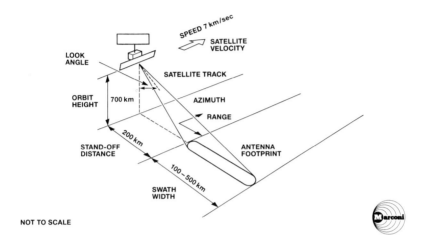

governed by several factors, but principally by the orbit height and sensor viewing angle constraints. LEO orbits are practically constrained to altitudes between 500 and 1500km, high enough to minimise atmosphere drag and low enough to limit exposure to the Van Allen natural radiation belts. Although the horizon at, say, a 850km orbit exceeds 3000km, the technical limitations of both SAR and optical sensors constrains the observable region within a radius of less than 1000km. Within these very general constraints the different coverage available from optical and SAR instruments is typified in the performance of SPOT and ERS1 satellites. The SPOT1 optical mission is characterised by 60 × 60km images (of resolution down to 10m^2) from either side of the sub satellite track out to 400km. The principle of SAR coverage is illustrated in Figure 4. ERS1 will provide cover of a fixed 100km swath at a distance of 200km to 300km on a single side of the satellite track with resolutions below 30m^2. SARs currently under development in Europe will extend this swath width to over 500km with substantially improved resolutions. An example of such ground coverage capability over 24 hours is illustrated in Figure 5.

CFE
VERIFICATION FROM SPACE
TYPICAL 24 HOUR SAR COVERAGE WITH 500 km SWATH MODE

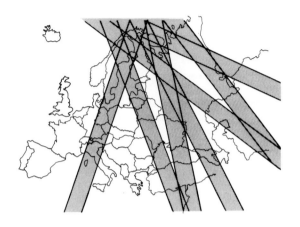

Revisit Times

The frequency of revisits to any given location is governed by satellite orbit height, its geographical latitude and the surveillance instrument's ground cover. Increases in orbit height result in increased orbit periods. At 850km the orbit period is around 100 minutes, which produces 14 orbits every 24 hours. For polar orbits, regions near the poles are viewed on every orbit, whereas tropical regions would receive less frequent cover. In an operational system, shorter revisit times can be achieved by using several satellites. The design aim would be to obtain optimum access to the specified surveillance area from a single satellite and then to phase additional satellites to reduce revisit times as necessary.

SAR SENSORS

Spaceborne SAR is characterised by these unique primary features:

- ☐ All weather, day/night capability.
- ☐ Flexibility; the possibility of a trade off between wide area cover at medium resolution and spotlight images at fine resolution.

The SAR Concept

The use of conventional radars for space surveillance is impracticable because of the antenna size required for fine resolution. SAR is able to overcome this limitation with antennas of practical size and power by summing coherently the whole sequence of radar pulse returns received from any given area on the ground in the period the satellite illuminates that area. The processing techniques effectively synthesis a radar of very long aperture (approximately 5km in the case of ERS1). It is this extended aperture which provides the enhanced spatial resolution in the along-track dimension. Fine resolution in the across-track dimension is obtained by means of pulse compression techniques. SARs are highly effective for imaging stationary or slow-moving targets and resolutions of $1m^2$ or less are theoretically feasible. SAR operates in a side-scan mode, normally illuminating only one side of the satellite's track at any one time.

The received signal pulses are demodulated and then individually converted from analogue to digital form. These digital words which contain the raw radar data, are formatted and reassembled into a data stream for transmission to a ground based processor in which the visual SAR image is produced.

European SAR Developments

The first European SAR will be flown on the European Space Agency's (ESA) ERS1 spacecraft which is scheduled to be launched in early 1991. ERS1, which is illustrated in Figure 6, will be launched into a near polar (98.5°), sun-synchronous plane to perform 14 orbits per day. ERS1 was initiated through Phase A studies 12 years ago in 1978, which serves as a reminder of the long gestation periods for complex collaborative projects. The principle objectives of this satellite are to exploit all-weather radar imagery of ice/ocean features for the prediction of climatic changes. The SAR provides a single fixed 100km swath offering a image resolution down to $30m^2$. The raw radar data is processed and transmitted to the DCGS at a data rate around 100Mb/s. ERS2, Europe's successor to ERS1, is planned to be launched in 1994.

More advanced SAR instruments are already under development in Europe which would offer capabilities closer to the verification mission. One candidate design is VSAR (Versatile SAR). This would provide greater operational flexibility over the ERS1/2 instrument which it would succeed in 1997, offering

FIGURE 6: ERS1 SPACECRAFT—EUROPE'S FIRST RADAR SATELLITE

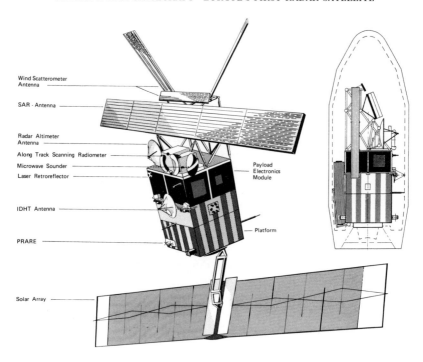

variable swath widths from 100 to 500km. SARs with resolutions of down to $20m^2$ are also being studied by ESA in their SAR 2000 project to meet longer term needs.

The associated technological developments, a larger steerable phased array antenna is one prime example, could be readily adapted to provide finer resolutions down to a few metres over a 'spot-light' area. These developments also provide for access to DRS, which itself has the capability to relay data traffic at up to 400Mb/s. These advanced SAR designs are currently driven entirely by civil earth observation and environmental monitoring objectives. However, the CFE space verification role would require no more than the optimisation of these existing sensor and processing developments.

In the military field, a SAR development programme is being considered which could lead to the realisation of instruments which would match the verification specification. This collaborative European SAR venture is expected to commence in 1990 as part of the Independent European Programme Group's (IEPG)

FIGURE 7: EVOLUTION OF EUROPEAN SAR TECHNOLOGIES

CFE
VERIFICATION FROM SPACE
EVOLUTION OF EUROPEAN SAR SATELLITE

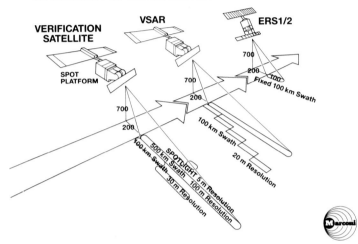

EUCLID (European Collaboration for the Long Term In Defence) Research & Development programme. The SAR specification which is beginning to emerge would offer 'spotlight' resolutions of well below 5m^2.

An illustration of the evolutionary programmes which are leading to a CFE verification capability is provided in Figure 7, while Figure 8 summarises the major European SAR specifications including a possible baseline specification for a verification instrument.

SAR Processing

The ground processing segment is driven by the need to obtain monitoring information in real-time. There are two stages to the chain; the SAR processor which generates images from the raw satellite data, and the post-processor for automatic feature extraction and change detection. A real-time SAR processor is currently under development in the UK which will process ERS-1 images as the data is received. It will then be possible to view and monitor the SAR image as the satellite passes overhead.

FIGURE 8: SUMMARY OF EUROPEAN SAR SPECIFICATION

CFE
VERIFICATION FROM SPACE
THE EVOLUTION OF SAR TECHNOLOGY

PROJECT	LAUNCH	GROUND COVER SCAN	SWATH	FREQ. BAND	SPATIAL RESOLUTION	POLAR-ISATION	ANTENNA	DATA RATE
ERS1 ERS2	1991 1994	FIXED STRIP	80 km	C	30 m	V	10 × 1 m W/G PLANAR ARRAY	100 Mb/s
VSAR	1997	STEERED BEAM SCANSAR	100 km 500 km	C	30 m 100 m	V or H	10 × 1.3 m ACTIVE PHASED ARRAY	100 Mb/s
SAR 2000	2000	STEERED BEAM SCANSAR	100 km 500 km	C	20 m 100 m	V/H	13 m × 2 m ACTIVE PHASED ARRAY	200 Mb/s
VERIFICATION SATELLITE	TBD	SPOTLIGHT STEERED BEAM SCANSAR	25 km 100 km 500 km	L/C/X	< 5 m 30 m 100 m	V/H	15 m × 3 m ACTIVE PHASED ARRAY	200 Mb/s
EUCLID SAR	2005	SPOTLIGHT STEERED BEAM SCANSAR	25 km 100 km 500 km	C or X	< 5 m 30 m 100 m	V/H	< 20 m LENGTH ACTIVE PHASED ARRAY	< 500 Mb/s

The large amount of data inherent in a SAR image requires an automatic post-processor. Conventional image processing techniques are inadequate. This projected real-time processor will receive and process images from successive or multiple passes and detect any changes occurring. Each change area must be examined and classified. The sheer bulk of image data enforces the maximum use of computer detection, but some level of human intervention will be required at this stage. Change detection algorithms and multi-image processors, capable of operating in such a system, are also currently under development within the UK.

PLATFORM/LAUNCHER CAPABILITIES

The instrument mass and power figures for the various European SAR projects above are listed at Figure 9 to show that all could be carried on the SPOT-4 platform or its evolved designs. SPOT-4 is a large modular expendable spacecraft, designed in its basic architecture to carry more than 1700kg of instrument mass and to be capable of launch with ARIANE 4 or ARIANE 5.

FIGURE 9: EUROPEAN SAR INSTRUMENTS: MASS/POWER

PROJECT	MASS	POWER
ERS 1/2	320 Kg	1.2 kW
VSAR	350 Kg	1.2 kW
SAR 2000	600 Kg	2.4 kW
VERIFICATION SAR	900 Kg	< 2 kW
EUCLID SAR	< 1000 Kg	< 2 kW

CONCLUSIONS

Space based surveillance systems have a vital role to play in CFE verification by virtue of their non-intrusiveness and durability, and their capability for large area cover, fine resolution and real-time response. Of the space surveillance instruments available for this CFE role, only SAR is able to offer all-weather and day/night capability.

All of the basic elements of a spaceborne SAR verification system have either been built or are under development in Europe; these include the surveillance satellite and its SAR instruments, data relay satellites, data receiving stations and ground image processing systems. Europe's first SAR instrument will be flown on the ERS1 spacecraft in early 1991 when the associated European-wide ground data processing network will also begin operation.

Development work is already underway in Europe on the next-generation systems, including SARs offering wider swaths and finer resolution as well as real-time image processors. However, these developments, are driven by the civil market and requirements which fall short of those imposed by CFE in terms of resolution and programme timescales. Nevertheless, these technological developments would require no more than some optimisation and acceleration in order to meet the CFE task.

The summary of conclusions to be drawn from European SAR developments is:

- [ ] A space based surveillance system has a unique role to play in CFE verification.
- [ ] Current civil space programmes demonstrate that Europe has the capability and technology to build a spaceborne verification system.

☐ The space system would require optimisation of existing sensor and processing technologies to meet the verification requirement. This is feasible.

☐ Existing European platforms (SPOT) and launchers (ARIANE) are adequate for the verification mission.

The Place of the Military in Regional Stability

'Things Will Never be the Same Again': Israel and the *Intifada*

DR ROSEMARY HOLLIS

Dr Hollis is a Research Fellow at the RUSI and has published various works on Israel and the Arab-Israeli conflict.

... [E]ven if a combination of Israeli military, economic and diplomatic achievements does succeed in reducing the level of violence in the territories, they will never return to the relatively easy and benign occupation of the first two decades.[1]

The Palestinian uprising, known as the Intifada or 'shaking off', which began in the West Bank and Gaza Strip in December 1987, two decades after Israel first occupied these areas, marked a turning point not only in the history of Palestinian nationalism, but also in the Arab-Israeli conflict. The Intifada and Israeli responses to it created the background for Arab and Israeli reactions to subsequent developments in East-West relations, the influx of Soviet Jewish emigres to Israel and, after 2 August 1990, the crisis in the Gulf. Here the focus will be on Israel: the logic of its traditional approach to the Palestinian problem; the challenge to that logic which the Intifada represented; and Israel's adherence to its traditional approach, once the initial shock of the uprising had worn off and divisions of opinion in Israel prevented it from developing a more innovative response.

While Israeli politicians explored the possibility of opening talks directly with the Palestinians and failed to agree on a way forward, Israel's actual conduct for three years has been contrived to contain, if not suppress, the uprising and reinforce Israel's hold on the land in dispute. Whether by default or design, therefore, Israel blunted the hopes of moderates both in the Jewish community and among the Palestinians, who advocated a 'land for peace' settlement. This set the stage for more bitterness and violence thereafter.

FROM CAPTURE TO INDEFINITE OCCUPATION

By 1987 Israel's occupation of East Jerusalem, the West Bank and Gaza had become a facet of the economic, social, political and military life of the Jewish state. Also, the experience of war with the armies of neighbouring Arab regimes, from the moment of Israel's establishment in 1948, through the Suez campaign of 1956, to the wars of June 1967 and October 1973, had established that the main Arab threat to Israel emanated from hostile Arab states. Even the organisations which represented the cause of Palestinians who had lost their lands in Israel or come under Israeli occupation operated from inside Arab states, on whose indulgence they relied for their continued existence.

Spoils of war

Because Israel had captured the Gaza Strip and Sinai Peninsula from Egypt, East Jerusalem and the West Bank from Jordan, and the Golan Heights from Syria, by defeating the armies of these three Arab states in the Six Day War of 1967, these conquests were treated as the prizes of war. That Egypt and Syria tried to win back their losses in a surprise assault during the Jewish Yom Kippur holiday in 1973 served to reinforce this characterisation. Then, when Egypt changed her approach and agreed to make peace in exchange for the return of the Sinai in the Camp David Accords and Egypt-Israel Treaty of 1979, this substantiated the perception that Israel could perhaps use the occupied territories, or parts thereof, as bargaining counters in a quest to reach accommodation with her Arab neighbours.

The Camp David Accords envisaged that a process could be set in motion, to settle the future status of the West Bank and Gaza Strip, through negotiation between the governments of Israel, Egypt and Jordan. Palestinian participation was invited, but initially only as members of the delegations of the Arab governments. In the meantime, it was proposed, a body elected by the Palestinian inhabitants of the West Bank and Gaza was to exercise a measure of self-government in these areas. The Accords stated that the solution reached through negotiation must "recognise the legitimate rights of the Palestinian people and their just requirements" and that agreement between Israel and Jordan "shall be based on all the provisions and principles of UNSC Resolution 242", which indicated an exchange of land for peace between Israel and Jordan. The lack of any more explicit undertaking to the Palestinians, or provision for their participation as a separate voice, rendered the Accords unacceptable to them and explains in part why the negotiating process failed to proceed. Subsequent attempts in the 1980s, notably by Israeli Labour leader Shimon Peres, to reach a bilateral agreement with Jordan, also foundered.

No voice for the PLO

Israel's attitude toward the Palestine Liberation Organisation (PLO) was apparent from the design of the Camp David plan for negotiations, which excluded the organisation from participation in the process. From its inception in 1964, one of the tenets of the PLO had been to seek the destruction of Israel. This and the terror tactics adopted by the organisation were among the grounds for Israel's refusal to contemplate any dealings with the PLO. One of the Israeli objectives in its invasion of Lebanon in 1982, meanwhile, was the elimination of the PLO's paramilitary bases and forces there. International intervention prevented their total destruction, but did ensure that the PLO leadership and commandos were dispersed to new locations scattered around the Arab world. Some, however, made their way back to Lebanon after the Israelis withdrew to what they called a "security zone", south of the Litani river, in 1985.

Palestinians on the sidelines

While Israel pursued its dual objectives of establishing a favourable modus vivendi with Arab neighbouring states and crippling the PLO, relations inside the occupied territories developed a momentum of their own. From the moment when Israel first captured the West Bank and Gaza Strip in 1967, the boundaries between these territories and 'Israel proper', the 'Green Line', were thrown open. Palestinians from the occupied territories were encouraged to cross the Green Line to take up employment as agricultural and construction workers inside Israel proper, some Israelis went in the opposite direction to set up settlements and business ventures.

By 1987, the year of the beginning of the Intifada, there were at least 107 Jewish settlements in the West Bank and 14 in the Gaza Strip. The total Jewish population of the West Bank stood at 67,000 and that of the Gaza Strip at 2,506, which was not, incidentally, as many as the Likud had hoped for.[2] These figures do not include Jewish settlers in East Jerusalem, estimated to number upwards of 70,000 by 1987.

The methods by which land was acquired by Israel in the occupied territories, either for settlement or for the direct use of the Israel Defence Forces (IDF), rested on Israeli interpretation and adaptation of laws governing land use since as long ago as Ottoman times and the period of the British Mandate, as well as Jordanian legal procedures. By the mid 1980s about 33 per cent of West Bank land had been declared state land and thereby available for Israeli use.[3] Various areas within and adjacent to such lands were directly requisitioned or rendered uninhabitable by being declared 'combat zones'. The Eastern part of Jerusalem, meanwhile, was deemed part of 'united Jerusalem, Israel's eternal capital' and brought under direct Israeli sovereignty from 1967 onwards.

In 1987 the Palestinian population of the West Bank stood at approximately 977,000 (not including the 140,000 or so living in East Jerusalem and some 90,000 residents living abroad).[4] These figures reflect a population growth of between 80 and 90 per cent since 1967. Of the total, 373,586 were registered as refugees with the United Nations Relief and Works Agency (UNRWA), 94,824 of them living in the 20 West Bank refugee camps.[5] Around 150,000 West Bank Palestinians, the vast majority of the work force, crossed the Green Line daily to work in Israel proper.[6] The Palestinian population of the Gaza Strip stood at 633,000 in 1987, having increased by over 60 per cent since 1967.[7] Eighty per cent of the Palestinian inhabitants of the Gaza Strip were registered refugees, well over half of whom lived in Gaza's eight camps.[8] Nearly half the Gaza work force of 92,000 worked in Israel proper.[9]

Resources for Israel

Initially the economic integration encouraged between Israel and the occupied territories produced an increase in development and growth in the West Bank and Gaza Strip. Improvements in health care and the provision of educational facilities, including universities, also took effect. However, over the years, most of the Israeli effort and funding were directed at developing an infrastructure tailored to the needs of the defence forces and Jewish settlers, to the neglect or detriment of Palestinians, especially in the case of communication networks and channelling of water resources. Restrictions were imposed on Palestinian businesses and agriculture so that Israeli ventures were protected from competition. As a result, by the 1980s, the Palestinian economy was dependent on Israel for goods, services and employment.[10]

In terms of administrative arrangements in the occupied territories, Israel has not allowed elections for local council members within the Palestinian community since 1976. In 1981 the Israeli government set up two types of administrative authorities for the West Bank and Gaza Strip: a Military Administration and a Civil Administration.

> The new division envisaged that the military commanders would remain responsible for security matters, while a civilian administration, subordinate to the Defence Minister, would be responsible for civilian matters and for relations with the Arab inhabitants.[11]

This structure remained in place until the Intifada began. It did not encompass annexed East Jerusalem, which came under the same laws as Israel proper. Jewish settlers in the occupied territories, meanwhile, held the same rights as all other Israelis.

Intifada Breaks the Mould

The *Intifada* delivered a rude shock both to Israel's domestic political scene and to its foreign policy posture. It upset the status quo and underlying assumptions about Israel's hold on the occupied territories and challenged the logic of Israel's policies toward the Arabs.

Taken by surprise

Throughout the 20 years following Israel's occupation of the West Bank and Gaza Strip, Palestinians in these areas had staged protests against Israeli rule and violent demonstrations had taken place periodically. However, the riots which began in the Gaza Strip on 8 December 1987, following the deaths of four Palestinians when an Israeli lorry collided with their car, were on a wholly unprecedented scale. Within days of the first outburst, Palestinian men, women and children were staging mass demonstrations, burning tyres and hurling stones at the Israeli troops sent to disperse them with an arsenal ranging from tear gas to live ammunition.

By mid–January 1988 the rioting had spread to Jerusalem and the West Bank and Palestinian casualties included some 40 dead and hundreds wounded. Television coverage of the uprising sent pictures around the world of civilian demonstrators clashing with Israeli armed forces. Some of the beatings meted out by IDF soldiers were shown in graphic detail and Israel was widely criticised for brutality and unnecessary use of force. As studies were subsequently to confirm, the Israeli armed forces and government were taken completely by surprise by the uprising and took weeks to organise a coordinated response.[12]

The Palestinian demonstrators adopted nationalist slogans and displayed the Palestinian flag in defiance of Israeli regulations. Within a few weeks, an underground leadership, the Unified National Leadership of the Uprising (UNLU), came into being and issued directives for the movement, distributed by leaflet, throughout the occupied territories. The tactics they called for included strikes, boycotts of Israeli products, non-payment of Israeli taxes and mass resignations of Israeli-appointed Arab local officials and police.

The PLO was apparently as surprised by the *Intifada* as the Israelis. However, it rallied to the cause and began issuing pronouncements designed to capitalise on international criticism of Israeli actions. The UNLU declared its allegiance to the PLO and the leadership of its chairman Yasser Arafat. The Islamic Resistance Movement or Hamas, which operated in the Gaza Strip, was somewhat of a power unto itself, however, although it did not, initially, present a challenge to the role of the more secular UNLU in the West Bank.

Closing in of Options

During the course of 1988 the Intifada provided the impetus for a series of new developments in the geopolitics of the Arab-Israeli conflict. On 31 July King Hussein of Jordan announced:

> Since there is unanimous conviction that the struggle for liberating the occupied Palestinian territory can be bolstered by disengaging the legal and administrative relationship between the two banks, then we must perform our duty and do what is required of us.[13]

The old Jordanian House of Representatives, whose members had included West Bank Palestinians, even though there had been no elections since the occupation, was dissolved and some Jordanian-appointed officials with West Bank responsibilities were retired. The King also stipulated that his moves would not affect Jordanian citizens of Palestinian origin in the kingdom, and:

> Jordan is not Palestine and the independent Palestinian state will be established on the occupied Palestinian territory after its liberation, God willing.[14]

On 15 November 1988 the Palestine National Council (PNC) met in Algiers and drew up a Palestinian Declaration of Independence. On 8 December 1988 a joint statement issued in Stockholm by a Palestinian delegation led by Yasser Arafat and a group of five representatives of the American Jewish community offered clarification of the PNC Declaration and accompanying communiqué. The PNC, it said, was calling for a two-state solution to the Israeli–Palestinian conflict and thus accepted the existence of Israel alongside the newly declared Palestinian state. Furthermore, the Palestinian leadership was now rejecting and condemning terrorism in all its forms, including state terrorism. These new positions were considered sufficient to remove US objections to holding direct talks with the PLO and at the end of 1988 a dialogue was opened between the US Ambassador in Tunis and PLO officials.

One year on from the beginning of the Intifada, the uprising had settled into a way of life for both the Palestinians and the Israelis. By then it was clear that the Palestinian inhabitants of the West Bank and Gaza Strip had become the driving force of Palestinian nationalism, even as they pledged allegiance to the PLO. The latter, meanwhile, had attained new respectability in the international community. None of Israel's Arab neighbour states was prepared to speak on their behalf and Jordan had renounced its claims to the West Bank. The main principles behind Israel's policy on the Palestinian question and Arab opposition to its existence had been seriously undermined. Its control of the occupied territories and subordination of the Palestinians there had been proven incomplete, if not unsustainable, without substantial changes.

Attempt at an initiative

Pressure mounted on the Israeli government, both on the domestic front and in the international community, to find a new political way forward. No such initiative was forthcoming until after the Israeli Knesset elections of November 1988, and the formation of a new coalition government between the Labour Party and the Likud, who received almost equal support in the polls.

The coalition leadership agreed that Israel should still aim for a regional peace agreement, based on the principles of the Camp David Accords. Since neither Jordan nor Egypt were prepared to speak on behalf of the Palestinians, however, they were obliged to find a new partner with whom to open a dialogue. Objections to direct dealings with the PLO in the Likud and Labour leaderships ruled out that possibility, so attention focused on finding an alternative interlocutor for the Palestinians.

The initiative proposed by Prime Minister Yitzhak Shamir on 15 May 1989 called for elections among the Palestinians in the West Bank and Gaza Strip. As had been proposed in the Camp David Accords, the elected Palestinian body was to join in negotiations with Israel and Jordan to decide on a permanent solution. Whereas the Accords expected Palestinian participation in the process to take place after negotiations had begun between Israel, Jordan and Egypt; the Shamir initiative anticipated that negotiations would open with an Israeli–Palestinian dialogue, to include the Egyptians and Jordanians only if they so wished. Included in the wording of the initiative were the following stipulations:

> Israel opposes the establishment of an additional Palestinian state in the Gaza district and in the area between Israel and Jordan; Israel will not conduct negotiations with the PLO.[15]

Since these stipulations rendered the initiative unacceptable to most Palestinians, the US and Egypt took up the task of trying to find an accommodation acceptable to both sides and sufficient at least to allow a dialogue to begin.

After months of behind the scenes diplomacy and much public debate in Israel, the coalition government finally collapsed on 15 March 1990, over the issue of whether to go ahead with talks in Cairo on terms brokered by US Secretary of State James Baker. The Likud balked at the inclusion of East Jerusalem Palestinians in the process, and Shamir claimed that his elections and autonomy plan had been hijacked and distorted by the US, in collusion with Labour and the PLO. Labour advocated going ahead on US terms, hoping perhaps that the Americans would ultimately protect Israel from PLO demands. The efforts of Labour leader Shimon Peres to form a new coalition with small left wing and religious parties, committed to going ahead with talks in Cairo, failed however.

Following more tortuous negotiations between Knesset members, a government was finally formed in June 1990, dominated by the Likud and including both religious groupings and the small, ultra-right-wing parties opposed to Palestinian self-rule. This constituted the most hardline government in Israeli history, firmly committed to the retention of all the occupied West Bank.

SUSTAINING THE COSTS OF CONTAINMENT

While Israel's politicians cast about for an appropriate policy to deal with the new political developments, the defence and security forces were charged with containing the Palestinian uprising in the West Bank and Gaza Strip. Divisions, not only between the Labour and Likud parties, but across the spectrum of opinion in Israel, frustrated attempts to find a political solution to the Intifada. After a year or so the Israelis began to grow used to living with it.

Counting heads

In terms of casualties, the Palestinians took a far larger toll than the Israelis, but this provided little cause for satisfaction in Israel, since every Palestinian death created a martyr for the cause and both deaths and injuries could only fuel Palestinian resentment and international criticism of Israel. According to IDF figures issued at the end of the second year of the Intifada, 535 Palestinians had been killed, including 69 children aged 14 and under.[16] Another 136 Palestinians had been killed by their compatriots for alleged collaboration with the Israelis. Over the same period eight IDF soldiers and 11 Israeli civilians had died as a result of the Intifada. The number of Palestinian wounded was put at 8,938 by the IDF, though other estimates put the numbers in the tens of thousands. The IDF estimated that 1,637 soldiers and 803 Israeli civilians had been wounded. In the first months of 1990 the numbers of Palestinian deaths and injuries continued to mount, but at a reduced pace, until violence exploded anew in May 1990. The most dramatic escalation occurred in the midst of the Gulf crisis, when rioting at Temple Mount in Old Jerusalem was put down by Israeli security forces firing live ammunition, resulting in the deaths of 20 Palestinians in one day alone.

During the first two years of the Intifada, 50,000 Palestinians were arrested and by the end of that period 9,000 were being held in 'administrative detention', that is, for up to one year at a time, without trial.[17] Jails in the Gaza Strip were reported to be full to the point of overflowing. Some 58 leading Palestinians had been deported, 248 Palestinian houses had been demolished and another 118 sealed, as a punishment. The drawback for the Israeli authorities of all such measures was the politicising effect they were likely to have on those concerned, and the deportations may have served to dilute the ranks of potential moderates in the Palestinian leadership.

Military deployment

Responding to the Intifada had a variety of implications for the IDF. From January 1989 the IDF split responsibility for the occupied territories into three divisional commands, one each for the northern West Bank (Samaria), the southern West Bank (Judea) and the Gaza Strip. Both reserve and regular units were deployed to undertake police duties in these areas, regardless of whether they were trained as paratroopers, gunners or engineers. Since the rioting was initially widespread and almost continuous, extra reserves had to be called up and reserve duty was extended from one to two months a year.

To meet the requirements of fighting a civilian insurgency, new rules of engagement were developed, largely through trial and error, and special training programmes instigated. Troops were equipped with an array of different types of ammunition, including rubber bullets (containing steel cores), plastic bullets (metal bullets with plastic tips) and tear gas grenades. Machines designed to shower rioters with gravel and plastic-coated steel marbles were also used. Measures such as these served to reduce the likelihood of Palestinians being killed outright during street riots, though the so-called plastic bullets proved lethal on a number of occasions and many Palestinians were seriously wounded by this array of IDF implements.

By the end of the second year of the Intifada, the IDF claimed a number of achievements for its counter–insurgency campaign, amongst them a reduction in the total number of Palestinian deaths in clashes with troops, as opposed to internecine killings for alleged collaboration. With respect to IDF activities in the West Bank in the latter half of 1989, a variety of accomplishments were cited, including: the arrest of about 100 'most wanted' persons (another 40 were apparently still at large); the entry of IDF forces into all parts of the region, including the most remote; a reduction in the number of marches, processions, and villages declaring independence; an increase in security on the major arteries, following the construction of 41 IDF 'strongpoints' in 'sensitive areas'; the halting of tax revolts (the case of Beit Sahur included); the capture of groups engaged in hostile activities of a terrorist nature, such as kidnapping; and an increase in the feeling of security among Jewish settlers.[18]

Set against this record, according to the IDF itself, was the persistence of passive civilian revolt among the majority of the residents of the occupied territories. Notwithstanding the numbers of deaths, detentions and deportations of activists, in December 1989 an Israeli field analysis reportedly concluded:

> the Intifada in the territories will continue mainly because of the activity of a hard core of activists estimated at between 10,000 and 20,000 people. These activists and the recognised leadership of the Intifada are looking for new means and strategies to strengthen the uprising and bring it back to the crowd levels that characterised the beginning of the period.[19]

That the fears expressed here were warranted was demonstrated in May 1990, when the murder of seven Palestinian labourers by one apparently deranged Israeli sparked furious rioting not only in the occupied territories, but among Israeli Palestinian citizens inside the Green Line, and in Jordan.

Effects on morale

The effects on the IDF of having to take on a counter-insurgency role have been carefully documented by Israeli analysts. One consequence was a loss of prestige for the IDF, at least in the short term. Criticised by Jewish settler organisations on the one hand for being too 'soft' on the insurgents, and by Israeli civil rights activists on the other for being too brutal, the IDF lost some of the near unanimous support from Israelis that it had previously enjoyed. The demands of the Intifada certainly reduced the amount of time the forces could devote to training units in handling new weapons technology, designed for the conventional battlefield. Duties such as running detention centres required wholly different skills from those needed for conventional combat.

Contrary to some expectations, examination of the psychological effects on young Israeli soldiers of dealing with Palestinian rioters and a hostile civilian population did not reveal a severe drop in morale. New recruits reported that they treated duty in the occupied territories as one of their professional obligations and tried to keep a sense of detachment to reduce the emotional impact on themselves. They were apparently aided in this by the IDF strategy of identifying a hard core of Palestinian activists who could be singled out from the rest of the population as enemy targets. According to the head of the IDF's Behavioural Studies Department, far from causing soldiers to 'crack' under the stress, the Intifada had measurably increased the motivation-to-serve of some 41 per cent of soldiers in 1988, and of 35 per cent the following year. Those who reported a drop in their motivation stood at 16 per cent in 1988 and 19 per cent in 1989.[20] In order to contain the levels of stress experienced by reservists, in February 1990 the IDF announced that reserve units would serve no more than one tour a year in the occupied territories.[21]

The intelligence net

The fact that the Israelis were taken by surprise by the outbreak of the Intifada indicates a failure in the security apparatus that should have been able to predict it. The grass roots nature of the rebellion and the elusiveness of the underground leadership, which issued instructions for the conduct of the uprising as it went along, apparently made it difficult for the security forces to penetrate to the core of the movement thereafter. In time, however, evidence of the effects of security force activity became more apparent.

Having been taken off-guard, the various Israeli security and intelligence units with responsibility for monitoring the Palestinian community in the occupied territories had to map a whole new strategy and expand their strength and activities. Two years on, police officers from forces inside Israel proper were still being called upon for secondment in the occupied territories and all the relevant organisations were spread thinner than previously. In March 1990 it was announced that the military intelligence corps was to become a full branch of the IDF and the best intelligence officers were being assigned for duty in the occupied territories.[22]

By the second year of the Intifada the security forces were in a better position to identify their targets or 'wanted persons' and single them out for capture or 'elimination'. They would enter villages and town districts along with regular IDF forces on patrol or responding to demonstrations. Alternatively, they acted under cover, disguised as tourists, journalists or other civilians and driving cars with Arab number plates (blue and green in the West Bank and white in the Gaza Strip, as distinct from the yellow plates used inside the Green Line). Meanwhile, as the economic hardship of the Palestinians intensified, more collaborators could be recruited for money and were allowed to carry firearms for their own protection.[23]

Allowing the distribution of firearms to Palestinians, whether collaborators or not, might be considered counterproductive from the Israeli point of view. However, as the number of killings of alleged collaborators by fellow Palestinians grew, this was greeted by some Israelis as an indication that the Intifada was turning in on itself and laying the groundwork for its own destruction. The pursuit of 'wanted persons', meanwhile, also had its drawbacks. Palestinian youths who had previously been 'part time' activists, were driven underground and in some cases formed into new and violent cells.[24] In addition, some Israelis expressed alarm at the fact that after over two years of counter–insurgency, the numbers of hard core activists identified by the security forces still remained in the thousands.

Economic factors

Prior to the outbreak of the Intifada, Israel benefitted from the resources, cheap labour, tax revenues and markets provided by the occupied territories. None of these economic benefits was wholly lost as a result of the Intifada, however, they had to be weighed against some of the new costs accrued.

Deployment of the IDF in the occupied territories increased the budget requirements of the defence ministry at the same time as deflecting existing funds and manpower resources from other IDF functions. According to the Israeli Chief of the General Staff, in 1989 the costs to the armed forces of fighting the Intifada amounted to Shekels 1m (approximately £300,000) per day.[25] Increased requirements for reservists, meanwhile, had consequences for the civilian sector, deprived of reservist labour for an extra 30 days per year. However, by the second year of the Intifada, the IDF was able to reduce its deployment in the occupied territories below the levels required in 1988.

According to a survey produced by one of the main Israeli banks, the overall economic impact of the Intifada on the Israeli economy was less damaging in 1989 than 1988.[26] In its first year, the uprising represented a loss of an estimated 1.5 per cent to Israel's $42 million economy, and less than 1 per cent the following year. The economy had suffered most from low growth, a high budget deficit and as much as 22 per cent unemployment, only indirectly attributable to the Intifada.

Over the first year of the Intifada, Palestinians had repeatedly failed to arrive for work inside Israel proper because of strikes or curfews. Estimates indicated that the Palestinian workforce in Israel was reduced by 30 per cent. By the end of 1989, however, absenteeism had dropped and some of the remaining shortfall had been made up by replacing the cheap labour with machinery or Israeli workers. Ostensibly, the increased costs to industry of this adjustment had been somewhat defrayed by improved quality and productivity. Palestinian boycotts of Israeli products damaged Israeli sales in the occupied territories, and even in the internal Arab Israeli market, but reliance continued on Israeli sources for some commodities and manufactured goods. Returns from tourism were severely damaged in the occupied territories, less so in Israel proper, where Israelis themselves increased their visits to resorts. Loss of tax revenue from the Palestinians was gradually recouped through enforcement of payment and fines.

Legal procedures and Israeli norms

The effect of the Intifada on Israel's reputation as a democratic state with a higher regard for civil rights and legal procedures than any of its Arab neighbours, was pronounced. A distinction had always been made between what the authorities could decree in the occupied territories and practices inside Israel proper. After 1987, however, 'due process' was more often sidestepped and 'emergency measures' were used to override existing legal constraints.

In the case of the IDF, the rules of engagement were changed in keeping with the evolution of its strategy and the evolving character of the uprising. In the early days, soldiers were frequently deterred from firing on civilian demonstrators, armed only with stones, for fear of prosecution. After a year or so, when mass demonstrations were comparatively infrequent and the main IDF target became the masked youths and 'wanted persons', the rules of engagement were changed to allow shooting on the basis of suspicion of a criminal act, provided efforts were made to halt the suspect and a warning shot fired in the air.[27] This change was first introduced in Gaza and thereafter in the West Bank.

Some of the measures used to contain the uprising in its early stages, such as holding detainees for up to a year without trial, closing schools and universities, and demolishing or sealing houses were justified on the basis that they would bring the Intifada to a speedy end. When they failed to do so, the Israelis faced a double dilemma. To desist with these practices would mean relinquishing some of the control that had been gained; to continue with them meant further erosion of the claims of the Israeli authorities to represent the rule of law.

The distinction traditionally drawn between East Jerusalem and other territories occupied by Israel in 1967 was jeopardised by the increased resort to emergency procedures there. According to one commentator:

> The police, for their part, freed themselves from a long list of prohibitions that they had imposed on themselves during the pre-Intifada period, as part of the attempt to present to the world a united Jerusalem, under Israeli sovereignty, where the rules were different. Curfews were imposed, areas were closed off, schools were shut down, rubber bullets and even real ones were fired, and detainees were not handled with kid gloves and sometimes were even treated with brutality.[28]

During the course of the Intifada the nature of the struggle and related incidents changed in East Jerusalem, as elsewhere. In the case of Jerusalem, street demonstrations and stone throwing gave way to anonymous, night time arson attacks on cars and buildings, before erupting again in October 1990.

As the Intifada dragged on and Israeli emergency procedures became a way of life, international interest in the situation ebbed somewhat, to re-emerge only when spectacular new developments hit the headlines, such as the riots in Nazareth and the killings at the Temple Mount.

Despite diminished media coverage, impeded in any case by Israeli restrictions on the free movement of journalists, it became ncreasingly apparent in 1990 that Israel's international reputation had been damaged irrevocably by her efforts to suppress the Intifada. Sympathy for the Palestinians, and respect for their fortitude and determination, had increased meanwhile, notwithstanding the posture adopted by the PLO during the Gulf Crisis.

Most crucial in this regard was the shift in government and public opinion in the US, including within the Jewish community there. As the US government examined its budget priorities in 1990, continuance of aid to Israel at the customary high level came under scrutiny. When Yitzhak Shamir succeeded in forming a narrowly based, hardline government in Israel in June 1990, the US administration demanded that he demonstrate a palpable interest in furthering the cause of peace and entering a dialogue with the Palestinians. The US commitment to the defence of the Arab Gulf states, following the Iraqi invasion of Kuwait, compounded this trend, by making Washington doubly sensitive about its traditional links with Israel, and in October the US joined other members of the UN Security Council in censuring Israel for the shootings at Temple Mount.

While signs of US impatience with Israel became more marked, the members of the European Community increased their efforts to forge more direct links with the Palestinian community in the occupied territories, by-passing the Israeli government. Framing a new European initiative on the Israeli–Palestinian conflict was designated one of the priorities of the EC when Italy assumed the presidency of the Community in July 1990.

In Israel, meanwhile, the members of the various peace movements and left-wing political parties desirous of an accommodation with the Palestinians were despondent at the advent of Shamir's hardline government. Their discomfort was compounded by the findings of public opinion surveys which revealed a decline in popular interest in events inside the occupied territories. At the end of the second year of the uprising, an article in the Israeli daily *Haaretz* reported:

> Many observers, who believed that during the long-lasting intifada the uprising would rouse the Israeli public against its ramifications on the military and the rest of society, were proven wrong.[29]

A survey conducted by the Institute for Policy Planning in Israel–Diaspora Relations revealed that in 1989 only 44 per cent of Israelis disagreed with the statement: 'every slight danger to national security justifies strict limitations on democracy'. In 1987 a majority, 56 per cent, had opposed this view.[30]

Palestinian reactions to the Gulf Crisis, when many of them identified with the Iraqi position, to varying degrees, undermined the position of Israelis who had previously advocated negotiating 'territory-for-peace' with the PLO.

THE STAGE IS SET

By the time Israeli's coalition government collapsed in March 1990, changes in Eastern Europe and the Soviet Union over-shadowed all other events on the international stage. Thereafter, until Iraq's invasion of Kuwait, the focus of attention, both in Israel and increasingly in the Arab world, was the influx of Soviet Jewish emigres to Israel.

Suddenly, on 20 May 1990, the killing of seven Palestinians by one deranged Israeli brought the Intifada back into the forefront with a vengeance and accumulated tensions and anxieties exploded anew. For the Palestinians, the strategy of their 29 month old Intifada had yielded no tangible gains and much suffering. Meanwhile, the prospect of a sizeable increase in Israel's Jewish population indicated that even time and demographic trends were perhaps no longer on their side. An attempt to launch an armed assault on Israel's beaches by the Palestine Liberation Front on 30 May 1990, signalled a return to the type of Israeli–Palestinian conflict characteristic of pre-Intifada days. For the Israelis this, Arab objections to the influx of Soviet Jews, and Palestinian support for Saddam Hussein, indicated that most Arabs were still fundamentally opposed to the existence of Israel and its raison d'etre.

With the formation of Shamir's hardline coalition government, committed to retention of the occupied territories, the stage was thus set, not so much for movement toward a settlement of the Israeli–Palestinian dispute, but for a new round of hostilities in the Arab–Israeli conflict. Even though the Intifada had made Israel's position in the occupied territories more costly to maintain, it had also served to re-emphasise divisions between Jews and Arabs, whether in the occupied territories or in the broader regional context. In some senses it had turned Israel back on itself.

In terms of its economy Israel had been obliged to find a way to rely less on the Palestinian labour force and market and more on its own devices. The strategy devised by the IDF and the security forces for fighting the Intifada had led them to identify and isolate a new Arab enemy, the 'wanted persons' or underground cells, and to pursue these with the operational precision and professional commitment that they had traditionally used to eliminate external enemies. A significant proportion of the Israeli population, if not the majority, wanted the Intifada crushed more than they wanted democratic norms upheld, at least in respect of Israel's dealings with the Palestinians.

Even though the lesson drawn from the Intifada by many Israelis was that a political situation was urgently required, they were not powerful enough to override those who refused to make any move which might signal a withdrawal from territory, let alone the creation of a Palestinian state in the West Bank and Gaza. The Gulf crisis then complicated the situation, raising fears in Israel, not only of a new round of violence between them and the Palestinians, but also of increased pressure from outside to reach an accommodation with the Palestinians, once the situation in the Gulf had been contained, when Israel was becoming even less inclined so to do.

NOTES

[1] Yosef Goell, 'Things will never be the same again', *Jerusalem Post*, International Edition, 16 December 1988, p. 8.
[2] Meron Benvenisti and Shlomo Khayat, *The West Bank and Gaza Atlas*, West Bank Data Base Project, Jerusalem, 1988, pp. 32, 33, 64, 109.
[3] Ibid., p. 61.
[4] Ibid., p. 28.
[5] UNRWA, Map of UNWRA's Area of Operations (Vienna: UNRWA Public Information Division, 1988).
[6] According to the *Financial Times*, 21 August 1989.
[7] Benvenisti and Khayat, *The West Bank and Gaza Atlas*, p. 109.
[8] Ibid.
[9] Ibid.
[10] Simcha Bahiri, *Construction and Housing in the West Bank and Gaza*, West Bank Data Base Project, Jerusalem, 1988, p. 18.
[11] Elie Rekhess, 'Palestinian Issues: West Bank and Gaza Strip', *Middle East Contemporary Survey*, Vol.V (1980-81), p. 337.
[12] See, Zeev Schiff and Ehud Yaari, *Intifada*, Simon & Schuster, New York, 1990.

[13] King Hussein's speech 'To the Arab Nation', *Amman Domestic Service*, 1701 GMT, 31 July 1988, reproduced in translation, FBIS-NES-88-147.

[14] Ibid.

[15] 'A Peace Initiative', *Jerusalem Post*, 15 May 1989, p. 2.

[16] Joel Greenberg, 'The year the Intifada turned on itself', *Jerusalem Post*, 16 December 1989, p. 3.

[17] Ibid.

[18] 'IDF Predictions for Third Intifada Year', *Haaretz*, 28 November 1989, reproduced in translation, JPRS-NEA-90-007, 29 January 1990, p. 29.

[19] 'IDF Estimate Intifada Not Dying Down', *Haaretz*, 7 December 1989, reproduced in translation, JPRS-NEA-90-009, 7 February 1990, p. 34.

[20] Joshua Brilliant, 'One stint per year in territories for reservists', *Jerusalem Post*, International Edition, 24 February 1990, p. 7.

[21] Ibid.

[22] 'Shahor on IDF Intelligence Changes, Intifada', *Bamahane*, 31 January 1990, reproduced in translation, JPRS-NEA-90-014, 7 March 1990, p. 23.

[23] 'Security Measures Allegedly Spawn Violent Cells', *Davar*, 22 December 1989, reproduced in translation, JPRS-NEA-90-011, 21 February 1990, p. 37.

[24] Ibid.

[25] Figure derived from statement made by Brig. Gen. Michael Navon, economic adviser to the Israeli Chief of the General Staff and Director of the Defence Ministry's Budget Department. See Kenneth Kaplan, 'Intifada costs NIS1m. a day', *Jerusalem Post*, 12 July 1989.

[26] 'Bank Hapoalim Estimates Costs of Intifada', *Jerusalem Post*, 13 February 1990, p. 2.

[27] Yizhar Beer, 'Killing under the cover of procedure', *Haaretz*, 2 November 1989, reproduced in translation, JPRS-NEA-90-002, 9 January 1990, p. 17.

[28] Nadav Shraguy, 'Incendiary Statistics', *Haaretz*, 8 October 1989, reproduced in translation, JPRS-NEA-90-002, 9 January 1990, p. 21.

[29] 'Israelis "Indifferent" to Intifada', *Haaretz*, 26 December 1989, reproduced in translation, JPRS-NEA-90-011, 21 February 1990, p. 36.

[30] 'More Israelis Reportedly Indifferent to Democracy', *Yediot Aharonot*, 25 January 1990, reproduced in translation, JPRS-NEA-90-017, 21 March 1990, p. 35.

Cambridge Review
of
International Affairs

The Journal of the Centre of International Studies, Cambridge University.
Published twice annually.

Past Contributors:

Sir Harry Hinsley	The European Communities and the International System
Zara Steiner	Foreign Services and Modern Diplomacy
Javier Perez de Cuellar	The United Nations in a Changing World
Jonathan Eyal	Gorbachev and Eastern Europe
Ian Clark	Britain and the 'Special Relationship'
Hugh Macdonald	The 'Domestication' of International Politics

Forthcoming Contributors:

Professor Georges Soutou (University of Paris); *Dr Tony Kemp-Welch* (Nottingham University); *Professor Paul Wilkinson* (St Andrews University).

For details of advertising rates, institutional subscription rates and for submissions of articles and reviews contact

The Editor
Cambridge Review of International Affairs
History Faculty
West Road
CAMBRIDGE CB3 9EF
England

Cambridge Review of International Affairs, History Faculty, West Road, CAMBRIDGE CB3 9EF, England

Please enter me for a one year ☐ three year ☐ subscription.

NAME

ADDRESS

POST CODE

COUNTRY

Subscription Rates:
UK: individual £6.00 (1 year) / £15.00 (3 years).
Rest of World: individual £9.00 (1 year) / £24.00 (3 years).

The Rise and Fall of Syria's Quest for Strategic Parity

DR EFRAIM KARSH

Dr Karsh is Lecturer in Regional Security at the Department of War Studies, King's College, London.

However focal in the study and practice of international politics, the idea of a 'balance of power' is seldom used in its original meaning, namely, an even distribution of power among the actors in the international system. For the *status quo* powers this concept implies 'the principle that my side ought to have a margin of strength so as to avert the danger of power being unevenly distributed'.[1] Revisionist actors, for their part, seek this 'margin of strength' for the opposite reason: the subversion of an existing international order. Finally, from a hegemonistic point of view, the balance desired 'is the one which neutralises other states, leaving the home state free to be the deciding force and the deciding voice'.[2]

The equation of the balance of power with advantage or superiority is not difficult to understand. Since preponderance provides wider security margins and greater international prestige than equilibrium, why opt for the latter if the former is within reach? Even those who conceive of the balance of power in its original sense are not driven by a principled disdain for predominance, but rather by a recognition of their inability to obtain more than equilibrium at a given moment.

Given this ambiguity about the concept of a balance of power, Syria's mid-1970s decision to reach 'strategic parity' with Israel, to enable the Arabs to press for a 'just peace' from a position of strength, was bound to create speculation about the essence of Syria's strategic goals and the operational means for their attainment. What is President Hafiz al-Asad's interpretation of a 'just peace'? Would he be amenable to a separate Syrian-Israeli peace agreement on the basis of the pre-1967 borders, or would he be adamant on the complete 'elimination of the predatory Zionist presence in Palestine', namely, the dismantling of the State of Israel? Similarly, does 'strategic parity' mean 'defence sufficiency' that would enable Syria to contain an Israeli attack on her own, or does it imply the ability to launch war against Israel independently? Or, perhaps, the alleged quest for strategic parity is merely a political ploy aimed at rallying public support behind the régime, rather than at matching (or surpassing) Israel's power?

By way of addressing these questions, I will discuss the origins of Syria's quest for strategic parity and its actual implementation; analyse the Syrian perception of 'just peace' and the consequent operational requirements; examine the attitude and practice of the Soviet Union, Syria's staunchest international supporter, towards this objective, and assess the reasons for the demise of Asad's ambitious grand-design.

THE EVOLUTION OF THE QUEST FOR STRATEGIC PARITY

Syria's concept of 'strategic parity' originated in the deep anxiety attending the conclusion of the second Egyptian-Israeli disengagement agreement in September 1975. Until then, and despite vehement declarations of readiness to confront 'the Zionist enemy' at all costs, Damascus's awareness of its military inferiority to Israel had driven it to anchor Syrian grand strategy to that of the largest Arab state. The formation of the Cairo-Damascus axis in 1973 accounted for the Arabs' most successful military initiative to date, the October 1973 War, and was therefore perceived by Asad as a prerequisite for the further advancement of the Arab cause.

The disengagement agreement, which in effect opened the door for a separate Egyptian-Israeli peace treaty in the future, was therefore bound to alarm the Syrians. Although Asad clearly gained a higher status in the Arab world as a result of Egypt's growing isolation, he perceived Sadat's move both as a betrayal of the Arab cause and as a personal offence by a comrade-in-arms. In Asad's view, the removal of Egypt from the Arab-Israeli conflict upset the regional balance of power in favour of Israel and left Syria alone, as 'an orphan', in the frontline of the Arab struggle.[3] Wary of King Hussein, distrustful of the Iraqi leadership, and concerned over the domestic deterioration in Lebanon, Asad gradually came to the conclusion that, by way of restoring the strategic balance, Syria had to rely primarily, though not exclusively, on its intrinsic resources. This meant both an uncompromising political posture on the issue of a partial settlement and a major drive to enhance Syria's military potential to enable it to lead the Arab campaign and, if necessary, to fight Israel on its own.[4]

Notwithstanding Asad's grim realisation of the changing strategic landscape in the Middle East, he did not lose hope of reconstructing the strategic alliance with Egypt. On 18-21 December 1976 he paid an official visit to Cairo, where the two leaders decided to establish a unified political command as a preliminary step on the road to Syrian-Egyptian unification. The harbinger of the renewed bilateral co-operation was the joint call for the reconvening of the Geneva Peace Conference by March 1977, with the full participation of all parties, including the PLO.

As things turned out, the revived Egyptian-Syrian alliance did not advance very far. Asad's categorical insistence on a joint Arab delegation to Geneva was totally unacceptable to Sadat who resented the idea of constraining Egyptian diplomacy; this dispute injected a strong element of mutual distrust into Syrian-Egyptian relations, poisoning them from the outset. The brief rapprochement between Cairo and Damascus was brought to an abrupt end in November 1977 following Sadat's historic visit to Jerusalem. For Syria, the visit was traumatic. Not only did Sadat violate the most sacred political and ideological Arab taboo, but his move also undermined Syria's ability to advance her own national goals. Differences, distrust and hostility apart, Asad never forgot that it had been the alliance with Egypt that had made Syria's greatest achievement—the October War—possible. Now that Sadat had broken the 'rules of the game', Asad was forced again to the conclusion (which he had already reached two years earlier but to which he remained reluctant to give effect) that the strategic balance between the Arabs and Israel had been seriously upset and that Syria *alone* would have to shoulder the burden of confronting Israel. In the words of the Syrian minister of information, Ahmad Iskandar Ahmad:

> The balance of power has been tipped in favour of the Zionist enemy following Sadat's step and his attempt to isolate Egypt from our Arab nation and wipe out Egypt's Arab and national aspirations. Syria is seeking to build a defence capability that would achieve a strategic military balance between itself and the Zionist enemy. Syria considers that, even if Syria's national voice remains alone as the voice struggling against the enemy, it will remain steadfast and will cling to the rights which, naturally, are Arab rights.[5]

Yet it required two more years and the conclusion of a separate Egyptian-Israeli peace treaty before Damascus's drive for strategic parity gained full momentum: in August 1979 Syria took the first delivery of T-72s (comprising some 80 tanks). Two months later Asad went to Moscow to sign Syria's largest arms deal ever, thus setting in train an accelerated process of military expansion, unprecedented in scope and intensity even when compared to the post-1973 rehabilitation programme.

In qualitative terms, the Syrians received a wide variety of items from the latest generation of Soviet weaponry, including T-72 tanks, 122mm and 152mm self-propelled guns, MiG-25 aircraft, Mi-24 assault helicopters, and SA-8 surface-to-air missiles. Quantitatively speaking, and by the completion of the implementation of this large arms deal in mid-1982, the Syrian ground forces had absorbed some 1,400 tanks (including 800 T-72s), nearly 2,000 armoured vehicles, and approximately 1,700 artillery pieces. This equipment enabled the substantial reorganisation and modernisation of the Syrian ground forces, most notably by the establishment of two additional armoured divisions.[6] Syria also received some 200 combat aircraft, including 25 MiG-25s, 30 SU-20/22, and an unknown number of improved MiG-23 interceptors which the Syrians had not previously utilised. The Syrian air defence system was similarly augmented, doubling in strength from 50 to nearly 100 surface-to-air missile batteries. The Syrian navy was also reinforced through the addition of four OSA-2 missile boats.

The 1982 Lebanon War constituted another milestone in Syria's military expansion. Not only were Damascus's war losses fully replaced but its military potential was significantly enhanced and upgraded. Between the end of the Lebanon War in June 1982 and the beginning of 1984, Syria's aerial and air defence forces were strengthened by the arrival of around 140 fighting aircraft, and approximately 70 surface-to-air missile batteries (mainly SA-6s and SA-8s). The Syrian Army received some 600 tanks, a few hundred armoured vehicles, and about 1,000 artillery pieces.[7] These large quantities of arms enabled Syria to expand the order-of-battle of its army from six to eight divisions and the overall size of the regular Armed Forces from 310,000 to 450,000-500,000 troops.

Syria's strategic posture was decisively buttressed during 1983 by the arrival of two SA-5 surface-to-air missile brigades and an unspecified number of SS-21 surface-to-surface missiles.[8] Apart from the prestige attending their arrival, the SS-21s, with a range of 120 km and far greater accuracy than anything in the Syrian arsenal, improved Syria's ability to hit military and economic targets in northern Israel, thereby partly counterbalancing Israel's long-range bombing capacity. In addition, the extended range of the SA-5 (250-300 km) improved the Syrian air defence capability, in particular against high-flying reconnaissance, intelligence and electronic-warfare aircraft. Finally, the Soviets supplied Damascus with SSC-1 long-range anti-ship missiles which significantly improved Syria's coastal defence capabilities.[9]

With the expansion of the Syrian armed forces completed in early 1984, Soviet arms transfers to Syria dropped sharply. From 1984 to date, the amount of major weapons systems at the disposal of the Syrian armed forces has remained essentially unchanged, though their quality has been enhanced following the absorption of new weapons systems (such as MiG-29 and SU-24 aircraft, submarines, and SA-13 surface-to-air missiles). As will be shown shortly, this dramatic slowdown in arms supplies to Syria has been essentially motivated by Mikhail Gorbachev's (and Chernenko's) anxiety to curb Asad's tireless quest for strategic parity; however, it has also reflected Damascus's diminishing capacity for military expansion as a result of severe manpower and economic constraints.

First, since the mid-1980s Syria has faced a most unfortunate combination of steep economic decline, higher weaponry prices, and reduced ability, and willingness, of the Arab oil states to subsidise Syria's military acquisitions following both the oil glut and Syrian support for Iran in its war with Iraq. Second, by the mid-1980s Syria's regular army had developed into a nearly 500,000 strong force, larger by 11 per cent than the Egyptian armed forces, although Syria's population (c. 11.5m) is merely one fifth of that of Egypt (c. 54m). Since the Syrian regular forces—over one-quarter of whom are delayed-release conscripts and reservists—account for nearly 20 per cent of the labour force, the heavy burden imposed by the military build-up on the Syrian economy becomes more than evident.[10] Finally, despite the large size of the Syrian armed forces, they have been unable to master the tremendous amount of weaponry at their disposal. For example, according to several assessments, only 2,800 tanks out of the 4,000 in the Syrian arsenal are fully operational; the rest are employed as static anti-tank weapons or stored in large stockpiles.[11] It is against this backdrop that Asad has been forced to recognise that the legs of the Syrian economy are too weak to carry too large an army. Accordingly, from late 1986 onwards, a process of cutbacks in the Syrian ground forces has been implemented, with regular units being dismantled and transferred to reserve status and their weaponry put in storage.

While military build-up has undoubtedly constituted the most important single factor in Damascus's quest for strategic parity, the Syrian perception of this concept extends beyond the purely military sphere to comprise other elements of national power such as social cohesion, economic resilience and international backing. A major role in this comprehensive effort has been, naturally, assigned to the Soviet Union, Damascus's staunchest international ally. Thus, from late 1978 onwards it became increasingly evident that Asad had made up his mind to tie the USSR to Syria through a defence treaty: on 7 September of that year, following reports that the US intended to sign a defence pact with Israel to allay the latter's apprehensions over her national security and thus strengthen her willingness to make territorial concessions, the-then Syrian foreign minister, Abd al-Khalim Khaddam, called upon the Arab states to respond in kind by entering into defence agreements with the USSR.[12] A month later, during a summit meeting in Baghdad of the Front's foreign ministers, Khaddam reportedly threatened that Syria would join the Warsaw Pact should it fail to receive the necessary support from its Arab allies.[13] Similar reports on Syria's interest in a defence pact with the USSR that would provide, *inter alia*, for the dispatch of Soviet ground forces to Syria in case of dire emergencies, were carried by the Arab and foreign press throughout 1980.[14]

To Asad's deep dismay, Syria's growing eagerness to sign a bilateral treaty was not matched by Soviet enthusiasm for such an agreement. However important, a bilateral treaty with Syria had never been perceived by the Soviets as a top priority foreign policy goal. Until October 1973, while the Soviet Union was preoccupied with the prevention of a new Arab-Israeli conflagration, Syria was not viewed as important enough to justify a large Soviet campaign to push it into a bilateral treaty. Conversely, given Syria's ascendancy in Soviet Middle Eastern interests in the aftermath of the October War, the Soviet Union was careful not to antagonise its major regional ally by pushing the issue of a treaty (to which Asad was then opposed) too hard.

The significant weakening of Asad's domestic and regional position in the late 1970s further restrained the Soviet drive towards a bilateral treaty. A treaty with a confident and strong Syria playing a leading role in the Arab world was one thing, but an accord with an isolated leader who faced an imminent threat of dethronement was quite another. Furthermore, familiar with Asad's propensity for independent conduct, the Soviets apparently feared that a precipitous reaction on his part to the threats facing the regime might drag them into an undesirable predicament. Therefore, not only was a defence pact inconceivable from Moscow's point of view, but, from 1979 onwards, the Soviets surrendered the initiative in the quest for a treaty to Syria and adopted an essentially reactive position on the issue.[15]

The outcome was the Friendship and Co-operation Treaty of 8 October 1980 which constituted the lower common denominator between Damascus's ambitious desire and Moscow's restrictive wishes. Reluctant as it was to sign a treaty at that particular time, the Soviet Union could not afford to turn down its major Middle Eastern ally. Syria, for its part, unable to harness an unequivocal Soviet commitment to its national security, in the form of a defence pact, had to content itself with a 'standard' Third World Friendship and Co-operation Treaty. Consequently, it was not long before this uneasy compromise was to lead to conflicting interpretations of Soviet military and strategic obligations towards Syria. Whereas the Syrians depicted the treaty as embodying a far-reaching Soviet undertaking to redress the strategic imbalance caused by Egypt's desertion of the Arab camp, by ensuring that 'any aggression to which Syria will be exposed will not be faced by Syria separately',[16] the Soviets sought to play down the extent of their commitment by highlighting the international, rather than the bilateral, ramifications of the treaty.[17] Whilst Syria viewed the provision for consultations and co-operation as a means to harness Soviet support for its foreign policy ventures, the Soviet Union regarded this stipulation as a useful mechanism for tension reduction and crisis management.

STRATEGIC PARITY: WHAT FOR?

We have seen that the Syrians conceive strategic parity as the ability to fight Israel on their own following Egypt's 'betrayal' of the Arab cause. But what is the political purpose of such a war and what would its resultant military requirements be? In the Syrian view, the Arab-Israeli conflict is a mortal struggle over 'existence' and 'destiny', a zero-sum game that must eventually be settled in favour of one of the two sides: 'Either we Arabs exist in this part of this world ... or the Zionist enemy exists at the expense of Arab territories, Arab nation, and Arab rights'.[18] This is because Israel is 'an imperialist-linked colonial-settler state implanted in the heart of historic Syria at the expense of Syria's southern Palestinian cousins'[19] with the aim of subjecting the entire Middle East to their domination. As Asad put it:

> The ambitions of racist Zionism are as clear as the sun ... They do not want Palestine alone or a piece of land here or there. They do not want only another Arab country. They want the land from the Nile to the Euphrates ... They want the Israeli state from the Nile to the Euphrates to impose their hegemony beyond that until it covers the entire world.[20]

Accordingly, 'the Arab-Israeli conflict did not start in 1967. It originated in 1917, with the Balfour declaration, when international Zionism, in league with international imperialism, started moving into Palestine and displacing its people to establish the Israeli state'.[21] Hence, and since the 1967 war is merely 'a consequence of the Zionist presence in Palestine', the recovery of the territories lost in that war would not resolve the Arab-Israeli conflict because 'before 1967 no Egyptian and Syrian territory was occupied but the dispute was there'.[22] In these circumstances, Syria has no other alternative but to

> work to prevent the Palestinian issue from being transformed into *mere elimination of the traces of the* 1967 *aggression.* This must be done by rejecting peace and recognition of the Zionist entity and by not relinquishing the Arab lands under any circumstances ... [There is also] a need to work to promote the Palestinian personality and to *support the right of the Palestinian people to establish a national independent authority on liberated Palestinian land, and to continue the struggle to liberate all Palestinian soil.*[23]

As for the inter-relationship between the prospective Palestinian state and Syria, Asad has made it clear that 'Palestine is not only a part of the Arab homeland but a basic part of southern Syria. We also believe that it is our right and duty, and we cannot concede right or abandon our duty, to be determined that Palestine should remain a liberated part of our Arab homeland and of our Syrian Arab region'.[24]

The Syrians concede that the elimination of Zionist presence in Palestine may not be within their immediate reach. However, given Asad's perception of the conflict as involving 'nothing less than the Arabs' national existence',[25] he believes that the Arabs should adopt a long-range historical perspective; they should exert the utmost effort to redress the strategic imbalance with Israel, while bearing in mind that this process may be a very prolonged and tiresome one. In his own words:

> I regret to say that some of us, as Arab citizens, are seeking the shortest, easiest and least difficult roads, which at the same time are the most prone to failure . . . we view the matter from the perspective of the future of the nation and not that of the next few hours, months or years in which we shall live . . . If we, as a generation, fail to do and to achieve what must be done, there will be future generations which will deal with this issue in the proper manner . . . What I am saying here is not new. I am just reviewing some facts in our history. Let us go back to the Crusaders' invasion. Although they fought us for 200 years, we did not surrender or capitulate. They, too, were a big power and had scored victories, while we had been defeated. After 200 years, however, we triumphed. Why are we now expected either to score a decisive victory in approximately 30 years or completely surrender?[26]

In short, however long it may take, the ultimate Arab triumph over Israel is a foregone conclusion:

> The facts of history, the given facts of reality, and the elementary truth of right and logic confirm that . . . the Zionist invasion is bound to be defeated and its imperialist colonisation plan shall fail. Palestine is bound to be returned to its people as a purely Arab state.[27]

The quest for strategic parity, then, seeks neither to enable Syria to ward off an Israeli attack (which, in the Syrian view, is bound to come sooner or later), nor to win back the Golan Heights or even all the territories lost in 1967. Rather it aims at returning Palestine 'to its people as a purely Arab state'. In military terms it means the ability to inflict a mortal blow at Israel, either through a protracted war of attrition or a dynamic war of movement and manoeuvre.

Apart from this perception of the conflict which makes anything short of military superiority worthless for the attainment of Syria's ultimate goal, the equation of 'parity' with superiority in the Syrian mind can also be inferred from the fact that since the mid-1970s Damascus has had the ability to fight a defensive war on its own. For example, between February and May 1974 Syria conducted a fully-fledged war of attrition against Israel along the Golan Heights in which there was neither victor nor vanquished. Similarly, during the 1982 Lebanon War, despite a limited defeat

TABLE 1—EXPANSION OF THE SYRIAN AND ISRAELI ARMED FORCES
1975–1990

		1975	1979	1982	1984	1986	1990
Tanks	Sy.	2,200	2,600	4,000	4,100	4,200	4,050
	Is.	2,700	3,050	3,600	3,650	3,660	3,790
Armoured Vehicles	Sy.	1,200	1,600	3,500	3,500	3,600	3,850
	Is.	3,300	4,000	4,400	6,400	6,400	6,400
Artillery Pieces	Sy.	800	900	2,600	3,500	3,800	2,500
	Is.	660	660	670	1,000	1,150	1,400
SAM Batteries	Sy.	40	50	100	150	150	150
	Is.	15	15	15	45	45	45
Combat Aircraft	Sy.	350	400	600	650	650	650
	Is.	461	576	634	640	629	574
Attack Helicopters	Sy.	n.a.	n.a.	62	80	100	130
	Is.	n.a.	n.a.	n.a.	55	58	77
Missile Boats	Sy.	9	14	18	22	24	22
	Is.	18	19	27	23	23	26
Submarines	Sy.	—	—	—	—	—	3
	Is.	2	2	3	3	3	3
Manpower & Formations							
Manpower,	Sy.	178	247	310	450–500	450–500	500
Total (000')	Is.	375*	400	500	440	440	440
Armoured Divisions	Sy.	2	2	4	5	5	5
	Is.	3	8	11	11	11	12
Mechanised Divisions	Sy.	3	3	2	3	3	3
	Is.	3	3	3	n.a.	9	5
Special Operations/	Sy.	n.a.	—	—	—	1	1
Airborne Divisions	Is.	n.a.	—	—	—	—	1
Independent Brigades	Sy.	6	9	10	17	10	7
	Is.	14	14			10	16

*Figures refer to Israeli strength on full mobilisation. The size of the regular/conscript is approximately one third of the total strength.
*Source: IISS.

on the ground and the public humiliation following its un-
matched losses in the aerial and air defence fields, Syria managed
to frustrate the Israeli campaign, and, moreover, to attain this
objective alone, without proper air cover and in the face of
Israel's overwhelming superiority on the ground. Above all, as
shown in Table 1, Syria enjoys a quantitative advantage over
Israel in most major weapons systems including artillery and
surface-to-air missiles (since the early 1970s), as well as tanks,
fighter aircraft and attack helicopters (since the early 1980s). This
material superiority may not suffice for the initiation of a
full-scale war; it is, nevertheless, more than enough for the
conduct of a defensive campaign.

The Syrians are fully aware that they have not reached the
ability to move to the offensive against Israel on their own; and
they have few qualms over pointing to the party which, in their
view, bears the main responsibility for this state of affairs: the
Soviet Union.

STRATEGIC PARITY: THE VIEW FROM MOSCOW

Syria's decision to opt for strategic parity was received by the Soviets with mixed feelings. On the one hand, Moscow's unequivocal acceptance of Israel's right to exist and its overriding interest in regional stability precluded approval of the ambitious Syrian programme which, if successful, could undermine these two foundations of Soviet Middle Eastern policy. On the other hand, the development of Syria into the Soviet Union's most prominent regional ally following the Egyptian drift from Soviet orbit seriously constrained Moscow's ability to ignore Damascus's requests for military support. Hence, the Soviets chose the middle way: they praised the 'principled' Syrian struggle against Egypt's 'capitulationist course', voiced in private their understanding of Syria's intention to restore the strategic balance upset by Sadat's Jerusalem visit, and agreed to conclude a $500 million arms deal in February 1978. Yet, they would not support Syria in moving beyond the level of 'defence sufficiency' to the ability to overwhelm Israel militarily; whenever Syria appeared to near the offensive option, the Soviets quickly reduced their arms supplies.

At the same time, the Soviets went to great lengths to point out to Damascus the advantages of a negotiated settlement, indicating unequivocal reluctance to commit themselves to Syria's defence in the case of another conflagration. Thus, just as Asad's October 1979 visit to the Soviet Union led to the conclusion of the largest arms deal until then, so it also marked a watershed in Soviet and Syrian approaches towards the issue of a bilateral treaty. If until that visit it had been the Soviet Union that had been interested in a bilateral treaty, from that time onwards it was Syria that worked to bring it about. Hence, it is very likely that Brezhnev's evasion of Asad in October 1979, explained by the Soviets on grounds of poor health, emanated from his reluctance to give a flat refusal to Syrian requests for a bilateral treaty.

The events preceding the 1979 agreement demonstrate Moscow's wariness of Syria's quest for strategic parity and this gave rise to an open clash between the two parties. In November 1978, following a Soviet pledge of military support given to Asad a month earlier, the Syrian chief of staff, Hikmat Shihabi arrived in Moscow to work out the details of a new large-scale arms deal, only to be confronted by an unexpected refusal to supply Syria with the promised sophisticated weapons systems (i.e., T-72 tanks, MiG-25 aircraft). While it has been argued that the Soviet cold shoulder to Shihabi was merely a tactical ploy aimed at pressuring Syria into a bilateral treaty, this move appears to have reflected Moscow's apprehensions of the escalatory potential of the sudden reconciliation between the embattled Syrian and Iraqi regimes that took place at the time.[28] Enabling Syria to withstand the Israeli threat on its own was one thing, but the Soviets were reluctant to provide the same sophisticated weapons systems to a more powerful Syrian-Iraqi union which might launch a military campaign or provoke Israel to risk a pre-emptive strike.

Syria responded vehemently to the Soviet change of heart. 'Maybe the Soviet Union now believes that it can achieve a strategic balance for Syria without providing the necessary weapons', commented Ahmad Iskandar Ahmad, but 'we believe otherwise . . . we are the only frontline state left and they [Israel] are choked with arms; so our demand for a strategic balance is a fair one'.[29] Therefore, he argued, the only criterion for befriending Syria could be the extent of support for its attempts to re-establish the regional strategic balance.[30] Syria's criticism was paralleled by concrete moves, aimed at demonstrating its irritation with Soviet behaviour: on 28 November 1978 the Syrian ambassador to Moscow, Jabr Kafri, was summoned to Damascus 'for consultations'; and in December Asad reportedly called off a visit to Moscow which he was due to make together with Iraq's vice president, Saddam Hussein.[31]

Damascus's rage had little effect on Moscow, and it was only in the summer of 1979, six months after the signing of the Egyptian-Israeli peace treaty, that the Soviets agreed to elevate Syria's military potential to a higher qualitative and quantitative level. This decision, nevertheless, did not reflect Moscow's acceptance of the Syrian interpretation of strategic parity; rather, it resulted from a series of successive events which weakened Syria's regional and domestic position, namely, the collapse of the Syrian-Iraqi *rapprochement* and the unprecedented rise in violent domestic opposition to the Asad regime. With the need to consolidate the rejectionist camp stronger than ever, following the conclusion of the Egyptian-Israeli peace treaty, and the likelihood of a Syrian-Israeli conflagration significantly reduced, due to Syria's much weakened position, the Soviets no longer saw any reason to starve Damascus of arms. Hence, the major breakthrough in Soviet-Syrian procurement relations in 1979. Similarly, the abundant Soviet support for Damascus during and following the 1982 Lebanon War did not imply acceptance of

Asad's view regarding the desirable extent of Syria's military expansion. Rather, Moscow had several important reasons to support a substantial build-up of Syrian armed forces. First, the chill between Moscow and Baghdad at the time, and the deterioration in Soviet-Iranian relations, highlighted Syria's prominence for Soviet standing in the Middle East, and made the recovery of the Syrian armed forces from their (however limited) debâcle a vital Soviet objective. This goal became especially urgent given the likelihood of resumed Syrian-Israeli hostilities and the strong position of Israeli forces in Lebanon, deployed merely 4km from the Syrian-Lebanese border and less than 30km from Damascus. Second, by destroying 20 surface-to-air missile batteries and by shooting down 90 of Syria's front-line interceptor aircraft without suffering a single casualty, the Israeli Air Force had exposed the weakness of a Soviet-type air defence system, dealing yet another painful blow to the reputation of Soviet weaponry. Given the Soviet Union's own reliance on much the same system for the defence of its own airspace, a prompt response to the challenge posed by Israel became not only a matter of recovering lost prestige but also a pressing operational need.[32] Finally, the Soviets could hardly afford to remain indifferent to the growing American activity in both the Lebanese and Middle East arenas which threatened to push the Soviet Union to the sidelines of regional politics yet again.

Against this backdrop, it is hardly surprising that the Soviets would curtail their military support for Syria once their circumstantial dependence on this important regional ally decreased. Thus, when Vice President Rif'at Asad arrived in Moscow in May 1984 to discuss a new arms agreement following the implementation of the huge deals signed with Brezhnev and Andropov in the summer and autumn of 1982, he was bluntly told by Konstantin Chernenko that there was no need for expanded Soviet support since 'the Arabs possess all necessary means for foiling the schemes of US imperialism and its Israeli partners'.[33] A visit of Asad in person to Moscow four months later, the first of its kind since the historic October 1980 one, during which the Friendship and Co-operation Treaty had been signed, was equally disappointing from the Syrian point of view. Not only did he fail to mobilise Soviet support for Syria's quest for strategic parity but the Soviets declined his request for a moratorium on Syria's military debt[34] and, moreover, took the exceptional step of linking their support for Syria with Damascus's willingness to assist 'other Arab nations in every way in their work for a just and

lasting peace in the Middle East'.[35] This linkage was galling for
Syria for two reasons. First, because it indicated the Soviets'
determination to go ahead with a new arms deal with Jordan,
whose relations with Syria were very poor at the time,[36] and
second, because it implied an erosion in Syria's position as
Moscow's most prominent ally. Indeed, during the visit Asad was
apparently informed by Chernenko of the latter's intention to
withdraw Soviet air defence units from Syria and transfer control
of the SA-5 missiles to the Syrians. While this decision may be
considered a Syrian achievement—the equipping of the Syrian
armed forces with important weapons systems not previously
under their direct control—it certainly reflected Moscow's de-
creasing readiness to take risks on Syria's behalf.[37]

But the most formidable Soviet pressures on Syria to desist from
its persistent drive toward strategic parity have undoubtedly been
applied during the Gorbachev era. During Mikhail Gorbachev's
first meeting with Asad in June 1985 the newly-established Soviet
leader declined a Syrian request for a new generation of
weaponry, the MiG-29 fighter aircraft in particular, lecturing
Asad instead on the futility of Syria's quest for 'strategic parity'
with Israel. A second visit by the Syrian president to Moscow in
April 1987 turned out to be no less disturbing. To be sure, in
contrast with the 1985 visit, the second meeting between Asad
and Gorbachev bore concrete and positive fruit: it produced a
series of bilateral agreements on technical and economic co-operation, as well as a reported Soviet agreement to reschedule Syria's
$15 bn debt and to conclude a new arms deal, which apparently
included the contested MiG-29 aircraft.[38] However, Gorbachev
did not fail to indicate to Asad the tight strings attached to
Moscow's support for Syria by emphasising that 'the reliance on
military force in settling the Arab-Israeli conflict has completely
lost its credibility'.[39] While this statement was partially directed
towards Israel, and even though the belief itself had been
preached by the Soviets to their Arab allies from the early 1970s
onwards, the futility of reliance on military force was stressed by
Gorbachev 'with more conviction and vigour than ever before'.[40]
This view was supported by a joint communiqué on the importance of the 'convocation of a fully-fledged international conference with full powers under the aegis of the UN', and by
Gorbachev's reference to the abnormality of the absence of
Soviet-Israeli diplomatic relations.[41]

Asad's visit was followed by outspoken Soviet criticism of the
Syrian concept of 'strategic parity'. 'In our view', argued

Izvestiya's Middle Eastern commentator, Konstantin Geyvendov, in an interview with the Kuwaiti newspaper *al-Anba* on 12 September 1987, 'the talk about strategic parity aims at diverting attention from the question of achieving security and peace in the Middle East ... [It just] does not have any meaning'. And Vladimir Vinogradov, a former Soviet ambassador to Egypt, Iran, and the Geneva conference, had an equally dismissive view of the Syrian quest for strategic parity:

> I would like our Arab friends to get rid of a false psychological feeling that Israel is besieging them. In fact, the opposite is true ... I have always thought that the balance was, and still is, in favour of the Arabs. A quick look at the balance of power affirms this fact insofar as the size of population, the quantity and quality of arms, and the extent of the area concerned.[42]

This outspoken criticism has been accompanied by concrete manifestations of Soviet indignation with Damascus's rejectionist stance. In a visit to Damascus in July 1988, the Soviet deputy foreign minister, Yuliy Vorontsov, urged the Syrians to resume the dialogue with the PLO and emphasised Moscow's determination to 'actively contribute to the search for a just settlement of the Arab-Israeli conflict based on a balance of interests among all sides'.[43] A strongly-worded message from Gorbachev to Asad three months later reiterated the USSR's unequivocal rejection of the military option and called upon the Syrian leader to display greater openness towards a possible territorial compromise over the Golan Heights.[44] This message was augmented by a slowdown in Soviet arms transfers to Syria and a significant reduction in the number of Soviet advisors in the Syrian armed forces.[45]

A visit to Moscow in November 1988 by the Syrian Minister of Defence, Mustafa Tlas, did not deflect Soviet pressure. Not only did Tlas fail to secure the smooth flow of Soviet arms to Syria, but he was lectured about the grave risks attending Syria's quest for strategic parity. Any expansion of Syria's military potential at this stage, the Soviets told Tlas, would only be counterproductive; it would further constrain Syria's dire economic position, provoke Israel into a pre-emptive attack, and frustrate the evolving political process in the Middle East. And in any event, argued the Soviets, there was no need for Syrian concern, given its Friendship and Co-operation Treaty with the Soviet Union. Accordingly, instead of focusing on the consolidation of its military might, Damascus had better improve its relations with the moderate Arabs and collaborate with them in the pursuit of a political settlement.[46] The same position was presented to the Syrians, though probably in a milder form during visits to Damascus by Foreign Minister Shevardnadze and Defence Minister Yazov in February and March 1989 respectively.[47]

CONCLUSIONS AND OUTLOOK

Asad's remarkable tactical pragmatism notwithstanding, his fundamental position on the Arab-Israeli conflict has remained essentially unchanged during his term in office. Thus, not only has Asad failed to reconcile himself to Israel's existence but his adaption to the changing international arena has been extremely slow and tortuous: he has not concealed his irritation with Gorbachev's 'new thinking' on the Middle East, has harshly criticised the PLO's 'capitulationist' recognition of Israel in late 1988, and has refrained from recognising the self-declared Palestinian state. 'We do not ignore or belittle the importance of world public opinion', Asad responded to the PLO's move, 'but we will not allow ourselves to concede our rights for the sake of winning its support'. 'What is the use of asking others to support our legitimate rights', he reasoned, 'if we ourselves concede these rights'?[48]

Yet there has been precious little Asad has been able to do to check the new political dynamics in the Middle East. At the turn of 1990s Damascus found itself weaker and more isolated than on any other occasion during the last two decades. After all, Syria's rise to prominence during the Asad years owed no less to the regional vicissitudes (e.g., Egypt's reassessment of its leading role, Iraq's preoccupation with the Gulf War) than to Asad's political acumen; once this favourable conjuncture disappeared, Syria has had to reoccupy its 'real' place in the Arab world. With Saddam Hussein bent on avenging Syria for its anti-Iraqi policy during the eight-year Gulf War; the PLO well outside Syria's control; the situation in Lebanon chaotic; Egypt back in the centre of inter-Arab politics;[49] and Soviet pressure steadily intensifying, Asad has been forced to bow to reality.

The outcome has been the actual, albeit publicly unacknowledged demise of the quest for strategic parity. As shown earlier, Asad's recognition of Syria's economic plight drove him, as early as 1986, to reduce the size of the Syrian armed forces. Three years later, in a major break with a decade of vociferous condemnation of the Egyptian 'betrayal', Asad (unconditionally) re-established diplomatic relations with Egypt thereby implicitly admitting Syria's inability to impose its solution regarding Israel alone. Moreover, in the early months of 1990 Damascus signalled to Jerusalem (via the American channel) its readiness to reach an agreement on mutual reductions of their chemical arsenals and, moreover, to enter into negotiations over the future of the Golan Heights. These signals were coupled by reports on an (unofficial) meeting in Switzerland between Syrian and Israeli representatives.[50]

It remains to be seen whether these developments are merely a tactical ploy to prevent Syria's isolation in a future negotiating process (or alternatively, to reconstruct the Cairo-Damascus axis for a new military initiative against Israel), or whether they reflect a fundamental reversal in Asad's perception of the Arab-Israeli conflict in the direction of acceptance of Israel's legitimacy. Either way, they imply the total bankruptcy of Syria's quest for 'strategic parity' by demonstrating Damascus's implicit acknowledgement of its inability 'to return Palestine to its people as a purely Arab state' on its own, and her keen recognition that, if at all, such development would only be possible through a concerted Arab effort.

NOTES

[1] M. Wight, *Power Politics*, Penguin, London, 1979, p. 175.
[2] N.J. Spykman, *America's Strategy in World Politics*, Harcourt, New York, 1942, pp. 21-2.
[3] E.R.F. Sheehan, *The Arabs, Israelis, and Kissinger*, Reader's Digest Press, New York, 1976, p. 196; 'Ba'th Party Statement on the Disengagement Agreement', *Damascus Domestic Service*, 3 September 1975.
[4] See, for example, Asad's interviews with *Time*, 1 December 1975 and *Newsweek*, 14 September 1975. See also, *Financial Times*, 13 October 1975.
[5] Interview with *al-Rai al-Amm* (Kuwait), 14 February 1978. For further references to the need to achieve strategic parity with Israel see, Abd al-Khalim Khaddam's declarations, as brought by *Damascus Domestic Service*, 17 September 1977, 13, 24, 27 January 1978; Khaddam's interview with *al-Rai al-Amm* and *Events*, 8, 10 February 1978 respectively.
[6] The overall order of battle of the Syrian ground forces, though, grew by only one division, since one of the two additional armoured divisions was previously a mechanised one. Thus, by mid-1982, the Syrian army comprised four armoured and two mechanised divisions, as compared with two and three respectively in 1979.

[7] Figures include war replacements.

[8] Arriving in January and October 1983 respectively, the SA-5s and SS-21s were initially operated by independent Soviet units. By mid-1985, having completed the transfer of these weapon systems to the Syrians, the Soviet units, totalling some 2,000 troops, left Syria. See, *International Herald Tribune*, 5 January, 9, 23 February, 10 October 1983; *Foreign Report* (London), 17 November 1983; *The Daily Telegraph*, 9 May 1985; *Jane's Defence Weekly*, 11, 25 May 1985.

[9] P. Seale, *Asad of Syria: The Struggle for the Middle East*, (I.B. Tauris, London, 1988), p. 399.

[10] *The Middle East Military Balance*, 1986 (Tel Aviv), p. 177.

[11] *The Military Balance*, 1986-1987 IISS, London, 1987, p. 109.

[12] *Financial Times*, 8 September 1978.

[13] *Al-Mustaqbal* (Paris), 16 December 1978.

[14] See, for example, *al-Bayraq*, 21 July 1980; *al-Hawadith* (Beirut), 3 October 1980; *Ha'aretz* (Tel Aviv), 18 November 1980.

[15] The last Soviet attempt to persuade Syria to sign a bilateral treaty was made during Asad's visit to Moscow in October 1978.

[16] Ahmad's interview with *Monday Morning* (Beirut), as brought by *Damascus Domestic Service*, 9 November 1980.

[17] See, for example, *Pravda*, 3 December 1980; *Moscow Domestic Service in Russian*, 12 October 1980.

[18] Mashariqah's interview with *al-Ba'th*, 8 March 1987.

[19] R.A. Hinnebusch, 'Revisionist Dreams, Realist Strategies: The Foreign Policy of Syria', in B. Korany and A.E. Hillal Dessouki (eds.), *The Foreign Policies of Arab States*, Westview, Boulder, CO, 1984, p. 294.

[20] Asad's Ramadan Address, *Damascus Domestic Service*, 13 May 1988.

[21] Khaddam's interview with *Monday Morning*, 14-20 May 1979.

[22] *Ibid,*; Khaddam as cited by *SANA*, 4 February 1978.

[23] *Damascus Domestic Service*, 4 August 1975 (emphasis added).

[24] *Ibid.*, 8 March 1974.

[25] Seale, *Asad*, pp. 185-6.

[26] Asad's interview with *al-Rai al-Amm*, as brought by *Damascus Domestic Service*, 13 December 1981.

[27] Mashariqa's interview with *al-Ba'th*, 18 March 1987. For further Syrian references to the essence of the Arab-Israeli conflict see, for example, Asad's interview with *al-Nahar* (Beirut), 17 March 1971; speech on Lebanon, *Damascus Domestic Service*, 20 July 1976; interview for the Kuwaiti press, as brought by *Damascus Domestic Service*, 13 December 1981; interview with *Liberation* (Paris), 14 February 1986; his speeches on the anniversary of the Ba'th revolution as brought by *Damascus Domestic Service* on 8 March 1988 and 1989. See also Vice-President Khaddam's interview with *Monday Morning* (Beirut), 14-20 May 1979; comments on the conflict, as cited by the *Syrian Arab News Agency* (*SANA*), 4 February 1978; Vice-President Zuhair Mashariqa's interviews with *al-Ba'th*, 24 January 1987, 8 March 1987; Farouq al-Shara's interview with *Damascus Domestic Service*, 31 May 1989. See also statement of the 13th National Congress of the Ba'th Party, *Damascus Domestic Service*, 25 August 1980.

[28] On 24 October 1978, in response to an invitation by the Iraqi leadership, Asad flew to Baghdad, where he signed a 'Charter for a Joint National Action' as the first step on the road towards a union between the two countries; the visit was followed by intensive consultations in late 1978, designed to prepare the infrastructure of the projected integration.

[29] *The Observer*, 17 December 1978.

[30] *Le Monde*, 28 November 1978.

[31] *The Guardian*, 9 December 1978.

[32] C. Roberts, 'Soviet Arms-transfer Policy and the Decision to Upgrade Syrian Air Defences', *Survival*, July-August 1983, p. 155.

[33] *TASS*, 29 May 1984; *SANA*, 29 May 1984. For further Soviet and Syrian accounts of the visit see, for example, *Radio Moscow in Arabic*, 25 May, 2 June 1984; *TASS*, 28 May 1984; *Damascus Domestic Service*, 29 May 1984. For Western accounts see: *The Guardian*, 30 May, 4 June 1984; *The Times*, 31 May, 1 June 1984.

[34] *Foreign Report* (London), 22 November 1984, p. 8.

[35] *Radio Moscow in English*, 17 October 1984. While the Soviet-Syrian joint communiqué contained no reference to Syria's relations with other Arab countries, *Pravda's* report of the 18 October Politburo meeting reiterated this linkage.

[36] Indeed, in late 1984 the Soviets signed an arms deal with Jordan. L.C. Napper, 'The Arab Autumn of 1984: A Case Study of Soviet Middle East Diplomacy', *Middle East Journal*, Vol. 39, No. 4 (Autumn 1985), p. 743.

[37] *New York Times*, 26 January 1986; *Jane's Defence Weekly*, 11, 25 May 1985. For further discussion of this issue see below p.

[38] For Soviet accounts of Asad's talks with Gorbachev see: *Moscow Domestic Service in Russian*, 24 April 1987; Joint Soviet-Syrian Statement on Asad's visit, *TASS*, 26 April 1987; Y. Potomov, 'USSR-Syria: Realistic Approach', *New Times*, No. 18 (May 1987), p. 8. On Moscow's agreement to Reschedule Syria's debt see, *The Financial Times*, 14 May 1987.

[39] *Moscow Domestic Service in Russian*, 24 April 1987.

[40] Potomov, *USSR-Syria*, p. 8.

[41] *Moscow Domestic Service in Russian*, 24 April 1987.

[42] Vinogradov's interviews with *al-Anba* (Kuwait), 12, 29 June 1987.

[43] *Pravda*, 21 July 1988 (emphasis added).

[44] *Ma'ariv* (Tel Aviv), 16 October 1988; *Ha'aretz* (Tel Aviv), 24, 30 October 1988.

[45] *Ma'ariv*, 16, 17 January 1989.

[46] On Tlas's visit see: *TASS*, 29 October, 1 November 1988; *Krasnaya Zvezda*, 1, 3 November 1988; *Jerusalem Post*, 12 December 1988; *Ha'aretz*, 13 December 1988; *Ma'ariv*, 23 December 1988.

[47] On Shevardnaze's visit see: *Damascus Domestic Service*, 17, 18, 19 February 1989; *Damascus Television*, 19 February 1989; *New York Times*, 19, 20 February 1989; *Financial Times*, 17, 20 February 1989; *International Herald Tribune*, 28 February 1989. On Yazov's visit see: *Damascus Domestic Service*, 25 March 1989; *TASS*, 27, 28, 30 March 1989; *Krasnaya Zvezda*, 28 March 1989; *al-Majalah* (London), 5-11 April 1989.

[48] *Damascus Domestic Service*, 8 March 1989. For further Syrian criticism of the PLO's recognition of Israel see: *Damascus Domestic Service*, 19, 20 November, 30 December 1988.

[49] Asad managed to prevent Egypt's participation in the Arab summits in Amman (1987) and Algiers (1988). However, following the Amman summit all Arab states, with the exception of Syria, Libya and Lebanon restored diplomatic relations with Egypt. In May 1989 Egypt took part in the Arab summit in Casablanca for the first time since its expulsion from the Arab League a decade earlier following the conclusion of the Egyptian-Israeli peace treaty. In October 1989 Mu'amar Kaddafi paid an official visit to Egypt, and two months later Asad re-established diplomatic relations.

[50] *Yediot Acharonot* (Tel Aviv), 19 January 1990.

The Changing Military Balance in The Gulf:

Iraq's Invasion of Kuwait and its Aftermath

ANTHONY H. CORDESMAN

Anthony H. Cordesman is an Adjunct Professor of National Security Studies at Georgetown University, and Legislative Assistant for National Security to Senator John McCain. He is the author of numerous books on the region, including The Gulf and the West *(Westview/Mansell, 1988), and* The Lessons of Modern War *(Westview/Mansell, 1990).*

On August 2, 1990, Iraq invaded Kuwait. In doing so, it has triggered events that will change the military balance in the Gulf in ways that no one can now predict. An international effort has already been launched to contain its aggression that involves over 300,000 foreign troops, over 1500 tanks, over 100 combat ships, and over 500 aircraft. It has created a situation whereby the United Nations is seeking to force Iraq to withdraw from Kuwait through an international embargo and blockade, but where a United States-led military coalition of Arab and Western states may go to war with Iraq at any moment. If that war does occur, no one can predict its intensity or results. It could be a limited conflict to liberate Kuwait, a conflict involving a massive strategic bombing effort to destroy much of Iraq's military potential and ability to build and deliver weapons of mass destruction, or an all out war to force fundamental changes in Iraq's régime.

The aftermath of this crisis is equally unclear. If Iraq should triumph, it would leave an aggressor in control of 20 per cent of the world's proven oil reserves, and with the military power to intimidate every nation in a region with nearly 60 per cent of all the world's oil. If Kuwait should be liberated, but Iraq's forces were left largely intact, some kind of military presence must be created that can provide Kuwait and the southern Gulf states with long term security. This kind of military presence would probably have to be large enough to include substantial numbers of Arab military forces from outside the Gulf—possibly several

Egyptian divisions—and substantial United States air and ground forces. A small international peace keeping force would almost certainly lack the teeth to be effective. If Iraq's actions force an invasion of its own territory, it becomes almost impossible to predict what forces will be required, or how this will reshape the military balance in the Gulf. Iran could suddenly re-emerge as a major military power, and new threats to regional stability could be created.

These sudden changes have occurred in a region where most nations believed that the August 1988 ceasefire in the Iran-Iraq War had brought a new period of peace and stability. That war ended in an Iraqi military victory which did little more than restore the strategic situation that existed before Iraq's invasion of Iran in 1980. All the Gulf states that had existed at the time of the British withdrawal from the area in the late 1960s still existed. With the exception of Iran, the régimes that existed then have the same general character. They pursued most of the same force development and procurement policies that they had pursued since British withdrawal from the region and the oil boom of the 1970s. Iran, Iraq and Saudi Arabia continued to dominate the regional military balance, and to compete in building up modern military forces. The smaller southern states continued to develop their own military forces with few serious efforts at collective security. Each state continued to build up its forces in ways which reflected a complex mix of different—and sometimes conflicting—motives for military procurement. These motives included the desire for weapons that offer prestige, that enhanced political or military ties to states outside the region, that strengthen internal security, and/or which supported efforts to build up forces that can deal with external threats.

The Gulf of the 1990s will not, however, be the Gulf of the past. Unless Iraq is decisively defeated—which would require a massive conflict—it will remain a major threat to Gulf stability. A liberated Kuwait cannot be secured without major new efforts at collective security by the southern Gulf states, efforts that go far beyond the empty rhetoric and tokenism of the Gulf Cooperation Council in the period before Iraq's invasion of Kuwait. Those states will have to accept the continued presence of foreign forces—both Arab and Western, to compensate for their military weakness. While Iraq will inevitably be the near-term focus of attention, Iran is likely to remain an unstable nation that gradually restores its military power while going through a succession of radical political changes as its revolution leads to new features in the character of Iran's leadership.

There are a number of major developments that will change the regional military balance, and the pattern of military deployments and procurement policies, within the Gulf states. While the full implications of these developments remain unclear, the broad patterns involved have already begun to affect the strategic position of all the Gulf states, as well their military forces and capabilities:

☐ *Changes in weapons capability and technology*: Gulf military forces now include large numbers of first line weapons which are roughly equivalent to those of most NATO and Warsaw Pact countries. While command, control, communications, and intelligence (C^3I) capabilities do not rival those of NATO and Pact forces, they are steadily improving. Some countries— most notably Iraq—have developed effective logistic and support forces to match their strength in weapons. All the larger Gulf states have, or are acquiring, significant numbers of modern strike aircraft capable of long range missions, and most now have advanced air ordnance. Most Gulf states have at least a token strength of long range anti-ship missiles, and some have considerable military capability. Many have large armoured forces equipped with modern main battle tanks. Naval strength is more erratic. Iran has the ship numbers, but most of their ships have limited capability to operate their sensors and missiles. Iraq has not yet taken delivery of most of the modern combat ships it ordered from Italy before the Iran-Iraq War and it will take years to develop a significant naval capability. Whilst Saudi Arabia has a significant number of modern combat ships, its navy still has only limited effectiveness.

☐ *The Proliferation of Weapons of Mass Destruction*: The Iran-Iraq War triggered an arms race between Iraq and Iran to acquire chemical, biological and nuclear weapons, and long range missiles—a race that led to major Iraqi chemical warfare attacks on Iranian forces in 1984, and to a missile war in 1987. Saudi Arabia acquired its own long range missiles in 1988, and Iraq and Iran have since continued actively to improve their chemical warfare capabilities, deploy effective biological weapons, and develop the ability to produce nuclear weapons. Iraq already has the capability to strike virtually any target in the Gulf with long-range missiles which will soon have chemical and biological warheads, if they do not already possess them.

Many peripheral states are actively involved in some form of proliferation. These states include Egypt, India, Israel, Libya, Pakistan, Syria, and the Yemens. Much of this effort is covert or limited, but the efforts of India, Israel, Pakistan and Syria have already acquired significant military capabilities. As a result, an increasing number of states can reach a wide range of highly vulnerable targets in the Gulf, including oil facilities, water facilities, power plants, population centres, and military bases.

☐ *Changes in military politics and internal security*: The character of the rivalries for power in the Gulf states is changing. The southern states are far less threatened by external political pressures and radical movements. Arab socialism is effectively dead, and the Islamic revival has not yet posed a serious threat to them. Domestic political movements in the southern Gulf have tended to demand democratic evolution and/or increased adherence to Islam, rather than revolutionary change and hence the southern states face far less of a risk from a 'man on horse back' from within their own military forces than they did in the 1950s and 1960s. In consequence, they are willing to put more trust in military professionalism—although always within the authority of a senior member of the ruling family and subject to surveillance by internal security forces.

Iraqi military politics have been dominated by Saddam Hussein's personal ambitions and authoritarianism, and there has been some conflict between Ba'athist ambitions and military professionalism, but the Iran-Iraq War clearly showed Iraq the advantages of professionalism. Iran is the only Gulf state in which internal politics directly oppose military professionalism: after a decade of attempts to resolve the political struggles between revolutionary and professional military leaders, these struggles remain as divisive and crippling as they were at the start of the Iran-Iraq War.

☐ *Iraq's emergence as a regional 'Superpower'*: Iraq has strikingly reversed the balance of power in the Gulf—although it is unclear whether it will be able to retain this military position if it forces a conflict with the international forces that oppose its invasion of Kuwait. During the period between February and August 1988, Iraq decisively defeated Iran's ground forces, capturing or destroying at least 40 per cent of their armour and major combat equipment. At the same time, Iraq built up a relatively effective air force, massive long range missile capabilities, and an effective chemical corps.

Since the partial ceasefire in August 1988, Iraq has imported nearly three times as many arms as Iran, steadily adding modern weapons and technology to a battle-proved force structure that suffered only minimal losses during the final phase of the Iran-Iraq War. Iraq has also aggressively sought biological, more advanced chemical, and nuclear weapons, and missiles and aircraft capable of delivering weapons of mass destruction anywhere in the region. Its only major remaining limitations in military capability lie in its lack of naval, amphibious, and power projection forces and any ability to sustain large scale military operations outside its own borders.

□ *Iran has in some ways emerged as the 'sick man' of the Gulf*: Long before its climactic military defeats in 1988, most of Iran's air force and heavy surface-to-air missile forces had ceased to be operational. It had lost most of the armour and helicopter forces it possessed under the Shah—because of combat and a lack of spare parts. Much of its navy had ceased to be fully operational, and its remaining inventory of Western supplied missiles had aged beyond their rated shelf life. During 1987 and 1988, Iran lost most of the new land force equipment it had been able to obtain from North Korea and the People's Republic of China (PRC). Its navy suffered severe losses to the United States, and its forces became even more divided because of conflicts between and among its revolutionary and regular forces. Iran has been able to do almost nothing to change this situation since the cease fire. Its economic problems consume most of its resources: it has cut its post-war defence budgets and foreign procurement efforts by nearly 40 per cent; it has not been able to fund major arms imports or find a supplier of advanced modern weapons and its remaining Western inventories average more than 15 years in age, requiring massive rebuilding—not simply spare parts. Its limited chemical warfare and missile capabilities do not approach those of Iraq, and it still lacks an effective military organisation and anything approaching a cohesive concept of force modernisation.

□ *Saudi Arabia has not emerged as a balanced military power, but it has had nearly two decades in which to build up the core of a modern air force, effective active and passive air defences, and mechanised land forces*: Saudi forces can scarcely match those of Iraq, but they do have some significant self defence capabilities and the ability to both provide significant air support to its smaller conservative neighbours and dominate the Southern Gulf. Saudi Arabia has become both the protector of—and potential threat to—the other southern Gulf states. The resulting tensions have been most serious in terms of Saudi and Omani relations, although these tensions have not gone beyond low level political rivalry.

Saudi military strength must not be exaggerated. The Saudi Air Force is in a period of transition where it will be at least five years before it can acquire the modern combat aircraft it needs and fully absorb them. The Saudi Air Defence Force has only limited proficiency in operating its surface-to-air defences. The Army is poorly organised and equipped and only half of a relatively small force has the mix of armour and artillery it needs. The Saudi National Guard is only trained and equipped for light infantry combat and the Saudi Navy still have very low overall combat readiness. While Saudi forces must be the core of any effort at collective security in the Gulf, they are at least a decade away from being strong and ready enough to form a major deterrent to Iraqi military action.

☐ *The smaller southern Gulf states have joined Saudi Arabia in some limited efforts towards collective security, but remain divided and weak*: Bahrain, Kuwait, Oman, Qatar, Saudi Arabia, and the United Arab Emirates (UAE) increased their strategic and military cooperation, and banded together to create the Gulf Cooperation Council (GCC) in 1981. Their military cooperation, however, is still little more than a hollow shell. Actual efforts at common military planning, exercises and training and the creation of integrated military forces have been far more limited than the rhetoric of the GCC has implied, and many long standing quarrels between ruling families, and over border issues, still divide them. Nevertheless, these states were gradually developing the potential capability for collective defence, and Iraq's invasion of Kuwait has already catalysed them into a far greater degree of cooperation than existed before the invasion.

Unfortunately, however, even the best cooperation would not give them adequate security. The smaller states have only limited military capabilities, and many of their forces and procurements are poorly organised and lack effectiveness.

While their forces are now far better manned and trained than a decade ago, the steady increase in the sophistication of their military technology and in their numbers of advanced weapons systems has outpaced the ability of their forces to absorb new technologies and systems. Few arms sales have actually resulted in a high level of military capability or effective technology transfer. Thus, like Saudi Arabia, the smaller southern Gulf states are a decade away from having balanced and effective military forces of the kind needed to deal with a threat as sophisticated as Iraq.

☐ *The changes in the nature of the Arab-Israeli conflict, and in the character of Arab politics, have sharply reduced both the possibility that any of the Gulf states will become militarily involved in some future Arab-Israeli conflict and the political problems each faces in dealing with the Palestinian movement*: Egypt's commitment to peace, the emergence of a strong Arab liberation movement on the West Bank and Gaza, and Syria's growing problems in financing its military forces have reduced the risk that a major Arab-Israeli conflict will occur—particularly a conflict involving more than Israel and Syria. All the Gulf states continue to support at least some aspects of the Palestinian movement, but the prospects of the southern ones being dragged into some form of direct military action are far less likely than in the past.

The wild card is Iraq. Iraq has emerged as a conventional military power that could have a significant impact on the Arab-Israeli balance, and may yet be driven to provoke Israel in its efforts to marshal Arab support for its conquest of Kuwait and against the international forces that are trying to make it give up its conquest. There is also a growing risk that Iraqi acquisition of long range missiles, strike aircraft, and weapons of mass destruction could involve the Gulf in a future Arab-Israeli conflict in ways that were previously unthinkable.

☐ *The potential threat from the Yemens and Red Sea States must still be considered*: The civil war in the People's Democratic Republic of Yemen (PDRY) in the late 1980s, and Soviet disengagement from the PDRY, left a régime that was forced largely to abandon Marxism, allow political parties, and partially free its press. This régime reached a unity agreement with the Yemen Arab Republic (YAR) on 22 May 1990.[1] The YAR, in turn, has maintained a surprising degree of political stability, and the military build-up in both states has slackened significantly since the early and mid-1980s. Nevertheless, significant border clashes took place between Saudi Arabia and the PDRY in 1988 and 1989, and tensions between Yemen, Saudi Arabia, and Oman remained high in 1990. The new unified Yemen is also the only state in Arabia that backed Iraq in its conquest of Kuwait.

As for the other states in the Horn of Africa and Red Sea, Somalia has never been a significant threat and is consumed in a growing tribal civil war. The Sudan is an economic and military basket case wrapped up in its own civil war and with negligible chances of becoming a regional military power. Ethiopia is equally sick in economic terms and has lost most of its recent military encounters with the rebel groups in the north. Whereas Ethiopia threatened to become a major regional military power in the mid-1980s, it is now a decaying one that has lost most of its Cuban and Soviet support.

☐ *The Soviet Union is collapsing inward, rather than expanding as a military threat*: In a few short years, the Soviet Union has been transformed from a superpower, which steadily sought to expand its military and political power in the region, to an inwardly-oriented state whose primary goal is economic reform. While it has not yet cut its naval forces, it has sharply cut its naval presence in the Indian Ocean, Gulf, and Red Sea Area. It has virtually cut off military aid to Iraq, Syria and the Yemens, and has insisted on oil or cash for most arms sales. It has withdrawn from Afghanistan, largely disengaged from the PDRY, and ended most of its advisory role to Ethiopian combat forces. The forward deployment facilities which the Soviet Union had begun to develop in Ethiopia and Yemen now exist only at token levels, and it has cut back much of its presence in Cam Ranh Bay—its major staging base for power projection into the region. It has begun to make significant cuts in the total forces it can deploy against the Gulf and South-west Asia, and faces a significant series of ethnic problems from Islamic and other minorities in the Soviet republics in the relevant border area that may yet take the form of separatism.

☐ *The United States is now firmly committed to a regional presence based on informal cooperation with friendly states like Bahrain, Kuwait, Oman, and Saudi Arabia, backed by over-the-horizon reinforcement*: The United States no longer sees the Gulf or the Middle East as an area of confrontation with the Soviet Union, and has slowly improved its ability to work with the southern Gulf states in achieving regional security on a basis in which they do not feel their sovereignty is at risk.

The US generally worked well with the southern Gulf states during its deployment of naval forces into the region during Operation Earnest Will in 1987 and 1988. Long before it reacted to Iraq's invasion of Kuwait, America had developed considerable 'over-the-horizon' capability. It completed the creation of a major staging base at Diego Garcia, and has deployed stocks and equipment for Army and Air units, and prepositioned ships with major combat equipment and stocks for an entire Marine Expeditionary Force (MEF). The United States also completed a smaller pre-positioning effort at Masirah, off the coast of Oman, and developed a contingency base on that island. It has also developed informal working arrangements with the military forces of Bahrain, Kuwait, Oman, and Saudi Arabia.

The key issue for the future is whether the United States can build upon this base to marshal the kind of regional and international action necessary to defeat Iraq's efforts to retain Kuwait, and can then create an international force to secure the Gulf in the future. In practice, this is likely to require not only a considerable degree of resolution and endurance, as well as military sacrifice, but will require America to work with Arab states like Egypt and Syria, other Western states, and possibly the Soviet Union. The future military stability of the Gulf will depend heavily on its ability to shift from a superpower, acting in a largely unilateral manner, to the leadership of a broadly sustained international military force that recognises regional political sovereignties.

☐ *Oil has growing strategic importance, and the Red Sea is increasing in importance as a trade route, although oil prices and external dependence on Gulf oil continue to fluctuate*: Much of the importance of Iraq's invasion of Kuwait lies in the extent to which it suddenly forced the world to confront its strategic dependence on Gulf oil. In 1990, the Gulf region had roughly 77 per cent of the Free World's proven oil reserves and over 50 per cent of all the proven oil reserves in the world. Free world dependence on the region was indicated by the fact the United States imported 11 per cent of its oil from the Gulf, Europe imported 27 per cent, and Japan imported 62 per cent. This percentage seems almost certain to increase, since virtually all the oil exporters in other areas have, or will soon have, declining reserves. During 1989, American dependence on oil imports increased by 5 per cent. Europe already imports 66 per cent of its oil, and Japan imports 100 per cent.[2]

The overall importance of Gulf oil exports is illustrated by the fact that over 20 per cent of the world's oil consumption passes through the Straits of Hormuz at the mouth of the Gulf, or through pipelines from the Gulf area to the Mediterranean or Red Sea. Iraq can deliver another 1.7 million barrels per day (mbd) of oil to the Mediterranean via pipelines through Turkey. The Saudi Petroline to the Red Sea has a capacity of over 3 mbd, and Iraq has a parallel pipeline with a capacity of 1.645 mbd. The Saudi Petroline will be expanded to nearly 5 mbd capacity by the late 1990s. Additionally, some 20-30 major ships transit the Straits of Hormuz each day, and 40-55 major ships transit the Red Sea and Suez Canal.[3]

THE DYNAMICS OF THE MILITARY BALANCE IN THE GULF AREA

The recent trends in the military balance in the Gulf are shown in Tables 1-5.[4] The past trends shown in these tables provide a good summary picture of the relative military power of each Gulf state, and each Gulf nation's military expenditures, force levels, and arms imports. The projections, however, predate the Iraqi invasion of Kuwait and there is no way as yet to revise them, although the changing strategic conditions affecting the Gulf are likely to trigger a massive new military build-up in the Southern Gulf, as well as major new procurement efforts.

The Iraqi threat has increased to the point where every other Gulf state must react or risk losing its sovereignty or independence

TABLE 1: DEFENCE EXPENDITURE ($m)

	1978	1979	1980	1981	1982	1983	1984	1985	1986	1987
Iran	23,510	14,700	12,540	13,820	15,570	13,590	18,960	21,120	17,000	17,000
Iraq	8,823	10,000	17,460	21,680	22,090	22,260	22,850	16,710	16,500	16,500
Iran-Iraq total	32,333	24,700	30,000	35,500	37,660	35,850	41,810	37,830	33,500	23,500
Saudi Arabia	9,629	12,390	14,990	18,410	22,040	24,800	20,400	21,340	17,290	10,490
Kuwait	649	806	939	903	1,179	1,473	1,505	1,606	1,369	1,330
Bahrain	108	143	157	215	281	166	148	151	161	160
Qatar	260	475	604	720	948	1,790	1,213	2,308	1,800	1,800
UAE	822	1,197	1,724	2,090	1,980	1,973	1,932	1,901	1,580	1,700
Oman	687	699	1,057	1,355	1,510	1,742	1,891	1,935	1,728	1,516
GCC total	12,155	15,710	19,471	23,693	27,938	31,944	27,089	29,241	23,928	16,996
Gulf total	44,488	40,410	39,471	59,193	66,598	67,794	68,899	67,071	57,428	50,496

TABLE 2—TRENDS IN ARMS IMPORTS ($m (CURRENT))

	1972	1974	1976	1978	1980	1982	1984	1986	1988	1990	1992	1994
Iran	525	1,000	2,000	2,200	410	1,600	2,400	2,200	1,550	2,100	1,800	2,000
Iraq	140	625	1,000	2,400	2,500	6,500	9,300	3,800	4,800	3,700	4,000	4,100
Iran-Iraq total	665	1,625	3,000	4,600	2,910	8,100	11,700	6,000	6,250	5,800	5,800	6,100
Saudi Arabia	100	340	440	1,500	1,800	3,100	3,100	3,800	3,300	3,400	3,500	3,500
Kuwait	5	10	80	320	40	110	450	130	550	600	640	690
Bahrain	2	2	4	6	40	5	40	50	80	70	70	75
Qatar	3	2	5	20	90	270	200	80	190	230	240	260
UAE	10	50	100	60	170	50	190	30	190	180	170	170
Oman	5	10	10	270	100	130	310	10	240	230	230	250
GCC total	125	414	639	2,176	2,240	3,665	4,290	4,100	4,550	4,710	4,850	4,945
Gulf total	790	2,039	3,639	6,776	5,150	11,665	15,990	10,100	10,800	10,510	10,650	11,045

of action—and no state can predict whether Iran will re-emerge as a major threat. If the Soviet threat has decreased, Saudi Arabia continues to need the United States and other outside forces as a counterbalance to Iraq. The smaller Gulf states too need the United States as a counterbalance to both Iraq and Saudi Arabia. The regional arms race will be driven by the ongoing competition between Iraq and all its neighbours, the uncertain future political and military situation in Iran, the dominant role of Saudi Arabia in the southern Gulf and the new need for collective security in the southern Gulf. In the case of the smaller southern Gulf states, each must simultaneously improve its independent military capability while finding ways to integrate these forces with those of the United States and/or Saudi Arabia.[5]

THE IMPACT OF IRAQ AND IRAN[6]

The tensions between Iran and Iraq, and Iraq's emergence as a Gulf 'superpower', are likely to remain the key factors shaping the level of military tensions in the Gulf during the 1990s— almost regardless of the outcome of the current crisis over Iraq's invasion of Kuwait. Even if Iraq is driven out of Kuwait, and even if Saddam Hussein should fall, no one in the region will be able to predict the future character and action of Iraq's leadership. No one will be able to predict either whether Iran and Iraq can move towards a stable peace, whether Iran can recover its former military strength relative to Iraq and its southern neighbours, and whether the proliferation of weapons or mass destruction and long range strike systems in Iran and

TABLE 3—SOURCE OF ARMS IMPORTS BY MAJOR SUPPLIER 1983-1987 (US$m (CURRENT))

	Total	USSR	US	France	UK	FRG	China	Poland	Czech.	Italy	Bulgaria	Other
Iran	8,865	100	10	—	70	—	1,800	20	40	—	650	5,610
Iraq	29,865	13,900	0	4,800	40	700	3,300	460	700	370	625	5,000
Iran-Iraq total	38,730	14,000	10	4,800	110	700	5,100	480	740	370	1,275	10,610
Saudi Arabia	18,320	0	7,200	6,400	2,400	0	0	0	0	320	0	2,000
Kuwait	1,275	240	220	525	110	170	0	0	0	0	0	10
Bahrain	425	0	230	60	5	120	0	0	0	0	0	10
Qatar	555	0	10	525	20	0	0	0	0	0	0	0
UAE	610	20	320	0	220	0	0	0	0	20	0	30
Oman												
GCC total	21,185	260	7,980	7,510	2,755	290	0	0	0	340	0	2,050
Gulf total	59,915	14,260	7,990	12,310	2,865	990	5,100	480	740	710	1,275	12,660

TABLE 4—TRENDS IN MILITARY MANPOWER ('000)

	1975	1976	1977	1978	1979	1980	1981	1982	1983	1984	1985	1986	1987	1988	1989
Iran	385	420	350	350	415	305	660	640	640	735	745	705	700	654	480
Iraq	155	190	140	362	444	430	392	404	434	788	788	845	1000	1000	750
Iran-Iraq total	540	610	490	712	859	735	1052	1044	1074	1523	1533	1545	1700	1654	1230
Saudi Arabia	75	75	75	75	79	79	79	80	80	95	96	97	95	95	95
Kuwait	25	25	10	10	11	12	12	13	13	15	16	18	20	21	22
Bahrain	2	2	2	2	2	2	2	2	2	3	3	3	4	4	4
Qatar	5	5	5	5	6	6	6	6	6	6	7	9	11	12	12
UAE	21	27	25	25	25	44	44	44	44	44	44	43	44	44	44
Oman	12	12	12	12	13	15	15	15	20	25	25	26	27	28	28
GCC total	140	146	129	129	136	158	158	160	165	188	191	186	201	204	205
Gulf total	680	756	619	841	995	893	1210	1204	1239	1711	1724	1731	1901	1858	1435

TABLE 5—TRENDS IN MILITARY EQUIPMENT

| | Main battle tanks | | | | | | Combat aircraft | | | | | |
	1973	1979	1982	1984	1989	1992	1973	1979	1982	1984	1989	1992
Gulf												
Iran	920	1735	1110	1000	900	1250	159	447	90	95	70	110
Iraq	990	1800	2300	4820	5500	5400	224	339	330	580	513	535
Iran-Iraq total	1910	3535	3410	5820	6400	6650	383	786	420	675	583	645
Bahrain	0	0	0	0	54	70	0	0	0	0	12	18
Kuwait	100	280	240	240	275	290	34	50	49	49	36	50
Oman	0	0	18	18	39	50	12	35	37	52	63	70
Qatar	0	12	24	24	24	30	4	4	9	11	13	20
Saudi Arabia	85	350	450	450	550	600	70	178	191	203	179	219
UAE	0	0	118	118	136	160	12	52	52	43	65	72
Total GCC	185	642	850	850	1078	1200	132	319	338	358	368	449
Total Gulf	2095	4177	4260	6670	7478	7850	515	1105	758	1033	951	1094

Source: Estimated by the author using various editions of the IISS, *Military Balance*, and ACDA, *World Military Expenditure and Arms Transfers*.

Iraq will fundamentally change the arms race throughout the region.

In spite of Iraq's recent efforts to reach a peace settlement with Iran in order to allow it to concentrate on its conquest of Kuwait, even the best peace between Iraq and Iran is unlikely to prevent a continuing political struggle between the two countries, and a future struggle for influence over the southern Gulf states. Regardless of the outcome of the current crisis, Iraq will probably try to consolidate its present military superiority over Iran, try to become the dominant military power in the region, and try to expand its influence over the southern Gulf states. Iran is likely to try to rebuild its military forces and at least to seek parity with Iraq, although it may fall back on weapons of mass destruction as a way of creating such parity if it cannot compete in the area of conventional forces.

IRANIAN ABILITY TO COMPETE WITH IRAQ

The military balance between Iran and Iraq at the start of Iraq's invasion of Kuwait is shown in Table 6. It is obvious from the force ratios in this table that Iran faces major problems in competing with Iraq. Further, Iran cannot seem to decide on the future shape of its military forces, the extent to which these should be 'regular' or 'revolutionary' or how to exploit its potential advantage in manpower—Iran's population is now over 54m and is growing at over 3 per cent per year, but Iran can only deploy the same number of forces as Iraq, a nation with approximately one-third of its population.

There have been major changes in Iran's high command. President Rafsanjani has made repeated efforts to reorganize his Iranian forces. While he was still acting Commander-in-Chief, he created the General Command Headquarters, and then attempted to combine the regular armed forces and Iranian Revolutionary Guards Corps (IRGC) into a single Ministry of Defence and Armed Forces Logistics. In spite of the creation of this command, however, and the setting up of a Supreme National Security Council, which Rafsanjani has headed since he became president on 2 September 1989, the IRGC is highly independent and its politics have ensured that it remains a weakly organised force with no standardisation of its units, poor military discipline, inadequate training, and far too little modern equipment. The high command of Iran's forces remain unstable and the constant series of changes in the political and military leadership of the armed forces reflects continuing shifts in the relative influence of 'moderate' and 'radical' political factions.

The military situation in Iran may be summarized as follows: Iran never effectively competed with Iraq in building up its military forces during the Iran-Iraq War. During the period between 1982 and 1989, Iran has only imported about $17 billion worth of arms, versus $42.8 billion worth of arms for Iraq. Iran has only been able to import about $2.4 billion worth of these arms from advanced arms sellers like Western Europe and the Soviet Union as opposed to $30 billion for Iraq. Iran was unable to import spares and replacement equipment for most of its American and West European supplied equipment, and much of this equipment ceased to be operational. Iraq was able to import parts freely for its existing equipment, but these imports were incremental to its existing pool of military equipment, while Iran's imports failed to replace the equipment it already had but could no longer operate.[7]

The battles of 1988 made this situation far worse for Iran. By the time of the cease-fire in August, 1988, it had been decisively defeated on the land and in the air. It lost at least 40 per cent of its remaining major land combat equipment in the battles of 1988, and its air force reached the point where most of its combat aircraft were largely inoperable. Iran was only able to import about $1.2 to $1.5 billion worth of arms in 1989. Many of these deliveries, and many of Iran's outstanding orders, consisted of artillery, Scud missiles, and ammunition. Iran received only limited supplies of T-54/55, Type 69 and T-72 tanks, and has been unable to rebuild anything approaching effective armoured forces. Iran may have received a few F-7 and/or F-8 fighters, but these are very poor Chinese substitutes for older Soviet fighter designs. Iran has not received any modern fighters, or restored many of its American-made fighters and surface-to-air missile units to combat effective status. Further, Iran's deepening economic crisis has forced it to cut its defence budget by 30-50 per cent in 1989/1990 and 1990/1991, and to make similar cuts in its hard currency budget for arms imports.

Iran has lost much of its power projection capability. Equally importantly, the United States defeat of the Iranian Navy—and Iran's nearly decade-long lack of ready access to parts, munitions, and weapons modernisation—may soon transform the naval balance in the region. A full cease-fire would

TABLE 6—THE TRENDS IN IRANIAN AND IRAQI MILITARY FORCES: 1980-1990

Force category	1980/81 Iran	1980/81 Iraq	1990/91 Iran	1990/91 Iraq
TOTAL ACTIVE MILITARY MANPOWER SUITABLE FOR COMBAT	24,000	242,250	400,000-600,000	500,000-750,000
LAND FORCES				
Maximum regular army manpower				
Active	150,000	200,000	305,000	600,000
Reserve	400,000 +	256,000	350,000	480,000
Revolutionary Guards/			250,000	
Basij/People's Army			175,000	400,000?
Hezbollah (home guard)			2,500,000	
Arab volunteers		6,000		?
Division equivalents				
Armoured (divisions/brigades)	6 + 4	12 + 3	?	3 (b)
Mechanized	3	4	4? (a)	3 (b)
Infantry and mountain	0	4	6 (a)	40 (b)
Special forces/airbourne			1/1 (a)	20 (b)
Pasdaran/people's militia			(c)	—/15
Major combat equipment				
Main battle tanks	1,740	2,750	700	5,500
Other armoured fighting vehicles	1,075	2,500	650-800	5,800-9,800
Major artillery	1,000 +	1,040	800-1,000	2,800-3,700
AIR FORCES				
Maximum air force manpower	70,000	38,000	35,000	40,000
Combat aircraft	445	332	70-190 (c)	510-775 (e)
Combat helicopters	500	41	?	150-170
Total helicopters	750	260	120-370	360-4303
Surface to air missile batteries (f)			12	70
NAVY				
Navy manpower	26,000	4,250	14,500	7,000
Destroyers	3 (g)	0	3 (g)	0
Frigates	4 (h)	1 (i)	3 (h)	5 (i)
Corvettes	4 (j)	0	1-2 (j)	4 (k)
Missile patrol craft	9 (l)	12 (m)	6 (m)	8 (m)
Major other patrol craft			4	6
Mine warfare vessels		5	1	8

Hovercraft	14	0	6	0
Landing craft and ships	—	17	8	6
Maritime patrol aircraft	6 P-3F	0	1-5 P-3F	0

(a) Estimates differ sharply. One detailed estimate of the regular army in mid-1989 showed 7 mechanized divisions with 3 brigades each and a total of 9 armoured and 18 mechanized battalions. Also 2 special forces divisions, 1 airborne brigade, plus eight Revolutionary Guard divisions and large numbers of other brigades and battalions. A recent Israeli estimate says there are about 10 regular divisions and 20 Pasdaran divisions. The latest JCSS estimate shows four corps with four armoured and 29 infantry divisions, plus 3 independent special forces brigades, and two airbourne divisions. This is equivalent to 13 regular armmy and 20 Pasdaran divisions.

(b) The Iraqi order of battle began to change rapidly in late 1988, and its future structure remains unclear in mid-1990. A heavy emphasis is being placed on elite forces with a heavy component of regular forces. In late 1989, there were three armoured divisions, one infantry division, and one commando brigade in the Presidential Guards. The seven 'mechanized divisions in the regular army were mechanized/armoured divisions'. The infantry divisions include 4 mountain divisions. There were two independent special forces divisions, 9 reserve brigades, and 15 People's Volunteer Infantry Brigades.

(c) The IRGC or Pasdaran is being re-organised. One plan drafted in late 1988 indicated that it would have 21 infantry divisions, 15 independent infantry divisions, 21 air defence brigades, three engineering divisions, and 42 armoured, artillery, and air defence brigades.

(d) In early 1990, force strength included a maximum of 20-35 F-4D/E, 20-45 F-5E/F, 10-14 F-14A, 5 RF-5, and 3 RF-4E operational aircraft. Large numbers of additional combat aircraft are in storage due to lack of parts. Some Argentine A-4s and PRC or North Korean F-6 and F-7 may have been in delivery. The number of attack helicopters still operational was unknown, but armed helicopter strength was negligible.

(e) In early 1990, air strength probably included 7-12 Tu-22, 8-10 Tu-16, and 4 H-6D (PRC); 17 FGA squadrons with 4/64 Mirage F-1EQ5 (some with Exocet and some Mirage F-1EQ200 with extended range fuel tanks), 4 FGA squadrons with 70 MiG-23BM/MiG-27, 3 with 50-80 Su-7 and Su-17/20/22, 2 with 30 Su-25, and 2 with 40 J-6. There were 1 recce squadron with 8 MiG-25; and 16 interceptor squadrons with 25 MiG-25, 70 MiG-21, 80 J-7, 18-25 MiG-29, and 30 Mirage F-1EQ. Estimates of Mirage strength varied sharply according to assumptions about delivery rates and combat attrition. Typical combat helicopters were 40-50 Mi-24, 50-70 SA-342 Gazelle (some with HOT), 30 SA-316B with AS-12 and 44 MBB BO-105 with SS-11. Major air munitions include R-530, R-550 Magic, AA-2, AA-6, AA-7, and AA-8 AAMs, and AS-30 Laser, Armat, Exocet AMN-39, C-601 Silkworm, AS-4 Kitchen, and AS-5 Kelt ASMS.

(f) The number of operational SAM units on each side is unknown. Many of Iran's 12 Hawk batteries are not operational. Iran also has extensive holds of SA-7s and some RBS-70. Iraq has shown very limited ability to use its Soviet made SAMs and some sites do not seem to be fully operational. Counts of Iraq's missile strength are controversial but Iraq seems to have roughly 20 SA-2 (120 launchers), 25 SA-3 (150 launchers), and 25 SA-6 batteries. It also has SA-7, SA-9, SA-13, SA-14 units and some 60 Roland fire units.

(g) None fully operational. 3 equipped with Standard Arm SSMs. One Battle-class and two Sumner-class in reserve.

(h) Alvand-class ships quipped with Sea Killer SSM. Three seem to have at least limited operational capability.

(i) 4 Hittin (Lupo)-class with eight Otomat-2 missile launchers, 2 X 3 ASTT, 1 AB-212 ASW helicopter, and one 127mm gun. There is 1 Yugoslav training frigate. (i) 6 Wadi-class Italian made 650 ton corvettes. The Hussa el Hussair class ships each has 1X4 Albatros/Aspide. 2 have 2 Otomat-2 and 1 helicopter each; 4 have 6 Otomat 2 SSMs.

(j) Up to two Bayander-class (ex-US PF-103). At least one is largely non-operational.

(k) There are two Hussa el Hussair-Class with one AB-212 helicopter and 2 Otomat SSM launchers, and two Hussa el Hussair with 6 Otomat 2 launchers and 2 x 3 ASTT. The ships are based on the Italian Assad class.

(l) Equipped with Harpoon surface to surface missiles. No missiles currently available.

(m) Equipped with Styx missiles.

Adapted from various editions of the IISS: *The Military Balance*, JCSS, *The Middle East Military Balance*, and work by Drew Middleton for the *New York Times*.

mean Iraq's modern major combat ships in Italy can transit to ports in Iraq. Once Iraq makes such vessels operational, it is unclear how Iran could rebuild its former naval supremacy.

Iran has discussed various plans to rebuild its forces by 1995, but these involved arms purchases costing at last $25 billion and none have yet been funded. Iran keeps examining different forms of military organisation, but both its regular forces and IRGC forces have continued to drop in manning and readiness since its 20 August 1988 cease-fire with Iraq. Even if Iran could obtain access to the arms it wants, it would be unable to salvage most of its United States and British-made equipment. In many cases, parts are no longer available and years of wear and neglect would require total rebuilding of the equipment. While Iran is not saddled with anything approaching Iraq's foreign debt, and has enough money to make some major new arms purchases, it is now earning slightly less revenue from oil exports than Iraq, yet it must meet the needs of a population more than three times as large. The Iranian revolution has not brought order to Iran's post-war economy, and tax revenues and other foreign exchange earnings remain low.

In contrast, Iraq was able to obtain massive imports of new arms to supplement a victorious force structure after the cease-fire, and emerged far stronger from the war than it was at the war's beginning. In spite of a foreign debt in excess of $60 billion, Iraq spent nearly $2 billion on arms imports in the 18 months following the August 1988 cease-fire, largely on imports from the Soviet Union. Iraq's purchases included high technology weapons like the Su-24, Su-25, and Su-22, and additional Mirage F-1 fighters. They have also included Silkworm anti-ship missiles, T-72 tanks, and additional surface-to-air missiles and advanced radars. In mid-1990, in the period before its invasion of Kuwait, Iraq was considering purchase of up to three squadrons each of Mirage 2000 and Alphajet fighters, or Su-27 Flankers, and there were reports that the Soviet Union might sell Iraq advanced SA-10 surface-to-air missiles.

At the same time, Iraq has attempted to build up a massive defence industry. Iraq already can produce artillery, small arms, long range missiles and rockets, and chemical weapons. At the time of its invasion of Kuwait, it was seeking to produce T-72 main battle tanks and other armoured fighting vehicles, multiple rocket launchers, trainer aircraft, RPVs, and small combat ships. Iraq already had the most modern air defence and air attack systems in the Gulf. It had built up a long range missile strike force, vast chemical warfare capabilities, and was developing biological and nuclear weapons.

Iraq had at least three major chemical and biological weapons production facilities at Samarra, Habbaniyah, and Salman, and five major chemical weapons storage sites at the time it invaded Kuwait. Its army was divided into seven corps, deployed north to south along the Iranian border, with 48 infantry divisions, four mechanized divisions, eight armoured divisions, and one special forces division. The combat ready strike aircraft in its 770 aircraft Air Force included seven Tu-22 and eight Tu-16 bombers; 24-33 MiG-29 fighters, 10 Su-24 long range strike fighters, 24-33 Su-25 attack fighters; large numbers of MiG-23s, MiG-25s, and Su-20/22s; and roughly 170 armed helicopters—largely Mi-8s and Mi-24s. It had nine fixed long range missile launch sites, and many of its missiles were on mobile launchers. While Iraq did not capture most of Kuwait's air force during its invasion of Kuwait, it did capture most of the Kuwaitis 275 main battle tanks, including 165 Chieftains, its 670 other armoured vehicles, 82 major artillery weapons, and other armoured equipment. It also captured Kuwait's Improved Hawk surface-to-air missile forces, and its eight missile patrol boats, all of which were equipped with Exocet anti-ship missiles.

Nevertheless, Iraq faced military problems even before the United Nations embargo cut it off from further arms imports. Its forces were organised, trained, and deployed largely for defensive warfare along the border with Iran, and for reliance on large nearby rear area logistic and supply bases and massive artillery fire bases. Only a limited number of élite units were properly trained for offensive combat, and Iraq had major command and control problems unless it had days to organise a defence and weeks to plan an offensive. The Iraqi Air Force had little training or experience in air-to-air combat and the readiness and proficiency of Iraqi surface-to-air missile defences was poor. The Iraqi Navy was a weak and obsolescent force. Iraq has had to cut its active strength sharply after the cease-fire in order to try to rebuild its economy. It must now rely on a large number of unproven conscripts and untried reserves. There have been many reports that Saddam Hussein has come into conflict with some of his senior officers and that this has led to executions, imprisonments and, possibly, to assassination attempts. Iraq had problems in meeting its debt payments and this affected its access to foreign arms during 1989 and the first six months of 1990.

Iraq's invasion of Kuwait was anything but a model of effectiveness, although it committed 10 full divisions to deal with Kuwaiti forces that numbered only 20,300 men and which provided more the image of military capability than the substance. Even though Iraq initially used many of its élite Republican Guards forces, it failed to secure largely undefended palaces and strong points, many units lost their way or broke down, and when small engagements did take place, Iraqi forces tended to fire indiscriminately and with little initial military effect. Iraq also proved unable to deploy rapidly the support and supply forces it needed to support the combat units in its occupation forces, and even in mid-September 1990, many forward-deployed units in Kuwait still had supply problems with basics like food and water. While Iraq did succeed in rapidly deploying large numbers of surface-to-air and Silkworm missiles into Kuwait, it did not succeed in integrating these into an integrated air defence system. Iraq soon encountered problems with the operational readiness of its air force the moment it attempted to sustain high readiness levels in reaction to the deployment of American units and other parts of the international force in the Gulf.

Iraq has all the military equipment and supplies it needs for a prolonged war, but now faces major future problems in obtaining parts and new weapons. It will also experience major strategic problems if it cannot continue to occupy Kuwait. Iraq would lack naval bases and sea ports that would give it a secure ability to use the Gulf, and its access would remain uncertain even if it should somehow obtain access to Bubiyan or Waribah, or Kuwaiti permission to make unrestricted use of the Kor Abdullah Waterway between Umm Qasr and the Gulf. Like the Shatt al-Arab, this would still leave ships passing through these channels totally vulnerable to Iranian land-based anti-ship missiles. While Iraq's pipelines through Turkey and Saudi Arabia have offered it an alternative to shipping oil through the Gulf, these lines were shut within days of Iraq's invasion of Kuwait, and Iraq's oil production facilities will become progressively more difficult to defend as Iran rearms with long range strike systems.

The final trend affecting the military balance between Iran and Iraq is proliferation. Both Iran and Iraq are continuing to expand their gas warfare capabilities and now have extensive stocks of mustard and non-persistent nerve gases. They probably have some stocks of biological weapons and toxins. Iraq is actively pursuing a nuclear weapons development effort using centrifuge enrichment systems, and is probably about three to eight years away from acquiring usable nuclear weapons.

Iraq has chemical weapons stored in binary shells, bombs, and warheads of multiple rocket launchers. It has large numbers of Scuds with a range of 300km and a Circular Error Probability (CEP) of about 1000m, and of Al Husayn missiles with a range of 600km and a CEP of about 2000m. It is beginning to deploy the new Al Abbas missile with a range of about 900km and a CEP of a little over 3000m. Iran probably has similar, if less sophisticated, weapons. Iraq probably has missiles equipped with gas warheads and has already deployed long range missiles at nine fixed sites near its north-central, western, and southern borders.

Iran is less advanced than Iraq, although it now has a substantial capability for chemical warfare and at least some biological warfare capabilities. It lacks anything approaching Iraq's air and missile strength, but it is seeking to produce extended range Scuds and possibly an indigenous long range missile. Iran also has a nuclear weapons effort, but is unlikely to have an actual weapon until after the year 2000.

THE MILITARY CAPABILITIES AND VULNERABILITIES OF THE SOUTHERN GULF STATES[8]

This mix of Iraqi strength and Iranian weakness has destroyed the former balance of power in the northern Gulf, and undoubtedly contributed to Iraq's willingness to take the risk of invading Kuwait. It has created a situation where the best that the southern Gulf states can probably hope for is that the United Nations embargo, and possibly military action by the coalition of Arab and Western states, drives Iraq out of Kuwait and weakens it both militarily and politically. No matter what happens, the southern Gulf States face the prospect of dealing with an Iraq and Iran which are scarcely likely to be stable friends and allies, and whose régimes are likely to remain sufficiently unstable to become active threats at any time.

The current size of the forces in the southern Gulf or Gulf Co-operation Council (GCC) states is shown in Table 7. This table shows the forces Kuwait once contributed to the southern Gulf states, and any comparison of these forces with those in

TABLE 7—THE SIZE AND MILITARY CAPABILITIES OF THE SOUTHERN GULF STATES IN 1990

Country	Size (Sq. Km.)	Population (1,000s)	GDP ($B)	Defense ($m)	Active Military Manpower	Tanks	Combat Aircraft	Major Combat Ships
Bahrain	676	497	3.5	194	3,350	54	12	6
Oman	212,380	1,305	7.5	1,300	25,500	33	63	12
Qatar	11,000	469	5.4	420	7,000	24	13	3
Saudi Arabia	2,149,690	16,109	74.0	16,000	65,700	540	179	24
UAE	83,600	2,115	22.0	1,800	43,000	131	61	6
Total	2,457,346	20,495	112.4	19,714	144,550	782	328	51
Kuwait	*17,818*	*2,008*	*19.1*	*1,560*	*20,300*	*245*	*36*	*8*
Iran	1,648,000	53,867	93.5	5,000	600,000	700-900	100-175	15
Iraq	434,924	18,074	34	11,000	750,000	5,000-5,500	550-750	9
Total	2,082,924	72,941	127.5	16,000	1,350,000	5,700-6,400	650-925	21
Yemen	517,218	9,446	5.51	860	64,000	1,144	227	14

(Adapted from: The IISS, *Military Balance*, 1989-1990; JCSS, *Middle East Military Balance*, 1988/1989; ACDA computer data base for *World Arms Transfers and Military Expenditures*, 1988; Tony Banks and James Bruce, 'Country Survey: Gulf States', *Jane's Defence Weekly*, 31 March 1990; John Aronson and Inge Lockwood, 'Background Materials on the Persian Gulf Region', Washington, The Middle East Institute—Sultan Qaboos Center, December 1987; CIA, *The World Factbook*, 1989, WF 89-001 Washington, GPO, 1989.)

Table 6 shows how weak the southern Gulf states really are. Even those few countries where the total number of major combat equipment is impressive clearly lack the active military man-power necessary to make it effective.

The southern Gulf states have only three ways to react to these tensions and uncertainties, and to create a significant deterrent to possible threats from Iraq and/or Iran. The first, is to band together in co-operative defence efforts that go beyond political symbolism and have actual military effectiveness. The second, to use their oil wealth to buy superior technology and take advan-tage of the geography of the Gulf to use air power and advanced technology to compensate for their weakness in land forces and air strength. The third, is their ability to draw on external support from other Arab states and the West—principally the United States.

Unfortunately the procurement policies and deployments of the southern Gulf in the period before Iraq's conquest of Kuwait scarcely set the kind of precedent that the southern Gulf states needed. Once one probes beneath the surface of the military deployments and procurement policies of those states, there are only limited signs of prior progress in military co-operation and few signs of military effectiveness. They will have to make dramatic changes in their behaviour if they are to create an effective regional deterrent, be able to make effective use of the 'force multiplier' effect of advanced technology, or even to support properly any outside powers in coming to their defence. This does not mean that they have not made progress since the early 1980s. Bahrain, Kuwait, Oman, Qatar, Saudi Arabia, and the United Arab Emirates have each improved their relative forces during the last decade, and they moved in the direction of collective security by founding the GCC on 25 May 1981. The GCC states held numerous common military exercises since their first Peninsula Shield exercise in 1983—although these were largely ineffective 'set piece' displays, and Oman, Dubai, and other elements of the GCC often failed to participate. The GCC states also formed a two-brigade Peninsula Shield Force on 27 November 1984. This established the core of a small integrated force which was based at King Khalid Military City, about 30 miles due south of Hafr al Batin in Saudi Arabia—although it scarcely proved able to help Kuwait when Iraq invaded.[9]

The current deployments of the military forces of the southern Gulf states lend themselves to future co-operation built around the forces of Saudi Arabia. Several of Saudi Arabia's land combat units are deployed near its Gulf border. Saudi Arabia can also provide many elements of a regional air defence system. The Saudi air base at Dhahran has some 70 combat aircraft, including squadrons of F-15s and Tornadoes, and Dhahran can be rapidly reinforced by forces of the other major Saudi bases at Tabuk, Taif, and Khamis Mushayt. Saudi Arabia has eight Improved Hawk (IHawk) batteries along the Gulf coast, and four Crotale batteries. Another IHawk battery is deployed at Hafr al-Batin. Saudi Arabia has roughly half of its navy—including four Al-Badr Class guided missile patrol boats and seven As-Siddig Class guided missile patrol boats, both of which are equipped with Harpoon—based on the Gulf coast at Jubail.

The five smaller southern Gulf states are forced to locate their forces near the Gulf coast, creating what could someday become a belt of integrated land, air, and naval forces along the rest of the southern Gulf. In the north-east, a liberated Kuwait could provide the force necessary to defend the 'hinge' of the southern Gulf—providing that it was given strong Arab and Western reinforcements and support. Qatar and Bahrain could defend the central Gulf, the United Arab Emirates the eastern or lower Gulf, and Oman the mouth of the Gulf (the Straits of Hormuz) and its southern approaches from the Indian Ocean. These states deploy a total of 13 additional army units, have six additional naval bases, nine air bases, and deploy six additional IHawk batteries, three SA-8 batteries, two Rapier squadrons, a Crotale battery, and an RBS-70 battery.

Nevertheless, the southern Gulf states do not yet act as a bloc. There are still major political divisions between them, and many elements of their forces are ineffective. Their land forces lack armoured strength and the ability to manoeuvre effectively or conduct joint operations. Most air defence and fighter-attack units have low effectiveness and limited sustainability. Command and control integration is negligible, and there is nothing approaching an integrated air control and warning or maritime surveillance system. Saudi forces did fly E-3A airborne warning and air control systems (AWACS) missions over the southern Gulf during the Iran-Iraq War, but this was only made possible by the fact that American crews flew similar missions over the upper Gulf. The failure of Western contractors like Boeing to provide effective command and control and air defence systems, in spite of years of expenditure on systems like Peace Shield, is an international scandal. There is little standardization of equipment, munitions, and logistics, and many units have very limited military effectiveness.

The basic factors shaping the future deployments, procurement policies and military capabilities of the southern Gulf states may be summarised as follows:

□ *First, the geography of the Gulf may force the southern Gulf states to concentrate their forces near the coast, but it also creates serious problems*: Kuwait, Bahrain, Qatar, and the UAE lack strategic depth and are vulnerable to Iranian or Iraqi attacks. None of the smaller Gulf nations can hope to succeed in defending its territory by itself in any confrontation with a northern Gulf power, even if it uses all its air and naval capabilities to defend its own airspace and waters. Kuwait, Bahrain, and the UAE will face particularly serious problems because of the small size of their military forces relative to the threats they face, and the location of the border area and territory they must defend. The geography of the southern Gulf also ensures that a radical takeover of any one of the southern Gulf states might cripple both any regional efforts at collective defence and Western ability to deploy reinforcing units.

□ *Second, Saudi Arabia is the only southern Gulf state with sufficient military forces to cross-reinforce the other Gulf states*: Saudi Arabia's geography also makes it the only state with the lines of communication and strategic depth to make such reinforcement possible and to deploy at least some of its forces where they are safe from attack. Even Saudi Arabia, however, has a low ratio of forces to the space they must cover to defend its critical areas. It has also had major problems in obtaining the military equipment it needs and has often received poor support in absorbing and maintaining this equipment from the West. The problems with the air defence variant of the British Tornado fighter, the American-supplied Peace Shield system, and French-supplied missile 'frigates' are all cases in point.

□ *Third, the problems inherent in the lack of military force in the southern Gulf states are compounded by the fact that their forces enjoy little standardisation and have poor interoperability*. While the forces of each state are gradually improving in individual military capability, many are still 'showpiece' forces which cannot operate effectively except in carefully planned exercises. They have few native combat troops, and have whole foreign manned combat units with little loyalty to the nation or régime. Once again, these problems have been compounded by the desire of Western states and companies to maximise sales at the cost of military effectiveness in the nations they are supposed to aid.

☐ *Fourth, the smaller conservative Gulf states suffer from major dis-economies of scale*: The smaller Gulf states may spend a great deal on defence, but each faces special problems in building up an adequate deterrent or defence capability. Bahrain is small, relatively poor and ethnically divided. Kuwait, as we have seen, is highly vulnerable to both Iranian and Iraqi attacks, and is an extraordinary prize, since its small territory and population make it militarily vulnerable while it has massive oil and gas resources. Oman is acutely limited in the amount of modern heavy weaponry it can buy and operate effectively. Qatar is small, and has too small a native population to create significant military forces. The defence efforts of the UAE are so divided because of tensions between the individual Sheikdoms, that it is making little progress in coalescing them into an effective force. Further, the individual Sheikdoms have taken very different stands about whether to organise to defend against Iran or appease it. The only way to improve the present situation is for the southern Gulf states to integrate their training, procurement, infrastructure, and major defence systems.

☐ *Fifth, there are still significant rivalries between the southern Gulf states*: Qatar and Bahrain continue to squabble over control of the Hawar Islands; considerable tension remains between Oman and Saudi Arabia; and the military forces of the UAE are divided by long standing rivalries between Abu Dhabi, Dubai, and Sharjah.

☐ *Sixth, all of the southern Gulf states have bought at least some of their major weapons to enhance their prestige or out of rivalry with neighbouring states, rather than to get maximum benefit in improving their deterrent or combat capabilities*: Most of the military forces in the smaller southern Gulf states have inadequate warning sensors, and weak command and control systems. Most armies lack modern communications, battle management, and target acquisition systems. There is little helibourne or amphibious capability to move troops rapidly. There are few airborne early warning (AEW) systems and no air control and warning assets. Most ships have inadequate air defence and no anti-missile defence. The smaller GCC navies have no mine warfare capability, and poor ability to conduct combined operations. There are few modern reconnaissance and intelligence assets. The various states and military services differ sharply in sheltering and passive defence capability. Only Oman has pipelines that allow it to avoid dependence on ship movement through the Gulf.

☐ *Seventh, the southern Gulf states generally lack the skilled personnel and technicians necessary to operate their equipment in sustained combat, and many have poor outside advisory support*: While Saudi Arabia and Oman have reasonably effective Western military advice and support, the other southern Gulf states have fared badly in getting the kind of outside support they need, or have refused either to purchase it or let it be effective. At the same time, many outside arms sellers have failed either to make good their promises regarding equipment performance or to provide effective support.

☐ *Eighth, the military expansion and modernisation of the southern Gulf states has been sharply affected by the changes in oil prices.* The total oil revenues of the southern Gulf states shrank from about $150-163 billion in 1981, to $45-55 billion in 1985. According to some estimates there were around $40-43 billion in 1986, and although they were probably above $50 billion in 1987, the rapid drop in the value of the dollar in the fall of 1987 brought their purchasing power back down to something approaching the 1986 level. These drops in income were cushioned by nearly $160-200 billion in investment abroad, but virtually all of these investments were held by Saudi Arabia, Kuwait, and Abu Dhabi. Bahrain and Oman were dependent on Saudi Arabia and Kuwait to finance their military modernisation. This led to a slowdown in military modernisation during the mid-1980s, although oil revenues and defence spending seemed to be on the rise again in 1989.[10]

☐ *Ninth, the geography of the southern Gulf ensures that a radical takeover of any one of the southern states might cripple both regional defence efforts and Western ability to deploy reinforcing units*: The Iraqi seizure of Kuwait has already illustrated these risks, and much will depend on whether Kuwait can be liberated. Fortunately, most of the southern states seem to be relatively secure against immediate internal threats to their political security of the kind that could overthrow their present régimes, or turn them into hostile radical states. All, however, are vulnerable to outside pressure and threats unless they can count on strong outside assistance.[11]

☐ *Tenth, the southern Gulf states ultimately cannot deal with proliferation or with the acquisition of long-range strike systems by the northern Gulf states without reinforcement or support from the United States.*[12] Nothing the southern Gulf states can do will secure them against missile attacks using weapons of mass destruction, missile attacks on their tanker traffic, or the risk that a significant number of attacking aircraft can get through with chemical, biological, or smart warheads to attack key targets like oil facilities, desalinisation and power plants, and population centres. The smaller Gulf states are 'one target' countries, and even Saudi Arabia is so vulnerable to limited attacks that it might otherwise have to give way to blackmail by its neighbours in the northern Gulf.

☐ *Eleventh, the southern Gulf states must rely on Western power projection capabilities as their ultimate defence, but these capabilities have severe limits*: Important as regional military capabilities are, the balance is ultimately stabilised by Western power projection capabilities. The forces that Britain and France can project are limited to low intensity war, however, and even US capabilities have important limits. Successful Western power projection depends on being able to have forces or equipment in place, and substantial co-operation from the threatened southern Gulf states in terms of the use of facilities, ports, air bases, and supply. The US is the only power capable of deploying division and wing sized combat units, but it cannot act as the policeman of the Gulf without substantial outside military and financial aid. It is also important that the Gulf states maintain and improve their popular support. Outside powers will not intervene in low intensity conflict, most forms of insurgency, or petty regional quarrels. No Western state will act to save an unpopular Gulf regime from its own people. Ultimately, Western security guarantees are informal, contingency dependent, and only as strong as states in the region care to make them.

REGIONAL THREATS TO THE GULF AND THE PROCESS OF DETERRENCE

The current mix of strengths and weaknesses in the military forces of the various Gulf states, and their deployments and procurement policies, present major military problems for regional stability regardless of how Iraq's invasion of Kuwait is resolved. If Iraq should somehow triumph in spite of the United Nations' actions and the international military coalition that is now building up to force Iraq to give up its conquests, the results would be a disaster. Iraq would clearly dominate the region, and the temptation to deal with an aggressor on an aggressor's terms would be almost irresistible. This confronts the West and other states outside the region with the need to build some form of regional coalition that can protect the southern Gulf states while they improve their own military capabilities, and with the need to restrict future arms transfers to Iraq and Iran while exerting every possible pressure to slow down their acquisition of weapons of mass destruction.

The world must not only deal with the ethical problem of resisting conquest and aggression, it must deal not only with the fact that it is dependent on Gulf oil, but that, regardless of the Iraqi régime that emerges from the present crisis, the Gulf region has a long history of unpredictable wars which have been fought to intensities far beyond the level justified by their strategic purpose. The proliferation of weapons of mass destruction, long range missiles and aircraft, anti-ship missiles, and advanced munitions seems almost certain to make this worse by creating a growing threat that any conflicts could escalate rapidly and take on highly unpredictable forms.

The sad fact is that the ability to use force is still the only way to achieve security and stability in the region, and that states will only be secure to the extent that they and friendly states have sufficient military force to halt any challenge. This inevitably means that a stable military balance will only exist if the southern Gulf states can unite far more effectively than they have to date, and if outside military forces remain in place to support them for many years to come.

NOTES

[1] The new nation will have 13m people (10m coming from the YAR) and be the poorest state in Arabia. The president will be General Ali Abdullah Saleh, the former president of the YAR. The Prime Minister will be Haiddar al-Attas, the former president of the PDRY. The political capital will be Sana and the economic capital will be Aden. Approximately two million Yemenis work abroad. *Economist*, 26 May 1990, p. 45.

[2] General H. Norman Schwarzkopf, *Witness Statement Before the Senate Armed Services Committee*, USCENTCOM, Washington, D.C., 8 February 1990, p. 9.

[3] *Jane's Defence Weekly*, 31 March 1990, pp. 588-590; Statement and testimony of the Director of the Central Intelligence Agency, William H. Webster, before the Senate Armed Services Committee, January 23 1990; and telephone conversation with US Department of Energy, International Affairs.

[4] The defence expenditure and arms transfer data shown in Table One represent estimates by the CIA, as reported in the US Arms Control and Disarmament Agency (ACDA) document, *World Military Expenditures and Arms Transfers*, 1989, Washington, GPO, 1989. These data are generally more accurate than those produced by the IISS and SIPRI, but have several important uncertainties. They do not reflect loans or off-budget accounts. The Gulf states have very large accounts based on oil revenues that do not show up on central government budgets. Several countries, particularly Iraq and Saudi Arabia, have massive military debts that do not appear in ordinary government reporting. The total Iraqi war debt, for example, is often reported as equalling $60bn, although much of this went to civil expenditures and is drawn from loans by southern Gulf states that are unlikely to ever be repaid. The arms import data represent the estimated dollar value of actual imports and not orders or the prices actually paid.

[5] The flow of oil revenues has generally been the key factor setting a cap on Gulf states' military and arms expenditures. Total OPEC oil revenues rose from $20bn in 1973 to nearly $220bn in 1980, and then fell to $60bn in 1986, as world demand fell and OPEC developed a net surplus. World demand for oil has increased at roughly 2 per cent annually since the collapse of world oil prices in 1986, and OPEC now produces about 21-22m barrels a day (MBD). Many projections indicate that demand will rise to the point where OPEC will need to produce about 33 MBD in the mid-1990s, which could lead to major price rises. Such predictions have, however, been made for years and prices have not risen to anything like the level predicted. (Economist Publications, *A Survey of the Arab World*, 12 May 1990, pp. 17-18.)

The oil revenue patterns of the Gulf states are shown in the table below. They provide a good picture of each state's relative buying power before the shifts in oil exports, and increases in oil prices, resulting from Iraq's invasion of Kuwait and the resulting international embargo.

TABLE A

PETROLEUM EXPORTS INCOME FOR SELECTED MIDDLE EASTERN COUNTRIES: 1980-1988[a]

(In billions of nominal dollars)

Country	1980	1984	1985	1986	1987	1988
Bahrain[b]	1.2	1.2	1.1	0.8	0.7	0.7
Iran	13.3	12.3	13.1	7.2e	10.5e	8.2e
Iraq	26.3	9.4	10.7	6.9	11.4e	11.0e
Kuwait	17.7	10.7	9.8	6.4	7.5	6.3
Oman[c]	3.0	3.7	4.3	2.7	3.3	2.8
Qatar	5.4	4.4	3.1	1.7	1.8e	1.7e
Saudi Arabia	105.8	34.2	24.2	17.0	19.3	20.5e
U.A.E.	19.6	13.0	11.8	7.4	8.7e	7.4e

a. Estimates provided by Dario Scuka, Congressional Research Service, 15 March 1990.

b. Revenue from total exports. Bahrain relies heavily on imports, notably from Saudi Arabia. Bahrain is not a member of OPEC.

c. Estimates are calculated by the Congressional Research Service and are drawn from CIA unclassified data.

e = estimate.

[6] The estimates made in this section are drawn primarily from interviews in the region, London, and Washington; press sources and computerised defence data bases; and the relevant country chapters of International Institute for Strategic Studies (IISS), *Military Balance*, 1989-1990, London, Brassey's (UK), 1989; Anthony H. Cordesman, *The Lessons of Modern War, Volume II: The Iran-Iraq War*, Boulder, Westview, 1990; Anthony H. Cordesman, *The Gulf and the West*, Boulder, Westview, 1989; the DMS computerised data base on foreign military markets for the sections covering the Middle East and Africa; Shlomo Gazit and Zeev Eytan, *The Middle East Military Balance*, 1988-1989, Boulder, Westview Press, 1990; The 'International Navies' issue of *Proceedings*, Annapolis, Naval Institute Press, March 1990, pp. 138-143; Tony Bank editor, 'JDW Country Survey: The Gulf States', *Jane's Defence Weekly*, 31 March 1990, pp. 583-602; Arms Control and Disarmament Agency, *World Military Expenditures and Arms Transfers*, 1988, Washington, GPO, 1989. The data also draw on Joseph M. Kelly, 'And in this Corner: The Strategic Balance in the Northern Gulf', unpublished research paper by a student at

Georgetown University, May 1990; p. 6 and James Bruce and Paul Beaver, 'Latest Arab Force Levels Operating in the Gulf', *Jane's Defence Weekly*, 12 December 1987, pp. 1360-1363. Data on ethnic and religious divisions are taken from the CIA, *World Factbook*, 1990; and the *Middle East Review*, 1985 and 1988, World of Information, Saffron Walden, England, 1988. For additional background see the author's *The Gulf and the Search for Strategic Stability*, and Thomas L. McNaugher's 'Arms and Allies on the Arabian Peninsula', *Orbis*, Volume 28, No. 3, Fall, 1984, pp. 486-526.

[7] Figures based upon data provided in Richard F. Grimmett, 'Trends in Conventional Arms Transfers to the Third World by Major Supplier, 1982-1989', Congressional Research Service, Report 90-298F, 19 June 1990, pp. CRS-46 to CRS-47.

[8] It is important that the reader understand that there is no consistency in the statistical data provided on the Middle East. The author has used a wide range of sources throughout this article, and has often had to make his own estimates. The data on the GCC countries are, however, particularly uncertain, and the author has often had to change sources to get consistent or comparable data on a given point. This leads to the use of contradictory data for the same measurement, often because of differences in definition or time of estimate, but sometimes simply because accurate data are not available. The reader should be aware that such statistical information is better than no information, but must be regarded as approximate and should be checked with at least three to four different sources before being used for specialised analytic purposes.

[9] Estimates of the strength of this force often disagree in detail. It seems they have about 7000 men and to include the 20th Saudi Mechanised brigade, the 5th Kuwaiti mechanised regiment, an infantry battalion or two companies from Bahrain, a light mechanised company from Qatar, the 1st Infantry Battalion and small artillery elements from the UAE, and an infantry company or battalion from Oman. This force has some integral air defence capability, and Kuwait, Oman, Saudi Arabia, and the UAE have committed airlift to give the force some 'rapid deployment' capability.

[10] These estimates are made by the author, and are based on working data from Wharton, the EIU, and US Department of Energy. Such estimates differ sharply according to source.

[11] The military data in this section are based primarily on interviews in the region, London, and Washington; press sources and computerised defence data bases, and the relevant country chapters of IISS, *Military Balance*, 1989-1990, London, Brassey's (UK), 1989; Anthony H. Cordesman, *The Gulf and the West*, Boulder, Westview, 1989; the DMS computerised data base on foreign military markets for the sections covering the Middle East and Africa; Shlomo Gazit and Zeev Eytan, *The Middle East Military Balance*, 1988-1989, Boulder, Westview Press, 1990; The 'International Navies' issue of *Proceedings*, Annapolis, Naval Institute Press, March 1990, pp. 138-143; Tony Bank editor, JDW Country Survey: The Gulf States, *Jane's Defence Weekly*, 31 March 1990, pp. 583-602; Arms Control and Disarmament Agency, *World Military Expenditures and Arms Transfers*, 1989, Washington, GPO, 1989. The data also draw on James Bruce and Paul Beaver, Latest Arab Force Levels Operating in the Gulf, *Jane's Defense Weekly*, 12 December 1987, pp. 1360-1363. Data on ethnic and religious divisions are taken from the CIA, *World Factbook*, 1990; and the *Middle East Review*, 1985 and 1988, World of Information, Saffron Walden, England, 1988. For additional background see the author's *The Gulf and the Search for Strategic Stability*, and Thomas L. McNaugher's 'Arms and Allies on the Arabian Peninsula', *Orbis*, Volume 28, No. 3, Fall, 1984, pp. 486-526.

[12] In singling out the US, the author does not mean to underestimate the value of British and French forces, or collective action by the West. No other Western or Free World state can, however, project enough power or deal with the military and technical risks involved.

SLOVO: a Journal of Contemporary Soviet & East European Affairs

An interdisciplinary journal, gathering the best work of a wide range of scholars, young academics and postgraduates to study the development of the USSR and Eastern Europe

SUBSCRIPTION details from:

SLOVO

SSEES,
University of London
Senate House
Malet Street
London WC1E 7HU
Britain

Recent Articles:

The Past in Contemporary Romania - DENNIS DELETANT

The Perestroika of History in the Soviet Union - JUDITH SHAPIRO

Civil Soviety and the Polish Opposition - MAREK MATRASZEK

The Private Sector and Policy Change in the Soviet Union - TERRY COX

Dismantling a Patronage State - ZYGMUND BAUMAN

The Gay Community in the USSR - JIM RIORDAN

The United States and the Persian Gulf in the Bush Administration

PROFESSOR BERNARD REICH AND
MAJOR STEPHEN H. GOTOWICKI, USA

Professor Bernard Reich is Chairman of the Department of Political Science at George Washington University in Washington, D.C. He is the author of various works on United States policy in the Middle East and on Middle East politics.

Major Stephen H. Gotowicki is a United States Army Middle East Foreign Area Officer currently serving as a Southwest Asia analyst in the Department of Defense and a PhD Candidate in Political Science at George Washington University.

The views expressed in this article are those of the authors and do not necessarily reflect the official policy or position of the United States Army, the Department of Defense or the United States Government.

The United States is a relative newcomer to the Persian Gulf sector of the Middle East (sometimes referred to as South-west Asia) and has been an active participant in Gulf affairs only in recent decades, primarily since the British withdrawal East of Suez. During this time the United States' perception of its interests, and the policies it has adopted in support of those interests, has varied considerably. Several overriding factors have dominated the United States' approach to the Persian Gulf since the Second World War: concern about possible Soviet domination of the region; access to oil; the stability and security of friendly states and moderate regimes; the relationship of all such factors to other concerns in the broader Middle East region (i.e., the Arab-Israeli conflict); and, more recently, concern over weapons proliferation. The policies and priorities developed in response to these interests and concerns have varied with each administration. There has been a desire to ensure the maintenance of open sea lanes for transporting oil and the development of political and economic co-operation with the Arab world. The US has also sought to limit regional conflicts (such as the Iran-Iraq War) that might affect other interests. Another closely linked concern has been the preservation of an independent and secure Israel. Although there has been widespread agreement on these interests, there has been little agreement on their relative priority.[1]

POLICY DEVELOPMENT

Until the British Government announced, in the late 1960s, that it would withdraw its forces from the Persian Gulf by the end of 1971, the British special relationship with the Gulf states and the British presence in that sector served, to a significant extent, as a proxy for the United States.[2] The British generally represented United States interests and created and fostered conditions of calm and stability. The era of British prominence in the Gulf coincided with a period in which the United States did not take a major part in the political/security affairs of the sector, and was active primarily in unofficial, non-political and non-strategic spheres that might best be described as philanthropic, missionary, humanitarian, educational, cultural, and commercial in nature.

By the time Britain had decided to withdraw its forces from east of Suez, the United States posture in the Gulf had evolved considerably from the very limited individual and commercial dealings that had characterised its involvement in the nineteenth and early twentieth century. Commercial activity involving oil had become the main US concern. Although the Gulf sector was not seen as vital to the United States, there was a growing realisation that it was important to United States' interests. This development and perceptions of a potential Soviet threat, combined with the British withdrawal to produce a re-evaluation of United States' policy and the assumption of new commitments and obligations for the area. The British withdrawal seemed to create a vacuum in a sector of importance at a time when Soviet influence appeared to be growing in the broader Middle Eastern region, in such places as Egypt, Iraq and South Yemen. This, combined with Soviet activities elsewhere and a declining American desire to serve as the world's policeman, led to the promulgation of what later became known as the Nixon Doctrine:

> We shall provide a shield if a nuclear power threatens the freedom of a nation allied with us . . . we shall furnish military and economic assistance when requested in accordance with our treaty commitments. But we shall look to the nation directly threatened to assume the primary responsibility of providing the manpower for its own defense.[3]

The adoption of the Nixon Doctrine led to a Persian Gulf policy which sought to create and support surrogates to ensure regional stability. The 'two-pillar policy' focusing on Iran and Saudi Arabia was conceived in part as a response to a potential threat from the Soviet Union and its allies. Although the Nixon Doctrine was not designated specifically for the Middle East, it was applied to the Gulf sector and authorised the Shah of Iran a virtually blank cheque for the acquisition of US military equipment to build Iran's strength and capability, to help ensure stability and security in the Gulf. The Shah of Iran was particularly pleased with this concept since it comported well with his view that Iran could and should play the dominant role in the Persian Gulf after Britain's withdrawal, and that there was no power vacuum because of Iran's presence and capability. Saudi Arabia moved more circumspectly at the outset and was ill-suited to the role as a pillar of United States policy, given its military capability and policy inclination.

The policy of the United States as delineated by the Nixon Doctrine was carried into the Ford administration and the early days of the Carter tenure, during which attention initially focused on the Arab-Israeli conflict and its resolution.[4] Carter's attention shifted to the Gulf sector with the Iranian revolution, the overthrow of the Shah, the taking of American hostages, and the Soviet invasion of Afghanistan. Taken together, these changes undermined the concepts underlying the twin pillar policy and the Nixon Doctrine, and raised new concerns about Soviet intentions and policies. At the same time, Middle Eastern oil was becoming more important, both as a natural resource and a source of Western financial strength. Regional tensions and instability seemed to be growing.

The Soviet invasion of Afghanistan in December 1979 dramatically altered American thinking and policy because it involved direct Soviet military action. The Soviet move raised questions not only about Afghanistan, but also about the potential threat to the Persian Gulf, as well as the Arab-Israeli sector. The invasion convinced President Jimmy Carter that the Soviet Union was a hostile, rather than a benign, power that sought regional domination and whose threatening posture had to be countered. The United States' reaction to the altered regional situation developed into the Carter Doctrine. It asserted that the Gulf was vital to the United States and its allies, and that all action necessary, including military force, would be utilised to protect that interest from a Soviet threat. In his State of the Union Address to the Congress on 23 January 1980, Carter said the Soviet move into Afghanistan threatened a region of great strategic importance which contained more than two thirds of the world's exportable oil. The President outlined the

United States' response (dubbed the Carter Doctrine) in these terms:

> Let our position be absolutely clear: An attempt by any outside force to gain control of the Persian Gulf region will be regarded as an assault on the vital interests of the United States of America, and such an assault will be repelled by any means necessary, including military force.[5]

To Carter, the Soviet invasion of Afghanistan represented but one more step in a broader Soviet move toward the Persian Gulf. The Iranian revolution and the hostage crisis assisted the USSR in achievement of this goal by reducing American influence in the area, and by distracting the administration from the immediate threat posed by the USSR to American interests in the region. The problem complicating implementation of the doctrine, however, was operational: the United States lacked the capacity to put it into practice effectively.

The Carter Doctrine was accompanied by the establishment of the Rapid Deployment Joint Task Force (RDJTF) at MacDill Air Force Base in Florida on 1 March 1980. This was a permanent military force designed to deploy rapidly into the region to respond to contingencies threatening US interests, specifically threats to Persian Gulf oil. The RDJTF evolved from a concept originally called the Rapid Deployment Force (RDF). The RDF had been in the planning stages since 1977, when Presidential Directive 18 (PD-18) had called for the formation of a 'deployment force of light divisions with strategic mobility.'[6] At its inception, the RDJTF (commonly referred to as the Rapid Deployment Force) was frequently criticised as a 'paper tiger', lacking the force structure and firepower to engage projected Soviet force deployments in the region effectively, and without sufficient strategic mobility. The RDJTF would later become the United States Central Command (CENTCOM) during the Reagan Administration.

When Ronald Reagan became President in 1980, he maintained Carter's emphasis on the Persian Gulf-Arabian Peninsula sector, but his approach to the Middle East and its problems derived from a different set of assumptions. The Reagan Administration held a broader and more negative view of the Soviet challenge worldwide (including the concept of an 'evil empire'). Reagan believed that the fundamental threat to peace and stability in the region was not from the Arab-Israeli conflict (especially since Egypt and Israel were moving toward implementation of the Egypt-Israel Peace Treaty as scheduled) but the Soviet Union and its policies. Unlike Carter, he assumed the main focus of American interest in the Middle East to be in the Persian Gulf sector. The Soviet invasion of Afghanistan represented a direct threat to the security of the Gulf. Reagan's policy toward Afghanistan maintained that while the United States would employ no military force (given, in part, that it was unable to secure the support of its allies), it would nonetheless provide aid to the Afghan rebels to pressure the Soviet Union to withdraw its forces.

The Reagan Administration introduced the concept of 'strategic consensus', which called for the regional states, from Pakistan to Egypt, to co-operate with Washington and amongst themselves to oppose the common Soviet threat. The challenge for the Reagan Administration was to convince the regional states that the primary threat to their security came from the Soviet Union. Strategic consensus required access and a regional network of support facilities for US military forces. A principal incentive for implementation of the strategic consensus concept was to be the expansion of US arms sales to co-operative countries. For this purpose the Reagan Administration supported the sale of 60 F-15 and 5 AWACs aircraft to Saudi Arabia. Except for Israel, none of the regional states embraced the concept. Regional and domestic concerns were perceived by them as greater threats than those from the Soviet Union.

In January 1983, the RDJTF formally became CENTCOM. CENTCOM was organised as a unified command with a broad and continuing mission focused on an area of responsibility (AOR) that includes the Northern Tier from Iraq to Pakistan, the Arabian Peninsula, Egypt, Jordan, and the Horn of Africa including Kenya and Sudan. CENTCOM has responsibility for all military activities and crisis military operations within its AOR. Major forces available to CENTCOM to respond to regional contingencies include five Army divisions and two separate Army brigades; one Marine Expeditionary Force (comprising a Marine division and an air wing) and a Marine Expeditionary brigade; 21 Air Force tactical fighter squadrons; three carrier battle groups and one surface action group; B-52 squadrons; and five squadrons of maritime patrol aircraft.[7] The availability of these forces remains dependent on the absence of a concurrent crisis in another area of the world as most of these units are earmarked for multiple contingencies.

The Reagan Administration was also concerned by the negative effects of the Iran-Iraq War and it adopted the view that US interests in the region would not be served by a decisive victory by one side or the other. A victory by Iraq might encourage Soviet military intervention into Iran. A victory by Iran would risk the spread of Iranian Islamic fundamentalism into the Gulf and the Arabian Peninsula. As the Iran-Iraq War expanded into the Gulf and attacks against non-belligerent shipping increased in 1987, the US agreed to the reflagging of Kuwaiti oil tankers and provided them with US naval protection in Operation EARNEST WILL. Force levels of the Middle East Force (MIDEASTFOR) which has been operating in the Persian Gulf routinely since the 1940s, with a flag ship and four surface combatants, were substantially increased in size with the deployment of the Joint Task Force Middle East (JTFME) in support of EARNEST WILL. At the height of the protection action, as many as 40 US naval vessels were operating in the Persian Gulf and the Arabian Sea.[8]

The last years of the Reagan Administration and the advent of the Bush Administration coincided with the accession to and consolidation of power in the Soviet Union of Mikhail Gorbachev. This, in turn, led to a modification of American perceptions of the evil empire and, later, of the Cold War. The Bush Administration began its tenure in office as developments in the region and world moved in previously unexpected directions. These major developments included the Soviet withdrawal from Afghanistan; a cease-fire in the Iran-Iraq War; the collapse of the Soviet bloc in Eastern Europe; developing Soviet internal political and economic transformation; an assessment of diminished Soviet military capability to threaten the South-west Asia region; and increasing US and allied dependence on Persian Gulf oil. These and related developments led the Bush Administration to reassess its perspectives of the Gulf and of related Middle Eastern issues.

Oil remains an element of United States strategic/political concern in the region, and as United States oil dependency grows, so does the significance of the Persian Gulf. The United States has had a gradual increase in oil and energy consumption in recent years and with it have come increases in net oil imports. Because of declining American reserves and production, as well as a price that has not been sufficiently high to promote alternative energy sources and the development of new oil finds in the United States, there is a growing need to import oil from abroad. The increasing dependence on imported oil necessarily links the United States to an increasing requirement for Middle Eastern (i.e., essentially Persian Gulf) oil since this is where most of the world's oil reserves, excess production capacity, and available oil for export are located. Some estimates suggest that in the coming decade the increased dependence of the United States on imported oil will grow to between 50-60 per cent of its total oil consumption and the Gulf will become the primary source for that oil. The United States requires 'secure stable sources of energy supply'. Thus, the United States has 'a stake in the stability of the Persian Gulf and the moderation of Gulf oil policies over the long term'.[9]

The stability of the moderate regional states has been a concern of previous administrations in the light of Islamic fundamentalism, expatriate Palestinians, terrorism and the minority ruling élites in some of the region's states. With a cease-fire in the Iran-Iraq War, the Bush Administration has been concerned with the potential for instability in the region created by Iran and Iraq, the sector's most dominant powers. Iraq now has the largest and most battle-experienced military force in the Arab world and has the capability to create significant tensions in the region. Iran, although militarily defeated in the latter months of the Iran-Iraq War, continues to possess the capability to disrupt maritime traffic in the Persian Gulf, and to destabilise regional states through its support of terrorism or the export of its Islamic revolution. The Gulf Co-operation Council (GCC) is not strong enough to confront either Iran or Iraq effectively without external assistance.

Despite *perestroika* and *glasnost*, the Bush Administration has also been concerned about Soviet diplomatic advances in the region. The Soviet Union maintains embassies in four of the six GCC countries: Kuwait, Oman, Qatar, and the United Arab Emirates, and there have been growing contacts with Saudi Arabia despite the absence of formal diplomatic links. While increasing its diplomatic relationships with the moderate Arab states, Moscow continues to maintain a military presence and influence in Ethiopia, Libya, Iraq, Syria, and South and North Yemen. In June 1989, the Soviet Union formalised its developing relationship with Iran during the Moscow visit of Ali Akbar Rafsanjani, then Speaker of Iran's parliament. During Rafsanjani's visit, formal economic and military agreements were signed between the two countries.[10] The military agreement was undertaken by the Soviet Union with 'the explicit understanding that this will not injure the security of third countries nor make for a change in the power balance in the region'.[11]

The Bush Administration's enunciated interests in the Persian Gulf sector, in light of these factors, include the security of the oil and its free passage out of the Gulf, the security and stability of friendly regional states, and because of uncertainty concerning Soviet intentions, there remains the need (generally unstated) to contain Soviet advances. These interests do not deviate substantially from those of earlier administrations, but US goals appear to reflect the changed circumstances in the region and beyond. Stated goals include maintaining stability in the region; preventing either Iran or Iraq from dominating the region; preventing the spread of radical Islamic fundamentalism; and reducing the threat of terrorism from and in the region.

DIPLOMATIC STRATEGY

The Bush Administration has continued to rely on both diplomatic and military approaches in its Gulf strategy. The Gulf sector poses a number of inter-related policy issues in the political-military arena for the United States. These tend to revolve around America's past and future relationship with Iran and Iraq and their roles and activities in the region.

Iraq-US relations remain a dilemma. Iraq's poor human rights record, American concerns about its development of weapons of mass destruction, and its use of chemical warfare weapons during the war with Iran and against dissident Iraqi Kurds have contributed to existing problems. These have been further heightened by the execution of Farzad Bazoft, an Iranian-born journalist living in Great Britain, accused of spying; Iraq's attempt to acquire krytons (nuclear trigger devices);[12] and Saddam Hussein's threats to retaliate with chemical weapons against an Israeli strike on Iraq. Baghdad's drive to acquire weapons of mass destruction and other sophisticated systems has become a particularly sensitive issue. Iraq is believed to be one of the largest producers of chemical warfare agents in the Third World and far less dependent on foreign assistance in its chemical weapons programme than any of the other regional states. It could soon have a largely indigenous chemical warfare production capability.[13] Iraq also has a capable arsenal of short range ballistic missiles with its 650 km *Al Hussein*, a locally modified Soviet SCUD-B, the 900 km *Al Abbas*, and the recently claimed 2,000 km *Al Tamuz*.[14] All of these systems currently use conventional explosive warheads and have poor accuracy. This gives them only limited military utility, their optimum use being as 'citybusters'. Iraq demonstrated few reservations in using either its chemical weapons or ballistic missiles during the Iran-Iraq War. Added to these concerns is Iraq's potential nuclear development programme. Although Iraq is a signatory to the non-proliferation treaty and allows International Atomic Energy Agency safeguard inspections of its nuclear facilities, Washington is increasingly concerned that Iraq may seek to develop a nuclear weapon in the future. The spring of 1990 US/UK seizure of krytons destined for Iraq heightened this concern.

Bush Administration policy has been to try to alter Iraq's behaviour and to seek to influence Iraq to move in a more positive direction rather than to penalise it:

'Our policy toward Iraq has been to attempt to develop gradually a mutual beneficial relationship with Iraq in order to strengthen positive trends in Iraq's foreign and domestic policies.'[15]

On 12 April, a delegation of United States Senators lead by Robert Dole visited Iraq to talk to Saddam Hussein and lessen the tension between the two countries. Reflecting the Administration's approach, Senator Dole said 'there might be a chance to bring this guy around'.[16]

The US-Iran relationship revolves around a range of issues that include the restoration of diplomatic and other relations, the Iranian threat to regional (and other) states, Iranian support of international terrorism, and the Iranian role in the continued captivity of American hostages in Lebanon. The adversarial role of the United States during the later stages of the Iran-Iraq War remains a factor in poor relations. To limit Iran's ability to pursue the Iran-Iraq War, the United States initiated Operation STAUNCH with its allies to embargo the flow of weapons to Iran. These sanctions were to continue in force until Iran had accepted UN resolution 598 and renounced terrorism as a state policy. The sanctions remain in place and Iran sees these continued war-related sanctions as evidence of US hostility toward Iran.

The US has little leverage on Iran and there is little prospect for improved relations in the near term. The Bush Administration appears to have accepted that it can do little but wait until the Iranians decide that the time is right to re-establish relations with

Washington. It is still widely assumed that Iran's need for Western technology and investment will eventually drive it toward closer relations with the West. The Bush Administration seeks to contain Iran's Islamic fundamentalism to keep it from spreading to the Arabian Peninsula, and to convince Iran to end its support of international terrorism. It remains a longstanding and public policy that the United States government is prepared to engage in a dialogue with any authorised representative of Iran to discuss the issues that divide the two governments with no pre-conditions. Improved relations, however, are conditional on Iran stopping its support for terrorism and on using its influence to bring about the release of the US hostages held by pro-Iranian groups in Lebanon. On 15 August 1989, President Bush said:

> ... we don't have to be hostile with Iran for the rest of our lives. We've had a good relationship with them in the past. They are of strategic importance. They would be welcome back into the family of law-abiding, non-terrorist-sponsoring nations.[17]

In Washington's view, US interests would best be served by a strong, prosperous, non-aligned Iran. The emerging Iranian-Soviet relationship works against this prospect.

The members of the GCC (Saudi Arabia, Kuwait, Qatar, Bahrain, Oman and the United Arab Emirates) generally have positive relations with the United States. These were enhanced by the United States' role during the later stages of the Iran-Iraq War and particularly by the United States' reflagging of Kuwaiti ships and actions to assure freedom of navigation in the Gulf. Continued expansion of the relationship remains a goal of the United States as it seeks to assure the security of these states, their stability, and the flow of oil from the region to the United States and its allies. Nevertheless, the Gulf states will probably continue to be reticent concerning basing and access for US forces.

At the international level, Washington has been seeking to expand responsibility for the security of the region. It has strongly supported United Nation's peacekeeping activities in the region. Another initiative toward this end has been what Secretary Baker refers to as creative responsibility-sharing. This concept is based on the success of allied co-operation in EARNEST WILL which included British, French, Italian, and Dutch naval forces as well as American. Responsibility-sharing is a broader concept than burden sharing and calls for a division of responsibility for a wider range of security needs between America's friends and alliance partners.

> We must learn to pool our various strengths. Countries having different capabilities, experiences, and know-how can lend each of these capabilities, experiences, and know-how toward meeting the security challenges which we together face.[18]

Secretary Baker specifically related this concept of responsibility-sharing to protection of vital shipping lanes in the Persian Gulf, co-ordinated responses to terrorism and to building barriers to halt the proliferation of weapons of mass destruction.

MILITARY STRATEGY

General H. Norman Schwarzkopf, Commander of CENTCOM, in testimony before the Senate Armed Services Committee, on 8 February 1990 outlined a US peacetime military strategy that encompasses 'three pillars': security assistance, US presence, and combined exercises.[19] Underlying these three pillars is the continuing US efforts to increase access for its military forces in the area. Security assistance is the transfer of arms, services, training and provision of economic assistance to strengthen the capabilities of friendly governments. Security assistance is also beneficial to enhance bilateral relations, increase access for US training and support personnel, and to demonstrate US resolve and determination to support friendly states. The countries of the Persian Gulf region have generally been cash customers for US weapons systems for which they express a preference. However, in recent years, US Congressional refusals to sell weapons to the Gulf countries has reduced their confidence in US reliability as an ally and forced them to turn to other sources such as Great Britain, France, Eastern Europe, and the Soviet Union. Congressional inhibitions seem to be changing. In July 1988 Congress approved the sale of 40 F/A-18 fighters and 300 Maverick air-to-surface missiles to Kuwait worth $1.9 bn.[20] It had previously agreed to sell F-16 fighters to Bahrain. Systems under consideration in 1989-1990 include 40 F/A-18 fighter aircraft for the United Arab Emirates,[21] 200 M-1A2 tanks for Kuwait and 315 M-1A2 tanks (valued at $3 billion) for Saudi Arabia.[22] The Saudis are also expected to seek replacements for their aging fleet of 110 F-5 fighter aircraft in the near future and may ask the US to sell them F/A-18s or F-16s.[23]

With no permanently assigned forces based in the region, US presence is limited to the JTFME. Since the Iran-Iraq cease-fire, the US has been quietly reducing the naval forces in the JTFME in the Persian Gulf to the levels of the pre-1987 Middle East Force. This force will remain in the area as a symbol of America's continued commitment to the region and to support deployment of larger US forces into the area as necessary. As for exercises, CENTCOM will continue to sponsor and conduct major combined exercises with the countries of the region. Exercise BRIGHT STAR is one such example. As General Schwarzkopf told the Committee, these exercises foster increased cooperation, interoperability, and demonstrate US resolve and commitment to the host country. They also bolster American access and allow US combat forces to train in the unique terrain of the region.

In addressing wartime military strategy, the Department of Defence has undertaken a major shift in its approach to Southwest Asia. This is reportedly reflected in the instructions contained in the Defence Planning Guidance (DPG), a classified publication which provides strategic planning guidance to the military services and the Joint Staff for the period 1992-1997.[24] The DPG directed that contingency planning be focused away from a possible Soviet invasion of Iran or the Arabian Peninsula to defence of the Middle Eastern oil fields from a range of regional threats. Planning would continue to consider the contingency of a Soviet attack, but at a lower priority. General Schwarzkopf told the Senate Armed Services Committee that he had directed his planners to put the contingency plans for facing a Soviet invasion onto the back burner. His primary planning focus in the future was the defence of the Peninsula's oil fields and to respond to inter-state conflicts, such as the Iran-Iraq War, which could spill over into the Peninsula. This reorientation in Department of Defense thinking has developed over several years and is based in great part on assessments of Soviet military failures in Afghanistan. In attacking Iran, the Soviets would face terrain as difficult as Afghanistan but in an area twice as large with three times the population. Other disincentives for the Soviet Union would probably be the loss of the political momentum it has achieved with the moderate Arab regimes in the region; a setback in its improving relations with the United States and Western Europe; and the high probability of an increased US military presence in the area, if not a direct US military response to the Soviet invasion. Such a Soviet attack would incur great cost for little benefit.

Despite these disincentives, Soviet military operations in the region cannot be totally discounted. The Soviets maintain up to 30 divisions in its Southern Theatre of Military Operations (STVD) in the North Caucasus, Transcaucasus, and Turkestan military districts.[25] Soviet Backfire bombers staging from bases in the South-Central Soviet Union could threaten oil facilities in the Gulf, and US naval forces in the Gulf and Arabian Sea.[26] In the naval sphere, the Soviet Indian Ocean Squadron (SOVINDRON) operates in the Arabian and Red Seas from anchorages off the island of Socotra, and facilities in Aden, South Yemen and the Dahlak Archipelago of Ethiopia. SOVINDRON strength routinely averages 12-17 ships, which generally includes only 2-3 surface combatants.[27] SOVINDRON is essentially no match for the US and Western naval forces steaming in the area; it is faced with shortfalls in air defence, logistics support, and anti-submarine warfare capability.[28] Thus, the Soviet naval presence in the region would seem to imply that Moscow is either unwilling or unable to challenge Western naval supremacy in this sector.

In addressing a regional threat, CENTCOM must focus its attentions on Iran and Iraq. The populations of both Iran and Iraq are seen as war-weary and unlikely, in the near term, to support aggressive adventures. Nonetheless, CENTCOM must plan against their capabilities. Iran's military, decimated by Iraq in the last months of the war, will be incapable of a major regional ground offensive for some years to come, although its naval and air forces will provide it with sufficient capabilities to pose a threat to maritime traffic in the Persian Gulf. This threat is enhanced by its possession of Chinese Silkworm missile which it has deployed abreast of the Strait of Hormuz in permanent sites such as Kuhestak.[29] Iran's possession of, and willingness to use, its chemical warfare and ballistic missile capabilities must also be included in any assessment of potential regional threats. Iraq's military strength coupled with its former hegemonic designs make it a potential threat in the region as well as to US interests. With the Gulf War cease-fire, Iraq is freer to pursue its regional objectives, but it still needs to repair its economy, repay at least part of its massive war debt, and rebuild its war-damaged cities, so it is seen as unlikely to want to antagonise its Arab neighbours in the near future.

PROSPECTS

The future of the United States' approach to the Persian Gulf as well as other policy areas will depend to a significant degree on its assessment of the Soviet Union and its intentions. The Bush Administration has already undergone a substantial metamorphosis on this question although it does not seem to have reached its final conclusion concerning the nature and intent of Soviet policy in the Middle East as elsewhere. Noteworthy is the absence in most recent statements and policy surveys of references to the Soviet Union as a threat in the South-west Asia sector, although concern about the continued Soviet role, if not presence, in Afghanistan remains, as does a lingering suspicion of Soviet motivation and intent. Nevertheless, the focus of policy concern seems to be associated more with regional developments and the need for resources than with a Soviet military threat.

In addressing a military strategy for South-west Asia without a Soviet military threat, the US faces some crucial problems. It must convince the regional states to co-operate in contingency planning and increased basing and access for US forces. Washington failed to do this with 'strategic consensus' and probably has less potential to accomplish it with only local threats on the horizon in the near term. Because of the compact geography of the region and the heightened military readiness of Iraq, Israel, Syria and, to a lesser degree, Iran, warning of an impending attack in the region might be too short for the US to respond adequately.[30] This situation is complicated by the low readiness of Saudi Arabia and the other GCC states, the heavily armoured threat forces in the region and the hesitance of regional states to request or allow deployment of US combat forces until attacked.[31] Under these conditions, the capability of the United States to transport sufficient heavy forces quickly some 6,500 to 8,000 nm by air, or nearly 12,000 nm by sea,[32] to oppose a major regional power effectively, is problematic.

Domestic considerations will also serve to limit America's strategy in the Persian Gulf. The mounting US government debt and Congressional calls for a 'peace dividend' as a consequence of the 'end of the cold war', suggest cuts in the US force structures, overseas deployments and major improvements to strategic mobility. There is significant discussion of shrinking the force and cancelling, scaling back or stretching out major weapons programmes. If the suggestions of former Secretary of the Navy John F. Lehman Jr. strike a chord in Congress, critical worldwide naval deployments could be reduced. In testimony before the House Armed Services Committee on 27 March 1990, Lehman recommended that the Navy reduce its operational tempo throughout the world. He proposed abandoning the six month deployment cycle for naval battle groups, mothballing older ships, and increasing reserve manning of vessels. The end result would be a fleet sufficient in the latest technologies and large enough to deter the Soviets, but with longer times to mobilise.[33] A reduced naval presence in the region would make it even more difficult to respond to fast developing crises in the Gulf.

America's interests and goals have changed little over the years, but the Bush strategy has changed to respond to the perceived contemporary realities in the region.[34] The Bush Administration has moved away from, but not totally abandoned, the Cold War focus on containing the Soviet Union and has begun to approach the Middle East and the Persian Gulf more on their own terms, than as a subset of the global East–West competition. To a great degree, it appears that the United States lacks a grand strategy for the region; policies are oriented bilaterally rather than regionally, and tend to be reactive rather than active. The Gulf balance of power centres around Iran and Iraq and the Bush Administration will continue to seek improved relations with both of these countries. Logically and fiscally, the Administration's initiatives on burden-sharing and Allied involvement in the region are appropriate to this approach. Nevertheless, several major problem areas remain: the anti-Islamic appearance of US policies in the region will hinder expansion of its influence;[35] the US orientation toward defending the status quo risks antagonising successor generations to the detriment of relations in the longer term; and US-Israeli relations, and progress in the Arab-Israeli peace process, will continue to influence its broader relations throughout the region.

The views and policies of the Bush Administration changed only with Iraq's invasion of Kuwait—an action that was not predicted and generated a policy that in many respects ran counter to the pre-invasion approach. The embargo and the deployment of forces to the Peninsula and the Gulf is in many respects quite different from the pre-invasion view of Saddam Hussein described in this article.

NOTES

[1] For further discussion see Bernard Reich, 'United States Interests in the Middle East' in Haim Shaked and Itamar Rabinovitch, Editors, *The Middle East*

and the United States: *Perceptions and Policies* Transaction Books, New Brunswick 1980, pp. 53-92.

[2] For further details of United States policy in the period prior to the British withdrawal see Bernard Reich, et. al., *The Persian Gulf* Research Analysis Corporation, McLean, Virginia, 1971.

[3] See 'Informal Remarks in Guam with Newsmen, 25 July 1969' in *Public Papers of the Presidents*: *Richard M. Nixon* 1969, US Government Printing Office, Washington, D.C., 1970, p. 359; and 'Annual Foreign Policy Report, 18 February 1970', in *Public Papers of the Presidents*: *Richard M. Nixon* 1970, pp. 118-19.

[4] See Bernard Reich, 'United States Middle East Policy in the Carter and Reagan Administrations', *Australian Outlook* 38, August 1984, pp. 72-80; Bernard Reich and Alexander J. Bennett, 'Soviet Policy and American Response in the Middle East', *Journal of East and West Studies* 13 (Fall-Winter 1984) pp. 79–114; Bernard Reich, 'United States Middle East Policy in the Carter and Reagan Administrations', *Middle East Review* 17, (Winter 1984/1985), pp. 12-23, 60-61; and Bernard Reich, 'The United States and the Middle East', in *The Political Economy of the Middle East*, US Congress, Joint Economic Committee, 1980, pp. 373-399.

[5] State of the Union Message by President Carter, 23 January 1980, in *Department of State Bulletin*, February 1980, page B (special insert).

[6] Zbigniew Brzezinski, *Power and Principle*: *Memoirs of the National Security Adviser* 1977-1981, Farrar, Straus, Giroux, New York, 1983, p. 177.

[7] See Department of Defence, *Soviet Military Power*: *Prospects for Change* 1989, US Government Printing Office, Washington DC, 1989, p. 122.

[8] Assistant Secretary of State for Near Eastern and South Asian Affairs Richard W. Murphy interview on NBC-TV's 'Meet the Press' on 23 August 1987 in *Department of State Bulletin*, October 1987, pp. 44-45.

[9] Statement of Assistant Secretary of State for Near Eastern and South Asian Affairs John H. Kelly before the Subcommittee on Europe and the Middle East of the House Committee on Foreign Affairs, 28 February 1990. 'Toward Stability in the Middle East and South-west Asia', *Current Policy* No. 1259, Department of State, March 1990, p. 3.

[10] USSR Ministry of the Foreign Affairs, 'The Foreign Policy and Diplomatic Activity of the USSR (April 1985-October 1989)', *International Affairs* January 1990, p. 93.

[11] *Ibid*.

[12] On 8 May 1990 Saddam Hussein asserted that Iraq had acquired a secret electronic device that could detonate a nuclear bomb and it was able to make the detonators itself. See Paul Lewis, 'Iraq Says It Made an Atom 'Trigger'', *New York Times*, 9 May 1990.

[13] See W. Seth Carus, *The Genie Unleashed*: *Iraq's Chemical and Biological Weapons Program* The Washington Institute for Near East Policy, Washington, D.C., 1989 [Policy Papers Number 14]; Robert Pear, 'Iraq Can Deliver, US Chemical Arms Experts Say', *New York Times*, 3 April 1990; and Michael R. Gordon, 'Greater Threats From Lesser Powers', *New York Times*, 8 April 1990, p. 1.

[14] For details of Iraq's (and Iran's) missile capability see Martin S. Navias, 'Ballistic Missile Proliferation in the Middle East', *Survival* Volume 31, No. 3 (May/June 1989), pp. 225-239; and Thomas G. Mahnken and Timothy D. Hoyt, 'Missile Proliferation and American Interests', *SAIS Review* Volume 10, No. 1 (Winter/Spring 1990), pp. 101-116.

[15] Statement of Assistant Secretary of State for Near Eastern and South Asian Affairs John H. Kelly before the Subcommittee on Europe and the Near East of the House Foreign Affairs Committee, 26 April 1990, 'US Relations With Iraq', *Current Policy* No. 1273, Department of State, May 1990, p. 2.

[16] See Patrick E. Tyler, 'US Working to Lessen Tension With Iraq: Antagonism Could Add to Mideast Instability, White House Decides', *Washington Post* 23 April 1990, p. 1.

[17] *Weekly Compilation of Presidential Documents*, 21 August 1989, p. 1243.

[18] Secretary Baker's address to the National Press Club, 8 June 1989, in *Department of State Bulletin*, August 1989, p. 57.

[19] Testimony of General H. Norman Schwarzkopf before the Senate Armed Services Committee, 8 February 1990. See elements of General Schwarzkopf's testimony in Patrick E. Tyler, 'Soviets Said to Be 'Pouring' Arms, Equipment Into Afghanistan', *Washington Post* 9 February 1990, p. A 21.

[20] See 'Global Briefs', *New York Times* 29 August 1988, p. D8.

[21] See *Wall Street Journal* 16 February 1989, p. A 16.

[22] See Richard A. Clarke, 'US Sale of Abram Tanks to Saudi Arabia', *Current Policy* No. 1235, United States Department of State, Bureau of Public Affairs, Washington, D.C., December 1989; 'Fact Sheet: Proposed Sale of the M1A2 Tank to Saudi Arabia', October 1989; 'Background Information: Sale of the Abrams Tank to Saudi Arabia', 12 October 1989. Written and published jointly by the Department of State and the Department of Defence.

[23] See David B. Ottaway, 'No New Aircraft Sales to Saudis Planned This Year, US Says', *Washington Post* 3 February 1989, p. A 4.

[24] See Patrick E. Tyler, 'US Finds Persian Gulf Threat Ebbs', *Washington Post*, 7 February 1990, p. A 1.; Michael R. Gordon, 'Discount Soviet Peril to Iran, Cheney Tells His Strategists', *New York Times* 7 February 1990; and Patrick E. Tyler, 'New Pentagon 'Guidance' Cites Soviet Threat in Third World', *Washington Post* 13 February 1990, p. A 1.

[25] *The Military Balance* 1988-1989, IISS, London, 1989, p. 42; and Department of Defence, *Soviet Military Power: An Assessment of the Threat* 1989, p. 121.

[26] *Soviet Military Power: An Assessment of the Threat* 1988, p. 119.

[27] *The Military Balance*, p. 42; and Department of Defence, *Soviet Military Power*: 1988, p. 119.

[28] Department of Defence, *Soviet Military Power*: 1989, p. 121.

[29] See. R.K. Ramazani, 'Gulf Peace and Security: Rethinking US Policy', *Middle East Insight*, (Fall 1988) pp. 3-8.

[30] See Amitav Acharya, *US Military Strategy in the Gulf*, Routledge, London, 1989, p. 125, 151.

[31] See Anthony H. Cordesman, *The Gulf and the West: Strategic Relations and Military Realities* Westview Press, Boulder, 1988, p. 141; and Amitav Acharya, *US Military Strategy*, p. 125.

[32] Mileage derived from Department of Defence, *Soviet Military Power*: 1988, p. 119.

[33] See Patrick E. Tyler, 'Navy Urged to Bring Ships Home to Cut Costs: Ex-Secretary Says US Should Rely More on Reservists, Hold the Line on Carriers, Battleships', *Washington Post* 28 March 1990.

[34] On the Bush and Baker 'vision' see Marjorie Williams, 'Jim Baker', *The Washington Post Magazine* 29 January 1989, pp. 17-22, 36-38; Robert S. Greenberger and Walter S. Mossberg, 'Despite His Successes, Baker's Critics Say He Lacks a Broad Strategy', *Wall Street Journal* 16 May 1990; and Maureen Dowd and Thomas L. Friedman, 'The Fabulous Bush & Baker Boys', *The New York Times Magazine* 6 May 1990, pp. 35-36, 58, 62-67.

[35] See James A. Bill, 'Populist Islam and US Foreign Policy', in *SAIS Review* (Winter/Spring 1989), pp. 25-39.

United Nations Peacekeeping After the Cold War

ROLAND PARIS

The author has studied at the Sorbonne and the University of Toronto, and is currently a graduate student of International Relations at Cambridge University.

Over the past four years, the United Nations (UN) has helped to resolve long-standing regional disputes in the Persian Gulf, Afghanistan, Namibia and Central America; and new UN operations may also be in the works for Cambodia and the Western Sahara. These peacekeeping successes, combined with the East-West *rapprochement* and the spirit of cooperation among the permanent members of the Security Council, have fueled hopes that the UN will play an increasingly useful role regulating and resolving international conflicts in the 1990s.

Whether the permanent members of the Security Council—Britain, France, China, the United States and the Soviet Union—will continue to use the instruments of the UN to settle regional disputes is, in this period of international flux and uncertainty, a matter for conjecture. The UN's current flurry of peacekeeping activity depends largely on the continued willingness of the Soviet Union to reduce the financial and political costs of supporting unstable regimes in the Third World, and to use the UN to fill the 'power vacuums' it leaves behind. This willingness depends, in turn, on the future of both Mikhail Gorbachev and the Soviet state. Furthermore, even if the demand for international peacekeeping remains high, regional organisations rather than the UN may soon be the preferred vehicle for peacekeeping; in particular, the Organisation of American States, the Arab League, the Organisation of African Unity, and the yet-uncrystallised defence arrangements for Europe.

This article does not attempt to make these sorts of predictions. Rather, it seeks the 'lessons' of the UN's peacekeeping past, and attempts to set out guidelines for efficacious peacekeeping in today's post-Cold War world, should the great powers continue to turn to the UN for help. The implicit question when we discuss UN peacekeeping in the 1990s is, I think, whether or not the

267

organisation will be able to tackle inveterate international disputes where: (a) the great powers' Cold-War divisions previously blocked any direct UN intervention, and (b) the dispute still acts as a source of international tension, despite the apparent end of the Cold War. Indeed, conflicts of interest between the great powers are likely to continue, particularly in areas where they have traditionally been at odds with each other. The UN's ability to cope with these conflicts may, more than any other factor, determine the extent of its peace and security role over the next decade.

A leading role for the UN will require success at a particular type of peacekeeping—what I shall call 'maximum' peacekeeping—which involves complex assignments in chronic international hot-spots where great-power interests are directly involved. 'Minimum' peacekeeping, on the other hand, involves relatively straightforward tasks in essentially local disputes, and is likely to continue no matter what happens on the world scene. Although every UN operation displays elements of both types of peacekeeping, a quick glance at the record reveals that most operations have been of the 'minimum' variety. There is a good reason for this: the best example of 'maximum' peacekeeping, the Congo operation in 1960-64, was so controversial that the UN never tried anything like it again, or at least not until last year's Namibia operation. By contrast, the most widely known UN peacekeeping operation—the multinational force in Cyprus, which has successfully separated the island's Greek and Turkish communities for almost 27 years—cannot help us very much if we mean to examine 'maximum' peacekeeping. Despite the fact that the Cyprus operation has generated a wealth of useful information about peacekeeping in general, the dispute is between two members of the same alliance—NATO—and therefore tells us very little about the interaction of UN peacekeeping and great-power rivalries. Consequently, this article will not attempt to summarise every UN operation since 1945, but will instead concentrate on the experiences which, I believe, can best guide us today: Suez in 1956 and the Congo in the early 1960s.

There is every reason to be excited about the UN's new potential in the security field. As former UN Under Secretary Brian Urquhart says, 'we are just getting in sight of the starting line on which we all believed we were in 1945'.[1] However, the record of UN peacekeeping suggests that our excitement should be tempered by a healthy awareness of the organisation's inherent limits and warns of the dangers, both to the organisation and to the great powers themselves, of overestimating the UN's capabilities.

THE IDEA OF PEACEKEEPING AND THE SUEZ CRISIS

The United Nations has been through periods of optimism and enthusiasm before. At the time of the Organisation's creation in 1945 there was widespread hope that the new system of collective security enshrined in the Charter would surmount the problems which had immobilised the League of Nations in the inter-war years. What followed is an old and familiar story. The Security Council, which is responsible for 'determining the existence of any threat to the peace'[2] and to call upon members of the UN to take action against intransigent states,[3] was premised on a continuation of amicable relations among the wartime allies (and China). All five were made permanent members of the Council and given a veto. Meanwhile, the war in Europe was over and Soviet-American relations were fast deteriorating;[4] their respective vetoes and the growing litany of mutual recriminations disabled the security system and have since prevented the Council from undertaking any bona fide 'enforcement actions'.[5]

The second spell of optimism followed Secretary-General Dag Hammarskjöld's 1956 attempt to carve a new niche for the UN in the field of international peace and security. Faced with a potentially explosive situation in the Middle East arising from the Anglo-French landing at Suez and the simultaneous Israeli advance in the Sinai, Hammarskjöld joined forces with Canada's Lester Pearson to devise the first full-fledged UN peacekeeping operation. The United Nations Emergency Force (UNEF)[6]—a lightly armed contingent of third-party, middle-power intermediaries—was sent to Egypt 'with the consent of the nations concerned' and empowered 'to secure and supervise the cessation of hostilities . . .'[7] The force was allowed to slip through the legal lacunae of the Charter: if what was written in the Charter rendered the operation of the collective security system impracticable in cold war conditions, then the only answer was to find some security role for the UN on the basis of what was *not* written there. Peacekeeping was not 'enforcement action' under Chapter VII; therefore the General Assembly, in lieu of the Security Council, could approve UNEF's formation.[8]

Before 1956, thinking about the security function of the United Nations was locked into the idea of enforcing the peace by military means.[9] The key concept was united opposition to 'aggression' and the archetypal 'aggressor' was Nazi Germany. But the rise of the Cold War changed international conditions in ways that the framers of the Charter could not have foreseen. First, as the two blocs entrenched their respective positions, the conflicts which did emerge were mainly low-intensity local affairs not involving the Superpowers directly, in which the assumption that a clear line could be drawn between 'aggressor' and 'defender' was often wrong. Second, once the Soviet-American relationship stabilised as an uneasy armed truce, the greatest danger to international peace was no longer a re-enactment of the Second World War—premeditated, aggressive *Blitzkrieg*. Rather, it was the destructiveness of the nuclear weapons themselves, and the risk that local turbulence outside the orbit of the Superpowers' private defence arrangements might lock the nuclear rivals into an escalating spiral of confrontation.

This was the thinking that underlay Hammarskjöld's doctrine of 'preventive diplomacy', and peacekeeping was its concrete result. Hammarskjöld's aim was to have the UN fill the gap between the Charter and traditional diplomacy—between the empirical realities of the Cold War and the normative vision of world government enshrined in the UN's constitution—by giving the organisation a more active role in the unstable, peripheral areas of the Cold War, primarily in the third world. The UN, he wrote,

> must aim at keeping newly arising conflicts outside the sphere of bloc differences . . . Preventive action in such cases must in the first place aim at filling the vacuum so that it will not provoke action from any of the major parties.[10]

'Preventive diplomacy' seemed to prove its worth during the Suez crisis. Britain and France needed an honourable excuse to withdraw their troops from Egypt after facing unexpected political opposition from the United States, and the arrival of UN forces provided a suitable pretext. The Americans wanted their NATO partners out of Egypt and were concerned by the Soviet Union's apparent intention to send 'volunteers' to fight alongside the Egyptians. And the Soviets, although opposed to the UN operation in principle, were willing to stand back as long as it led to the departure of foreign forces.[11] It was, in essence, a face-saving operation that seemed to please everyone, including the Egyptians and even the Israelis.[12] Combined with the success of a smaller UN observation mission in Lebanon two years later (the UN Observer Group in Lebanon, UNOGIL) UNEF fueled the idea that the organisation could make an important contribution to the preservation of world peace despite the failure of collective security. It also propelled Hammarskjöld to a level of influence and personal support never previously enjoyed by a UN secretary-general.[13] Buoyed by expressions of confidence in the UN, Hammarskjöld was soon to launch a new and ambitious peacekeeping mission in the former Belgian Congo. What followed was one of the principal international crises of the post-war period, which drew the Superpowers to the brink of confrontation and threatened to undo the United Nations itself.

THE CONGO CRISIS: PEACEKEEPING GONE WRONG

Shortly after the Congo achieved independence on 30 June 1960, pockets of Congolese soldiers began mutinying against their Belgian officers. The violence soon spread to bases throughout the country and to the capital, Léopoldville. Belgian troops were deployed from their bases to protect the white population,[14] and the leader of the Congo's wealthy Katanga province, Moïse Tshombé, declared his province's independence. The Congo was slipping quickly into chaos, and the president and prime minister, Joseph Kasavubu and Patrice Lumumba, turned to the United Nations for help.

Hammarskjöld immediately convened a meeting of the Security Council and proposed the creation of a new peacekeeping force, ONUC (Opération des Nations Unies au Congo). The Council called on Belgium to withdraw its troops and authorised the secretary-general to provide the Congolese government with UN military assistance.[15] Unlike UNEF, whose task was clear and limited—to supervise the cease-fire and the withdrawal of foreign troops, and then to patrol the border between Egypt and Israel—ONUC's mandate was open-ended and ambiguous. There was no time limit on the withdrawal of Belgian troops, no definition of 'military assistance', no description of the 'task' ONUC was to help the government to achieve, no mechanism to deal with disagreements which might arise between the Congo government and the UN, no suggestion of how Hammarskjöld was to ensure the withdrawal of the Belgians without interfering

in the Congo's internal affairs, and until a second resolution was passed on 22 July there was no mention of the
secessionist province of Katanga or the Congo's territorial
integrity.

None of the Security Council powers opposed sending a UN
force to the Congo; they all agreed with Hammarskjöld when he
talked about insulating Africa from the effects of the Cold War.
The problem lay in what the Superpowers and Hammarskjöld
understood by 'insulation'. For the Secretary-General it meant
providing the newly-independent Congo with disinterested UN
assistance, filling the power vacuum left behind by the Belgians
and preventing the Congo from becoming a surrogate battlefield
for the Superpowers. For the United States, which saw Moscow,
not Brussels, as the primary threat to Congolese independence,
'insulation' meant keeping the Russians out of the Congo. After
the largely favourable experience of UNEF, American officials
were quietly confident that the UN could achieve American
policy goals in the Congo at a fraction of the political cost of direct
US action.[16] The Soviets, not surprisingly, held a different view.
Premier Khrushchev's doctrine of 'peaceful coexistence' with the
West meant, in this case, competition for the hearts and minds
of the emerging African states, whom he hoped would pursue a
policy of 'positive neutrality' and foster increasingly close economic, political, and cultural ties with the Soviet Union.[17] 'Insulation' did not necessarily mean the immediate removal of
Western influences from the Congo, but it certainly meant the
expulsion of Belgian troops. And the creation of ONUC seemed,
in the wake of Suez, the best means to this end. It also gave the
Soviets an ideal opportunity to display their anti-colonialist
credentials to the neutral Afro-Asians.

ONUC's mandate was, as a result, deliberately imprecise; both
the Americans and the Soviets placed the difficult task of
interpreting it squarely on the shoulders of the secretary-general.
At the early stages at least, one historian writes,

> both superpowers were willing to approve or reaffirm ambiguous measures
> so long as they could be re-evaluated in the clearer light of national-policy
> considerations when the problems of implementation arose.[18]

And when the problems did arise they came at a time when
neither the Soviets nor the Americans were in the mood to
compromise. The brief détente following Khrushchev's 1959 visit
to the United States dissolved when an American U-2 spy plane

was shot down over Soviet territory in April 1960, wrecking the much-anticipated Paris summit before it could even begin, and severing the already strained communication links between the Superpowers.

In the increasingly factious Congo, it was nearly impossible for the UN to avoid influencing, in one way or another, the internal politics of the country. Their actions or lack of action elicited protests from local leaders, and each protest drew the Superpowers and the UN deeper and deeper into the morass of Congolese politics. Relations between Prime Minister Lumumba and Hammarskjöld steadily declined as it became clear that the secretary-general would not allow UN troops to end Katanga's secession by force, despite the continued presence of Belgian officers seconded to Tshombé's army. Lumumba's subsequent appeal to the Soviet Union for military equipment, and Khrushchev's agreement to deliver trucks, transport planes and other matériel directly to the prime minister, tied Soviet prestige to Lumumba's fate. It also confirmed Lumumba's 'communist' tendencies in the eyes of American officials, whose growing concern was echoed by the CIA station chief in Léopoldville on 18 August: 'Anti-West forces [are] rapidly increasing [their] power [in the] Congo and there may be little time left in which to take action to prevent another Cuba'.[19] A classic Cold War confrontation was brewing in the Congo and Hammarskjöld was anxiously searching for a formula that would lead to the departure of the remaining Belgian officers, and maintain law and order in the country, in a manner that was satisfactory to both Superpowers and without influencing the internal affairs or political future of the Congo.

No timely solution was in sight. A constitutional crisis in early September pitted American-backed Kasavubu against Lumumba. Fearing an outbreak of violence, the UN representative in the Congolese capital closed the radio station and all of the Congo's airports, and unintentionally aided Kasavubu's cause. (Kasavubu, unlike Lumumba, could transmit radio messages to his supporters from the station in Brazzaville, across the Congo River.) Lumumba suffered the first of several defeats, and the Soviets were humiliated and furious: 'The outrageous colonialist behaviour of the representatives sent by Hammarskjöld to the Congo really knows no limits'.[20] But from this point onwards they were effectively shut out of the Congo. Colonel Joseph Mobutu's 'peaceful revolution' and 'neutralisation' of the Congo's politicians on 14 September was in fact a further victory for American interests, as he immediately expelled the Soviet and other communist embassies.[21]

While the Congo teetered on the edge of civil war, the United Nations seemed equally close to disintegration. News of Lumumba's murder in February 1961 fueled Soviet demands that a 'troika' representing the Western, communist and neutralist states should replace the office of Secretary-General, and sparked a vituperative Soviet campaign against Hammarskjöld personally. After Hammarskjöld died in an aeroplane crash in September 1961, the Soviets reluctantly agreed to elect a new Secretary-General as an 'interim measure' until the 'troika' question could be settled. Growing divisions among the powers also hamstrung both the General Assembly and the Security Council on the Congo issue. However, a consensus gradually emerged among the Americans and some Afro-Asians that Katanga's secession should end (in American eyes, to prevent a return of Soviet influence to Léopoldville). This gave UN officials the political leeway to remove Tshombé by force, although the operation itself was legally justified by the putative need to maintain ONUC's 'freedom of movement'.

In his final report on ONUC in June 1964, Acting Secretary-General U Thant announced the departure of the force on the grounds that it had completed its job and that, despite the reappearance of sectarian fighting, the 'current difficulties in the country reflect conflicts of an internal political nature . . .'.[22] Yet these problems—namely, instability and disorder—were largely the same as those which Hammarskjöld had called a threat to 'international peace and security' when the Congolese leaders first appealed for UN assistance. Granted, the Belgian troops were gone by 1964, but in 1960 Hammarskjöld was less concerned with the Belgians than with the potential for Superpower conflict over the Congo. If U Thant did not share this concern in 1964, it was because the Congo government was by then firmly in Western hands, and because the damage to Soviet-American relations had already been done. The peacekeeping mission failed to insulate the Congo from the Cold War, or the Cold War from the Congo. Rather, it brought the Soviet-American rivalry to bear directly on the United Nations and *exacerbated* that rivalry. And naturally, the widening rift between the Superpowers after their initial agreement on ONUC handcuffed the UN's freedom to pursue a non-partisan solution to the Congo's internal problems.

This is not to say that the UN operation did not help the Congo: it provided a measure of stability, famine relief, technical expertise and, finally, a unitary state, albeit one that was held together by the thinnest of threads. But what distinguishes peacekeeping from civilian assistance is its concern with the global, rather than the local, consequences of regional turbulence. The Congo crisis was, above all else, an American victory and a Soviet defeat, during a particularly sensitive period in post-war Soviet-American relations. Khrushchev's 'peaceful coexistence' doctrine was crumbling. He had failed to advance his disarmament proposals or build a socialist-neutralist alliance in the UN, and the Berlin Wall (built in 1961) was a concrete reminder of his failure to oust the western powers from Berlin. Moreover, he faced growing criticism both at home and from the Chinese, who accused him of 'betraying the revolution' and appeasing the 'imperial' powers.[23] The Congo crisis was one of many setbacks that led Khrushchev, desperate for a foreign policy victory, to install nuclear missiles in Cuba, provoking the Soviet-American dispute of October 1962 which took the world to the brink of nuclear war.[24]

Yet there was little the United Nations could have done to prevent this deterioration; the organisation was, and is, little more than a collection of nationally-minded states. No amount of peacekeeping 'machinery', no collective security system, no standing international army, not even the most dynamic and persuasive Secretary-General could have kept the Congo operation from becoming a focus and ultimately a source of Superpower rivalry. Only the Superpowers themselves, and the other permanent members of the Security Council, could have created the necessary spirit of co-operation in the UN. Their mistake was to send ONUC into the turmoil of the Congo—into conditions which were vastly more complex than at Suez—without first reaching a consensus on what these troops should do once they got there.

THE CONGO'S LEGACY

Five lessons can be gleaned from the experience of ONUC. First, agreement to initiate a peacekeeping operation may in fact mask deep-seated differences between the great powers. Second, these divisions are more likely to surface if the operation's purpose, in part or in whole, is to support a government which is itself unstable or disunited. Third, in the words of Ruth Russell, 'the success of a given peacekeeping operation will be in direct ratio to the degree of political accord that underlies it'.[25] Fourth, the continuing presence of a controversial UN force in conditions of worsening great power relations may, in addition to creating operational difficulties for the force, act as an added source of tension between the powers. And fifth, UN successes (like UNEF) can focus international attention on the instruments of peace-keeping, play down and obscure the need for political consensus as a foundation for future peacekeeping operations, and might thus encourage the great powers to agree on new and more ambitious UN action before, or in lieu of, settling their political differences.

Do these lessons apply today, 30 years after the events from which they are drawn, in a post-Cold War security environment? There is no reason why they should not. Despite the slackening of international tensions, peacekeeping still concerns itself with the global, rather than the local, implications of regional conflicts. And the first goal of peacekeeping—to 'insulate' local conflicts from the Superpower relationship—remains the same. Perhaps the only difference, viewed in this light, is that peacekeeping no longer aims to maintain the stability of the Cold War, but rather to prevent local turbulence from sparking Superpower disputes which could, in turn, sabotage the current trend towards Soviet-American comity. The Congo reminds us that the UN will be capable of mounting effective peacekeeping missions in contested areas only insofar as the powers continue to cooperate, and warns us of the perils of assigning UN troops and negotiators complex tasks that are not supported by concrete agreements between the powers.

THE RECENT RESURGENCE OF 'MAXIMUM' PEACEKEEPING

The UN Transition Assistance Group in Namibia (UNTAG) was a 'maximum' peacekeeping operation that worked, despite its ignominious and unsettled début, mainly for two interrelated reasons: it enjoyed the unwavering support of the Security Council, and the force's mandate was clear from the start. For over 20 years the United Nations had demanded that South Africa end its 'illegal occupation' of Namibia. But the South African Government refused so long as Cuban troops remained in neighbouring Angola.[26] Meanwhile, the battle between the Soviet-backed Namibian guerrilla movement (SWAPO) and

South African regular troops continued and was complicated by the civil war in Angola, where government forces, supported by Cuban troops, fought South African- and American-backed UNITA rebels. In December 1988 the Superpowers agreed to end the Cold War drama in south-western Africa. Their joint *démarche*, and the fact that the conflict had settled into a military stalemate, led South Africa, Cuba and Angola to sign two agreements for Namibian independence and the withdrawal of Cuban troops from Africa.

On 1 April 1989, as members of UNTAG began arriving in Namibia, a large group of SWAPO guerrillas crossed over the border from Angola in violation of the peace accords.[27] By 3 April approximately 1,200 guerrillas, and only 921 peacekeepers (out of 4,650), had entered Namibia.[28] With UNTAG too weak to take any decisive action, Secretary-General Javier Pérez de Cuéllar temporarily allowed South African troops to leave their bases and engage the guerrillas. On 9 April South Africa announced a 'de facto' suspension of the peace plan.[29] Events were slipping beyond the UN's control. As one unnamed diplomat reportedly said when the trouble first broke, 'This is an incident from which he, the Secretary-General, may never recover'.[30]

In the end, Pérez de Cuéllar was saved by the great powers, who were determined to see the linked agreements survive. In the Congo, unanticipated disturbances had been exploited by local factions who drew their great power patrons, themselves deeply divided, ever deeper into the Congo's indigenous rivalries. In Namibia, similar disturbances had the opposite effect: the great powers collectively put the political screws on SWAPO and South Africa to suppress and settle their long-standing enmity.[31] On 15 May UN officials were able to confirm that all the guerrillas had returned to Angola and were confined to their camps;[32] and on 16 August South Africa announced that it was recalling to base its counter-insurgency units in northern Namibia.[33] Six months later Namibia's new constitution was approved and the path was cleared for the country's first elections on 21 March 1990.

As the operation in Namibia reached a successful end, the five permanent members of the Security Council were trying to negotiate a comprehensive settlement to Cambodia's 16 years of internecine violence. At the time of writing, the powers have agreed on the need for free elections in Cambodia, but have been unable to resolve their differences on details of the transition period leading to the elections. The network of great power commitments in the area is labyrinthine. The Americans back the

exiled Prince Norodom Sihanouk, who is allied with Pol Pot's
Khmer Rouge, and Son Sann, the former Cambodian prime
minister; China supports and arms the Khmer Rouge, while
Vietnam and the Soviet Union endorse the regime currently in
power in Cambodia. The sticking point in the negotiations is the
Soviet-Vietnamese opposition to the participation of the Khmer
Rouge in the transitional care-taker government, and China's
insistence that they do take part. (The Khmer Rouge is thought
to have killed somewhere between one million and three million
Cambodians from the time they took control of the country in
1975 until they were ousted from power by the Vietnamese in
1979.)

It is too early now to foresee the outcome of these negotiations,
but the five powers have been inching towards an Australian
proposal to have the UN, not a collection of rival factions,
administer Cambodia until the elections. In the light of the
Congo experience, however, this seems like a dangerous non-sol-
ution; it falls back on the great powers' agreement to use the UN
before the outlines of a real consensus are in sight. Unlike
Namibia, where the UN supervised South Africa's administration
of the territory in the transitional period, the Australian plan
assigns administrative tasks in Cambodia to 12,000 UN officials,
who would be aided by 5,500 military peacekeepers.[34] As one
newspaper editorialist pointed out, there is 'desperation and
unreality' in the proposal. It places too great a logistical, political
and military burden on the UN and it demands 'an unprecedented measure of sophisticated balancing among warring Cambodians and wary regional players and great powers alike'.[35]
Hasty expediency in the current negotiations may risk more than
a continuation of disorder in Cambodia. Ultimately, it may
damage the UN and strain relations between the great powers.

THE PRACTICAL POLITICS OF PEACEKEEPING

There are some who argue that, with the Cold War now over,
the UN's peacekeeping function must be strengthened and made
more consistently effective; for instance, by removing the requirement that all parties must consent to the stationing of a UN
force,[36] or by reviving the stillborn Military Staff Committee,[37] or
by creating a permanent UN force.[38] But like the Australian plan
for Cambodia, these proposals focus on the instruments of
peacekeeping and direct attention away from the UN's essential

and unavoidable dependence on *Realpolitik*. The danger, as I have argued, is mainly cognitive: in order to maintain the effectiveness of the UN's peace and security role, the great powers must perceive a continuing need for political compromise.

This is not to say that UN peacekeeping should not be strengthened in other ways. It would certainly benefit from increased and more reliable funding, an independent fact-finding agency, and the earmarking and training of more national contingents to perform peacekeeping tasks at short notice. But it must be clear that any new peacekeeping 'machinery' will function in conjunction with, not independently of, the underlying political process. The problem with more far-reaching proposals is that they attempt to rehabilitate elements of the collective security system (standing army, etc) which falsely suggest 'automatic' security guarantees.

Herein lies the paradox of peacekeeping. Because it is seen as the 'poor relation' of collective security, rather than as an entirely different approach to problems of international violence; because it operates in the shadowy gap between the empirical 'what is' and the normative 'what should be'; because it is so ill-defined as to mean anything from the smallest group of unarmed observers to large armies backed by jet fighters; because of all these things, successful peacekeeping operations, like UNEF and UNTAG, bolster efforts to institutionalise, formalise and expand the UN's peacekeeping role. But these efforts seem to obscure the inherently political nature of peacekeeping and undermine its general effectiveness as a tool of pacific settlement.

The fact that peacekeeping is, as one commentator has written, 'an uncertain, unpredictable, and unregulated international operation,[39] is both its strength and weakness. Its versatility, resilience, and requirement for political consensus before and during each operation, allow the peacekeeping mechanism to adjust to changing international conditions in a way that collective security never could, and thus provide the UN with an important safety valve in periods of international tension. On the other hand, flexibility can lead to problems if the great powers, overly confident in the abilities of UN officials or hoping to deflect difficult negotiations, seek to push the UN into complex and precarious crises where a consensus for effective action does not exist. As George Kennan presciently wrote in 1958, two years before the Congo operation:

> No international organisation can be stronger than the structure of relationships among the Great Powers that underlies it; and to look to such an

organisation to resolve deep-seated conflicts of interest among the Great Powers is to ignore its limitations and to jeopardise its usefulness in other fields.[40]

The Cold War is over, ideology has taken a back seat in East–West relations, but conflicts of interest will continue. And it will be up to the great powers, not the UN, to resolve them.

POST SCRIPT

This article was written before the Iraqi invasion and annexation of Kuwait in the summer of 1990; as it goes to press, the possibility of large-scale fighting in the Middle East looms ominously on the horizon. The UN Security Council has so far responded with unprecedented and encouraging unanimity, isolating Iraq diplomatically and economically under the provisions of Article 41 of the Charter.

A successful international action against Iraq—one that is truly directed by the Security Council rather than solely by one of its members—may boost the UN's authority to new heights. However, as we saw earlier, success can engender its own problems if it creates false expectations of the UN's capabilities. Iraq's invasion of Kuwait left no doubt as to who was the 'aggressor'— the attack was premeditated, unprovoked, and was exposed to the full light of international scrutiny. But the odds are that this type of naked aggression—indeed, the model of 'aggression' implied in the UN Charter—will remain the exception rather than the rule. The UN should be prepared to deal with complex, ambiguous, low-intensity disputes, where Article 42 and the creation of UN campaign armies are inappropriate tools.

Secondly, if the UN fails to play a central and effective role in what has been touted as the first major international crisis of the post-Cold War era, then the organization may be forced to withdraw from the peace and security field for a long time. This type of 'defeat' could arise either if the great powers cannot agree on common objectives for UN policy in the Persian Gulf and pursue their own unilateral actions, seeking UN approval of these actions *ex post facto*, or the powers agree to undertake combined military action under the command of the United Nations (either 'peacekeeping' or 'enforcement action' under Article 42) but do not codify in precise detail the mandate, powers and command structure of the UN force.

NOTES

[1] Brian Urquhart, 'The United Nations system and the future', *International Affairs*, Vol. 65, No. 2, (Spring, 1989), p. 227.

[2] Article 39 of the Charter.

[3] Articles 41 and 42 of the Charter.

[4] For an account of Soviet-American relations in the immediate post-war period, see Daniel Yergin, *Shattered peace: the origins of the cold war and the national security state*, Boston, Houghton Mifflin, 1977.

[5] It is difficult to cite the Korean conflict as an example of 'enforcement action': the decision to send UN troops to war was taken in the absence of the Soviet delegate, and command of the UN forces was almost exclusively in American hands. For further reading, see Leland M. Goodrich, *Korea: a study of US policy in the United Nations*, New York, Council on Foreign Relations, 1956; Arnold Wolfers, 'Collective security and the war in Korea', *Yale Review*, Vol. 43, No. 4, (1954), pp. 481-496; and Trygve Lie, *In the cause of peace: seven years with the United Nations*, New York, Macmillan, 1954.

[6] For a good account of UNEF's creation, see Gabriella Rosner, *The United Nations Emergency Force*, New York, Columbia University Press, 1963.

[7] Resolution 998 (ES-I), *General Assembly Official Records*, First Emergency Special Session, Suppl. No. 1, (A/3354), 4 November 1956.

[8] Although the Soviet Union, fearful that the peacekeeping mechanism might be used against themselves in the future, argued that the operation should be considered enforcement action under Article 42. In the final vote on the creation of UNEF, however, they abstained.

[9] See Inis L. Claude, 'The peace-keeping role of the United Nations', in E Berkeley Tompkins, *The United Nations in perspective*, Stanford, Hoover Institute, 1972, pp. 49-63.

[10] 'Introduction to the annual report of the secretary-general on the work of the Organisation, 16 June 1959 - 15 June 1960' *General Assembly Official Records*, Fifteenth Session, Suppl. No. 1A, (A/4390/Add.1).

[11] See Indar Jit Rikye, *The theory and practice of peacekeeping*, London, C. Hurst and Co., 1984, p. 227.

[12] See Alan M James, 'Unit veto dominance in United Nations peace-keeping', in Lawrence S Finkelstein, ed., *Politics in the United Nations system*, London, Duke University Press, 1988, pp. 90-91.

[13] See Brian Urquhart, *Hammarskjold*, London, Harper and Row, 1972, p. 194.

[14] Belgian metropolitan troops intervened in 23 places between 10 and 18 July. See Catherine Hoskyns, *The Congo since independence: January 1960-December 1961*, London, Oxford University Press, 1965, pp. 124-7.

[15] UN document S/4387, *Security Council Official Records*, 14 July 1960.

[16] See Ernest W Lefever, *Uncertain mandate: politics of the UN Congo operation*, Baltimore, Johns Hopkins Press, 1967, pp. 76-8.

[17] See Alexander Dallin, 'The Soviet Union: political activity', in Zbigniew Brzezinski, ed., *Africa and the communist world*, London, Oxford University Press, 1964, p. 13.

[18] Linda B Miller, *World order and local disorder: the United Nations and international conflicts*, Princeton, Princeton University Press, 1967, p. 75.

[19] Cited in Madeleine G Kalb, *The Congo cables: the cold war in Africa—From Eisenhower to Kennedy*, New York, Macmillan, 1982, p. 53.

[20] Cited in Urquhart, *Hammarskjold*, pp. 449-50.

[21] For a discussion of the CIA's role in the Mobutu coup, see Kalb, pp. 92-8.

[22] Cited in Miller, p. 113.

[23] See Walter Lafeber, *America, Russia, and the cold war*, 1945-84, New York, Alfred A Knopf, 1985, pp. 199-200; and Joseph L Nogee and Robert H. Davidson, *Soviet foreign policy since World War II*, New York, Pergamon, 1981, *passim*.

[24] For further reading on Khrushchev's reasons for placing missiles in Cuba, see Nogee and Davidson, pp. 120-27; Adam B. Ulam, *Expansion and coexistence: Soviet foreign policy*, 1917-1973, New York, Secker and Warburg, 1974, pp. 668-77; and Anatol Rappaport, *The big two*, New York, Pegasus, 1971, pp. 182-3.

[25] Ruth B Russell, 'Commentary', in John M Paxman and George T Boggs, *The United Nations: a reassessment*, Charlottesville, Virginia, University of Virginia Press, 1973, p. 79.

[26] See Rikye, p. 155.

[27] Pretoria estimated that 600-800 SWAPO fighters crossed the border between 31 March and 1 April (*Financial Times*, 4 April 1989).

[28] *International Herald Tribune*, 4 April 1989; The force did not reach its full strength until 26 April.

[29] *Le Monde*, 9 April 1989.

[30] *The Daily Telegraph*, 5 April 1989.

[31] See C W Freeman, 'Angola/Namibia Accords', *Foreign Affairs*, Vol. 68, No. 3, (Summer, 1989), p. 139.

[32] *The Daily Telegraph*, 16 May 1989.

[33] *The Independent*, 16 August 1989.

[34] *Ibid.*, 23 May 1990.

[35] *International Herald Tribune*, 2 January 1990.

[36] This argument was made by Anthony Parsons, the former permanent representative of the United Kingdom to the United Nations; *The Independent*, 21 August 1989.

[37] This suggestion was made by Vladimir Petrovsky, the deputy foreign minister of the Soviet Union, *International Herald Tribune*, 6 October 1989.

[38] See Paul F Diehl, 'A permanent UN peacekeeping force: an evaluation', *Bulletin of Peace Proposals*, Vol. 20, No. 1, (March, 1989), pp. 27-36.

[39] V Venkata Raman, 'United Nations peacekeeping and the future of world order', in Henry Wiseman, ed., *Peacekeeping: appraisals and proposals*, New York, Pergamon, 1983, p. 372.

[40] George Kennan, *Russia, the atom and the west*, New York, Oxford University Press, 1958, p. 27.

Setback and Survival: Chinese Foreign Policy 1989-90

ALYSON J K BAILES

Alyson Bailes has been a member of the Diplomatic Service since 1969. She has served in Budapest, the UK Delegation to NATO, and Peking. Her current position is Deputy Head of Mission, British Embassy, Oslo. The views expressed in this article are the author's own and do not necessarily reflect the views of Her Majesty's Government.

Without fear of contradiction, Chinese Foreign Minister Qian Qichen could write in December 1988[1] that 'many world events have significantly improved the international situation', and sum up the past year as a very positive one for China. A date had been set for the historic Sino-Soviet Summit, while President-elect Bush would hasten to Beijing as one of his earliest foreign visits in February 1989. Rajiv Gandhi had been to China to inaugurate a new period of Sino-Indian détente. Benazir Bhutto would soon be visiting in her turn to complete the balance. Hardly a day passed without some Western (or Eastern) European Minister arriving in Peking with interesting offers of cooperation.

Less obviously, Chinese diplomacy was preparing itself in timely fashion to explore the new openings in Asia and the socialist community offered by Sino-Soviet reconciliation. The best prospect in a long while of an outcome in Cambodia acceptable to China had dawned with the exercise of Soviet pressure on Vietnam and the latter's commitment—though only partly as a result of this—to unilateral troop withdrawals. Looking beyond that to a peaceful and more complex regional constellation, China was making renewed efforts to normalise relations with Indonesia, had effectively normalised them with Laos, and was putting out bilateral feelers to Vietnam itself. It could build up trade relations with South Korea without fear, now, of driving the North into Moscow's arms. It had signed a new Border Treaty with Mongolia and was preparing an exchange of Foreign Ministers' visits that would herald State-to-State normalisation with Ulan Bator. It was boosting exchanges with Cuba and a fence-mending visit by the Albanian Foreign Minister was in prospect. All round, China's security seemed less

283

threatened and its international standing higher than at any time in the 40 year history of the People's Republic.

THE SETBACK

The dimming of this rosy perspective, curiously foreshadowed by a row over the dissident Fang Lizhi during Bush's February visit, was visible by the time Gorbachev arrived in Peking in May 1989 to find his programme disrupted by massive anti-leadership demonstrations. After the events of 3/4 June and the violent quelling of opposition, the transformation of China's diplomatic world—both in fact and in emotional and atmospheric terms—seemed complete. At the European Council on 27 June and the Economic Summit meeting on 15 July 1989 respectively, the European Twelve together with the US, Canada and Japan bound themselves to a series of measures against China the essence of which was a halt to all high-level visits, military dealings and preferential loans. Australia, New Zealand and several West European states took similar action on a national basis. Plans for $780 million of additional World Bank lending and various Asian Development Bank programmes were put on ice.

While no formal measures were announced in the cultural/educational area, most Western and Japanese students were withdrawn from China, plans for major arts events were set aside and some scientific cooperation schemes suspended. Popular reaction to the June events brought a sudden check to the flow of tourism, so that China's total earnings in 1989, projected to reach US$2.5 billion, fell back to about half the 1988 level of $2.2 billion. In the socialist world, the Hungarian, Polish and Yugoslavian Governments condemned Chinese use of force, suspended Party-to-Party exchanges and cut State-to-State traffic back to a minimum.[2] Gorbachev was careful not to take sides, but his refusal to let embattled East European Governments save themselves by force later in the year suggests what his true opinion must have been.[3]

THE LEADERSHIP REACTION

It would be idle to suggest that calculations of the possible international costs had played any serious part in Chinese leaders' decisions on how to solve their internal problems during May. Even so, the strength and specificity of the outside reaction probably surprised them. In the short term, it strengthened their inclination to blame the student-led 'rebellion' on United States and Taiwanese machinations, and to see Zhao Ziyang and his following as corrupted (although this was expressed more subtly[4]) by Yugoslav, Polish and Hungarian ideas. It prompted some extremely xenophobic utterances by leaders, including claims of the sort that had hardly been heard for a decade on China's ability to 'go it alone' without Western help. Imports of Western magazines were held up for a while, partial jamming of BBC and VOA broadcasts started and a series of new restrictions were introduced on foreign journalists. Gradually, pro-régime writers developed a systematic analysis of capitalist countries' treatment of China as part of a general 'diplomatic offensive', designed to 'bring the socialist countries into the international capitalist orbit' through insidious tactics of 'peaceful evolution'.[5] As Li Peng commented to the Nicaraguan Ambassador on 15 July:

> If China, a developing country with a population of 1.1 billion, took the capitalist road, it would inevitably become a vassal state of the developed capitalist countries in the West.

Yet even in the darkest post-June days there was another, contrasting theme to Chinese utterances. *The People's Daily* wrote immediately after the Economic Summit declaration:

> The Chinese Government and people will absolutely not change their basic policy of reform and opening up on account of the unfriendly acts of certain countries against us.[6]

Even the hardest-line analytical articles did not retreat from China's new standard view of the world scene as being dominated by détente, cooperation and growing multipolarity.[7] They merely warned of the new opening this gave unscrupulous capitalists and of the need for greater 'vigilance' if China was not to lose rather than gain from the process. China's own ideal remained, as it had been defined before, a 'new political order on the basis of the five principles of coexistence', where no State, whether socialist or bourgeois-liberal, would try to impose its system and standards on any other. Premier Li Peng's statement to the Spring 1990 National People's Congress meeting, which used this formulation, defined the enemy as 'hegemonism' rather than 'capitalism'.[8] In short, the theoretical latitude was there for China to continue cultivating foreign partners of every ideological shade in the interests of national independence, security and development. How far this licence was used, and how Peking's new authoritarian politics interwove with its now strongly-established pragmatism abroad, can best be assessed by looking at Chinese handling of individual foreign relationships after June.

BEIJING AND MOSCOW

Sino-Soviet relations were the clearest test. With the East European revolutions of the turn of the year, Gorbachev's 'subversion of socialism'—a term apparently used of him in Chinese Party documents, though for internal consumption only[9]—must have looked increasingly like a more insidious threat to the Chinese Party's survival than anything the West could do. But strategically, Gorbachev remained arguably the best Soviet leader China had got. Open criticism of him, still less any attempt to form a Chinese-led bloc of 'loyal' Communists, would have risked undoing all the gains of Sino-Soviet normalisation: the virtual disappearance of the Soviet conventional threat to China's borders; the new leeway given to Chinese diplomacy by the Pax Sino-Sovietica in Asia; and the hopes of mutual economic advantage especially through the rise in border trade.[10] Moreover, if Gorbachev were to fall, there was no guarantee that an equally pacific leader, or one better capable of controlling separatist pressures—with their risk of knock-on effects for China's non-Han populations in the West—would replace him.

By the autumn of 1989, therefore, Chinese leaders had clearly decided that, however lukewarm the political temperature, the perceived momentum of Sino-Soviet détente must continue or even accelerate. Bilateral exchanges agreed at the May Summit went forward as planned, including visits by senior Party functionaries.[11] Further rounds of the long-standing frontier demarcation talks were held in November 1989 and February 1990; two sessions of talks took place on defusing the military confrontation at the border; and in early April 1990 a senior Chinese Defence Ministry official[12] went to Moscow for the first 'normal' bilateral military visit in decades. The proclaimed success of Premier Li Peng's official visit to the Soviet Union in April thus came as no great surprise. Apart from the documents signed on scientific and space cooperation, the Chinese gained credits for Soviet consumer imports, the purchase of two Soviet nuclear power stations and regular foreign policy consultation. Li was also able to endorse 'basic principles' for Soviet-Chinese border force reductions and confidence-building measures, while the two Foreign Ministers agreed on early talks 'to work out a schedule and other details' for the latter. This was a step of some significance, given China's avoidance hitherto of specific national arms control commitments, and the general threat-consciousness of the Chinese military. It also suggested that any verdict on the post-June policy influence of the People's Liberation Army (PLA) and its putative directions had better be held open for the time being. However, the lack of a formal joint communiqué on the visit and the predictability of most of its practical results left many observers still wondering whether Beijing and Moscow had truly discovered a new spirit of cooperation, or whether they were not, rather, finding it hard going even to keep up the original pace.

It is tempting to see this phase of Sino-Soviet relations as harking back to the Sino-US model of Nixon's time, with strategic imperatives forcing internal policy contradictions under the carpet. The 'de-ideologisation' of Moscow-Beijing relations must, indeed, be regarded as irreversible in some respects. Both States have now explicitly forsworn in their external policy the notion of socialist 'blocs' or 'models', and both were sincere in disavowing any idea of a renewed 1950s-style alliance even before the events of June 1989. But ideology apart, no other two States in the region are closer to each other in the general scale and existential nature of the problems they must face, including their reasons for trying to defend some form of strong centralised authority. The Sino-Soviet interaction will continue to be more than a matter of diplomacy, and whether their domestic trends go on diverging or come back into step will matter for the internal, as well as foreign, policies of many of their neighbours.[13]

BEIJING AND THE EASTERN BLOC—
A DIFFERENT STORY

The same kinship can no longer be claimed between China and Eastern Europe, where new leaders started flexing their democratic muscles *inter alia* by dallying with Taiwan, Tibet and the Chinese dissident movement. Some East European observers are inclined to argue now that the attempt to apply their (ultimately unsuccessful) methods for patching up socialism in China's very different situation in the 1980s was an historical mistake. But

State-to-State relations remained intact between China and all her East European partners and some effort was already being made in early 1990 to keep economic, technological and foreign policy cooperation alive. An interesting illustration of Chinese practicality is that at Beijing's suggestion, trade with most East European countries—and with the Soviet Union—was switched from a virtual barter basis to hard-currency accounting with effect from 1990 or 1991. In the short term this is bound to depress turnover, but in the long run it offers the only chance for a more natural pattern of economic cooperation to emerge, based on competitiveness and comparative advantage.[14]

PEKING AND WASHINGTON

Sino-US relations were no bed of roses even before June 1989. American concerns over human rights and Tibet, other Congressional preoccupations and even some security-related disputes had already made Chinese warnings against American 'interference' a familiar refrain. In China's post-June inveighings against the West, the United States remained the primary target, not least because of the deadlock over Fang Lizhi's 'sanctuary' in the United States Embassy in Beijing. By 1990, Chinese analysts were also accusing the Americans of exploiting their military-political ascendancy over Gorbachev to start throwing their weight around again in classic 'big power' fashion, with the risk of driving the Russians so far into a corner that a new Superpower struggle could result.[15]

The deterioration in Peking-Washington relations was potentially all the more serious because the traditional safety-net of mutual strategic dependence, in face of the Soviet threat, had been removed.[16] Continuing US-Soviet détente, and the divergence of Soviet and Chinese domestic policies, left China at the remotest point of the famous 'triangle'. On the face of it, too, any interest in limiting the damage lay entirely on the Chinese side. It was just as true after June as it had been before, that United States and Western cooperation were vital for China's economic and technological development. It was perhaps even clearer that the Soviet Union and Eastern Europe offered no satisfactory alternative.[17] Whatever noxious influences entered through it, the open door to the West could not close if rapid modernisation was still the goal;[18] however galling the new

SETBACK AND SURVIVAL: CHINESE FOREIGN POLICY   289

Washington-Moscow entente might be in some ways, it must be encouraged to continue and produce disarmament results apt to consolidate China's peaceful environment.[19] By the end of 1989, the Chinese were making little attempt to conceal the problems that the Western credit freeze and fall in tourism were causing for their economy, particularly with a debt repayment peak of some £28 billion approaching in 1991-2.[20] They were lobbying openly for the resumption of World Bank and ADB loans, targeting the United States as the main obstacle. The one thing they would not or could not do was to buy their return to favour with anything like an apology for the June events. That would not only have gone back on the whole logic of 'non-interference', it would have whipped away all ideological underpinning from the already somewhat embattled post-June régime at home.[21]

LIMITED MEASURES

The interesting thing about the American and other Western measures against China was the thoughtful way in which they were limited from the start—affecting only transactions directly under government control and which could be construed as 'favours'; leaving ordinary trade flows, most unofficial exchanges and even technology transfer (other than defence sales) untouched. (In the event, China's foreign trade in 1989 showed a 10.5 per cent growth in exports and 7 per cent growth in imports, a slower growth rate than the previous year but resulting in a smaller deficit.) This approach was designed to avoid the weaknesses of earlier 'sanctions', and to make the package relatively easy to uphold without inter-allied quarrels, as indeed it proved.[22] It also reflected a conviction that China and the West needed to stay in touch, to trade and to cooperate on regional and global problems. The sheer 'dead weight'[23] of China made it impossible to think otherwise. For the sake of China's own future, too, the West should not be the first to cut off the flow of its own ideas and influences and should not give unnecessary pretexts for isolationism and xenophobia. All these ideas presumably had some part in President Bush's decision to veto Congressional proposals for new sanctions, to extend 'most favoured nation' treatment to China for a further year in June 1990, and to send not only unofficial emissaries like ex-President Nixon and Henry Kissinger, but also his own National Security Adviser, Brent

Scowcroft, on two visits to Beijing by the end of 1989. For the United States, an additional consideration may have been the importance of holding China to some degree of strategic pre-dictability, to put it at its lowest, at a time when so many other fixed points were shifting and the Soviet Union's future looked increasingly uncertain. Whether this joint interest in 'maintaining world peace and stability'[24], at best a pale replacement for positive strategic alignment, is actually sufficient to re-stabilise Sino-American relations is another question. It was raised afresh by frustration at the lack of results from Scowcroft's visits, and it will be looked at further below.

BEIJING AND WESTERN EUROPE

There is little to add on Sino-West European relations. China has, however, shown pragmatism in its close attention to the process of East-West restructuring in Europe and its appreciation of the important changes for Superpower and world politics that might result. German reunification concerns Beijing above all, for its relevance to the Korean question[25] and in the long run perhaps to China's own 'one country, two systems' concept as well as its strategic impact. Having leaned towards the GDR position and played down the self-determination theme in the late 1980s, in March 1990 Peking adopted the carefully judged public line that:

> China understands the wish of the people of Germany for German reunifi-cation, and favours a solution to this question that will not only benefit the people and the two German states, but also be conducive to peace and stability in Europe and the world.[26]

BEIJING AND JAPAN

In Sino-Japanese relations, both the existence and continuity of a kind of interdependence are easier to diagnose, though not simple to define. A cynic might have seen the June events and their diplomatic results as letting Japan off the hook in several ways—lessening the risk of its isolation through Sino-Soviet rapprochement,[27] improving its relative image with regional partners,[28] and leaving it as the only feasible arbiter for regional cooperation schemes and Europe-Asia dialogue.[29]

Prospects for Soviet-Japanese 'normalisation' certainly look better now than ever, though the role of the China factor in this, and the political and economic consequences, are difficult to quantify.[30] But Japan can never, in fact, rejoice at Chinese internal setbacks. Human rights concerns are less important here (and in Asia generally) than the risk of China turning to an isolationist course, which would leave a vast gap in Asian-Pacific growth and stability, or a spasmodically aggressive one which would actively threaten them. Again, although it is risky for an outsider to opine on these matters, it is not clear that Japan would prefer the prominence and self-reliance forced on it by a 'hermit' China (with all the consequences for defence policy and US-Japanese relations) to the more complex patterns that active, peaceful competition with Beijing for regional influence would allow. At any rate, from the outset the Japanese combined expressions of regret at the June events with urgings to China to return to an open, cooperative policy. They sent a number of high-level business delegations to Beijing under nominally non-governmental leadership (Deng Xiaoping, receiving one of them, detected 'some difference' between Japan's attitude and the rest of the G7).[31] Chinese State Councillor Zou Jiahua, responsible for science and technology, visited Japan in January 1990. The Japanese resumed negotiations soon after for a third major Yen loan to China, although with no particular commitment to an outcome. It was clear that Japan's perceived interest now lay in using a policy of active contact to prod or lure Chinese economic and external policies in a more productive direction.

THE ASIAN SPHERE

Elsewhere in Asia, continuity and even progress were the keynotes of Chinese diplomacy. Sino-Indian détente remained on course in early 1990 despite the New Delhi change of government (Qian Qichen paid a visit to pick up contacts soon after) and the Kashmir dispute (on which Beijing did not lean detectably towards Pakistan). Talks on border delineation made slow but steady progress towards defining acceptable principles. However, this did not prevent Chinese analysts starting to voice some concern about Indian strategic ambitions.[32] But Beijing's short-term response was simply to go on strengthening its own position in South-East Asia, notably through Sino-Indonesian normalisation which entered its final stages after March 1990.[33] A visit by Li Peng to Pakistan and Bangladesh meanwhile continued an already well established Chinese policy of balance between these countries and India.

On Cambodia and Vietnam, some interpreted China's failure to make concessions at the July 1989 Paris Conference as being linked to the ideological shift in Beijing. This author believes China was never seriously likely to give up its insistence on Khmer Rouge participation in a Cambodian coalition unless and until some other foolproof way could be found to guarantee the end of Vietnam's military presence and privileged political influence in Cambodia. That has been the consistent Chinese aim and it has nothing to do with ideology. In 1989-90 it proved compatible, however, with a certain easing of tension along the Sino-Vietnamese frontier,[34] a mounting interest in cross-border economic cooperation, and further visits by the Vietnamese Deputy Foreign Minister to Beijing from May 1990. The pattern was familiar from Sino-Soviet and Sino-Indian rapprochement and had less to do with any possible softening of Beijing's conditions than with the heightening of incentives for the other side to meet them. (This article went to press too early to permit a discussion of China's reaction to changes in the US's Vietnam policy in mid-1990.)

NORTH KOREA

Li Peng's foreign policy statement of 23 March gave pride of place to a friendship 'stronger than ever before' with North Korea. The glowing presentation of Kim Il-Sung's 'private' visit to China in November 1989 and General Secretary Jiang Zemin's visit to Pyongyang during the following March, symbolised this, but one may suspect their contents were less straightforward. Concern about leadership succession arrangements was mutual but its direction was different. North Korea would clearly prefer a hard-line Chinese leadership which was not too friendly with Moscow, while China's best option is still a pragmatic turn in Pyongyang, defusing intra-Korean tension and allowing real progress in reunification. Meanwhile political overtures between Seoul and Beijing were frozen in 1989, but trade on a non-governmental basis was permitted to continue. Sino-Mongolian 'normalisation' did not stop with *perestroika* in Ulan Bator, which actually made it more important for Beijing to monitor developments and prevent them spreading deliberately or osmotically to Inner Mongolia. The new Mongolian President, Ochirbat, paid a visit to China, cut short by his domestic preoccupations, in May 1990.

BEIJING AND THE THIRD WORLD

One obvious change in Chinese diplomacy after June 1989 was the zealous cultivation of contacts with African and other developing countries who, as Li Peng told four Ambassadors on 30 August, had shared China's experience of wrongful Western interference and thus were bound to sympathise. They certainly showed no propensity to criticise Chinese actions in June. High-level visitors from Burkina Faso, Ethiopia and Sao Tomé were the first into Beijing after the 'events' and over 1989 as a whole top-level visits were made to China from Mali, Burundi, Uganda, Togo, Ghana and Sierra Leone (there was also an important military visit from Nigeria).[35] Qian Qichen visited Botswana, Lesotho, Zimbabwe, Angola, Zambia and Mozambique in August-September 1989. China-Middle East exchanges were also active, with visits by Qian to Jordan, Egypt, Syria and Tunisia in September 1989 and Iraq, both Yemens, Qatar and Bahrain in early 1990. President Yang Shangkun visited Egypt, the UAE, Kuwait and Oman in December 1989.

But announcements of China's taking 'unity and cooperation with Third World countries, including African countries, as the fundamental foothold of its foreign policy' after June need careful interpretation. There was an air of *pis aller* about it as a policy, since the range of other States willing positively to strengthen their relations with Beijing was so limited. There was no great flood of new Chinese aid, except to Pacific States like Fiji, Vanuatu and Western Samoa where strategic (and anti-Taiwan) motives could explain it. China's actual policies on the Middle East and Southern Africa did not become more confrontational or tilted towards front-line States.[36] In Latin America the picture was similar: new Sino-Cuban warmth (based on a common view of the necessity of the June events) multiplied visits and brought new economic pledges, but not on a scale that would add up to formal alliance or imply Chinese substitution for declining Soviet aid. It coexisted with a Chinese diplomatic drive towards the region's capitalist States, with Party visits to Brazil and Venezuela, Parliamentary delegations to Bolivia and Mexico, a visit to China by the Ecuadorean Foreign Minister in May 1990 and visits by Yang Shangkun the same month to Mexico, Brazil, Chile, Argentina and Uruguay. Finally, China was no less active after June in the cooperation of the 'Permanent Five' at the United States Security Council, which had already brought one divergence of interest with African states into the open over the scale of the Namibian peacekeeping force. Beijing provided experts for the latter and in April 1990 sent military observers for the first time to a UN force—UN truce supervision organisation (UNTSO) in the Middle East. China was not, clearly, giving up its surviving great-power privileges for the sake of Third World solidarity any more than it was re-orienting its Asian policies on ideological lines. (China's reaction to the Gulf crisis has been entirely in line with this analysis.)

The circle was inevitably harder to square, and domestic factors harder to exclude, in China's dealings with those territories which were prospectively or theoretically parts of China itself. Taiwan was spurred to fresh efforts for separate recognition, and between June 1989 and April 1990 succeeded with Grenada, Belize, Liberia and Lesotho, with all of whom Peking then suspended or severed relations. The People's Republic of China (PRC) secured new recognitions only from the Federated States of Micronesia and Bahrain during this period. On the surface both Taipei and Beijing held by their policies of greater mutual contact, economic, touristic, administrative and perhaps even governmental. The Taiwanese Government had no need actively to criticise developments on the mainland in order for outsiders to draw the desired lesson: its growing economic strength, if nothing else, was eloquent enough at a time when the mainland seemed to be drifting backwards. Political point-scoring, moreover, might merely have encouraged the Taiwanese 'independence' movement which the régime was still pledged to resist at home. But the concern Li Peng expressed about that movement in his 23 March speech was well-placed. As he pointed out, 'The 1990s [ie the last stand of the post-war political generation] is an important historical period for advancing the great cause of peaceful reunification of the motherland'. If 1989 proves to have clinched the odds on this period passing fruitlessly in a mood of political alienation, peaceful convergence between Taiwan and the mainland will look more unlikely than ever and there are no very palatable alternatives.

CHINA AND HONG KONG

Mainland-Hong Kong relations over this period deserve a volume of their own and only the main lines can be sketched here. The essence of the problem was that the shock of June 1989 created new anxieties and demands in Hong Kong, while making

Beijing far less inclined to cater to them. China accused the Hong Kong people of violating the 'one country, two systems' principle by taking sides in the student rising and by alleged attempts after June to 'subvert' the mainland. But Beijing also set its face against the evolution of Hong Kong's own political system at the faster pace many demanded after June, and generally failed to appreciate the force of the 'confidence' factor that is an objective part of the Hong Kong scene, however subjective its origins. Again, the United Kingdom's 'nationality package', designed to meet (on a modest scale) new Hong Kong demands for British passports as an insurance, drew accusations from Beijing of trying to undermine Hong Kong's future. British initiatives to get other nations to help in this and to express general support for Hong Kong, in the European Community and Commonwealth contexts, were castigated by the Chinese as 'internationalising the Hong Kong question'. On the side of continuity, one may note London and Beijing's declarations of continued loyalty to the Sino-British Joint Declaration; the fact that the bilateral Joint Liaison Group resumed regular meetings, after a brief postponement in July-September 1989; the generally unexceptionable nature of the Basic Law passed in Beijing in April 1990 as Hong Kong's future constitution (it even gave a little extra on direct elections to the Legislative Council, though much less than demanded by the Hong Kong majority); and the limited, though still important, after-effects of June 1989 on mainland-Hong Kong economic relations and the Hong Kong economy generally. For all that, 1989 reopened—for a while at least—the original debate on the correctness of the Hong Kong solution, and while there were many voices to reaffirm its inevitability, uncertainties surfaced elsewhere which will not be easily or painlessly resolved. The lost time that should have been spent on practical, cooperative preparation for the hand-over in 1997 will not be easy to make up either, even when and if there is a new wind blowing from Beijing.

A VICTORY FOR PRAGMATISM?

The balance drawn above is already clearly in favour of pragmatism and continuity in China's own foreign policy, limited mainly by the change in other countries' positions. Should this be seen as the product of inertia and/or a rearguard action by Qian Qichen and his diplomatic cadres, who must have seen how much would have been lost by a simpler-minded approach? Or was it

actively willed by the top leadership, several new members of
which had considerable experience abroad (notably Jiang Zemin
and Li Ruihuan)? Did Deng Xiaoping himself cast the crucial
vote for conserving the gains of his years of 'open' diplomacy?
Or did the facts of the international situation simply leave no
other course available? Within the Chinese establishment, has the
influence of foreign-policy think-tanks been weakened or com-
mandeered by Zhao Ziyang's opponents and how should one
interpret the establishment of a new Foundation of International
Strategic Studies in January 1990 under State Councillor Ji
Pengfei?[37] Is the impression correct that the economically progressive regions and zones of China have largely won their case
for continued policy latitude and if so, will this bring a further
flowering of 'provincial diplomacy'?[38] Even if the PLA have not
influenced short-term policies, have they been promised resources
for a further naval expansion that could presage Chinese strong-
arm tactics, if not actual conflict, in the North Pacific and South
China Sea in future?[39]

  The second group of questions cannot be answered for lack of
information. Those in the first are difficult to tackle because,
across most of the field, objective facts, China's strategic interest
and the ideology professed by the new leadership do not actually
conflict. At one level China was arguably just following through
the logic of its insistence, ever since the time of the Sino-Soviet
split, that the 'socialist movement' has no normative or constraining character and that State-to-State relations are not made
'special' by ideological kinship or the lack of it. At another level,
the policy of building economic strength which still holds good in
Beijing—and in the name of which, indeed, the new leaders have
justified their tough measures against instability—is organically
linked with opening and the pursuit of peace in external policy.
This linkage is older and perhaps even more basic than that
between opening and 'reform', at least in the recently accepted
definition.

  In retrospect the particular international conjuncture of
1989/90, as well as Beijing's own policies, may have made it easier
for China to salvage a great deal of its diplomatic *acquis* and for
others to move back towards 'business as usual'. A *modus vivendi*
with the Soviet Union and Eastern Europe would have been
harder to find if Gorbachev had not, in the preceding years,
approved the elimination of ideology from inter-socialist relationships. If Asia had already developed a formal structure of
cooperation and obligation, or if China had already entered on

more than a minimum of international commitments (including membership of non-UN global institutions), the sanctions operation would have been on a quite different scale and China could hardly have got away with so many of her spheres of operation unaffected.[40] Had the international situation been less uncertain, with the changes in Europe not yet started or already resolved, would the case for conserving relations with Beijing have looked so strong in Moscow or Tokyo, let alone in Washington?

CONCLUSION

The dichotomy between Chinese diplomacy and internal politics, which suited most partners pretty well in 1989-90, could become harder for them to accept and for China to sustain if present trends towards formal political cooperation on the basis of shared values, and deeper economic interpenetration, should continue. Their force will depend to some extent on whether the Soviet Union upholds or turns back from its new-found commitment to the process. At any rate it is hard to imagine the world's top 20 or so countries switching their allegiance to the arid, essentially non-integrationist 'new international political order' advocated by China in which no state would have the right to comment on anything within another's borders. There is a not insubstantial group of countries—Asian, African, Arab and South American—who have been happy to accept China amongst them on that basis, and who may remain so for some time to come. But can these countries supply all that China needs to reach its full potential for growth—in spiritual and intellectual as well as material/technological terms? Is the status of a global power, to which China reasonably aspires given its size and regional influence, within their gift, or does it not rather require the acceptance of responsibilities and restraints that would set China apart from them? More concretely, can Asia itself remain immune much longer to the integrationist process and the spread both internally and internationally of concern over human rights? The Chinese are quite capable of anticipating that problem, as shown by their declarations in late 1989/90 that any Asian system of cooperation should remain non-obligatory and should stretch across ideological differences.[41] But China is particularly poorly placed at the moment to dictate such an outcome. In its diplomacy, as in its internal affairs, the solutions found in 1989/90 may turn out to be transitional at best, certainly inadequate, and arguably ill-suited to achieve the fullest realisation of China's destiny in the world.

NOTES

[1] *Beijing Review*, 26 December 1988 - 1 January 1989, translating a *People's Daily* article of 16 December.

[2] See the author's 'China and Eastern Europe: A Judgement on the "Socialist Community" ' in *The Pacific Review* No. 3, 1990 and 'Eastern Europe II: The China Connection' in *The World Today*, July 1990.

[3] Gerald Segal, 'Northeast Asia: all aboard the détente train?' in *The World Today* Vol. 46, No. 3, March 1990.

[4] For example, through the reprinting by *People's Daily* on 22 August 1989 of a speech made by Deng Xiaoping in 1956 warning against Polish and Hungarian notions of 'big democracy'. Several of the official accounts of Zhao Ziyang's 'crimes' alleged a plan to dissolve the Communist Party from within, using terminology clearly influenced by East European developments.

[5] See, for example, Qian Qichen's and Wu Xiongcheng's articles in *Beijing Review* of 11-17 September 1989; Wang Jingpiao, 'West European "Strategy of Integration" Towards the Soviet Union and Eastern Europe', *International Strategic Studies* (published by the Beijing Institute for Strategic Studies) No. 4, December 1989; and several articles in *International Strategic Studies* No. 1 of 1990. A Xinhua (New China News Agency) publication of summer 1989 called *Important Western Political Figures on Peaceful Evolution* traced the Western strategy of integration through infiltration as far back as Dulles.

[6] *People's Daily* overseas edition, 17 July 1989.

[7] This is well summed up in Banning N Garrett and Bonnie S Glaser, 'Chinese Assessments of Global Trends and the Emerging Era in International Relations' in *Asian Survey* April 1989. For an interesting Soviet account see S Goncharov and A Vinogradov, 'The Evolution of PRC's Foreign Policy Concept', *Far Eastern Affairs* No. 5, 1988.

[8] Full text in SWB Special Supplement FE/0720 C2/1 of 23 March 1990. The significance of the word 'hegemonism' was that it could apply to over-mighty socialist as well as capitalist states, and had in practice been used by Beijing more against Moscow than against Washington.

[9] Patrick L Smith in 'The Chinese-Soviet Impasse: Efforts for Asia Peace May Suffer', *International Herald Tribune*, 16 January 1990 quotes an internal Chinese Party document of December 1989 as using this phrase but as going on to say that Gorbachev should not be criticised openly.

[10] See for example Michael B Yahuda, 'The People's Republic of China at 40: Foreign Relations' in *The China Quarterly* No. 119 of September 1989; Sheldon W Simon, 'The Sino-Soviet future: some PRC Perspectives' in the *Third World Quarterly* of July 1989; and Dr Laura Newby, 'Sino-Soviet Rapprochement and its Implications for China's Foreign Policy' in *RUSI/Brassey's Defence Yearbook* 1990.

[11] The Director of the Chinese Party's International Liaison Department went to Moscow in September 1989 and the Director of its Propaganda Department in March 1990. The Deputy Director of the CPSU International Department visited China in April 1990.

[12] Major-General Song Wenzhong, Director of the Ministry of National Defence Foreign Affairs Bureau. See SWB FE/0731 A2/1, 5 April.

[13] Similar points are made in Gerald Segal, 'Sino-Soviet Relations', in Gerald Segal ed., *Chinese Politics and Foreign Policy Reform*, Kegan Paul International for RIIA 1990.

[14] Barter trade is not excluded and China is making new efforts to encourage it on a province-to-province basis, but it will not be counted towards the targets in official trade agreements. On this and other aspects of future Sino-East European relations see the first article cited in Note 2 above.

[15] This point was made in Li Peng's NPC statement referred to in Note 8 above, and developed at more length in Chai Chengwen, 'The Situation Tending Towards Relaxation, the Struggle Being Acute and Complicated', *International Strategic Studies* No. 1, March 1990.

[16] A point well made by Michael B Yahuda, 'Sino-American Relations', in Gerald Segal, *Chinese Politics* op. cit.

[17] This is admitted in Shao Wenguang, 'China's Relations with the Superpowers', *Survival* Vol. XXXII No. 2, March/April 1990.

[18] Kim Il-Sung is said (by diplomatic sources) to have remarked to the visiting President of Zimbabwe at the Pyongyang Youth Games in Autumn 1980: 'When Comrade Deng opened the door I advised him to put up a mosquito net. Now all sorts of insects have flown in and stung him on the nose.'

[19] See details in Harry G Gelber, 'China's New Uncertainties: Security Prospects' in *The Pacific Review* Vol. 3, No. 1 1990.

[20] On 2 November 1989 the Chinese MFA spokesman welcomed the informal US-Soviet Summit and expressed hope that the two sides would do 'more down to earth work in promoting relaxation and stability of the international situation'. Chinese positions on disarmament generally did not harden after June but even moved forward a little, with Qian Qichen's announcement that China would send an observer to the Fourth NPT Review Conference in August 1990 (vide his speech of 27 February 1990 at the CD in Geneva, quoted in an unpublished paper by Wang Houkang for the RIIA, 'China and Disarmament'). China's position on entering talks about reducing its own nuclear weapons remains, however, that the time for this will come only after the two Superpowers have pledged themselves to stop all testing, production and deployment of nuclear systems (cf. Qian Qichen's remarks to journalists on 28 March 1990).

[21] The linkage between foreign-policy and domestic ideological themes post-June is noted by Jean-Luc Domenach, 'Ideological Reform', in Gerald Segal, *Chinese Politics . . .* op. cit. He concludes, however, that this use of ideology is 'essentially defensive' and has only 'partly and temporarily halted the progressive decline in the role of ideology in Chinese foreign policy'.

[22] At the time of writing (May 1990) the Western consensus has held solid in the main for nine months. The principal departures, agreed or unilateral, from

it have been the two visits by US National Security Adviser Scowcroft to China in July and December 1989, the recent Australian and New Zealand decisions to renew Ministerial visits, the approval of a World Bank loan to China for earthquake rehabilitation in early 1990, and the resumption of discussions (though without commitment) on Japan's third Yen loan. There has also been some readjustment in 'grey areas' of the measures covering defence-related supplies, export credit cover and the demarcation line between 'new' and 'ongoing' soft loans. (Most of the 12's measures against China were lifted, by agreement, on 24 October 1990.)

[23] Michael B Yahuda, op. cit.

[24] Formulation used by the then Chinese Ambassador to Washington, Han Xu, in a speech at Palm Beach on 24 July 1989.

[25] Discussed in Jin Park, 'Korean Reunification and the New German Question', *The Pacific Review* Vol. 3, No. 1 1990.

[26] From Li Peng's NPC speech cited in Note 8.

[27] See for instance François Joyaux, 'Vers un nouvel équilibre international en Extrême-Orient' in *Politique Etrangère* No. 1, 1989 and Dick Wilson, 'A Whole New Power Game—With Japan the Joker in the Pack' in *China Review* February 1989.

[28] Laura Newby, 'Sino-Japanese Relations' in Gerald Segal, *Chinese Politics*, op. cit.

[29] Nobuaki Tanaka, 'The Impact of the Historic Changes in East-West Relations on the Far East', *IIGP Policy Paper*, Tokyo 25 December 1989. He argues that Asia needs a 'concept' for future inter-continental cooperation if it is not to lose touch with the West, that the 'isolationist' States like China risk being left even further behind in the process and that Japan must take the lead in evolving active policies towards Eastern Europe.

[30] See Gerald Segal, 'North East Asia . . .' op. cit. in Note 3 above.

[31] The occasion was a visit by Masayoshi Ito and others on 19 September 1989.

[32] Chen Feng in 'An Assessment of the Trend of Development of the Security Situation in the Asian-Pacific Region in the 1990s', *International Strategic Studies* No. 1, 1990, lists Indian military improvements and concludes that they have 'far surpassed the defensive need of India'. He does not rule out further India-Pakistan hostilities or conflict over the Sino-Indian border.

[33] According to Chinese MFA statements, Sino-Indonesian talks in December 1989 and in March 1990 resolved respectively the technical problems in the way of recognition and the bulk of outstanding debt questions. A visit to Peking by Indonesian Foreign Minister Alatas was seen as the completion of the process but its timing was still not clear at the time of writing.

[34] The Communist-run Hong Kong newspaper *Wen Wei Po* made this point in an article of 4 April 1990, alluding also to improvements in Chinese relations with Burma, Thailand, Singapore, and Brunei among others. See also Gary Klintworth, 'The Outlook for Cambodia: The China Factor', *The Pacific Review* Vol. 3, No. 1 1990.

[35] Qian Qichen in an interview with 'Chinafrique', translated in *Beijing Review* No. 49, 4-10 December 1989.

[36] On the Middle East China continued to support the Palestinian cause and criticise Israeli rigidity, while advocating a peaceful settlement through an

international conference. On Southern Africa, Qian Qichen argued during his summer 1989 tour for moderation and dialogue between Pretoria and the ANC and South Africa and the front-line states. In March 1990 he welcomed the SAG's release of Mandela and agreement to talks with African nationalist groups, while stressing that China could still not recognise South Africa diplomatically. Even so, a few non-governmental exchanges took place between China and South Africa after June 1989 (eg a South African MPs' visit to China and a visit to South Africa by the Chinese Association for International Understanding) and there was growing interest in trade. Similarly, Chinese and Israeli representatives at the UN started a dialogue and agreed in February 1990 on exchanging language students.

[37] Reported in *China Daily* 17 January 1990. Previously, the only institute in Peking specifically devoted to strategic questions was the BISS, linked with the Ministry of National Defence. Its Chairman Xu Xin and Foreign Minister Qian Qichen both took part in the FISS's inaugural meeting.

[38] See David S G Goodman ed, 'China's Regional Development' (RIIA/Routledge London 1989) and Peter Ferdinand, 'Regionalism', in Gerald Segal, *Chinese Politics . . .* , op. cit. in Note 13 above.

[39] Gerald Segal, 'As Soviet Power Wanes, China's Military Reach Is Expanding', *International Herald Tribune* 3 May 1990. For a Chinese analysis which implicitly supports this view see Xu Shiming, 'Perspectives of Maritime Security in the Asian-Pacific Region', *International Strategic Studies* No. 1, 1990.

[40] Qian Qichen told a press conference in Harare on 5 August 1989 'of the 137 countries that maintain diplomatic relations with China, only about 20 reacted to the event that happened in China'.

[41] See for example an article by Qian Qichen in *Liaowang* (Outlook) magazine reproduced in *China Daily* of 25 December 1989.

Signposts

The PLO and The Gulf Crisis*

ANDREW RATHMELL

The author studied at Balliol College Oxford and continued his research at the George Washington University, Washington DC. He is currently researching for a doctorate on Middle Eastern terrorism at King's College, London.

Since Iraq's invasion of Kuwait on 2 August, the Arab world has experienced a series of political earthquakes. In an unprecedented move, Saudi Arabia has permitted the deployment of American, British and French troops on its territory. Syria, which only seven years ago was engaged in a bitter proxy war against the US, has aligned itself with the West. Jordan's King Hussein has alienated his former admirers in the West by siding with Saddam Hussein.

For the Palestinian movement, the regional realignments have been especially dramatic. To world opinion, both the leadership of the Palestinian Liberation Organization (PLO) and its followers in the streets of Jerusalem and Amman have appeared as stooges of Saddam Hussein. As a result, they have been ostracised by their erstwhile benefactors in the Gulf states and Egypt, as well as by the Israeli peace camp.

Perhaps the Palestinians have really dug their own grave. Maybe, 34 months after the outbreak of the *Intifadah* that thrust the PLO onto the world stage, the organisation has taken a stance that will exclude it from the Middle East 'peace process'. Whatever the outcome, as the international reaction to the Temple Mount killings on 8 October 1990 demonstrated, the Gulf crisis can only have a dramatic impact on the Palestinian question.

THE PLO'S DRIFT TOWARDS IRAQ

The Iraqi invasion of Kuwait came at a time when the Palestinian movement was rapidly sinking into frustration and despair. In the months preceding the invasion, it had become increasingly clear to many Palestinians that the 'peace process' was going nowhere. There was a widespread perception that the popular struggle in the occupied territories and the diplomatic

305

manoeuvres of the PLO leadership were futile. Many argued that even a war could not be worse than the status quo.[1]

These attitudes can be explained by the experiences of the Palestinians over the last decade. In 1982, the Israeli Defence Forces (IDF) crushed the PLO's military in southern Lebanon and forced over 14,000 Palestinian soldiers to leave Beirut. The rout was completed by Syria the following year when its client militias drove Arafat's *Fatah* from the Lebanese port of Tripoli. The effects of this expulsion from Lebanon were shattering for the PLO. The organisation lost its only remaining secure base. Its institutions and personnel were scattered across the Arab world. Their new host governments frequently prevented the Palestinian leaders from acting independently. Since there were no longer any military bases within striking range of Israel, the doctrine of armed struggle that had been at the core of the Palestinian movement since 1968 lay in ruins.

For a time, Arafat's position as leader was threatened as disagreements within the organisation erupted into internecine violence. Although Arafat retained his position as Chairman and succeeded in marginalising his Syrian-backed opponents, it seemed that the PLO was finished as an independent political force. The organisation's weakness was demonstrated at the 1987 Arab League summit in Amman, where Arab governments pushed the Palestine issue to the bottom of their agenda.

The *Intifadah*, which broke out in December 1987, suddenly and dramatically reversed this decline. Although initially taken by surprise, the PLO leadership rapidly took advantage of the uprising and was able to ride the wave of international support that it generated. On the strength of the *Intifadah*, Chairman Arafat persuaded the PLO to shift to a new approach. The essence of this new strategy was to draw close to the US-backed 'moderate' Arab regimes and to make concessions in the hope that the US would come to regard the PLO as an acceptable, moderate interlocutor. The aim was to persuade Washington to put pressure on Israel to accept the PLO as a negotiating partner and to begin substantive negotiations on the Palestine issue. The key components of this approach were attempts to cultivate good relations with Egypt, to generate a public image in the West of Palestinians as 'victims' rather than 'terrorists', to make concessions as demanded by the US, and to distance the movement from the 'radical' Arab regimes.

In accordance with this strategy, Arafat made historic concessions that thrust the movement into the diplomatic limelight. He opened the way for a dialogue with the US by recognizing Israel, renouncing terrorism and accepting both a two state solution and UN resolutions 242 and 338. In addition, the Palestinian movement benefited from closer relations with the European Community (EC) and from a dialogue with the Israeli left. In the Arab world, the *Intifadah* enabled the PLO to reassert its position as the sole legitimate representative of the Palestinian people, helped by Jordan's renunciation of its aspirations to lead the cause, exemplified by Jordan's severance of its administrative ties with the West Bank. Relations between the PLO and Egypt improved as Egypt mediated between the US, Israel and the Palestinians, while in return, the PLO facilitated President Mubarak's return to the Arab fold.

Besides revitalising the movement, the *Intifadah* gave hope to many Palestinians. The young activists in the occupied territories demonstrated to their compatriots in the Palestinian diaspora that it was possible to stand up to the Israeli Army and that the world community could be persuaded to sympathise with the Palestinians' plight. With the declaration of a Palestinian state in November 1988 and the opening of a dialogue with the US the following month, Palestinian hopes reached a peak.

During 1989 and 1990, however, the strategy appeared to be failing. Support for the *Intifadah* remained strong, but Palestinians in the occupied territories were ground down by the Israel Defence Forces' (IDF) 'iron fist' of repression. The US–PLO dialogue carried on at a low level but, as a senior Palestine National Council (PNC) official commented, 'it was more like a kind of tiresome courtesy visit', than a forum for substantive negotiations.[2] The National Unity Government in Israel produced an election proposal, but was unwilling to make the concessions that would have been necessary for the proposal to be acceptable to the Palestinians. Palestinian morale was also badly hit by the prospect of a flood of Jewish immigration from the USSR. This generated fears of a resurgent Israel and led to disillusionment with both of the Superpowers, as neither Washington nor Moscow made any serious attempt to stem the flow of immigrants. In March 1990, the Israeli government fell and after protracted negotiations was replaced by a new one dominated by Yitzhak Shamir's Likud party. Supported by an increasingly hardline public opinion, the Likud government has remained resolutely opposed to any form of negotiation that may lead to the acknowledgement of Palestinian national rights.

On 20 June, after Arafat had refused to condemn an abortive terrorist raid on Tel Aviv by the Palestine Liberation Front (PLF), President Bush suspended the US-PLO dialogue. Although some hoped that the suspension would be only temporary, for many Palestinians the American move merely confirmed their belief that the US and Israel were determined to deprive the Palestinians of their national rights. It was felt that all the sacrifices made since December 1987 had been wasted.

This feeling of frustration had several effects. Once again the Palestinian movement began to re-emphasise the armed struggle. The more extreme elements within the Palestinian movement, such as Ahmed Jibril's Palestinian Front for the Liberation of Palestine—General Command (PFLP-GC), had never assented to Arafat's diplomatic approach and had continued to launch commando attacks against Israeli targets.[3] However, the two major radical groups, George Habash's Palestinian Front for the Liberation of Palestine (PFLP) and Nayef Hawatmeh's Democratic Front for the Liberation of Palestine (DFLP), had halted their armed operations in order to give the diplomatic strategy a chance to work. As the peace process stagnated, these groups renewed the armed struggle with numerous attempts to infiltrate fighters into Israel from southern Lebanon. More importantly, the stagnation in the peace process led to growing calls for *Fatah* to turn the *Intifadah* into an armed insurgency. In the face of Israeli intransigence, many Palestinians came to believe that the Israelis would only listen to the 'logic of force'.

These calls for escalation became more insistent after 20 June, and were one indication that the PLO leadership in Tunis was gradually losing control of the uprising to more radical elements. This trend was further evidenced by the increase in the number of killings within the Palestinian community, despite orders by the Unified National Leadership of the Uprising (UNLU) to reduce the number of attacks on suspected 'collaborators'.[4] The PLO also came under increasing pressure from rival groups in the territories. The radical Islamic movement *Hamas*, which rejects any real compromise with Israel, has gained significant support over the last year and has competed with the PLO in organizing demonstrations and strikes.[5] In an attempt to co-opt the movement, the PLO leadership entered into negotiations in July 1990, but were unwilling to accept the movement's demand for 40 per cent of the seats in the PNC, which acts as the Palestinian 'parliament'.

With hindsight, the most significant result of the stagnation in the peace process has been the PLO's growing reliance on Iraq. Beginning in late 1989, Arafat gradually guided the PLO into an alliance with Iraq as he came to realise that his diplomatic strategy was failing. Despite a series of humiliating concessions, the PLO had made no concrete gains with its policy of moderation. Arafat's response to this failure was to edge the PLO towards the 'rejectionist' camp. As the Arab League summit held in Baghdad in May 1990 demonstrated, this camp was now led by Saddam Hussein. In moving closer to Saddam, Arafat hoped to compensate for the PLO's weak bargaining position by using Iraq's military might to counter Israel's military dominance. In his view, Israel would only have an incentive to compromise if its military pre-eminence was threatened by an Arab state. In 1990, Iraq was the only Arab power with the means and the will to stand up to Israel.

The disintegration of the Eastern Bloc regimes during late 1989 and early 1990 further influenced these geopolitical calculations. The PLO's military and diplomatic support from these sources rapidly evaporated, and it became clear that America was now the sole Superpower. The PLO leadership despondently predicted a resurgent Israel backed by untrammelled American power. In their view, Iraq was the only available obstacle to a new American-Israeli regional order—an order in which the PLO would be marginalised.[6]

During 1989 and 1990, the PLO gained both financially and militarily from its relationship with Iraq. Before the invasion of Kuwait, Iraq and Saudi Arabia were the only two Arab states to regularly fulfill their monetary pledges to the PLO. On the military side, at least 5,000 *Fatah* soldiers, along with their dependents, were based inside Iraq.[7] However, the PLO was careful not to break with the pro-Western Arab regimes as their financial support remained indispensable. Perhaps there was also a lingering hope that the diplomatic strategy could be picked up again at some future date, maybe after a change of government in Israel. In order to exploit any such opportunities, the PLO needed to remain on friendly terms with states such as Egypt, whose diplomatic orientations would facilitate negotiations with Washington and Jerusalem.

Thus, on the eve of the Iraqi invasion of Kuwait, the Palestinians were despairing of a negotiated solution. Radical groups and advocates of violence were gaining ground and the PLO leadership was tightening its links with Saddam Hussein in the belief that only he could resist the imposition of a *Pax Americana*.

THE PLO AFTER THE INVASION: MEDIATOR OR PARTISAN?

It is not clear whether the PLO leadership had foreknowledge of Saddam's intention to invade Kuwait. There have been as yet unsubstantiated rumours that the PLO was intimately involved in the planning for the invasion. According to one of these accounts, PLO support for Iraq was to be rewarded by a share of the loot plundered from Kuwaiti banks.[8]

The PLO's initial public reaction was supportive of Iraq, but was presented in the guise of a mediation effort. By the middle of August, the leadership had realised that they were dangerously isolated in the Arab world. Rather than change their policy, they responded by placing more emphasis on their mediatory role and by attempting to shift the focus of the intra-Arab debate onto the question of Western intervention. From the beginning of the crisis, the PLO had been unequivocally opposed to this intervention. Subsequently, this opposition was extended to those Arab regimes that were cooperating with the West. Despite some attempts at damage limitation, it now appears that the PLO has broken decisively with these regimes.

In many respects there was a striking continuity between PLO policy before and after the invasion. During the months of diplomatic skirmishing between Iraq and the West that preceded the events of 2 August, the PLO sided with Iraq. The organisation interpreted Western actions, such as the seizure of Iraqi nuclear triggers at Heathrow Airport and protests over the execution of the journalist Farzad Bazoft, as part of a concerted propaganda campaign aimed at undermining Saddam Hussein. PLO organs responded with vigorous defences of Iraq and denunciations of 'imperialist' plots. The Western reaction to the invasion of Kuwait enabled the PLO to claim that they had been right all along in discerning a plot aimed at destroying Saddam. The organisation's pro-Iraqi propaganda was stepped up, as exemplified by this broadcast on 9 August:

> This frenzied imperialist alignment [the deployment of US forces to Saudi Arabia] aims to subdue and humiliate the Arab nation. It is a prelude to

a comprehensive imperialist invasion of Arab identity with the aim of casting it into the abyss of absolute bondage to imperialism.[9]

There was also continuity in the PLO's self-appointed stance as a mediator. In the days before the invasion, Arafat had been instrumental in setting up the talks between Kuwait's Crown Prince Sheikh Saad and a senior Iraqi official that took place in Jeddah on 31 July. In the week following the invasion, Arafat was quick to suggest a peace plan. Although the plan came to nothing, Arafat's hectic schedule (he visited four capitals in five days) put him at the centre of Arab diplomacy in those crucial days. This continuity in behaviour reflected a continuity in policy. By August, the PLO was firmly within Iraq's sphere of influence. The relationship was so close that, even if he had not wanted to, Arafat had little choice but to play his part in Saddam Hussein's post-invasion diplomatic strategy. The objectives of this strategy were to prevent a united Arab reaction to the invasion and to forestall Western intervention.

The need for aggressive diplomatic action was clearly demonstrated to Baghdad when the Arab League ministerial council, meeting on 3 August, passed a resolution condemning the Iraqi invasion and demanding an unconditional withdrawal.[10] Iraq's reaction was, first, to declare this resolution void as it had not been adopted unanimously and second, to throw up a smoke-screen by announcing that its forces were withdrawing from Kuwait.[11] At the same time as these declarations were being made, Arafat began to carry out his part in the diplomatic offensive. His role was to travel the region with a Libyan-Palestinian peace proposal, the objectives of which were made explicit by the Libyan news agency Jana, on 4 August, '... [Colonel Qadhafi] has ... said that the Libyan-Palestinian peace plan, which is being conveyed ... by President Yasir Arafat, renders any Arab summit unnecessary [and] blocks the way to any foreign intervention'.[12]

The proposal served its purpose. An emergency summit, scheduled to meet in Jeddah on 5 August, was cancelled at the last minute. It was not until 10 August that a full Arab League summit met, at which it was decided to despatch an Arab force to Saudi Arabia. Arafat's efforts with the Libyan peace proposal were a major factor in delaying this decision by five days.

After the cancellation of the emergency summit, Arafat continued his round of visits to Arab capitals. His primary objectives continued to be to soften any criticism of Iraq and, above all, to forestall foreign military intervention. This policy was expressed in a radio broadcast on 5 August which stated that

> the Palestinian leadership ... began to co-ordinate with all the Arab capitals ... in order to prevent any foreign intervention in Arab affairs, especially as reports have been pouring in ... of the Zionists urging the United States to embark on a flagrant military intervention in the Arab area....[13]

The PLO clearly felt it imprudent to come out openly in support of Saddam's invasion. Its public statements tended to gloss over this aspect and instead focused on the threat of US intervention, as in this broadcast:

> in our talk here, we do not wish to touch on the question of the Iraqi invasion, whether to support it or condemn it, but we are puzzled by US double standards. ... The objective of the United States is the continuation of its hegemony over the oil-producing countries in the Arabian Gulf.[14]

On 7 August, President Bush despatched a squadron of F-15 fighters and detachments of the 82nd Airborne Division to Saudi Arabia. Recognising that its attempts to prevent foreign intervention had failed, the PLO shifted its attacks onto those Arab countries that had cooperated with the American move. On 8 August the Voice of Palestine radio station lamented that

> ... it is regrettable to see this frenzied campaign ... [of hostility to the Arab nation] ... from certain Arabs who are tolling the bells to welcome the US invasion of the Arab region instead of beating the drums of war to deter it....[15]

These attacks undoubtedly exacerbated the growing isolation of the PLO in the Arab world. The extent of this isolation became painfully clear at the Arab League summit held in Cairo on 10 August. The PLO was one of only three members to vote against the resolution to despatch an Arab force to Saudi Arabia, although several others did abstain. Their isolation was already beginning to cost the PLO dearly. The United Arab Emirates (UAE) had begun to deport leading Palestinians immediately after the invasion. After the Cairo summit, Saudi Arabia declared Arafat *persona non grata* and suggested that it would boycott the PLO for as long as he remained in power.[16]

Concern within the PLO at this isolation manifested itself in a series of contradictory statements regarding the organisation's position at the Cairo summit. On 13 August Saeed Kamal, the Palestinian Ambassador to Egypt, admitted that the PLO had rejected the resolution but said that it now condemned the Iraqi invasion. He was immediately contradicted by the Tunis press office. They claimed that the PLO had abstained from the vote. On the same day Al Tayeb Abdul Rahim, the ambassador to Jordan, dismissed these accounts and confirmed that the PLO stood by its opposition to the decision and '. . . view[ed] the Cairo summit resolutions as illegal.'[17]

Internal disputes continued to trouble the PLO over the following weeks. Palestinian communities in the Gulf whose livelihoods were directly threatened by their leadership's stance were especially concerned. On 15 September, a Palestinian newspaper based in the UAE argued that 'the Palestinian cause received a 'direct stab' from the Iraqi invasion' and accused the PLO leadership of terrorising 'anyone who tries to object to its policy.'[18]

After mid-August, the PLO did make efforts to reduce its isolation by emphasising that its refusal to condemn Iraq was due to its attempt to play the role of neutral mediator, and not an indication of support for the invasion.[19] As the PLO leadership stated on 16 August, 'the target of these efforts [to mediate a peaceful solution] has been . . . to avert the catastrophe of war . . . The goal is not to realise trivial financial or media gains or to curry favour with others. . . .'[20] On one occasion, a PLO official went so far as to say: 'it is essential to get the Iraqi forces out of Kuwait. The occupation is illegal.'[21] This policy of presenting a neutral face was accompanied by overtures to the Gulf states. On several occasions, PLO representatives declared their support for the Gulf regimes. In a letter to King Fahd of Saudi Arabia, Hani al-Hassan, political adviser to Arafat, wrote that Palestinians were prepared to 'sacrifice themselves for Saudi Arabia's defence, for the safeguard of its security and its sovereignity'.[22]

However, these nuances to the PLO's position represented a new propaganda approach, rather than any substantive change in policy. The overwhelming weight of evidence is that both the PLO's propaganda and actions continued to be rooted in the belief that Saddam's survival was vital to the Palestinian cause.

As well as their constant public attacks on the Western intervention as a 'Zionist-imperialist' plot to emasculate the Arab nation, the PLO helped Iraq in more concrete ways. A major element in Saddam's diplomatic offensive was his rapprochement with Iran. This freed over 300,000 troops for redeployment to southern Iraq, and opened up the possibility that Iran would become a conduit for the importation of embargoed goods. The PLO did its best to facilitate this rapprochement by despatching Sheikh Abdul Hamid al-Sayeh, the speaker of the PNC, to Tehran to negotiate the supply of food to Iraq across the Iranian border.[23] Subsequently it has appeared that President Rafsanjani is committed to implementing UN sanctions, indicating that Sheikh al-Sayeh's mission was not a success. Nevertheless, the fact that his visit took place at all indicates that the PLO leadership is concerned that Iraq should not be starved into submission.

In addition to behind the scenes diplomatic support, the PLO has frequently offered unequivocal public backing to the Iraqi government. On 24 August, Faruq Qaddumi, head of the PLO Political Department, stated that 'the State of Palestine stands firmly alongside fraternal Iraq in the glorious defence of its territory against all possibilities of foreign aggression . . . We stand alongside Iraq to defeat all these colonialist armies trying to harm it. . . .'[24] On 3 September Chairman Arafat himself said: 'to those who ask about the Palestinian position, we ask where Israel is in this war. . . . We can only be in the camp hostile to Israel and its imperialist allies. . . .'[25]

If, in the days after the Cairo summit, the PLO leadership had considered abandoning Iraq, such a move was made impossible by Saddam Hussein's initiative launched on 12 August. This three-point proposal called for the replacement of US forces by an Arab force, the lifting of sanctions and an Israeli withdrawal from the occupied territories. By linking a solution to the Gulf Crisis to the Palestinian question Saddam succeeded in igniting an explosion of popular support amongst Palestinians in Jordan, Lebanon, Israel and the occupied territories. As a result of this popular support, it became even more unlikely that the PLO would disengage itself from its alliance with Saddam. Any lessening of its support for Iraq would henceforth be regarded by the Palestinian masses as a betrayal of their cause.[26]

Saddam's linkage initiative thus had two results for the PLO. First, it locked the Organisation more tightly into Iraq's embrace. Although there were slight nuances in the PLO's position thereafter, there was little choice but to continue to act as Iraq's diplomatic front man. Second, the concept of linkage has increasingly seemed to promise some gains for the Palestinian movement. Arafat had originally pushed the PLO closer to Iraq in the belief that only Iraq's military weight stood any chance of pressuring

Israel and the US into making concessions over the occupied territories. As the crisis unfolded during September and October, it began to seem that his calculations might pay off.

PLO propaganda since 12 August has placed heavy emphasis on the benefits of a solution involving linkage. Qaddumi argued that

> ... the linking of all withdrawals, especially from ... occupied Palestinian land ... is a positive initiative that constitutes the basis for a just peace in the region. Without withdrawal from [the] occupied territories, there will be no peace in the land. ... [27]

In a message to a UN conference held on 29 August, Arafat further stressed this theme, saying:

> [the PLO seeks] the settlement of all the pending and chronic problems in the Middle East, whether in the Gulf, Kuwait, Palestine, Lebanon or the Golan Heights. ... Despite the Gulf crisis, the Palestine issue remains at the top of the agenda of the UN. ... [28]

The concept of linkage has been incorporated into the PLO's various peace proposals. On 29 August, Arafat put forward a five point plan. The points were that (1) the PLO should act as a neutral mediator; (2) there should be a comprehensive solution to all of the problems in the region; (3) a solution in the Gulf should be within an Arab framework; (4) US forces should be replaced by a UN force and (5) sanctions should be suspended against Iraq and imposed against any country that refused to withdraw from occupied territory. The preamble to these proposals made it clear that a central PLO demand was that Israel should be treated with the same vigour that the UN had shown with regard to Iraq.[29]

This approach was developed during a visit to Moscow in late September by Yasir Abd-Rabbuh, the PLO's Information Minister. Disappointed that the USSR had not asked the US for an international conference at the Helsinki summit, he sought Soviet assurances that Moscow still supported the principle of a comprehensive Middle East settlement. It was suggested that such a conference should be held under the auspices of the UN Security Council.[30] In a speech made on 7 October, Arafat claimed that 'there was an 'international consensus' on the need to establish a link between the Gulf, the Palestine issue, Lebanon and the Golan Heights.'[31] This link formed the basis of a new ten point peace plan that was presented to the PLO's Executive Committee on 10 October.

The PLO has been encouraged in its pursuit of linkage by the speed with which the idea has gained implicit acceptance from many non-Arab governments. All have denied that they would accept a direct trade-off, but the major powers involved appear to agree that some concessions may have to be made to the Palestinians. The USSR was the first to hint that some link may be possible. In a press conference on 4 September, Foreign Minister Shevardnadze described the Gulf crisis and the Palestine issue as 'interlocking'.[32] This was followed by President Mitterand who, in a speech before the UN on 24 September, proposed 'direct dialogues between the parties involved in other Middle East problems' as part of a settlement to the crisis.[33] On 1 October, President Bush suggested that after Iraq's unconditional withdrawal, there may be a chance for 'all the states and peoples of the region to settle the conflict that divides the Arabs from Israel'.[34] Finally, on 4 October, Douglas Hurd, the British Foreign Secretary, made it clear that he expected Israel to accept an international peace conference once the Gulf crisis was over.[35]

This implicit linkage was given visible expression in the wake of the killing of 18 Palestinians in Jerusalem by Israeli Border Police on 8 October. In a major break from its previous policy, the US did not veto resolution 672, which condemned Israeli violence and appointed a fact-finding mission. Paradoxically, for the PLO the passage of this resolution marked a tactical defeat. It was not strong enough to restrain Israeli actions in the occupied territories, but it was enough to preserve the unity of the anti-Iraq coalition. In a sign of its annoyance, the PLO recalled its permanent observer at the UN, Zehdi Labib Terzi.[36] Nonetheless, although it may have lost the battle over the resolution, the Temple Mount killings and UN 672 represented a strategic victory for the PLO. Together they provided further indication that the Western powers would have to consider concessions to the Palestinian cause, and probably accept an international conference.

MOTIVES, COSTS AND BENEFITS

The PLO certainly did not welcome the invasion of Kuwait, but after the event, felt it had no choice but to side with Iraq. Despite internal divisions, the leadership has maintained a consistently pro-Iraqi policy throughout the crisis. The costs of doing so have been extremely high. However, the costs of not supporting Iraq are deemed to be higher. A comprehensive accounting of these relative costs and benefits cannot be made until the crisis has been resolved. Nonetheless, certain costs are already evident.

The most significant has been the damage done to the organisation's foreign relations, particularly with the Gulf states and Egypt. Palestinians living in the Gulf bear little emotional attachment to their host countries. They resent their status as second class citizens, unable to gain citizenship and facing restrictions on their rights to own property.[37] The Palestinian concern to preserve good relations with the Gulf states is solely mercenary. Saudi Arabia is estimated to have given almost $10 billion in aid to the PLO over the last two decades. The other Gulf states also gave aid to the PLO, as well as to development projects in the occupied territories. Kuwait, for instance, reportedly donated $50 million every year to Palestinian institutions in the West Bank. Most of this aid is now being withheld. Although Gulf leaders still proclaim support for the Palestinian cause, they feel betrayed by the PLO leadership and are unlikely to renew their financial aid while Arafat remains in power.[38]

Apart from official aid, the Gulf oil economy provided a living for the over 700,000 Palestinians resident in the Gulf states. Remittances from these expatriates made up almost a fifth of the GNP of the West Bank and Gaza. In addition, the PLO benefited from a 5 per cent income tax levied on these individuals. As a result of the PLO's stand, Palestinian workers now face persecution and expulsion. Saudi Arabia has closed its borders to returning Palestinian residents and has expelled over 5,000 workers. The UAE and Qatar have both deported hundreds of Palestinian activists. The latter action led the PLO to warn Qatar that: '[the Palestinians] know how to return a stronger blow for any dealt to them . . . Rulers of Qatar: Beware. Do not harm the people of Palestine'.[39]

Palestinian relations with Egypt have been even more badly affected. By the beginning of 1990, the PLO had restored good relations with Egypt. This relationship was regarded as important because of Egypt's close relations with the US and the diplomatic weight that it enjoyed in the Arab world. As a consequence of his support for Iraq, Egyptian officials have made it clear that they can no longer work with Arafat. A vitriolic officially-backed media campaign has targeted Arafat and the PLO. The Voice of Palestine radio station in Cairo has been shut down, and Palestinian residents subject to increased harassment by security forces under the guise of 'anti-terrorist' measures.[40]

Syria has been hostile to the PLO for some years now. President Asad's alignment with the anti-Iraq coalition has exacerbated the tension. If the US continues to allow Syria a free hand in Lebanon, as it did in respect of the overthrow of General Aoun, this could be dangerous for the PLO. *Fatah* has recently been consolidating its military position around Sidon in southern Lebanon. In September, it captured a major refugee camp from Abu Nidal's Fatah Revolutionary Council, and it has exploited its position as a buffer between *Hizbollah* and *Amal* to extend its presence in south Lebanon.[41] In view of the new alignment of forces in the region, it is conceivable that Syria could receive tacit approval from Israel and the US to root out the *Fatah* presence. If this happened, it would be a major blow to Arafat.

The PLO's relations with Jordan are in a state of flux. During the late 1980s, King Hussein and Arafat were often at odds. In the current crisis, both are ostensibly on the same side. For the first time in years Palestinian public opinion is now expressing admiration for King Hussein. It is possible that good relations may endure. However, the vociferous support for the PLO amongst the Jordanian population may eventually lead to friction. King Hussein may increasingly find himself in competition with Arafat for the loyalty of the 60 per cent of Jordanians who are of Palestinian origin.

Enthusiastic Palestinian support for a leader who has often vowed to destroy Israel has alienated sympathetic Israelis. One of the benefits of the *Intifadah* and the PLO's new moderation had been that a growing minority of Israelis were engaging in discussions with Palestinians. For the first time, significant portions of the Israeli left had begun to accept the necessity for Palestinian national self-determination. In 1988, negotiations with the PLO were endorsed by *Mapam*, one of the parties that had been instrumental in founding the Zionist state. However, Israeli leftists were horrified by the PLO's support for Iraq. Palestinian enthusiasm for Saddam Hussein's threats against Israel persuaded many on the left that they had been mistaken in accepting at face value previous Palestinian moderation. Most have now broken off their contacts with Palestinians. For the majority of Israelis, who never believed that the PLO had renounced its professed intention to destroy them, Palestinian support for Saddam has merely confirmed their views. There is no doubt that the PLO's stand has retarded the process of building confidence between Palestinians and Israelis.[42]

Outside the Middle East, the PLO's relations with Western countries has also suffered. In the US, the *Intifadah* and the PLO's moderate image had begun to erode the instinctive pro-Israeli stance of public opinion. Events such as the Temple Mount killings will reinforce the sympathetic image of Palestinians as victims. But Palestinian support for 'the Butcher of Baghdad', as the American tabloid press have labelled Saddam, has eroded some of this sympathy. If the PLO were to side with Iraq in a military conflict against US forces, it is likely that any remaining popular sympathy would evaporate. However, although the Palestinians' public image in the US is important, in the short term, the attitude of the Administration is more significant. A minority of PLO leaders are concerned to appear neutral in the hope that the Bush Administration will see fit to restore its dialogue with the PLO. The majority believe that the US has no interest in dealing with the PLO. As one official put it: 'Our bridges with Washington are already burned. We should not fool ourselves'.[43] Proponents of this view argue that the PLO's relations with the US could not be worse than they already are. The impact of the crisis on US-Israeli relations cannot yet be determined. Optimistic Palestinians argue that the US must now recognise that Israel is not a strategic asset, but rather is a diplomatic embarrassment. Their hope is that the US will thus reduce its commitment to Israel.

The EC's relations with the PLO do not appear to have been too badly affected, though there is resentment at the pro-Iraqi stance. However, the belief that stability in the Middle East can only be consequent on a solution to the Palestine issue remains widespread and Iraq's ability to mobilise popular support around the Palestinian question has been used as an argument in favour of pushing harder for a solution.

Relations between the PLO and the USSR have not been dramatically worsened by the crisis, but this is because they were already on the wane. As a result of his 'New Thinking' in foreign policy and his desire to please the West, Gorbachev had been edging the Soviet Union away from its previous close relations with the PLO. In fact, this shift was one of the catalysts that led the PLO to adopt its diplomatic strategy. Since 2 August, Moscow has continued to express support for an international conference, but has basically fallen into line with America's wishes. Instead of backing the PLO, it has used the opportunity to improve its relations with Israel and the 'moderate' Arab states. The PLO's anger at Gorbachev's behaviour was expressed by Abdullah Hurani, a member of the PLO Executive Committee. He 'condemned' the Soviet Union's stance and said that 'It is no longer possible to consider the USSR a friend or ally of the world's liberation forces. . . . It is very difficult for the PLO to accept such a position from the USSR'.[44]

Thus, many of the financial and diplomatic costs attached to the PLO's stance in the Gulf Crisis are already evident. However, the greatest danger for the PLO would arise if Saddam Hussein were defeated. If he were to fall, it seems unlikely that the current leadership of the PLO would be able to survive, despite Arafat's proven ability as a political survivor. Although the cost to the PLO of an Iraqi defeat cannot be accurately predicted, it is clear that in choosing to support Saddam, Arafat is gambling for very high stakes. However, given the political realities that he faces, the choice is rational. He has already benefited from it and the potential gains are enormous. PLO officials have repeatedly stressed that their support for Iraq is a consequence of popular pressure. They argue that if Arafat had not responded to this pressure, he would have lost all credibility among his followers. This explanation for the PLO's behaviour is valid, but only up to a point.

Amongst Palestinians in Israel, the occupied territories, Jordan and Lebanon there has been mass popular support for Iraq. Frustrated by the stagnant peace progress, the majority in these areas have come to regard Saddam as their sole hope. Since his aggressive rhetoric on 2 April threatening to '. . . let our fire consume half of Israel . . .',[45] Saddam has emerged as a new Arab hero. He is regarded as the only leader willing to stand up to Israel and the West. Since the deployment of Western forces in the Gulf and Iraq's linkage initiative, there have been frequent mass demonstrations in support of Saddam Hussein. In the occupied territories the Iraqi flag and posters of Saddam Hussein have become ubiquitous symbols of resistance to the Israeli occupation. A poll conducted in late August by an Israeli media company indicated that 90 per cent of Palestinians supported Iraq.

Palestinian public opinion does not generally support the invasion as such. Neither are they sympathetic to the Iraqi regime itself; its brutality is widely recognized. The support is based more on the principle of 'the enemy of my enemy is my friend'. The frustration generated by US support for Israel is being expressed in support for America's enemy. As the West Bank Palestinian leader Faisal al-Husseini put it,

> the sentiment of the people is not first of all support for the regime of Saddam Hussein or the occupation of Kuwait. It is a feeling against the United States which has neglected us.[46]

Arafat has certainly felt the need to respond to this public pressure.[47] He has been afraid that the more radical *Hamas* may undercut support for the PLO if the nationalists do not back Saddam strongly enough. However, the current of public opinion that the PLO leadership have chosen to follow is at odds with the views of a large minority of their constituency. The 700,000 Palestinians living in the Gulf have not displayed much admiration for Saddam. Although their voices have been muted, many have complained bitterly that the PLO's stance is disastrous because of the damage it is doing to relations between the PLO and the Arab Gulf states.[48] These expatriates represent a powerful constituency. In economic terms, they are far more important to the health of the Palestinian movement than the 1.75 million Palestinians living under Israeli occupation. Aside from a few gestures, Arafat has done nothing to respond to the demands of this portion of Palestinian public opinion. So, the desire to maintain public support cannot be the sole motive behind the PLO's pro-Iraqi policy.

Another motive for Arafat's stance is his desire to maintain unity within the PLO. The PLO is an umbrella body for numerous guerilla groups which are often violently at odds. One of Arafat's main priorities during his 22 year tenure as Chairman of this unwieldy organisation has been to preserve its internal unity. He has proven himself to be a master at this. In recent months, his adoption of a pro-Iraqi line has enabled him to unite most of the different factions behind him. After the invasion, all the constituent members of the Palestinian movement rapidly adopted radically anti-Western lines. At a meeting entitled the 'Conference of Arab Popular Movements Against Western Military Intervention (and) in Solidarity with Iraq' held in Amman from 15 to 17 September, Habash and Hawatmeh made it clear that they supported Arafat's policy. They called for the withdrawal of foreign forces, an Arab solution and the linking of the Gulf Crisis to the Palestine issue. Many of the smaller groups took an even more radical line, threatening to launch armed attacks on the 'imperialists'. Thus the PFLP-GC proclaimed:

'. . . millions of Arabs will carry rifles, start a rebellion, and express readiness to fight and confront until their last drop of blood so that defeat might be inflicted on the imperialist troops . . .'.[49] This fiery message was repeated by, *inter alia*, the PLF, the Palestine National Salvation Front (PNSF) and the Palestine Popular Struggle Front (PPSF). Although Arafat has not endorsed this more radical line, by adopting a pro-Iraqi stance he has secured his position as the leader of both a united PLO and the wider Palestinian cause. If he had opposed Iraq, he would have lost popular support and undermined the PLO's unity.

These benefits have already been realised. But the PLO is expecting more from its support for Iraq. It hopes that Iraq's military might will pressure the West into finding a solution to the Palestine problem. If the policy of linkage can be made to work, then Arafat's gamble will have paid off. At last he may be in a position to wrest concessions from Israel.

IMPLICATIONS

The effects of the Gulf Crisis will reverberate throughout the Middle East for the foreseeable future. It is not yet possible to give a definite answer to the question originally posed, namely: have the Palestinians dug their own grave? The ultimate impact of the crisis on the Palestinians hangs very much on the fate of Saddam Hussein. The PLO leadership have certainly chosen a high-risk strategy, although it is difficult to see what else they could have done given their close ties with Iraq and the level of popular antipathy to the US. It is conceivable that Arafat's gamble will pay off, that Iraq will avoid defeat, lead the Arab world and persuade Israel to accede to Palestinian demands. However, if Iraq succumbs to the pressures of the coalition opposing it, this could lead to the fragmentation of the PLO and allow the US, Israel and the moderate Arab states to impose their favoured settlements on a weakened Palestinian movement.

No matter what, the damage already done to the PLO's foreign relations will not be easily overcome. However, if Saddam avoids humiliation and defeat, this will not matter so much. If he is able to win a leading role in the Arab world and persuade the great powers to convene an international conference, then the PLO may be able to take advantage of Iraqi support to negotiate from a position of strength. The danger inherent in this outcome is that Israel may be tempted to attack Iraq in order to reassert its military preeminence. While the results of such a war are unpredictable, it is fair to assume that they would not benefit the PLO.

However, the PLO would have serious problems if Saddam were forced to give up his ambitious plans. Their rejectionist strategy would have failed and a *Pax Americana* may well ensue. The Egyptians, Saudis and Syrians, who would form the core of any such *Pax*, would undoubtedly take their revenge on the PLO. Egypt is already cultivating an alternative to Arafat's leadership. In the case of an Iraqi defeat, they would probably try to oust him. If they succeeded, it is quite likely that the PLO would disintegrate as rival factions, backed by different Arab states, competed for control. Until another dominant leader emerged, the PLO would be too weak and divided to act as a credible representative of the Palestinian cause.

Even in this scenario, there would probably be movement on the Palestine issue. America and its allies may well take steps to push Israel into making concessions, if only to head off the wave of popular militancy that would probably sweep the Arab world after an Iraqi defeat. If an international conference were convened, the Arab states would seek to deal with a moderate and pliable Palestinian leadership, perhaps from within the occupied territories. Israel and the US would be in a strong position to impose a settlement favourable to them. The Palestinians would get something, but would hardly be in a position to press for the establishment of a sovereign state.

Whatever the outcome of the current crisis, the Middle East has entered a period of uncertainty and instability. In the near future, many regimes will be threatened by the destabilising forces that this crisis has unleashed. For the Palestinians, the uncertainty is magnified by the high-risk policy that their leaders have chosen. Depending on how events unfold, Arafat's current policy may be remembered either as a bold gamble, or as another humiliating defeat for the Palestinian cause.

NOTES

* The author would like to express his appreciation for the help given by Martin Kirk in the preparation of this article.
[1] 'We have nothing more to lose,' is a common view expressed by Palestinian supporters of Iraq's invasion. See for instance: Lamis Andoni, 'Frustrated with the West, Palestinians Rally Behind Iraq', *Jordan Times* (henceforth *JT*), 4 September 1990.

[2] 'PNC's "Abd-al-Rahman on Consequences of Crisis", *Svenska Dagbladet* (Stockholm), 5 September 1990, in *Foreign Broadcast Information Service* (henceforth *FBIS*), NES 7 September 1990.

[3] For a synopsis of the activities of these groups, see: US Department of State, *Patterns of Global Terrorism* (Department of State, Washington D.C., 1990).

[4] D. Kuttab, 'Occupied Palestine: The Need For a Rethink,' *Middle East International* (henceforth *MEI*), 3 August 1990.

[5] Ze'ev Schiff and Ehud Ya'ari, *Intifada* (Simon & Schuster, New York, 1990), pp. 220-239.

[6] An account of the PLO-Iraq alliance is given in L. Andoni, 'The PLO: Relying on Saddam', *MEI*, 11 May 1990. In an interview published on 5 September, PNC Central Council member As'ad 'Abd-al-Rahman explained the process by which 'little by little Iraq has become the PLO's base'. 'PNC's 'Abd-al-Rahman on Consequences of Crisis,' *Svenska Dagbladet* (Stockholm), 5 September 1990, in *FBIS-NES* 7 September 1990.

The PLO's fears of an American-Israeli imperialist alliance are demonstrated in almost every broadcast by the Voice of Palestine. See for instance: 'PLO Radio Comments on 'Reckless' US Intervention in Gulf Crisis', Voice of Palestine (henceforth VoP) (Baghdad), 9 August 1990, in BBC, *Summary of World Broadcasts* (henceforth cited as *SWB*) ME 11 August 1990.

[7] Tony Walker, 'PLO Tries to Please Riyadh and Baghdad', *Financial Times*, 21 August 1990.

[8] 'Saddam Gives Arafat $1 Billion for Help,' *Defense & Foreign Affairs Weekly*, 1-7 October 1990.

[9] 'PLO Radio Comments on 'Reckless' US Intervention in Gulf Crisis,' VoP (Baghdad), 9 August 1990, in *SWB/ME* 11 August 1990.

[10] The vote was 14 to 6 in favour of the resolution.

[11] This Iraqi declaration was only accepted by its allies. 'Yemen's Cabinet Satisfied by Iraq's Decision to Withdraw its Troops,' Republic of Yemen Radio, San'a, 4 August 1990, in *SWB/ME* 7 August 1990.

[12] 'Arab Consultations on Iraq-Kuwait Conflict,' Jana despatch (Tripoli), 4 August 1990, in *SWB/ME* 6 August 1990. The terms of the proposal stated that Iraq would withdraw from Kuwait in return for 'a response to Iraq's financial and security demands'. David Hirst, 'Invasion Throws up Unlikely Alliances Between Arabs', *Guardian*, 7 August 1990.

[13] 'PLO Broadcast Condemns US Role in Gulf Crisis', VoP (Algiers), 5 August 1990, in *SWB/ME* 7 August 1990.

[14] *Ibid.*

[15] 'PLO Radio Commentary Regrets Arab 'Welcome' for US Intervention', VoP (Baghdad), 8 August 1990, in *SWB/ME* 11 August 1990.

[16] 'Iraqi Agency reports 500 Palestinians Deported From UAE, Others Arrested', Iraqi News Agency (henceforth INA) (Baghdad), 16 August 1990, in *SWB/ME* 17 August 1990. 'Arafat Said Declared Persona Non Grata in Gulf', *Jerusalem Post*, 16 August 1990, in *FBIS-NES* 17 August 1990.

[17] Lamis Andoni, 'PLO Officials Clarify Stance', *JT*, 14 August 1990; 'Support of Invasion Creates a Deep Rift In PLO Leadership', *International Herald Tribune*, 14 August 1990. These differing interpretations may be partly explained by the fact that the vote at the summit was taken amidst scenes of great confusion, and that the ambassadors to Egypt and Jordan were aiming their remarks at different audiences.

[18] 'Palestinian-run paper in UAE attacks PLO on Gulf Stand', AFP (Abu Dhabi), 15 September 1990, in *SWB/ME* 18 September 1990.

[19] It was reported that *Fatah* leaders held discussions on 16 August in which the costs of the PLO's stance were discussed. 'PLO Holds Urgent Meeting Reassessing Stand on Gulf Crisis Says Gulf Agency', Wakh (Abu Dhabi), 17 August 1990, in *SWB/ME* 18 August 1990.

[20] 'PLO Issues Statement on Gulf Crisis,' VoP (San'a), 20 August 1990, in *SWB/ME* 22 August 1990.

[21] 'Al-Ghusayn Opposes Iraqi Invasion of Kuwait', Riyadh SPA (Abu Dhabi), 19 August 1990 and 'Further on Comments', Paris AFP (Dubai), 20 August 1990, in *FBIS-NES*, 20 August 1990.

[22] 'PLO Support', *Independent*, 13 September 1990.

[23] 'PLO Seeks Iranian Help to Circumvent Iraq Embargo', *JT*, 29 August 1990; 'PLO Aided Iran-Iraq Rapprochement', *JT*, 15 September 1990.

[24] 'PLO's Faruq Qaddumi Expresses Support for Iraq Against 'Foreign Aggression',' Republic of Iraq Radio (Baghdad), 24 August 1990, in *SWB/ME* 27 August 1990.

[25] 'Arafat: PLO Must Back Side Hostile to Israel', *JT*, 4 September 1990.

[26] On the initiative and Palestinian reaction to it, see: David Hirst & Simon Tisdall, 'US Spurns Saddam's 'initiative',' *Guardian*, 13 August 1990; David Horovitz, 'West Bank Hails Plan 'to End all Wars',' *Independent*, 14 August 1990.

[27] 'PLO's Faruq Qaddumi Expresses Support For Iraq Against 'Foreign Aggression','' Republic of Iraq Radio (Baghdad), 24 August 1990, in *SWB/ME* 27 August 1990.

[28] 'Arafat Message to UN Conference Proposes Comprehensive Middle East Settlement,' VoP (Algiers), 29 August 1990, in *SWB/ME* 31 August 1990.

[29] *Ibid.*

[30] Lamis Andoni & Sahar Qara'een, 'PLO Seeks Debate on all Mideast Problems,' *JT*, 27 September 1990.

[31] 'Arafat Says Gulf Crisis Linked to Palestine Issue by 'International Consensus','' Hashimite Kingdom of Jordan Radio (Amman), 7 October 1990 and Republic of Algeria Radio (Algiers) 5 October 1990, in *SWB/ME* 9 October 1990.

[32] Jonathan Steele, 'Moscow Seeks Israeli Link in Deal to End Iraqi Crisis', *Guardian*, 5 September 1990.

[33] Robert Swain, 'France: Mitterrand's Proposal', *MEI*, 28 September 1990.

[34] Peter Pringle & David Horovitz, 'UN 'Cannot Afford to Fail,'' *Independent*, 2 October 1990.

[35] Harvey Morris & Leonard Doyle, 'Hurd Attacks 'Misguided' Israel,' *Independent*, 5 October 1990.

[36] Robert Block, 'PLO Envoy to the UN is Recalled', *Independent*, 16 October 1990.

[37] Given this resentment, it is very likely that some Kuwaiti Palestinians are helping Iraqi forces in Kuwait. At the same time, others are fighting with the Kuwaiti resistance.

[38] Victor Mallet, 'Gulf Arabs Take Tough Line in Reassessing Their Friendships', *Financial Times*, 8 October 1990; 'Saudi Source Affirms Unswerving Support for Palestinian Cause', Kingdom of Saudi Arabia TV (Riyadh), 9 September 1990, in *SWB/ME* 11 September 1990.

[39] 'PLO Radio Warns Qatar Against Expelling Palestinians', VoP (Baghdad), 13 September 1990, in *SWB/ME* 17 September 1990. See also: Wafa Amr, 'Qatari Government Deporting Palestinians', *JT*, 4 September 1990; Hugh Carnegy, 'Economy of the Occupied Territories Feels the Pinch', *Financial Times*, 28 September 1990; 'Saudi Arabia to Expel Palestinians to Jordan', *Defense & Foreign Affairs Weekly*, 3-9 September 1990.

[40] 'PLO Radio Station in Cairo Closes', *Defense & Foreign Affairs Weekly*, 3-9 September 1990; 'Egyptian Officials, Media Attack PLO', *Defense & Foreign Affairs Weekly*, 1-7 October 1990; Michael Sheridan, 'Widening Gap Between Egypt and Arafat', *Independent*, 22 September 1990.

[41] 'Fateh Takes Control of 'Ain Al Hilweh Camp', *JT*, 11 September 1990.

[42] David Horovitz, 'Israelis Reject Call For Joint Pull-out', *Independent*, 13 August 1990.

[43] Lamis Andoni, 'PLO Unsure of Role in Gulf Crisis', *JT*, 27 August 1990.

[44] 'PLO Condemns USSR Stance on Gulf and Palestine Issue', Radio Monte Carlo (Paris), 27 September, in *SWB/ME* 28 September 1990.

[45] Nadim Jaber, 'The Iraq-West Confrontation: Background and reactions', *MEI*, 13 April 1990.

[46] Michael Sheridan, 'Palestinians Support Saddam by Default', *Independent*, 23 August 1990.

[47] One may even speculate that Saddam's 12 August 'initiative' was designed, at least in part, to lock in PLO support.

[48] See: Lamis Andoni, 'PLO Unsure of Role in Gulf Crisis', *JT*, 27 August 1990; 'Arafat and PLO Pay Heavy Price for Supporting Saddam', *Defense & Foreign Affairs Weekly*, 10-16 September 1990.

[49] 'PFLP-GC Condemns 'Defeatist' States for Sending Troops to Saudi Arabia', INA (Beirut), 15 August, in *SWB/ME* 17 August 1990.

Educational Establishments Teaching Strategic Studies

EDWARD FOSTER

The author is a researcher on the RUSI Western European Security Programme.

The following is a list of postgraduate options which may be of interest to those wishing to further their academic studies into areas within the scope of this yearbook. The normal requirement for eligibility on a Master's postgraduate course is a Bachelor's degree, class upper second or higher. However, candidates may still be considered favourably by some departments if they can demonstrate educational qualifications and competence appropriate to their proposed course of study. Where Diplomas are awarded, the work involved is substantially the same as for the MA or equivalent, but the Master's degree is conferred on candidates reaching a higher mark and may require a further stage of examination.

POSTGRADUATE COURSES IN STRATEGIC STUDIES

Department of International Relations
Edward Wright Building
University of Aberdeen
Dunbar Street
ABERDEEN AB9 2TY
Tel. (0224) 272725

In association with the Centre for Defence Studies, Aberdeen offers a one-year MLitt course in Strategic Studies for graduates in International Relations, Politics, Economics, Sociology or History, or those with appropriate career experience. The three terms are given over to Strategic Theory, Defence Economics, and Western European Security since 1945 respectively, and normally include visits to NATO (Brussels) and SHAPE. Enquiries should be directed to the course director, J. H. Wylie.

Graduate School of International Studies
University of Birmingham
PO Box 363
BIRMINGHAM B15 2TT
Tel. (021) 414 6517

The Graduate School of International Studies now offers a
Master's Degree in Defence Studies of one year's duration.
Students take one compulsory course in Strategic Theory and
Doctrine and two other courses chosen from a wide range of
options including United States Defence Policy and Soviet
Defence Policy. After examinations, students are required to
complete a 10,000 word dissertation. The course is taught by
members of the University of Birmingham and a number of
eminent external scholars and practitioners. The Graduate
School also offers Master's courses in International Studies, the
European Community, and Diplomacy. MPhil or PhD research
is also undertaken at Birmingham for a minimum of two years.
Study may be undertaken part-time. For further details, contact
the Coordinator of Defence Studies, Dr. Stuart Croft.

Department of Politics
University of Bristol
BRISTOL, BS8 1TU
Tel. (0272) 303030

The course leading to an MSc in International Relations offers
programmes in Competing Political Theories, Politics in the
Developed World, and those in the Developing World. Strategic
Studies and Political Implications of Modern Warfare are two
fields available for coverage. Research studies are also undertaken; details are available from the Department.

Centre of International Studies
University of Cambridge
History Faculty Building
CAMBRIDGE CB3 9EF
Tel. (0223) 335333

The Centre offers as its main programme an MPhil in International Relations which particularly emphasises the historical
background to this area of study and strategic studies. In addition
students sit papers on International History and Politics, the

Theory of International Relations, Strategic Studies, International Economics, and International Law. Those interested should contact the Centre's director, Mr R. T. B. Langhorne, or his deputy, Dr. P. A. Towle.

Department of International Relations
Keele University
STAFFORDSHIRE ST5 5BG
Tel. (0782) 621111

From October 1991, Keele offers three taught MA programmes, full-time or part-time: Security Studies, Diplomatic Studies and International Relations. A number of subjects relevant to Strategic Studies are either compulsory or optional for them.

Research is also conducted at MPhil or PhD level. Further details can be obtained from the Director, Dr. H. Suganami.

Board of Studies in Politics and International Relations
Rutherford College
University of Kent
CANTERBURY CT2 7NX
Tel. (0227) 764000

London Centre for International Relations
University of Kent
43 Harrington Gardens
LONDON SW7 4JU
Tel. (071) 487 4701

Two MA courses are offered here. The first is in International Conflict Analysis, which examines conflict theory and resolution, and the second in International Relations. Both involve optional modules in Strategic Studies. The period of study lasts for 12 months full-time or 24 months part-time and students offer a dissertation. Research students may also take advantage of the University's particular strengths in these fields to prepare theses leading to an MPhil or PhD over two or three years; those following the doctoral programme undertake a certain amount of course-work before beginning a thesis. A London Centre for International Relations has been established and teaches the MA in International Relations and accepts research students on both a full-time and a part-time basis. Teaching in the London Centre is organised so that students can follow the part-time degree by taking courses in the evening. Enquiries should be directed to

Professor A. J. R. Groom regarding courses based in Canterbury, and Professor Michael Nicholson regarding courses based in London.

Department of Politics and International Relations
Cartmel College
Lancaster University
LANCASTER LA1 4YL
Tel. (0524) 65201 (ext. 4261)

One year programmes in International Relations and Strategic Studies; Defence and Security Analysis; Science and Technology in International Affairs; Diplomacy; and Peace Studies. Each course contains a core compulsory element and electives from a wide range including Defence Analysis; Security and Modernity; Strategic Theory; Theory and Practice of Modern Warfare; Comparative Defence Analysis; Twentieth Century Peace Movements; Guerrilla War; Terrorism and Internal Security; The Military in Politics; and Technological Problems for Arms Control. Supervised research and facilities also for MPhil and PhD students.

Head of Department is Professor C. Clapham; the Director of Graduate Studies, David Travers; and the Graduate Studies Secretary, Susan Riches.

School of History
Leeds University
LEEDS LS2 9JT
Tel. (0532) 333612

The School is strong in military subjects of the nineteenth and twentieth centuries, which may be incorporated in the MAs in British History and International Studies. This may take the form of course work or research. More advanced research may also be conducted leading to MPhil or PhD. Details available on request from the University Admissions Office.

Department of War Studies
King's College
University of London
Strand
LONDON WC2R 2LS
Tel. (071) 873 2193/2178 Fax. (071) 873 2026

The Department of War Studies has an international reputation for inter-disciplinary teaching and research in all aspects of military affairs. Recent appointments have extended its coverage to technology and military affairs, regional security and sociological aspects of the military profession (historical and contemporary). The MA in War Studies is an extremely comprehensive one-year course combining both general and specific analysis. It includes a set paper on military history/theory, strategy, and society, including ethics and civil-military relations, plus a range of options and special subjects, from arms control to the literature of the First World War, which are examined by continuous assessment. In addition students are required to complete an extended essay on a subject of their choice. Diploma students follow the same course as for the MA but are not required to submit an extended essay. The Department is able to supervise research students for MPhil and PhD degrees over a wide range of topics. Further details can be obtained from the Departmental Secretary. From 1991 the Department will offer a BA in War Studies.

Department of International Relations
London School of Economics
Houghton Street
LONDON WC2A 2AE
Tel. (071) 405 7686

The MSc course in International Relations includes a paper in Strategic Studies. The course is of one year's duration, or may be completed part-time in two years. LSE also offers Diploma courses taking in Strategic Aspects of International Relations. MPhil or PhD research degrees also awarded. Enquiries should be made to the Graduate Administrator's Office.

Department of International Relations and Politics
Staffordshire Polytechnic
College Road
STOKE-ON-TRENT ST4 2DE
Tel. (0782) 744531

This college has developed working links with the services, NATO, and SHAPE, and offers graduates in suitable disciplines the chance to engage in research studies to MPhil or PhD subject to close supervision. Enquiries to Professor A. E. Thorndike.

Modern History Faculty
University of Oxford
Broad Street
OXFORD OX1 3BD
Tel. (0865) 277256

The MPhil is a two-year instructional course comprised of general, specialist, and research studies which may encompass lectures and seminars on Strategic Studies and the History of War, but a privately selected area of research could easily be combined with study into, say, British Foreign Policy. MLitt research is generally conducted over three years, DPhil over four years. Details are available from the Graduate Admissions Office.

Graduate School for European and International Studies
University of Reading
Whiteknights
PO Box 218
READING RG6 2AA
Tel. (0734) 318378

Papers on Strategy and Security in Europe, Defence Economics, Terrorism, Policing and Police Work, and International Relations in the Mediterranean are options open to those on MA courses in European, International, or Defence and Internal Security Studies. These may be completed full-time or part-time. MPhil or PhD courses may also be followed as research. Applications to the Secretary of the Graduate School.

Department of Politics
University of Southampton
SOUTHAMPTON SO9 5NH
Tel. (0703) 590000

The MSc or Diploma in International Studies is a one-year instructional course offering options in Arms Control and International Order, Soviet Foreign Policy, Revolution and International Order and Regional Security and Third World International Relations. It may also be taken part-time over two years. MPhil and PhD research may also be conducted at the Department. Details are available from the Postgraduate Studies Office.

Graduate Division of International Relations
University of Sussex
Falmer
BRIGHTON BN1 9RH
Tel. (0273) 606755

Suitably qualified graduates may apply for the MA course in International Relations, which includes second-term options such as The International Politics of World War II and Soviet Policy in Eastern Europe. Part-time students take two years over their MA rather than one. The Division also accepts applications for MPhil and DPhil Research degrees. Enquiries should be addressed to the University's Admissions Office.

COURSES IN SPECIALISED MILITARY FIELDS

Department of Military Studies
University of Manchester
MANCHESTER
Tel. (061) 275 3141

Postgraduate studies take the form of MPhil or PhD research into chosen areas of military theory or analysis carried out under close supervision. Graduates without a suitable academic background of military studies or military history may be advised to follow supervised studies into military organisation, psychology, philosophy and military evolution drawn from the department's course of undergraduate study. Enquiries should be addressed to Professor M. Elliott-Bateman.

Royal College of Defence Studies
Seaford House
37 Belgrave Square
LONDON SW1X 8NS
Tel. (071) 235 1091 Fax. (071) 235 0876

The RCDS is a military college run by the Ministry of Defence with an annual professional course for officers of Brigadier or equivalent rank of the armed forces of the United Kingdom, those of other friendly states and government officials. Study is made of the wider aspects of international security and defence and the way economic, strategic and social factors shape and limit national defence policies.

DEDICATED STUDIES IN PEACE AND ARMS CONTROL

Department of Peace Studies
University of Bradford
BRADFORD BD7 1DP
Tel. (0274) 733466

Two MA courses (Diploma for those without graduate entry qualifications) are offered: MA in Peace Studies and MA in International Politics and Security Studies. These degree courses may be followed full-time or part-time. Both courses cover nuclear issues, defence economics, global problems of resources and ecology, and on-going international and inter-communal conflicts. The MA in Peace Studies emphasises the philosophical dimensions of reflection on peace and war and practical approaches to conflict resolution; and it includes studies of peace and conflict at community and personal level. The MA in International Politics and Security Studies concentrates on international security problems, including economic and ecological security as well as political and military security, in a changing world of politics, economics and technology. There is a strong research section in the department with over twenty full-time doctoral students working on a range of topics including defence policies, air and naval arms control, American and Soviet foreign policies, international conflict resolution and mediation, Middle Eastern politics and Northern Irish politics. Part-time research is possible.

The Professor of Peace Studies is Professor J. M. O'Connell; Chair of Postgraduate Studies is Dr. T. Woodhouse.

Richardson Institute for Conflict and Peace Studies
Department of Politics
University of Lancaster
LANCASTER LA1 4YF
Tel. (0524) 65201

The Institute's MA in Peace Studies was the first of its kind to become available at a British university, and is open to qualified graduates or those with experience of 'Peace' work. Its papers on the Arms Race supplement those available for Lancaster's MA in International Relations (see above). For details, apply to the Administrator at the Richardson Institute.

NATO Defence Expenditures 1985-1989

EDWARD FOSTER

Researcher, RUSI Western European Security Programme

Defence accounting is not a universally standard science, but NATO computes the budgets of its member states according to a standard definition which gives the figures shown below. This is assessed as all spending on regular and reserve military forces, all national foreign military aid to other countries, pensions, host-nation support costs, expenditure on NATO infrastructure and civilian staff. It does not, however, include spending on paramilitary forces such as internal security or border units. Neither does it take into account the value of equipment received by countries benefitting from foreign military assistance.

When presenting this data, the fiscal year is denoted by the calendar year in which most of its months fall. Thus 1985 represents FY 1985-86 for Canada and the UK and FY 1984-85 for the US. The data displayed is that made available at the end of 1989, and the figures for that year are therefore estimates.

France is not a member of the Alliance's integrated military structure, and the figures given for it are therefore indicative only. Iceland has no armed forces and is thus absent from the tables.

TABLE 1—COMPARATIVE DEFENCE EXPENDITURES
OF NATO NATIONS 1985–89,
EXPRESSED AS A PERCENTAGE OF GDP[1]

Belgium	2.9	Netherlands	3.0
Canada	2.1	Norway	3.2
Denmark	2.1	Portugal	3.1
France	3.9	Spain	2.2
Fed. Rep. Germany[2]	3.0	Turkey	4.3
Greece	6.4	United Kingdom	4.6
Italy[3]	2.3	United States	6.3
Luxembourg	1.2		

[1] These figures are compiled using estimations for 1989.
[2] This does not include expenditure for the security of Berlin.
[3] Data for Italy for 1989 is unavailable; the average therefore reflects spending for that country in the years 1985–88.
Source: NATO

336   BRASSEY'S DEFENCE YEARBOOK

TABLE 2—DEFENCE EXPENDITURES OF NATO NATIONS 1985–89,
CURRENT PRICES

	1985	1986	1987	1988	1989[1]
Belgium					
Be Fr (millions)	144,183	152,027	152,422	150,647	155,164
Canada					
Can $ (millions)	10,331	10,970	11,715	12,335	12,611
Denmark					
Dan Kr (millions)	13,343	13,333	14,647	15,620	15,813
France					
Fr Fr (millions)	186,715	197,080	209,525	215,073	223,868
Fed. Rep. Germany[2]					
DMark (millions)	58,649	60,130	61,354	61,638	63,269
Greece					
Drachmae (millions)	321,981	338,465	393,052	497,236	521,209
Italy					
Lire (1000 millions)	18,584	20,071	23,788	26,590	n.a.
Luxembourg					
Lux Fr (millions)	2,265	2,390	2,730	3,163	3,143
Netherlands					
Gldrs (millions)	12,901	13,110	13,254	13,300	13,583
Norway					
Nor Kr (millions)	15,446	16,033	18,551	18,865	21,117
Portugal					
Esc (millions)	111,375	139,972	159,288	193,864	207,738
Spain					
Ptas (millions)	674,883	715,306	852,767	835,353	912,173
Turkey					
T Liras (millions)	1,234,547	1,867,990	2,476,869	3,788,920	6,104,534
UK					
£ (millions)	18,352	18,639	19,269	19,495	21,239
US					
US $ (millions)	258,165	281,105	288,157	293,093	300,325

[1]Figures for 1989 are estimated.
[2]Does not include expenditure for the security of Berlin.
Source: NATO

TABLE 3—DEFENCE EXPENDITURES OF NATO NATIONS 1985–89,
AS PERCENTAGE OF GDP

	1985	1986	1987	1988	1989[1]
Belgium	3.1	3.1	3.0	2.8	2.7
Canada	2.2	2.2	2.2	2.1	2.0
Denmark	2.2	2.0	2.1	2.2	2.1
France	4.0	3.9	3.9	3.8	3.7
Fed. Rep. Germany[2]	3.2	3.1	3.1	2.9	2.9
Greece	7.0	6.2	6.3	6.4	6.0
Italy	2.3	2.2	2.4	2.5	n.a.
Luxembourg	1.1	1.1	1.2	1.3	1.2
Netherlands	3.1	3.0	3.1	3.0	2.9
Norway	3.1	3.1	3.3	3.2	3.3
Portugal	3.2	3.2	3.1	3.2	3.0
Spain	2.4	2.2	2.4	2.1	2.1
Turkey	4.5	4.8	4.3	4.1	3.9
UK	5.2	4.9	4.6	4.2	4.2
US	6.5	6.7	6.4	6.1	5.8

[1]Figures for 1989 are estimated.
[2]Does not include expenditure for the security of Berlin.
Source: NATO